Creative Resources for School Age Programs

By

Donald Platz

and

Nancy Platz

Join us on the web at

EarlyChildEd.delmar.com

Creative Resources for School Age Programs

DONALD PLATZ AND NANCY PLATZ

THOMSON

DELMAR LEARNING

Australia Canada Mexico Singapore Spain United Kingdom United States

THOMSON

DELMAR LEARNING

Creative Resources for School Age Programs
Donald and Nancy Platz

Vice President, Career Education SBU:
Dawn Gerrain

Director of Editorial:
Sherry Gomoll

Acquisitions Editor:
Erin O'Connor

Director of Production:
Wendy A. Troeger

Production Editor:
Joy Kocsis

Director of Marketing:
Wendy E. Mapstone

Cover Design:
Joseph Villanova

Composition:
Pre-Press Company, Inc.

Cover Images:
© Getty Images

For permission to use material from this text or product, submit a request online at
http://www.thomsonrights.com

Any additional questions about permissions can be submitted by email to thomsonrights@thomson.com

Library of Congress Cataloging-in-Publication Data

Platz, Donald L. (Donald Lee)
  Creative resources for school-age programs / Donald Platz and Nancy Platz.
     p. cm.
  Includes bibliographical references and index.
  ISBN-13 978-1-4018-3726-6
  ISBN-10 1-4018-3726-3
  1. Creative activities and seat work 2. Activity programs in education. I. Platz, Nancy. II. Title.
  LB1027.25.P53 2004
  372.5--dc22

2004014330

NOTICE TO THE READER

Publisher does not warrant or guarantee any of the products described herein or perform any independent analysis in connection with any of the product information contained herein. Publisher does not assume, and expressly disclaims, any obligation to obtain and include information other than that provided to it by the manufacturer.

The reader is expressly warned to consider and adopt all safety precautions that might be indicated by the activities herein and to avoid all potential hazards. By following the instructions contained herein, the reader willingly assumes all risks in connection with such instructions.

The Publisher makes no representation or warranties of any kind, including but not limited to, the warranties of fitness for particular purpose or merchantability, nor are any such representations implied with respect to the material set forth herein, and the publisher takes no responsibility with respect to such material. The publisher shall not be liable for any special, consequential, or exemplary damages resulting, in whole or part, from the readers' use of, or reliance upon, this material.

Contents

Unit 2   Language Arts

Unit 3   Mathematics

Unit 4 Physical Activity

Unit 5 Science

Unit 6 Social Studies

Preface

I t is my first day. I have a number of pairs of eyes looking at me. I will be with these children for several hours. My question is, what will I do with them? Individuals who work in programs for school-age children look for ways to involve children in activities for fun and learning. The purpose of this resource book is to offer a variety of developmentally appropriate activities capable of being used in a variety of settings. Classroom teachers will find the activities helpful to fill in gaps in learning and to support learning concepts.

Staff members working in before- and after-school programs for children will find this resource book useful in planning daily or weekly activities for fun and to help reinforce school-based academic learning. Summer program staff members will find the activities useful in developing a well-balanced recreation program for school-age children.

School programs in recent years have adopted a number of local, state, and national standards that guide and direct the goals and outcomes for their programs. This new standards-based approach to curriculum has led teachers to seek out motivational activities that are aligned with standards and support the overall curriculum goals of their school. This resource book provides activities that relate to a variety of standards in the content areas including those from national organizations.

Programs for school-age children in before- and after-school settings may vary in their mission. Some programs are designed to provide safe, fun environments for children. Programs that adopt a fun-based mission normally utilize a number of arts and crafts and physical activities to engage children. Other programs for school-age children are designed to engage students in enjoyable as well as academically based activities. This resource book provides activities and resources that can be used by staff members who are responsible for meeting these varied missions. The activities included in this resource book draw from the areas of fine arts, language arts, mathematics, science, social studies, and physical activity.

In addition to the variation in missions of programs for school-age children, a number of other differences may be found. Group size, age levels, resource availability, space, and the amount of curriculum guidance are a few variables that also exist. The activities and resources in the book were selected and designed with these situations in mind, as well.

Five major considerations were addressed in designing activities and suggesting resources for this book:

1. providing activities that would be motivational for school-age children
2. providing activities that would support learning of standards-based curricula
3. providing activities that would be developmentally appropriate
4. providing activities that could be used by children individually or in small or large group situations
5. providing activities that limit the need for extensive resources

The Overview and Introduction sections to follow provide a more detailed explanation for each of the considerations addressed in the preparation of this resource book. We believe you will find that children will be motivated by these activities and that the activities will add to children's learning in whatever setting the activities are used.

Overview

This resource text offers a number of activities and sources that are appropriate for individuals who work with primary and intermediate school-age children. The activities are designed with the interest and learning potential of children in mind. This overview provides information on the basic considerations followed in developing the book, how the book is organized, how the book can be used by individuals who work with school-age children, and how the activities are outlined.

BASIC CONSIDERATIONS

Providing activities that are enjoyable and engage children in learning was a primary consideration in planning this resource book. The activities included allow children to be actively involved and provide opportunities for children to make connections with important learning concepts.

Content areas outlined in national standards were utilized in developing activities around areas of instruction for fine arts, language arts, mathematics, physical activity, science, and social studies. An overview of the national standards for each of these content areas is provided with each content area.

The activities were designed with the developmental ages of primary- and intermediate-level children in mind. Children at these levels still benefit from active learning, are gaining ability in problem solving, are learning how to collaborate and cooperate with peers, and are capable of becoming more independent in their learning activities.

The activities developed for the book can be used by children working independently, by children working in small groups, or by the class as a whole. The activities can also be used as choices for free time, for learning center options, or as the primary activity for the day's schedule.

A final consideration for the book was selecting activities that would require little time or money to implement. For classroom teachers who are responsible for carrying out their standard curriculum, less time may be available to bring together extensive materials for supplemental activities. For individuals involved in before- or after-school programs, limited resources may restrict the type of activities they can plan for children.

HOW THE BOOK IS ORGANIZED

The book is divided into six major units that contain activities for school-age children built around the six content areas of fine arts, language arts, mathematics, physical activity, science, and social studies. Each unit is broken down into chapters that reflect the national standards for the content areas. Each unit contains an introduction to the content area being addressed, identification of content selected based on national standards, and a brief discussion about the activities that are included.

HOW TO USE THE BOOK

Activities and resources in the book are set up to allow individuals to use the book in a variety of ways. Individual activities can be chosen to support a timely learning experience or to engage children in a fun way in an area of interest. Several activities from chapter strands can be grouped to form week-long experiences or mini-units to provide children with a more in-depth or continued learning experience.

HOW EACH ACTIVITY IS OUTLINED

Each activity follows the same outline to help individuals save time in reviewing and selecting activities from the book. The following components are included: title, description, learning, materials, steps, accommodations, and extensions.

✳ The *title* provides the user with a general idea of the type of activity.
✳ The *description* provides a quick overview of the nature of the activity.

* *Learning* identifies what concepts will be experienced and potentially learned by the children through their involvement in the activity.

* *Materials* indicates what is needed to carry out the activity.

* *Steps* provides directions for the user to follow when implementing the activity.

* *Accommodations* indicates how the activity may be modified to meet the needs of all children.

* *Extensions* offers suggestions of activities that could be used as follow-up activities to extend children's learning. Critical thinking challenge questions are also identified.

The Online Companion™ to accompany *Creative Resources for School Age Programs* is your link to early childhood education on the internet. The Online Companion™ contains many features to help focus your understanding of school age programs:

* Downloadable activities you can print from your computer

* Fine Arts Resources

* Language Arts Resources

* Mathematics Resources

* Physical Activities Resources

* Science Resources

* Social Studies Resources

You can find the Online Companion™ at
www.earlychilded.delmar.com

Acknowledgements

The authors would like to thank the following reviewers, enlisted by Thomson Delmar Learning, for their helpful suggestions and constructive criticism:

Irene Cook, M.A.
California State University, Bakersfield
Bakersfield, CA

Karen Callahan, M.Ed.
Central Piedmont Community College
Charlotte, NC

Sandra Hughes
Rainbow Express Child Care Center
Schenectady, NY

Marilee Cosgrove, M.A.
Rio Hondo College
Whitiler, CA

Jody Martin
Educational Consultant
Aurora, CO

This book is dedicated
to our sons:
Steve, Tom, and Mark

Introduction: Learning, Development, and Creative Resources

This introduction is intended to share with teachers a set of learning and developmental factors that should be considered when selecting, utilizing, or modifying the creative learning activities presented in this resource book. The resource activities included in this text were developed to help children learn concepts aligned in part with current curriculum standards deemed appropriate and essential for children in a nonthreatening environment.

Teachers introduce a variety of learning activities to children each day. To ensure that activities are beneficial, teachers should understand how to select, modify, and implement their instructional activities based on an understanding of how children learn and develop. The issue of how children come to learn and develop, however, is the subject of ongoing debate. A number of well regarded theorists such as Piaget and Erikson have outlined general sequential stages at which specific cognitive and psychosocial developmental behaviors emerge. Many local, state, and national curriculums outline standards and concepts at age- or grade-appropriate levels based on research and observations of children. Proponents of age- or stage-appropriate levels suggest that learning will be enhanced if teachers apply this knowledge when selecting learning activities for children.

More recent thinking by other educational professionals (Bredekamp, 1987; New, 1994; Lubeck, 1996) argues that while age and stage appropriateness is helpful to understand how children learn and develop, factors such as sociocultural learning, construct learning, learning styles, and intelligences must additionally be considered in setting up appropriate learning activities for children. Professional insight and experience suggest that learning and motivation to learn can be increased when the teacher makes connections between individual learner *profiles* and classroom learning activities.

Developing broad learning profiles on children will help teachers select activities that motivate children to learn at higher levels. It should also be remembered that in the classroom the selection of one activity may not meet the learning needs of all children equally. If activities over the course of the day or week consider profiles of all children, however, their motivation and learning can be enhanced. Alternatively, teachers can increase the value of selected activities if they provide several activities to choose from at one time. Teachers can also provide options to children as to how they carry out a specific activity. For example, children may choose to measure with a ruler several sets of objects given to them, or some children at a beginning level could move around the classroom measuring objects of their choosing with a nonstandard measure such as a shoe or string.

STAGE AND AGE APPROPRIATENESS

Many who have studied cognitive development of children have looked into and analyzed Piaget's four broad stages of development that children move through as they organize their environmental experiences. Many school curriculum guides, state and national standards, and developmental learning scales have drawn from Piaget's historic theory to form age- and grade-level learning goals for children. Table 1 provides a brief overview of the generally understood stages as presented by Piaget.

It becomes important for teachers to consider cognitive development in preparing activities for children. If a teacher decides to have four-year-old children learn to use the plus sign (+) as a way of learning to combine numbers, it may be completely inappropriate and extremely frustrating to children. A more appropriate activity based on Piaget's

Table 1 Piaget's Stages of Cognitive Development	
Sensorimotor Stage Birth–2 years	Infants begin to respond to their world through the use of their eyes, ears, hands, mouth, and nose. They learn through experiences and activities with real objects at a very basic level.
Preoperational Stage 2–7 years	Preschool and early primary age children continue to learn about their world through experiences with real objects. What they see is what they learn. As children grow older in the preoperational stage they begin to make use of symbols to represent what they are learning. They begin to understand that numeral 4 represents a certain quantity.
Concrete Operational Stage 7–11 years	Late primary and intermediate age children begin to use logic when learning about the world around them. They can begin to organize objects into hierarchies and to understand that what they see may not always be what is. If they have three pears and move the three pears further apart they still have three pears even though the appearance of the pears has changed and it may look like there are now more pears.
Formal Operational Stage 11 years to adulthood	Adolescents begin to use higher levels of reasoning to deal with abstract concepts such as the universe, infinity, and so forth. They can approach a problem and come up with a number of solutions. Investigations into advanced math are possible and students can understand symbols that do not represent real objects.

stages of cognitive development for this age would be to have the teacher ask children to take apples from one basket and apples from a second basket and show or tell how many apples were in the two baskets.

If activities planned by teachers do not consider the cognitive growth of children, the result will be frustration, inappropriate responses, and little to no targeted learning. If teachers keep in mind the simple rule of thumb that activities for young children should be based on the real, while activities for older children can be based on the more symbolic, the activities may have a greater chance of success in terms of child learning. Activities planned for children in the primary grades should be aligned with Piaget's preoperational stage, more of a hands-on approach. Activities for intermediate age children can allow for more symbolism to represent real objects and higher levels of thinking and problem solving as children organize information.

Teachers who rely on age- or stage-appropriate learning levels should be cautioned by the fact that age- and stage-level norms can be influenced by experiences and adaptations. For example, the concept of multiplication in years past was deemed an inappropriate developmental goal for first grade children. The thinking in the past was that learning "4×5" was too difficult for first grade children to understand because it was presented in a symbolic context. Current practice, however, has first grade children in some math curricula learning multiplication by presenting them with a math problem such as, "There are four plates on a table and each plate has four cookies. How many cookies are there on all four plates?" Children are given the option of identifying their answer after they draw out four tables with four cookies.

Another example relative to cautions surrounding age- or stage-appropriate goals can be drawn from the psychomotor skill of learning to ride a bike. Many gross motor developmental scales in years past identified the age range of seven to eight as a time when children begin to ride a two-wheel bike. As bikes became smaller and better balanced younger children became more proficient at riding two-wheelers.

Several key reminders associated with age- or stage-appropriate levels or development goals are:

1. Age- and stage-appropriate goals are helpful to teachers as they select learning activities for children.

2. Teachers should be reminded that age- and stage-appropriate learning goals are based on general norms of children and that some children will achieve the goals earlier or later.

3. Experiences or adaptations can influence age- and stage-appropriate goals, allowing for some goals to be introduced earlier.

SOCIOCULTURAL LEARNING AND THE CONSTRUCTIVIST APPROACH

Beyond stages and age-appropriate considerations, today's teachers are also encouraged to consider incorporating sociocultural and constructivist learning theory into the day-to-day activities they select for children. This new potential for teacher planning incorporates Vygotsky's sociocultural theory, which makes use of children's learning through their rich classroom environment. As teachers plan for learning activities in the social-constructivist classroom, they select activities that allow for them to work alongside of children to jointly develop understanding from the challenging activities presented. Children also have the opportunity to interact with their peers and exchange ideas to extend learning (Palincsar, 1998).

In constructing activities based on sociocultural theory, the teacher plans to be a part of the learning process. For example, if the teacher plans an activity to have children measure the width of a playground, the teacher may decide to have the children sit in a group or several small groups and raise questions like, "Would it or would it not be easy to use a 12-inch ruler to measure the width of our playground?" "What would be an easier way to measure the length of our playground?" "Can you give group A some reasons why you think their way of measuring our playground would be easier or harder?"

Constructivist theory, as applied to planning activities for the classroom teacher, applies Piaget's theory which views children as reflective thinkers who coordinate and organize their experiences with the world. Teachers who develop activities for the classroom based on the constructivist approach, provide children with the opportunity to question and rethink how they are attending to the problem or task being assigned. Older school-age children who have the opportunity to become involved in constructivist activities tend to gain in critical thinking, give more value to individual differences, and have more positive attitudes towards the learning tasks and school (Walberg, 1986).

Albert Bandura's social-cognitive approach to learning has some important ties to activities based on constructivist and sociocultural theories. Through the constructivist and sociocultural approaches children are encouraged to reflect, share, and respond to other children as they attend to activities with teachers. As children work through the activities they observe the self-praise and self-blame of others in determining their own worth. Through this process they develop personal standards and a sense of efficacy (Bandura, 2001). Bandura's theory becomes important for teachers to consider as they monitor activities that are based on constructivist or sociocultural theories. Teachers need to attend to comments that may build confidence in the form of approval or support for children and address comments that may reduce the perception of self-worth.

Several key reminders associated with sociocultural or constructivist approaches to learning include:

1. Building into teacher activities the opportunity for teachers and peers to share and reflect on learning can increase students' learning and motivation to learn.

2. Providing the opportunity for children to construct a process to solve a problem versus having children model a process given by the teacher, can increase childrens' critical thinking and reflection.

3. Children can develop personal goals and a sense of efficacy as they observe peers receive feedback from peers and the teacher when attending to assigned activities.

4. Older school-age children who have the opportunity to become involved in constructivist activities gain in critical thinking and give more value to individual differences.

LEARNING STYLES

Constructivism and socioculture theories have received attention recently in regard to classroom teaching practices. Learning styles is perceived to be a predecessor to these movements, which place an emphasis on teacher use of reflection and working through solutions by having children discuss, share, and reflect. A number of different perspectives and approaches to learning styles by McCarthy, Gregorc, and others have been developed over the decades. Learning style theories, as they relate to schooling, have a commonality in that all theories suggest that individuals have certain preferences in terms of the context in which they learn. In theory, instructional activities prepared by teachers should take into account the styles children bring to the classroom.

Bernice McCarthy's 4MAT system of learning promotes four distinct styles that learners may bring to the classroom. Teachers are asked to observe and assess children based on characteristics of the four styles. After the preferred style(s) of children are identified, teachers begin to design teaching activities with the styles in mind (McCarthy, 1980). As indicated earlier, while not all styles may be equally addressed in one lesson, the inclusion of activities that match different styles over the course of daily or weekly planning will motivate children and help all children to learn at a higher level.

McCarthy identifies the following four styles. Style one children are innovative learners who are motivated when they work in groups and share experiences. Style two children are analytic learners who are motivated when they gather information from the teacher and when information is presented in a logical manner that allows them to reflect and think through solutions. Style three children are common sense learners who like hands-on experiences and being involved in real life learning activities. Style four children are dynamic learners who are free thinkers and enjoy creating their own ways of learning.

McCarthy emphasizes that all four learning styles are equally valuable and have strengths and weaknesses. Children usually feel most comfortable in their dominant style and learn best through it. McCarthy indicates that while children may have a strong propensity for one style, they can still function when placed in classroom situations emphasizing other styles, but not as well. The implication of McCarthy's styles for the teacher is that the more students are taught in their styles, the more they learn and the more they enjoy the learning experience. Table 2 provides a brief overview of the characteristics of each of McCarthy's four styles.

A critical and age-old question of environment versus heredity, or nature versus nurture, is of importance in any discussion of learning

Table 2 McCarthy's Learning Style Characteristics	
Innovative Learners	Seek meaning and need to be personally involved through listening and sharing ideas. Learn through social interactions with others and are divergent thinkers who reflect on their own experiences. They ask why or why not types of questions.
Analytic Learners	Need to know what experts think. Function well in traditional classrooms. Less interested in people than ideas and concepts. Perceive information abstractly and process it reflectively.
Common Sense Learners	Need hands-on experiences and enjoy concrete learning. Learn by testing theories in ways that seem sensible. Want to learn how things work and like practical application of ideas.
Dynamic Learners	Adaptable to change and like variety. Excel in situations calling for flexibility. Tend to take risks and often reach accurate conclusions in the absence of logic. Approach problems in nontraditional ways.

styles. Supporters offer strong arguments for their opposing positions (Beck, 2005). The question is whether children are born with a dominant learning style, or whether early life experiences help mold the dominant learning style they enter school with. Those who argue that heredity/nature determines the learning style of the child suggest that exposing children to activities based on other learning styles at an early age would not help children accommodate the other styles to a greater degree. Contrarily, defendants of the environment/nurture theory argue that the more children are exposed to activities based on other learning styles at an early age, the more children will begin to accommodate and benefit from the experiences.

Several key factors to remember when applying learning style theory to classroom teaching activities include:

1. Learning styles identify preferences children have in ways they learn in the classroom.

2. If teachers match the learning styles of children to teaching activities, children will learn more and will be more motivated to learn.

3. Though it may not be possible to include elements for all learning styles in every activity, teachers can develop activities over the course of a day or week that include elements that support the learning styles of all children.

INTELLIGENCES

Howard Gardner (Gardner, 1983, 1993) constructed a model based on intelligences of children. Drawing from research on cognitive sciences, Gardner originally concluded that individuals have at least seven intelligences: linguistic, logical-mathematical, intrapersonal, spatial, musical, body-kinesthetic, and interpersonal. Consistent with McCarthy's learning styles, Gardner states that while individuals may dominate in one of the seven intelligences, they have some capability to work in the other six. More recently Gardner added an eighth intelligence, naturalistic. It is Gardner's perception that teachers in the past had a tendency to teach to the linguistic, logical-mathematical, and intrapersonal learner. Children who were dominant in the other intelligence areas were basically ignored in many classrooms. A brief explanation of Gardner's eight intelligences is shared in Table 3.

Table 3 Overview of Gardner's Intelligences	
Linguistic	Learns through stories, reading, and writing. Tends to love words and the sounds they make. Enjoys rhyming works and learns languages with ease.
Logical/mathematical	Uses reason and logic to solve problems. Manipulates numbers and symbols according to established rules and procedures. Works well with symbols.
Intrapersonal	Is a self starter and enjoys working alone, independently of peers and adults, and knows own strengths and weaknesses.
Spatial	Encodes memories in the form of images and pictures. Excels in visualizations and can see things in his or her mind as to what a final project will look like.
Musical	Loves music and likes to improvise and create own music. Learning is enhanced if it is aligned with musical options.
Bodily/kinesthetic	Can mentally form images about how the body and its parts move. Tends to enjoy activities that incorporate movement into the learning process.
Interpersonal	Works well with others and can empathize with others. Enjoys learning through interactions with others.
Naturalistic	Loves the study of nature and is sensitive to changes in the natural environment. Likes to learn when examples of the environment are included.

Gardner realizes the inherit difficulty of one teacher trying to teach to the intelligences when faced with twenty-some children in the classroom. If teachers begin to look at a series of activities they are planning, however, and target a few activities to each of the intelligences, more children will benefit over the course of the year. A teacher responsible for teaching children a set of vocabulary words could select the following activities to meet some of the intelligences identified by Gardner:

Musical: Ask children to think of a song or make up a song that includes a number of words to be learned.

Naturalistic: Have children find a nature scene and write captions using some of the vocabulary words to be learned.

Interpersonal & Linguistic: Put children on an editorial team and ask them to write a poem for the classroom newsletter including some of the words to be learned.

Gardner's main intent with his intelligences is to promote the use of a wide range of teaching activities that will bring a broader appeal to students in classrooms. Gardner also suggests that while he believes his intelligences are important for the classroom, good activities do not always need to fit into the boundaries of a specific intelligence. As with McCarthy's learning styles, Gardner feels that the more varied the activities children are presented, the more opportunity all children will have to learn and be motivated to learn.

Several key factors to include when applying Gardner's intelligences to teaching include:

1. Children come to the classroom with different intelligences that require different approaches to instruction on the part of the classroom teacher.

2. The more the teacher requires children to bring musical, spatial, logical, and the other intelligence performances into activities, the more involved children will be in learning.

3. Teachers should "think outside of the box" when it comes to involving children in daily learning activities.

4. Many activities selected or created by teachers can expand the boundaries of one or more intelligences.

CONCLUDING THOUGHTS ON LEARNING APPLIED TO ACTIVITY DEVELOPMENT

As teachers select activities for instruction, they need to consider the individual learning profiles of the children they are responsible for. Many of the activities included in this resource book address—or can be modified to address—the sociocultural, learning styles, and intelligences presented in this introduction. While many teachers may feel that one needs an accountant's aptitude to organize and implement all the components of learning shared in the preceding pages, the major need is for teachers to internalize the principles presented and reflect on a series of activities over time that can meet the profile learning needs of all children they are responsible for. The following principles might be internalized from the discussion in this introduction:

1. Plan activities that include you and children working together to problem solve (sociocultural).

2. Plan activities that allow for children to think of alternative ways of arriving at an answer (constructivist).

3. Plan activities that allow children to share ideas as they work through them (innovative learner, interpersonal intelligences).

4. At times allow children to work independently so they can reflect and organize their own thinking (analytic learner/intrapersonal intelligence).

5. Plan activities that are hands-on or allow for children to relate or apply the activity to a real-life situation (common sense learner).

6. Plan to have options for children, or allow children to develop their own activity to work on learning goals (dynamic learner).

7. Plan how activities that incorporate music, space, nature, logic, linguistics, and body movements into the procedures (musical, spatial, naturalistic, logical/mathematical, linguistic, bodily/kinesthetic).

8. Plan an informal or formal management system to ensure that activities selected over time (weekly) meet the learning profile needs of all children.

9. Remember that age- or level-appropriate learning goals can be influenced by other factors.

10. Evaluate how and which children were engaged and motivated by the activity once completed.

In preparing to select activities for children, it becomes important for teachers to view and consider how the procedures of the activity relate to the learning profiles of students. In addition to reflecting on the activity in the context of childrens' styles, intelligences, and so forth, it is also important to reflect on how children responded to the activity or activities completed. Of greatest importance perhaps is to remember that the selection of activities should offer variety in the way children are asked to participate and respond.

LEARNING AND DEVELOPMENT RESOURCES

Bandura, A. (2001). Social cognitive theory: An agentic perspective. *Annual Review of Psychology*, 52, 1–26.

Berk, L. E. (2005). *Infants, children, and adolescents*. 5th ed. Boston: Allyn and Bacon.

Bredekamp, S. (1987). *Developmentally appropriate practice in early childhood programs serving children from birth through age 8*. Exp.ed. Washington, D.C.: NAEYC.

Gardner, H. (1983). *Frames of mind: The theory of multiple intelligences*. New York: Basic Books.

Gardner, H. (1993). *Multiple intelligences: The theory in practice*. New York: Basic Books.

Lubeck, S. (1996). Deconstructing child development knowledge and teacher preparation. *Early Childhood Research Quarterly*, 11(2), 147–167.

McCarthy, B. (1980). *The 4MAT system: Teaching to learning styles with right/left mode techniques*. Oak Brook, Illinois: Excel, Inc.

New, R. (1994). Culture, child development and developmentally appropriate practices: Teachers as collaborative researchers. In B. Mallory & R. New (Eds.), *Diversity and developmentally appropriate practices: challenges for early childhood education* (pp. 137–154). New York: Teachers College Press.

Palincsar, A. S. (1998). Social constructivist perspectives on teaching and learning. *Annual Review of Psychology*, 49, 345–375.

Pressman, H., and Deblin, P. (1995). *Accommodating learning differences in elementary classrooms*. New York: Harcourt Brace.

Walberg, H. J. (1986). Synthesis of research on teaching. In M. C. Wittrock (ed.), *Handbook of research on teaching*. 3rd ed., 214–229. New York: Macmillan.

Unit 1

Fine Arts

In the document "National Standards for Arts Education: What Every Young American Should Know and Be Able to Do in the Arts," developed by the Consortium of National Arts Education Associations, the standards for arts education are set forth for these four areas of the fine arts: music, visual arts, theater, and dance. These are stated to be the broad areas that children should become competent in with regard to the fine arts.

✳ They should be able to communicate at a basic level in the four arts disciplines—dance, music, theater, and visual arts.

✳ They should be able to communicate proficiently in at least one art form.

✳ They should be able to develop and present basic analyses of works of art.

✳ They should have an informed acquaintance with exemplary works of art.

✳ They should be able to relate various types of arts knowledge and skills within and across the arts disciplines.

These broad goals are supported by more specific standards for different grade levels. After considering these broad areas of competence for the fine arts plus more specific standards for children from kindergarten through fourth grade also provided in the document, we have divided our fine arts activities into these three chapter topics:

❋ **Music and Dance:** The activities included in this chapter are designed to provide listening, singing, and movement experiences incorporating music making and a wide variety of musical styles into the learning. Children will be introduced to many musical concepts through activities that allow for creativity.

❋ **Visual Arts:** This chapter uses art projects to enhance the children's understanding of the various art mediums and techniques used by artists to create pieces of art and to support their understanding of composition and texture when creating and evaluating their own original works of art.

❋ **Creative Dramatics:** This chapter's purpose is to support the children's developing understanding of theater and acting with an emphasis on creative movement activities and simple plays and puppet shows.

The activities in these three chapters are meant to play a supportive role in the effort to raise children to the level of the national standards in the fine arts. They were created to be supervised by the classroom teacher with a somewhat limited grasp of the music and art components that are covered in far more detail by the specialists in these fields who are working with the children. It is our hope that these activities will encourage the children to view the arts as something everyone can enjoy and be a part of.

Chapter 1

Music and Dance

Activities in this chapter use listening, singing, and movement experiences to enhance and support the learning of musical concepts. The children will be involved in making music as well as experiencing the many and varied styles of music. Creativity with and excitement about music will be encouraged.

Make Your Own Music

Make Your Own Music allows the children to use their creativity to develop their own musical instruments.

LEARNING

❋ Music can be made in many ways using items easily available.

MATERIALS

❋ Various recyclable items and odds and ends that can be used to create musical instruments such as paper tubes, aluminum pie tins, rubber bands, jingle bells, plastic containers, seeds, beads, boxes, etc.

❋ Hole punchers, glue, ribbon or yarn, staplers, etc. to put the instruments together

STEPS

1. Gather the items together that could be used to create musical instruments such as paper tubes, aluminum pie tins, rubber bands, jingle bells, plastic containers, seeds, beads, boxes, etc. A note sent home describing this project will most likely bring in many and varied items that have the potential to become musical instruments for your creative children!

2. You will also need hole punchers, glue, ribbon or yarn, staplers, etc. to put the instruments together.

3. Before the children start to create, brainstorm ideas for making their instruments so that lots of ideas are given for children to consider.

4. Now let the children develop their plans. Older children can draw out their plans whereas younger children may explain their ideas to you before they begin. This will assure a doable plan.

   Now let the creating begin! Children may need help manipulating the materials and tools.

5. When the instruments are completed you will have an instrument for each child to use when you work on rhythms, sound effects, etc.

ACCOMMODATIONS

✔ Encourage children to help one another to come up with ideas and produce the instruments.

✔ Gear the materials used and the amount of materials available to the ages and abilities of your students. Too many choices can be overwhelming, and tools that are hard to use can be frustrating!

EXTENSIONS

✔ Group together instruments that make their sounds in similar ways (drums, rattles, woodwinds, etc.), and have the children create a tune with them.

✔ Compare the children's instruments with pictures of orchestra instruments while discussing the various types (woodwinds, string, percussion, etc.)

Musical Characters

Musical Characters challenges the children to represent characters in a story through sound.

LEARNING

* We can use sound to represent characteristics.

MATERIALS

* Rhythm instruments—either traditional or created—enough for each child to have one to represent a character. More than one child may have the same instrument

STEPS

1. Choose a familiar story in which the characters have definite character traits ("The Three Billy Goats Gruff," *The Grouchy Ladybug*, etc.).

2. Then decide what sound played on a rhythm instrument will represent each character. For example, someone who is timid might be represented by a triangle ding, and someone who is gruff might be represented by a strong thump on a drum. Allow the children to decide with your suggestions and guidance.

3. Depending on the number of characters and children, decide how many children will play each instrument.

4. Then, when you read the story, each time their character is mentioned they can make their sound.

ACCOMMODATIONS

✔ Length of story and number of characters should be adjusted to your age level and group size.

EXTENSIONS

✔ Sounds could also be created to represent actions in stories such as running, jumping, skipping, etc.

✔ Another idea would be to play a sound for the children that indicates it is time for them to do something physical, such as run, jump, or skip.

I'm in a Mood!

I'm in a Mood! allows children to represent their feelings with sound.

LEARNING

✳ Feelings can be represented with sound.

MATERIALS

✳ A rhythm instrument for each child in the group

STEPS

1. Allow each child to select a rhythm instrument.

2. Demonstrate, on an instrument you choose, sounds that you feel represent a few emotions. Sad may be represented by a slow, quiet beat on a drum, whereas excited may be represented by a quick, loud beat.

3. Then allow the children to play sounds on their instruments to represent other feelings such as angry, happy, sleepy, etc.

ACCOMMODATIONS

✓ Choose emotions or feelings that the children you teach can comprehend.

EXTENSIONS

✓ Allow the children to come up with the emotions they wish to represent through sound.

✓ Make up or read a story, such as "The Three Billy Goats Gruff," which involves some clearly portrayed emotions, and have the children play their instruments to represent emotions dealt with in the story. Creating a story about the children in your group using their names is sure to hold their interest!

Instrument Pantomime

Instrument Pantomime *involves considering how an instrument is played and pantomiming it for others to guess.*

LEARNING

✳ Instruments are played in many different and distinguishable ways.

MATERIALS

✳ Video featuring band and/or orchestra instruments

✳ Television with VCR

✳ Large pictures of the instruments with the names of the instruments on them

✳ Small cards with pictures of the instruments and their names

✳ A small container

STEPS

1. Find a video featuring the instruments of a band or orchestra to show to the children.

If the video doesn't do so, you should point out several instruments and how they are played along with telling the names of the instruments. Pictures of the instruments would also be helpful. These might be displayed in an obvious place.

2. Next demonstrate how to pantomime an instrument being played.

3. Pictures of the instruments on small cards should be placed in a small container.

4. Allow one child at a time to pick a card from the box and pantomime playing the instrument as the others try to guess which one it is. They can either say the name of the instrument or point to the larger picture of the instrument displayed. Having the name of the instrument under the large and small pictures will help children associate the instruments with their names.

ACCOMMODATIONS

✔ Vary the types and amount of instruments to suit your group's ability level.

✔ Having two children decide and perform the pantomime together may help children who lack confidence in taking part in the activity. Pairing a younger child with an older one may work well in multi-age groups.

EXTENSIONS

✔ Play music featuring a particular instrument, and allow all the children to guess which instrument it is and to pantomime playing that instrument.

What Do You Hear Now?

In What Do You Hear Now? *the children are challenged to use their listening skills to determine which musical instrument they hear without seeing it being played.*

LEARNING

❊ Each musical instrument makes its own distinct sound.

MATERIALS

❊ Rhythm instruments—either commercial or handmade

STEPS

1. Gather together several commercial rhythm instruments or instruments the children have made.

2. Have the children take turns playing each instrument separately while the other children listen to its distinct sound.

3. Now have the children turn around so that they cannot see the instruments being played. Select a child to play one instrument and then put it down.

4. Have the children turn around and allow one child to name or point to the instrument he or she thinks was played.

5. Allow the child who played the instrument to acknowledge whether the response was correct. If it wasn't, call on another child to make his or her guess until the correct instrument is given.

6. Allow as many children as possible to have a turn playing an instrument for the group to guess. It is okay if instruments get played more than once.

CRITICAL THINKING CHALLENGE

Can you distinguish more than one instrument's sound at the same time? How can you find out?

ACCOMMODATIONS

✔ Vary the number of instruments for the group's abilities.

✔ Use instruments that have very different sounds to make this activity easier.

✔ For children who are not able to give the names of the instruments played, allow them to point to the instrument they think they heard.

EXTENSIONS

✔ Use recordings and pictures of band instruments, and play the game in the same manner. A child could whisper to you which instrument he or she wants played.

✔ Invite children who play in the school orchestra or band to come in and play their instruments for the children to hear. The game could be played as before.

Musical Patterns

In Musical Patterns the children recreate the pattern they hear.

LEARNING

✳ Music often consists of patterns of sounds that are repeated.

MATERIALS

✳ One rhythm instrument for each child, such as homemade tambourines (easily made by stapling two paper plates together and adding a handful of large seeds before the last staple is secured), jingle bells, drums (drumming a hard surface would work, too), etc.

STEPS

1. Use one type of musical instrument to play a simple pattern.

2. Have the children repeat your pattern on the same instrument.

3. Allow each child to play his or her own pattern for everyone to replicate.

ACCOMMODATIONS

✔ You may need to help children play a definite pattern rather than just a long series of sounds.

EXTENSIONS

✔ The children could use two instruments when creating their patterns.

✔ Provide music to listen to that has very definite patterns and challenge the children to play these.

Musical Animals

In Musical Animals commercial or homemade rhythm instruments are used to depict the movements of different animals, and the children move in the manner of a specific animal when they hear a certain instrument played a certain way.

LEARNING

✻ Sounds can be used to express movements.

MATERIALS

✻ A variety of rhythm instruments
✻ A box or screen to hide the instruments behind

STEPS

1. Begin with a discussion and demonstrations of how certain animals move.

2. Then show how a rhythm instrument might be played to signify that movement. For example, a light ting-a-ling on a triangle might signify the flight of a small bird, and a hard thumping on a drum might signify an elephant's heavy movement.

3. Have the children decide on some animals they wish to make movement music for, and discuss what rhythm instrument might be played and how.

4. Then allow the children to move as the animals signified by each rhythm and instrument with the teacher producing the rhythms on the instruments. Each time the rhythm and instrument change, the children must change the animal they are imitating.

5. Once they have the idea, hide the instruments behind a box as you play them so that the children are listening to the sound and rhythm and not just changing movement because they see you change instruments.

6. Next allow some of the children to take turns playing the movement rhythms and instruments for the other children to move to as animals. Again, keep the instruments behind a box so they are out of sight of the movers!

CRITICAL THINKING CHALLENGE

Can you create musical sounds and movements for plants, machines, etc.?

ACCOMMODATIONS

✔ Use fewer instruments and simpler rhythms for younger children.

✔ The teacher might need to do all the playing of the instruments if playing the proper beat will be difficult for the children to do.

EXTENSIONS

✔ After the children have proven they can master this activity, try using one instrument played different ways for all the animals included in the activity.

Musical Bingo (Mingo)

Children play Musical Bingo (Mingo) by covering the picture of the instrument the caller says.

LEARNING

✳ Each musical instrument has its own specific name and appearance.

MATERIALS

✳ 1-by-1-inch square pictures of 25 marching band instruments (Clip art would work fine for this if you have access to a computer. Otherwise, catalogs from companies that sell musical instruments would provide you with small pictures.) on a 5-by-5-inch square sheet of paper, copied (one sheet for each child plus one extra sheet for the teacher)

✳ 5-by-5-inch square sheets of paper with blank 1-by-1-inch squares on them—five per row and five rows (one for each child)

✳ 25 (1-by-1-inch square) pieces of cardboard for the teacher to mount one set of pictures on to make the calling pieces

✳ Scissors and glue for the children to use to prepare the game cards

✳ A container for the calling pieces

STEPS

1. Arrange the instrument pictures on a 5-by-5-inch square sheet of paper that has five 1-inch squares across the page and five 1-inch squares going down the page, one picture in each small square.

2. Make copies of this sheet of paper—one for each child.

3. Also make copies of a squares sheet as described above but without the pictures—one for each child.

4. Have the children cut out the little pictures on the first sheet and arrange them in the little blank squares on the second sheet in any order that they choose and then glue them down.

5. While they are doing this, you will need to cut out a set of the little pictures, too, and glue them to small cardboard squares. These will serve as the calling pieces for the game.

6. Once these things are done, you are ready to play.

7. Place the calling pieces in a container.

8. Reach in and pull out one picture of an instrument, and call out its name.

9. The children will need some sort of markers (shelled corn works well) to use to mark the pictures of the instruments as they are called out by the teacher.

10. When a child has covered five squares in a row up or down, he or she should call out "Mingo!" If he or she has correctly covered all the squares, that card is a winner.

11. Have the children clear their cards and play the game again.

(continued)

Musical Bingo (Mingo) (continued)

12. Having a bigger-size picture of each instrument to show the children at first when you call out the name of an instrument will ensure that they cover the correct picture even if they are unsure of that instrument's name.

13. In no time, they will no longer need this crutch as they recognize each picture by its name.

14. At this point, the winner of the game could be the caller for the next game. If there is more than one winner, they can take turns calling for the next game.

ACCOMMODATIONS

✔ You can adjust the number of pictures and squares to suit the abilities of your group.

✔ Group a more capable child with one who needs more help, and have them play one card together.

EXTENSIONS

✔ Allow the children to come up with other ideas to use to make Bingo-type games, such as animals or methods of transportation.

You're the Conductor

In the activity You're the Conductor *one child conducts the rhythm orchestra while the other children play the rhythm instruments.*

LEARNING

✳ A conductor leads the orchestra, making sure the musicians are playing the instruments in the way he or she wishes.

MATERIALS

※ Video of a conductor with an orchestra

※ Television with VCR

※ A variety of rhythm instruments (for this activity it is fine if several are the same kind of instrument)

※ A baton for the conductor

STEPS

1. Show a video clip of an orchestra playing a piece. Point out the conductor and have the children pay particular attention to him or her and the movements he or she makes as well as how the musicians respond to the conductor's movements.

2. Now tell the children that they will have the opportunity to conduct their own orchestra of musicians playing rhythm instruments.

3. First decide on the motions that the conductor might use to tell the musicians to play more loudly, quickly, softly, or slowly, as well as when to begin playing and when to stop.

   Have all the children practice these motions.

4. Next choose a willing child to be the conductor, and assign the other children to play rhythm instruments. Seat the children with the same or similar instruments together as is done in a real orchestra.

5. Then have the conductor stand facing the orchestra with a baton in hand and direct the orchestra to play as he or she wishes using the signals decided upon earlier.

6. Let a few children have turns as conductors today and tell the rest they will get their chance to have a turn when the orchestra meets again.

ACCOMMODATIONS

✔ Keep the signals simple and to a minimum at first.

EXTENSIONS

✔ The children could pretend to conduct the musicians for a piece of recorded music they are familiar with.

✔ You might invite in a real orchestra conductor to tell about what he or she does when conducting.

New Year's Parade

In New Years Parade *the children use New Year's celebration noisemakers and hats to welcome in the New Year.*

LEARNING

✳ Music can be made with a variety of instruments.

✳ We celebrate some important events with parades that include marching bands.

MATERIALS

✳ Noisemakers and hats from New Year's Eve celebrations (ask parents to save and drop off used party supplies)

STEPS

1. Discuss how the movement of time from one year to another is celebrated all over the world. Ask the children how their families celebrate this. Tell the children that parades are often a part of important celebrations, and parades generally include music and marching bands.

2. Then allow the children to welcome the New Year with a parade complete with musical instruments (noisemakers) to play and hats to wear.

TEACHER NOTE

Consider the cultures represented by children in your group, and substitute parades that are more closely associated with their cultures.

 ACCOMMODATIONS

✔ Be sure each child can play the instrument he or she chooses or is given.

 EXTENSIONS

✔ Discuss ways that people celebrate New Year's around the world.

✔ Have parades to celebrate other important events in the children's lives.

Jump Rope Jingles

Jump Rope Jingles introduces children to the many jump rope jingles that are popular. They have a specific timing and beat that the children will feel as they chant and jump to the jingles.

LEARNING

❋ Jump rope jingles have a definite beat and rhythm we can respond to.

MATERIALS

❋ Jump rope jingles (such as those from *Anna Banana: 101 Jump Rope Rhymes* or ask the children which ones they are familiar with)

❋ Large sheets of chart paper and a dark, thick marker

❋ Jump ropes (optional)

STEPS

1. Take the book of jump rope jingles, and on the large sheets of chart paper write the jingles you wish to share with your group.

2. Read a jingle through to the children, keeping it in rhythm.

3. Now have the children chant the jingle with you.

4. Next have them pretend to jump rope to the beat while chanting the jingle.

5. If your group is up to the challenge, use actual jump ropes and have them chant the jingle while they jump rope. This is probably better done outside or in a gym.

6. It's great fun, great exercise, and a great way to work on rhythms and beats!

CRITICAL THINKING CHALLENGE

Can you create your own jingles? What makes for a good jumping jingle?

ACCOMMODATIONS

✓ Jumping rope is a skill that not all children might have, so jumping without a rope will be less frustrating for them. They could also chant the jingle while others actually jump rope. But encourage them to jump to the beat either way.

EXTENSIONS

✓ Add new jingles as the children hear of them. Their parents and grandparents may be good sources for jingles as they may have jumped rope when they were children.

✓ Have the children try jumping rope with two turning the rope and one jumping.

Music on the Move

Music on the Move has the children listen to music and rise up higher as the notes go up the scale and stoop down lower as the notes descend the scale.

LEARNING

* Music is made up of various pitches.

MATERIALS

* A xylophone or another instrument on which to play musical scales
* Music that contains fairly substantial changes in pitch throughout the piece

STEPS

1. Play a musical scale on a musical instrument such as a xylophone.

2. Instruct the children to rise up slowly as you play the notes going up the scale and to stoop down slowly as you go back down the scale. Tell them that the highness or lowness of a note is called its pitch.

3. Now jump around on the scale playing a high note and then a low note and having the children rise or stoop to the note played as compared to the one played before it. If it's a big jump between notes they need to make a big change in their body position, and if it's a small jump the change needs to be more slight.

4. Then play some music with lots of pitch changes and have them respond in a similar manner to the music played.

ACCOMMODATIONS

✓ Slower music will be easier for the children to move to.

EXTENSIONS

✓ Allow each child to play the xylophone, beginning with any note for the others to just listen to and then playing another note for them to move up or down to compared to the prior note.

Music That Makes Us Move

Music That Makes Us Move encourages the children to listen to classical music and to move creatively to the rhythm of it.

LEARNING

❋ Music can inspire movement.

❋ Choreography is the art of planning and designing the movements of a dance.

MATERIALS

❋ A piece of classical music that incorporates a variety of different rhythms (such as "Surprise Symphony," music from "Peter and the Wolf," etc.)

❋ Device to play the music—CD player, tape recorder, etc.—depending on the format the music is recorded on

❋ Scarves or streamers

STEPS

1. Play the piece of classical music.

2. First have the children listen to the music and think about ways they could move to the music. Scarves or streamers could be used in addition to body movements.

3. Then replay the piece allowing the children to move creatively to it.

4. Next have each child show how he or she moved to a particular part of the music.

5. Help the children decide on which of the movements they liked best.

6. Then move on to the next change in the rhythm of the music and repeat steps 4 and 5.

7. Do this for each different rhythm incorporated in the piece of music.

8. Now replay the music and have all the children move in the ways specified.

9. Discuss that this is choreography—the art of planning and designing the movements of a dance.

ACCOMMODATIONS

✓ Choose short pieces with very definite rhythms and rhythmic changes for younger children.

✓ For younger children, provide fewer choices as to what movements might be done and how many steps might need to be done to complete the movement pattern.

EXTENSIONS

✓ Provide lots of examples of classical music for the children to listen to during free time, snack time, etc. Always provide the name of the piece being played.

✓ Plan to attend a children's production of a musical program, such as a ballet, which incorporates choreography and classical music.

Musical Messages

In Musical Messages the children transform spoken messages into songs based on recognizable tunes.

LEARNING

✳ Writing lyrics involves putting words with tunes.

MATERIALS

✳ A familiar tune

✳ A message that you wish to send, written out to fit the tune

✳ Sheets of paper

STEPS

1. Using a familiar tune and the message you want to send to another class, develop a musical message that fits the tune's rhythm. For example, here's a message to fit the tune of "Twinkle, Twinkle, Little Star":

> Mrs. Johnson wants to know
> If it's time for reading to go.
> Yesterday we went at ten.
> Do we want to do that again?
> Tell us, tell us, what you choose
> And we'll relay this timely news!

2. Then have a small group of children practice the verse you have written down for them and deliver the musical message to the class or person who needs to get it. Writing the words out on a sheet of paper for the children to look at as they sing the words will be most helpful.

3. At first the teacher may have to figure out how the message can be written to fit the tune. Eventually, the children may be able to do this themselves.

 ACCOMMODATIONS

✔ If this message is too cumbersome, try a shorter message to a shorter tune.

✔ You may need to sing along with the children at first when the message is delivered. You may need to take all the children with you when you do this.

 EXTENSIONS

✔ Having a musical message service deliver a message to your classroom would be fun.

✔ You could also give directions with the words sung to a musical tune.

✔ Many idea books of activities to use with young children incorporate familiar tunes for songs to sing about many different topics. You could also teach the children these or have them develop their own songs to go with topics they are learning about. Putting words to music enhances our ability to remember them. Consider the ABC song!

It's All Music

It's All Music *introduces the children to the unique music of different cultures.*

LEARNING

✴ Every culture has music.

✴ Some things about the music make it specific to that culture.

MATERIALS

✴ Music characteristic of the culture you are emphasizing (recordings of traditional songs, different instruments)

STEPS

1. As you learn about different cultures of the world, highlight the musical traditions that are identified with the cultures. For example, Asian music has a sound of its own, as does Latin American music.

2. Sing the traditional songs of the culture in English or listen to them in the native language of the culture.

3. Teach the steps to simple folk dances of the culture or just move to the music if the steps are too complicated. Polka music from the German tradition is great to move to and the children will get a terrific aerobic workout to boot!

4. Square dancing is a great American tradition, and with the caller telling them what to do as they go, a simple square dance could be done with your group of children.

 ## ACCOMMODATIONS

✔ If teaching dance steps, adjust the difficulty of the dance to the children's abilities.

 ## EXTENSIONS

✔ Invite a square dance troupe in if there's one in your community.

✔ Many cultural groups are also willing to share their music and dances with children.

Let's Have a Parade

For Let's Have a Parade *the children march to the great marches of John Philip Sousa and others, as they move from one activity to another or to celebrate holidays when parades are generally held, such as the Fourth of July, Memorial Day, and city festivals.*

LEARNING

✳ Some composers wrote great marches that we regularly hear at parades.

MATERIALS

✳ Marching music (such as "Stars and Stripes Forever" by John Philip Sousa)

✳ Rhythm instruments to play or flags to wave

STEPS

1. Play the marching music.

2. Use this music as the children march from one activity space to another.

 ACCOMMODATIONS

✔ Hold your own classroom parades with the children marching to the music while playing rhythm instruments, waving flags, or pantomiming the playing of instruments. For students with physical special needs, ensure you choose an instrument that is appropriate—and make modifications in the room as needed.

 EXTENSIONS

✔ Encourage the children and their families to go to events where marching music is played, such as football games and band concerts.

Classical Cartoons

In Classical Cartoons the children are introduced to classical music through the old cartoons that incorporate it.

LEARNING

✳ Classical music is all around us.

MATERIALS

✳ Video-recorded children's cartoons that incorporate classical music scores in their sound tracks to go with the movements depicted (videotape older cartoons or locate them in a local video store)

✳ A variety of classical music pieces that have different tempos and rhythms

STEPS

1. Help the children identify the name of the musical score being played and then sit back and listen to the music as they enjoy the cartoon or portion of it where the music is played.

2. Have the children move to different classical pieces of music according to the speed and movement of the notes played.

3. Once the children are familiar with several different pieces of classical music, they will be able to suggest music to use with different movements they wish to make.

ACCOMMODATIONS

✔ Choose classical pieces that are very different in their tempos to use with different movements at first.

EXTENSIONS

✔ Invite the high school orchestra in to play some classical pieces.

✔ Play classical music during quiet work times.

The Music of the Week

Through The Music of the Week the children will be introduced to a wide variety of musical styles that they will come to recognize.

LEARNING

※ Music has many different and varied styles for us to enjoy.

※ Some music is instrumental and other music has vocals as well.

MATERIALS

※ Music of several different types, including classical, blues, jazz, pop, opera, etc. (Libraries often carry a nice variety of selections of good-quality musical pieces you could borrow.)

※ A good sound system

STEPS

1. Each week choose selections from one different style of music to feature during quiet work times, free time, lunchtime, etc.—any time music is appropriate and won't be overly distracting.

2. Some ideas of styles of music include:

classical	opera	folk
blues	show music	big band
jazz	country	patriotic
pop	rock and roll	

3. Combine instrumental and vocal music for each type. When using vocals, be sure the lyrics are appropriate for your listeners!

4. After the children have heard several types that you have identified over the weeks, along with the names of the musical pieces played, see if they can identify a piece they have not heard before by its type.

CRITICAL THINKING CHALLENGE

What is it about a particular type or piece of music that you like or don't like, and why?

ACCOMMODATIONS

✔ Play the music softly so that it can be enjoyed and yet won't be distracting as the children do other things.

EXTENSIONS

✔ Have a "share my favorite music" day each week when one child can bring in his or her favorite type of music to share. Send a note home so that parents will evaluate the music's appropriateness for the entire class to hear. If in doubt, listen to the music privately before playing it for the group. Vocals can sometimes raise inappropriate issues.

✔ Have the children write down the titles of the music scores they really like as you play them and then play the musical piece they liked the best when their turn comes up to share a favorite piece of music.

✔ The children could also vote on the piece they most want to hear again on Fridays.

Let's Dance

Let's Dance allows the children to experience the joy of dancing.

LEARNING

✳ Dancing is an enjoyable activity that anyone can take part in. There are many easy and fun dances that the children could learn to do.

MATERIALS

✳ Music for the dance songs, such as The Hokey Pokey, The Macarena, The Shoo-Fly Song, The Chicken Dance, The Mexican Hat Dance, etc.

✳ A large open space for dancing

STEPS

1. Teach the dances one at a time so that the children don't get confused with too many different steps. These dances are often done at weddings and other events, and the children will enjoy being able to join in at events where the dances are done.

2. Don't be too concerned if each step isn't just right. Keep it fun and lighthearted so the children will see the fun in dancing.

ACCOMMODATIONS

✔ Choose dances that are not too difficult for children to learn.

EXTENSIONS

✔ The children might also like to learn modern dances.

✔ Line dancing is also fun. There may be someone who teaches it who would come in to teach the dances to the children. Or children could go to a dance studio.

So Many Songs to Sing

So Many Songs to Sing introduces the children to a wide array of songs written for different reasons or about different topics.

LEARNING

✳ Songs are a rich part of our cultural heritage.

MATERIALS

✳ Selections of songs from many different categories, including camping songs, cowboy songs, sailing songs, patriotic songs, etc.

✳ Props to go with the categories (cowboy hats, sailboats, cradle, flags)

✳ A large chart

STEPS

1. Discuss with the children the many times an event or topic is associated with music and singing.

2. As you introduce the children to the different categories of songs, include fun props to denote each category. The children might wear cowboy hats or neckerchiefs when they are singing cowboy songs, and a fake campfire complete with logs and a red tissue paper fire would set the scene for all those songs kids sing at camp.

3. On a large chart, place a symbol for each category and under that symbol write the names of the songs they have learned that fit that category. A sailboat could denote songs about sailing, a baby's cradle could denote lullabies, and a flag could denote patriotic songs.

4. The idea is to introduce the children to all kinds of songs to show what a variety of songs there are.

 ACCOMMODATIONS

✔ Choose songs that are appropriate for the ability level of your group. Many of our patriotic songs contain concepts and words that are too difficult for younger learners.

 EXTENSIONS

✔ Try to find out something about the person or people who wrote the songs and when they sang them.

Chapter 2

Visual Arts

The visual arts chapter uses a wide variety of art activities to enhance the children's understanding of art concepts. Children will experiment with different art mediums and techniques that are used by artists to create a variety of different effects. They will be encouraged to evaluate their own works of art as they consider all the elements that go into creating original works of art.

Styrofoam™ Snowflakes

In Styrofoam™ Snowflakes Styrofoam™ packing "peanuts" can be used to make unique snowflakes to hang as if falling from the sky!

LEARNING

❋ We can recycle materials in art projects.

MATERIALS

❋ Wax paper sheets to cut into circles

❋ Styrofoam™ packing "peanuts"

❋ A piece of cardboard for each child cut a bit larger than the circles

❋ One squirt bottle of glue for each child

❋ Fishing line for hanging

STEPS

1. Cut sheets of wax paper into circles about the size you'd like the snowflakes to be.

2. Have the children arrange the packaging "peanuts" on the wax paper in the pattern each wishes to make, starting with a circular shape around the edge of the wax paper circle. Remind them that all the packing peanuts *must be* connected (each peanut must touch another peanut to form a continuous whole).

3. Once each child has decided on a pattern he or she likes, have him or her pick up one piece of Styrofoam™ at a time and squeeze a line of glue onto the wax paper before returning it to that spot.

4. Once all the pieces have been glued down in a connected whole, the snowflakes need to be placed in a safe place to dry. You will need to have a piece of cardboard under each circle when you begin this project so that the snowflakes can be easily moved to this area.

5. Once the glue is dry, which will probably take a day or two depending on how much glue was used (Being a bit generous with the glue is beneficial for this project!), the snowflakes can be peeled from the wax paper. Fishing line will work nicely for hanging the snowflakes and will give the illusion that the snowflakes are really falling from the sky, especially if you hang them at varying lengths!

ACCOMMODATIONS

✔ This project is easily adjustable to several age groups by varying the size and intricacy of the snowflakes.

EXTENSIONS

✔ You may want to compare these flakes with actual snowflakes. Using a magnifying glass and collecting real flakes on black construction paper will make this possible.

✔ You might also have the children come up with as many ideas as possible of things to make using packing "peanuts."

Colors of My Rainbow

Colors of My Rainbow *encourages children to create unique colors for rainbows.*

LEARNING

❋ By mixing the primary colors in different combinations, we can create many colors.

MATERIALS

❋ Red, yellow, and blue liquid tempera paint

❋ Styrofoam plates to use as paint palettes (one for each child)

❋ A paintbrush for each child

❋ Styrofoam™ cups to hold water for washing paintbrushes out after creating each new color and painting each stripe

❋ White and blue construction paper

❋ Scissors

❋ Glue

STEPS

1. Tell the children that you have a big problem. You want to paint some green grass but you only have blue and yellow paint. Lead them to the idea of mixing the yellow and blue paint to create green paint. Also show how the amount of each color mixed changes the shade of the new color.

2. Introduce red, yellow, and blue as the primary colors and discuss and demonstrate how many other colors (secondary colors) can be created by mixing these colors in different combinations and amounts.

3. Allow the children to experiment with mixing colors of paint on their Styrofoam™ palettes (plates) until they have each created six different colors of paint from the red, yellow, and blue paints.

4. Have them paint one stripe of each color they created to form rainbows on their sheets of white paper. (Use white paper to keep the colors true to what was mixed.)

5. Have the children cut out their rainbows when the paint has dried and mount them on sky blue sheets of paper.

ACCOMMODATIONS

✔ Have children mix fewer colors to make this project easier.

✔ The teacher could draw out arcs in rainbow fashion on the white paper to aid the children in creating a rainbow effect when painting.

EXTENSIONS

✔ The children could create rainbows of variations of all one color.

✔ Other objects could be added to the rainbow picture to make a complete outdoor scene.

Nature Prints

In Nature Prints many articles from nature (rocks, leaves, sticks, flowers, etc.) can be used to make interesting print designs when coated with tempera paint.

LEARNING

❋ Nature supplies us with many art materials that are free and unique.

MATERIALS

❋ Paper sacks to collect natural materials (one for each child)

❋ A variety of natural objects such as rocks, leaves, shells, feathers, etc.

❋ Tempera paint of various colors

❋ Paintbrushes and aluminum pie tins

❋ Construction paper

STEPS

1. Give each child a paper sack as you go on a nature walk. Remind the children not to pull plants up by the roots when collecting leaves or to take things that belong to others, such as landscaping materials.

2. When you return from your walk, have the children dump out the materials they've gathered to share with others. Leaves, if not used immediately, will need to be kept flat by placing a heavy book on them until it is time to do this project.

3. Tempera paint may be poured into aluminum pie tins and the objects used for printing dipped into the paint, or paint can be brushed onto the objects, which keeps the paint from being too thick and the impression from being lost. Be sure to demonstrate the proper technique to use to get a clear print on the paper—slow, careful, and firm.

4. Encourage the children to use several different materials to add interest and variety to their creations.

5. When the prints are finished and dry, have the children look again at all the materials used and try to figure out which objects others used to make their prints.

ACCOMMODATIONS

✔ If a nature walk is not possible, the teacher can collect objects ahead of time to share with the children, or the children can bring in objects from nature walks taken with their families.

✔ Adjust the amount and types of objects to the ages and abilities of your group.

EXTENSIONS

✔ Allow the children to experiment with different mediums other than tempera paint, such as stamp pad ink, powdered drink mix mixed with just enough water to dissolve it, etc.

✔ Children can also experiment with other stamping techniques, such as rolling rocks or sticks over the paper or swishing a feather back and forth on the paper.

✔ Different types of paper may also be used to get different effects.

Leaf Roll

In Leaf Roll leaves will be used in a unique manner to make printed wrapping paper.

LEARNING

✳ Materials from nature can be used to make inexpensive, appealing, and useful items.

MATERIALS

✳ A variety of fresh leaves (They need to be flat or should be flattened under heavy books before being used for this activity.)

✳ Tempera paint

✳ Blank newsprint paper

✳ Rolling pins or cylindrical blocks of rolling-pin length

STEPS

1. Gather several different types of fresh leaves.

2. Carefully paint the back of a leaf (where the veins show up better) with tempera paint.

3. Next lay the leaf painted side down on a sheet of newsprint paper.

4. Continue in this method until the child has the amount and pattern of leaves he or she likes. It is okay to overlap leaves a bit, but a part of each leaf needs to be touching the paper or it will not become a part of the finished design.

5. Now cover the leaves on the paper carefully with a piece of newsprint, and use a rolling pin to carefully roll over the paper and the leaves. Demonstrate this for the children.

6. After the paper has been completely rolled over, have the children lift up the newsprint on top and then carefully lift the leaves straight up and off the paper. Have them place the leaves on the piece of newsprint just removed for easy disposal and to avoid a big mess!

7. The bottom piece of newsprint should reveal the leaf patterns. When dry, this can be used for unique wrapping paper.

ACCOMMODATIONS

✔ The size of the paper and number of leaves can easily be adjusted to suit your group.

EXTENSIONS

✔ You may wish to work on identifying the leaves used by name or have the children figure out which leaves were used by comparing the leaf prints with unused leaves. Again, amount and difficulty should be adjusted to fit your group.

✔ Other objects may also work for this project, such as flat shape forms, cardboard patterns, etc.

Window Art

In Window Art using clear contact paper and various interesting flat objects, attractive window decorations can be made.

LEARNING

✻ Art can involve how we arrange things in an interesting, eye-catching fashion.

MATERIALS

✻ Clear contact paper (enough for each child to have two identical pieces)

✻ Construction paper to cut shapes out of, or flat materials like leaves, confetti, tissue paper strips or shapes, etc., which will stick to contact paper

✻ Construction paper for borders

✻ A hole punch and yarn or string for hanging

STEPS

1. For this project, cut the clear contact paper into shapes that are the same size. Each child needs two pieces.

2. Next the children need to choose what to use for their window decorations.

3. Have the children carefully peel back the covering from one of the two sheets of contact paper and lay the contact paper on the table sticky side up.

4. Now have them place their decorating materials on the contact paper as they choose. You may want to have them plan this out before they place anything on the contact paper, as it cannot be removed later.

5. Then they should carefully remove the cover paper from the other piece of contact paper and place it sticky side down on the pattern they just created to seal it in. They need to take care to line up the contact paper sheets, but edges that don't match can also be trimmed away without affecting the project if shapes enclosed aren't too close to the edges.

6. A hole can be punched through the contact paper now and a string attached to hang this from the curtain rod over a window, or it can be taped on the window with clear tape. (A border made out of construction paper will give the projects a finishing touch and can be glued on the edges or added before the two pieces of contact paper are stuck together.)

 ACCOMMODATIONS

✔ Size and materials should be altered to fit the group's abilities and tastes.

 EXTENSIONS

✔ Allow the children to experiment with materials to achieve different effects, such as cellophane, cloth, etc.

✔ Lead a discussion of the terms opaque, transparent, and translucent while dealing with the variety of materials that could be used with such a project.

Seeds Say It All

Seeds Say It All **helps children connect plants to the seeds that produce them.**

LEARNING

✳ Plants grow from seeds unique to each plant type.

MATERIALS

* A variety of seed packets. Children's families may have some to donate. Gardeners often have unused seed packets that contain seeds too old for planting but perfect for this project! Garden shops and other stores that sell seeds may be willing to donate seed packets left over after planting season, as well.

* Sturdy paper or cardboard

* White glue in bottles

* Crayons

* Small, flat container such as a jar lid (one for each child)

STEPS

1. Give each child an unopened seed packet.

2. Have each child identify the seed type from the picture of the plant found on the packet of seeds.

3. Have them carefully open their seed packets and pour the seeds into the small flat container.

4. Instruct the children to draw the plant and color it appropriately.

5. Next have them outline their drawings with glue and carefully place the seeds on the glue outline.

6. When the pictures are finished and dry, have the children compare the seeds and the plants they become with one another, discussing what type of plants their seeds will grow into.

ACCOMMODATIONS

✔ Larger seeds will be easier for younger children to work with.

EXTENSIONS

✔ If you actually plan to plant a garden using fresh seeds, these seeds can be used to make signs to show what is planted where by having the children print the plant names on small flat pieces of wood mounted on stakes. Then have the children outline the letters with glue and attach the seeds to the outlines. When these are dry you will want to cover each wooden sign with the name on it with a snack-size plastic bag that seals shut to protect them from the elements. (If printing is an issue for your group, you could do that and just have the children add the seeds.)

Two Halves Make a Whole

Two Halves Make a Whole *is actually an art activity in which the children each receive half of a picture to complete as they choose.*

LEARNING

✳ A complete picture tells the whole story.

MATERIALS

✳ Colorful pictures of interest to children, cut from magazines
✳ Sheets of white paper large enough to allow for the entire picture
✳ Scissors and glue
✳ Markers or crayons

STEPS

1. Take the magazine pictures and cut each one in half.

2. Glue one half of the picture to a sheet of paper, allowing room to complete the picture on the right or left side of the sheet of paper, whichever is appropriate.

3. Allow each child to choose a picture and instruct him or her to use markers or crayons to complete the picture already begun.

4. Display the pictures when completed.

5. The children may enjoy seeing how the person who had the other half of their printed picture completed his or hers. Display these two pictures next to each other.

6. Emphasize that each person had a different idea of how to complete the picture, and that's great!

ACCOMMODATIONS

✔ Vary detail and size of pictures to suit your group's abilities.

EXTENSIONS

✔ By choosing specific pictures you could introduce the concept of symmetry.
✔ Children could create stories to accompany their pictures.

Real Cool Trees

Real Cool Trees calls for the children to use real sticks from trees along with wallpaper samples to create unique trees never seen before.

LEARNING

✳ We can combine natural and man-made materials to create original works of art.

MATERIALS

✳ One 3-to-5-foot tree branch with smaller branches attached

✳ Wallpaper sample books (These can usually be obtained free from wall decorating stores once the styles in the books are out of print or out-of-date.)—Avoid wallpaper that has actual pictures of objects printed on it.

✳ Brown yarn

✳ Scissors for children and a hole punch

✳ A piece of earth-tone clay suitable for your branch size and a sturdy piece of cardboard to place it on

✳ Optional: real leaves of different shapes

STEPS

1. Place the large piece of clay on the piece of cardboard and stick the tree branch into it.

2. Using the samples from wallpaper books, have the children cut out leaf shapes to suit the size of the branch. Having real leaves for them to look at will help them to decide on shapes for their leaves. (Wallpaper that incorporates the colors we see in nature will work best for this activity.)

3. Help each child punch a hole in his or her leaf shape and string a piece of brown yarn through it.

4. Then he or she can tie his or her leaf to the tree branch to jointly create a class tree.

ACCOMMODATIONS

✔ The teacher may need to tie the leaves on the branches and punch the holes for some children.

EXTENSIONS

✔ Gather leaves from different types of trees, and provide books to help the children identify them. Then vote on a specific leaf shape to use to create the wallpaper leaves, and show the children how you can create a template for that leaf shape as well as how to use the template themselves to create their leaves. Label the tree with the name of leaf shape (tree type) they chose to use.

✔ Have a picnic or allow the children to take turns reading under the tree.

Ribbons and Color

Ribbons and Color *has the children use a unique technique to create symmetrical designs.*

LEARNING

❋ There are many techniques we can use to create symmetrical designs.

MATERIALS

❋ Two same-size and -shape sheets of construction paper for each child

❋ Tempera paint in squirt bottles

❋ Lengths of yarn or ribbon (any width will work) a few inches longer than the paper length

STEPS

1. Give each child two sheets of paper of the same shape and size.

2. Have each child squirt tempera paint on one sheet of paper, avoiding the edges.

3. Next instruct the child to lay a piece of ribbon or yarn on the paper with the ends hanging out on each end of the paper.

4. He or she should then place the second sheet of paper exactly over the first.

5. With one hand flat on top of the middle of the two piled sheets, have the child use his or her other hand to slowly pull the ribbon back and forth between the papers and then pull it all the way out.

6. Next he or she should carefully peel the two sheets apart to see the design created on each sheet and how they are the same.

ACCOMMODATIONS

✔ The teacher may need to hold the papers down for children so they can just concentrate on pulling the ribbon or yarn through.

EXTENSIONS

✔ Using two colors of tempera paint will allow you to show what happens when colors are mixed. Each child could choose different colors to use and speculate what color will be made when they are mixed.

✔ Another idea would be to create wrapping paper with this technique. You will need to use lighter-weight paper.

Wall Art Bulletin Board Backgrounds

Wall Art Bulletin Board Backgrounds *incorporates techniques used to paint real walls to create a bulletin board background.*

LEARNING

* Many materials and techniques can be used for painting.

MATERIALS

* Various painting supplies such as rollers, painting sponges, plastic wrap, and feather dusters, etc.
* Tempera or latex paint
* A large bulletin board covered with a sheet of heavy paper

STEPS

1. Cover a large bulletin board placed at the height of the children in your group with a piece of heavy paper.

2. On a separate piece of paper, demonstrate one or more techniques that could be used to paint the bulletin board, using the various painting supplies. These are all techniques used on real walls to create different effects.

3. Choose one technique to use and give each child the opportunity to try it.

4. Different bulletin boards could be used for different techniques or you could use a different technique each time you change the background of the bulletin board.

5. It would be fun to have an interior designer actually come to show the child how to do the various techniques and show pictures of walls he or she has painted using the techniques.

ACCOMMODATIONS

✔ The teacher may need to place his or her hand over the hand of the child to help the child master the technique used.

EXTENSIONS

✔ Children could use one of the techniques learned to create a cardboard backdrop for a play taking place in a room setting.

✔ Two colors of paint could be used to create a different effect.

Sand Paintings

Sand Paintings affords the children the opportunity to create sand paintings similar to those done by some Native Americans.

LEARNING

❊ We can recreate authentic art forms.

MATERIALS

❊ Authentic sand paintings or pictures of these

❊ Information to share about sand painting (such as *A Guide to Navajo Sandpaintings*, for example)

❊ Containers with tight-fitting lids (For each color you choose to make the sand, you will need one container of a size appropriate for that amount of sand.)

❊ Dry sand

❊ Several colors of liquid tempera paint

❊ A corrugated cardboard square for each child

❊ White glue in small squeeze bottles

❊ A tub for leftover sand

❊ A pencil for each child

❊ A self-adhesive label for each child

❊ Trays to keep colored sand separated nicely (TV dinner trays work well.)

STEPS

1. Show the authentic sand paintings, or pictures of them, to the children as you share information about them.

2. Place dry sand in the containers.

3. Add a different color of liquid tempera paint to each container. (Experiment beforehand to determine how much paint is needed to color the sand without making it wet and clumpy. It may be less than you think!)

4. Cover each container tightly with a lid and allow the children to shake them to turn the sand the color of the paint added to it.

5. Then have the children draw pictures on the brown corrugated cardboard using the small white glue bottles. Drawing the pictures they want with pencils first will keep them from making errors with the glue, which cannot be fixed. Drawing bigger and uncomplicated designs or pictures works best. Demonstrate this and remind the children when they begin drawing.

6. While the children are working on this, give each child some of each color of sand on a tray. Small groups of children sitting together could share a tray.

7. Demonstrate how to lightly sprinkle the sand over the glue picture in the colors you wish each thing in the picture to be.

8. When the children have completed "sanding" their glue pictures, leave them where they are to dry.

9. When dry, excess sand can be shaken off into a tub.

10. Sand paintings are generally labeled on the back with the artist's name and the date. It will work better to write this information on a self-adhesive label and to attach that carefully to the back without laying the sand painting facedown, which will rub sand off of it.

Sand Paintings *(continued)*

ACCOMMODATIONS

✔ If the child has trouble drawing a picture, a helper could draw what the child chooses.

✔ An adult helper could steady the hand of a child while he or she draws with the glue, if necessary.

EXTENSIONS

✔ Learn more about Native American artwork to share and attempt to replicate.

Decorative Garden Rocks

In this Decorative Garden Rocks activity the children create painted rocks to place in a garden as a decoration.

LEARNING

✳ Decorative rocks like the garden shops sell are easy and fun to create.

MATERIALS

✳ A rock for each child that is 6 inches to a foot in diameter and has a broad flat surface (Check with a quarry to see if rocks could be donated for this project, as bigger rocks are more visible in a garden. Otherwise, ask each child to bring in a rock of a certain size, if possible.

✳ Some rocks that are already decorated

✳ Tempera paint and brushes and/or permanent markers

✳ White glue and water

STEPS

1. Bring in the decorated garden rocks to show the children what they generally look like.

Some just have a picture and others include an appropriate saying such as "My Special Garden" or "No Weeds Allowed."

2. Brainstorm several ideas for decorating the rocks before the children begin so you can help those who struggle to decide what to do. Write these on the board, especially the sayings with correct spellings.

3. Have each child show you where he or she intends to paint his or her rock to ensure that a somewhat flat surface will be used.

4. Have the children use paint or permanent markers to decorate the rocks. Markers will work better than paint for writing sayings.

5. A thin mixture of white glue and water can be painted on once the rocks dry to safely seal in the artwork.

6. These would make nice gifts for Mother's Day or you could check with the city to see if the rocks could be donated for its gardens in the parks.

ACCOMMODATIONS

✔ Younger children could simply paint their rocks and the teacher could add a saying they like.

EXTENSIONS

✔ Take a walking field trip to a nearby garden shop to check out the garden rocks available there.

✔ Explore other forms of garden decorations such as bird baths, pinwheels, sundials, and the like.

Welcome Flags

Through the activity Welcome Flags *the children make flags of their own to hang by their front doors to welcome guests.*

LEARNING

✳ Welcoming guests into our homes is important. We can create our own flags rather than purchasing them for this purpose.

MATERIALS

✳ Enough light-colored fabric for each child to have a 7-by-10-inch piece

✳ One clear plastic sheet protector for loose-leaf paper sheets for each child with three holes punched on one side

✳ Fabric paints or fabric markers of a variety of colors (can be purchased at sewing supply stores)

✳ Enough sturdy wire for each child to have a 5-foot length

✳ A piece of corrugated cardboard a bit larger than the fabric piece for each child

✳ Four straight pins for each child

✳ Pinking shears

STEPS

1. Cut the fabric into 7-by-10-inch rectangles with pinking shears to prevent unraveling.

2. If you have commercial welcome flags you have purchased, bring them in to show, or ask parents to let you borrow theirs to show the children so they have an idea of what these generally look like. Many have seasonal themes.

3. Have the children decorate their flags (fabric rectangles) using fabric paints or fabric markers. Make sure the children draw with a long side of the fabric on the top. Pinning the corners of the fabric to a piece of cardboard will keep it from doubling up as the child draws on it.

4. When the paint is dry, the teacher must carefully slide the fabric into the plastic loose-leaf sheet protector. The holes need to be at the top of the picture.

5. Each child should slide the plastic sheet protector onto a 5-foot length of wire using the holes provided.

6. When the protector with the fabric inside is in the center of the wire, the teacher will need to bend the wire straight down on either side so there will be two feet of wire pointing down on each side of the flag. This is what is stuck into the ground.

7. Line the completed flags up in the grass so that the children can show parents what they made and how they are used.

(continued)

Welcome Flags *(continued)*

✓ ACCOMMODATIONS

✓ The amount of teacher involvement will vary with the ages and abilities of the children in the group. For younger children who will require more assistance, ask for parent volunteers to help, or allow older children to help younger ones.

EXTENSIONS

✓ Have the children watch for and report where they see welcome flags.

Plastic Bird Feeder

Through Plastic Bird Feeder the children will make a simple and attractive bird feeder and then draw the birds that come to it and identify them in a bird-watching book.

LEARNING

* We can help the birds have a ready food supply and enjoy nature and what it has to offer through the making of a bird feeder.

MATERIALS

* An 8-oz. or smaller plain plastic tub, such as whipped topping or margarine come in, for each child. Parents could be asked to supply a tub for their child.

* Enough string or fishing line for each child's feeder to have three equal-length pieces

* A hole punch and permanent markers

* Some sort of hook for each feeder to allow for hanging the feeder

* Birdseed

* A guidebook for bird-watchers. These can be purchased at a bookstore.

STEPS

1. Punch three holes around the top edges of each plastic tub at equal distances apart.

2. Have the children decorate the tubs using permanent markers.

3. Using heavy string or fishing line, tie a string to each hole of the length you would like the bird feeder to hang down from a branch.

4. Tie the three strings together at the other ends and add a wire hook to hang the feeder.

5. Provide a small amount of birdseed to each child to take home in a plastic sandwich bag so the feeder will be all set to hang when it is brought home.

6. Encourage the children to draw the birds that come to the feeders and bring their drawings to school so you can try to identify them with a bird-watcher's guide at school.

7. Keep track of all the different birds seen. Remind the children that it might take a while for the birds to find the feeders, so they need to be patient. They might also need to move the feeder to a different spot if no birds come in a week or two and they must be sure to keep seed in the feeder.

8. Why not make a feeder or two for the schoolyard while you are at it? A feeder outside a classroom window will allow bird-watching at school, too!

CRITICAL THINKING CHALLENGE

Why are organizations interested in the birds you see in your neighborhood?

(continued)

Plastic Bird Feeder *(continued)*

ACCOMMODATIONS

✓ Older children will be able to do more of the assembling of the bird feeders, whereas younger children will require more assistance from an adult or older child for this portion of the activity.

EXTENSIONS

✓ Watch for opportunities to report bird sightings from bird-watching organizations. At times these groups request public assistance in an attempt to determine how many or which birds are visiting feeders.

I'm Puzzled

I'm Puzzled allows the children to make their own puzzles out of their colorful drawings.

LEARNING

✳ It is possible to create puzzles using personal drawings we have made.

MATERIALS

✳ Tagboard cut into the size of puzzles you wish to have the children make

✳ Markers

✳ Decoupage sealant (which can be purchased at craft stores, or you can make your own by mixing white glue and water—see steps below for details)

✳ Heavy books

✳ Paper cutter

✳ Clear plastic self-sealing food bags

✳ Camera

✳ Clear tape

STEPS

1. Encourage the children to make colorful drawings on tagboard squares using markers.

2. Take a photograph of each picture. If you use a digital camera, you can enlarge the photograph to make it easier to see.

3. Next have the children paint over the pictures with decoupage sealant. If you don't buy the sealant, you can make your own using white glue mixed with water. Experiment with painting it on a small picture you've made with the same markers the children used to get the proper consistency to coat the picture without running the colors together (not too thin) and yet dry to a clear shine (not too thick).

4. When the pictures are dry, cover them with heavy books overnight to flatten them. The next day the teacher should use a paper cutter to cut each picture into puzzle pieces. The pieces will have straight edges rather than interlocking edges. This will encourage the children to really look at the pictures and the colors in them to put the puzzles together.

5. These pieces can then be stored in clear plastic self-sealing food bags. Tape the picture of the drawing taken with the camera to the bag.

(continued)

I'm Puzzled (continued)

✓ ACCOMMODATIONS

✔ To suit your group, vary the size of the tagboard for the drawings as well as the number of puzzle pieces you cut the pictures into.

✔ Another idea is to cut pictures from magazines to make the puzzles if drawing is an issue.

EXTENSIONS

✔ Provide commercial types of puzzles at the difficulty level suitable for your group of children. Older children may be able to work more complex jigsaw puzzles that take an extended period of time to do. Set these up on a table that won't be needed or disturbed for other activities. Finished puzzles can be sealed and hung on the walls.

Build Me a Sand Castle/Snow Sculpture

Children will use plastic containers to mold sand or snow into building blocks in Build Me a Sand Castle/Snow Sculpture.

LEARNING

✳ Materials such as sand and snow can be molded into forms to make building pieces.

MATERIALS

✳ Snow or sand of the consistency to hold together when molded

✳ Plastic containers of various sizes and shapes, (such as those that margarine, whipped topping, etc. come in. Plastic gelatin molds would also work well and add interest to the building pieces).

✳ Spray bottles filled with water dyed with food coloring (snow sculptures only)

STEPS

1. Gather clean, used plastic containers of varying sizes and shapes.

2. By adding water to your sand table or sandbox you can make sand of the consistency that will stick together when packed in these forms. If using snow you will need to wait until the snow that falls is of a packing consistency to do this activity.

3. Allow the children to use the containers to make molded pieces to build into castles,

forts, houses, etc. Encourage creativity and thinking about the whole that the pieces will create when put together. Snow allows for very big construction as the amount of material to work with is generally great. Sand at the beach would also allow for this.

4. With snow sculptures you can use spray bottles containing various colors of food coloring mixed with water to add color to the finished creations. Also, lightly spraying the snow sculptures with clear water from a hose after they are finished will cause them to freeze harder and last longer.

TEACHER NOTE

An important note of caution: do *not* allow the children to build sculptures that can be crawled into or are taller than they are, as this would be extremely unsafe should the sculptures collapse.

CRITICAL THINKING CHALLENGE

How can you make your snow/sand sculpture last longer?

(continued)

Build Me a Sand Castle/Snow Sculpture *(continued)*

✔ ACCOMMODATIONS

✔ Adjust the size of the containers to the abilities of the group. In this case, smaller containers may actually be more manageable for younger children.

EXTENSIONS

✔ Watch for snow-sculpture or sand-castle building competitions in your locale, and consider a field trip. Some will even allow your group of children to participate!

✔ Encourage imaginative dramatic play using the sculptures.

Cupcake Liner Flowers

Children will use cupcake pan liners to create unique Cupcake Liner Flowers.

LEARNING

✳ Many readily available household materials can be used to make attractive decorations and gifts.

MATERIALS

✳ Multicolored cupcake pan liners in two sizes. There should be enough for each child in the group to have one of each size for each flower the child wants to make, plus enough of the larger-size green liners to cut into leaf shapes. One green liner should be enough to make four or five leaf shapes

✳ One green pipe cleaner for every flower that will be made. The slightly larger and thicker pipe cleaners will work well for these flowers.

✳ A short length of yarn for each bouquet made

STEPS

1. Demonstrate to the children how a flower bloom can be made by gluing a small cupcake liner into the inside center of a larger liner.

2. Next poke a hole in the center of the flower and insert a green pipe cleaner into it. Twist the top of the pipe cleaner so it will stay in the hole.

3. Add leaves by cutting out leaf shapes from the green cupcake liners, poking the pipe cleaner bottom through these, and gently raising the leaves to the proper height.

4. Allow the children to create a small bouquet of flowers in this manner.

5. Group together the flowers that a child makes with a piece of yarn tied in a bow.

6. This would make a nice May Day gift for a special someone!

CRITICAL THINKING CHALLENGE

Why are flowers important to our world? Are flowers useful?

ACCOMMODATIONS

✓ The amount of adult assistance needed to do this activity will vary with the ages and abilities of your group members.

EXTENSIONS

✓ These same flowers could be placed in a vase made out of a painted tin can with a wad of clay in the bottom to hold the flowers in place. They could also be used to make a card with a 3D front.

✓ Now would be a great and practical time to discuss the parts of a flower plant and to teach the proper names of these.

Picture This!

*Children will use the mosaic technique to make a seed mosaic picture
in* Picture This!

LEARNING

❊ A mosaic is a picture or design made
with little pieces of material.

MATERIALS

❊ A variety of large garden seeds—about a cup
per child, depending on the size of the seeds,
such as corn, peas, sunflowers, and melons.
Garden shops may be willing to donate these
to you after the planting season.

❊ Clear plastic lids such as those from coffee
cans (one per child)

❊ White glue

❊ Water

❊ A container to mix the glue and water and a
spoon for mixing

❊ A cup with a pouring spout

❊ Pop top lids (one for each child)

❊ Permanent markers

❊ Hot glue gun

STEPS

1. Give the children a cup of mixed seeds, and
have them sort them by type.

2. Explain that they will be using these seeds
to create a picture.

3. Give each child a plastic lid and have him
or her write his or her name on the top of it

before the teacher hot glues a soda can pop
top on to use as a hook.

4. Explain that they will be arranging the
seeds in the lid to make an interesting design called a mosaic. If possible, show them
some real or pictured examples of mosaics
to give them a better feel for what a mosaic
really is.

5. Have them create their designs next to their
lids. When they have created the designs
they want, they should pour a puddle of
glue in the bottom of the lid and spread it
around to cover the bottom. Then allow
them to arrange the seeds in the lids in their
designs. Let these dry overnight.

6. The next day have them carefully pour a
mixture of white glue and water over the
seeds to seal them in and shine them up!
(Prior to this, experiment with your own lid
and seeds to find the consistency of glue
and water that will harden in the lid and
still let the seeds show clearly through it.)
Be extremely careful that they don't pour in
too much of the mixture, as an overflow
will wreck the designs they have created.
Also do this in a place where the lids can
stay undisturbed as you can't move them
easily once the mixture is added.

7. When the pictures are dry, they are ready to
be hung.

Picture This! *(continued)*

ACCOMMODATIONS

✓ Larger seeds will be easier for small children to handle.

✓ The teacher may need to do the pouring to avoid disasters!

EXTENSIONS

✓ Make mosaic designs using other materials such as small pieces of paper or cracked colored eggshells on paper.

✓ Point out mosaics to the children when you see them in artwork or decorations.

Paint Mystery

In Paint Mystery *the children will look at a painted sheet of paper and try to decide what instrument or item was used to paint it.*

LEARNING

✳ Painting with different instruments or items will create different effects.

MATERIALS

✳ Liquid tempera paint
✳ A variety of items to paint with—paint brush, cotton swab, feather, sponge, pine cone, little tire as from a toy car, wheat shaft, etc.
✳ Sheets of paper to paint on

STEPS

1. Paint with each of the several different items on separate pieces of paper.

2. Lay the items out where the children can easily see them.

3. Hold up a painted sheet and ask the children which item was used to paint on it.

4. Do this for each sheet, showing the correct item before going on to the next painting.

5. Discuss how the appearance of the paint gives us clues as to what was used to paint it on the paper. Each item gives a different effect.

ACCOMMODATIONS

✓ Use fewer items with very different characteristics when painting for younger children.

EXTENSIONS

✓ Send home a small amount of paint and a sheet of paper with directions to the parent that the child should paint on the paper using an item that will have an interesting effect. Have the child bring the sheet of painted paper back with the item used to paint it hidden in a paper bag. Then the other children can try to guess what was used.

✓ Find pictures of paintings that were done using different methods and discuss these with the children.

Edible Art

In Edible Art the children create edible snowmen.

LEARNING

❊ Art is everywhere. Even the foods we eat can be a form of artwork!

MATERIALS

❊ Large white marshmallows (three per child)

❊ Cookies frosted with white icing to use as a "snowy" base (one per child)

❊ Corn syrup

❊ Aluminum foil

❊ Small white paper plates (one per child)

❊ One black and one orange container of paste food coloring available at cake decorating supply stores

❊ Two toothpicks for each child

❊ One large gumdrop candy for each child

STEPS

1. Take out enough large marshmallows so that each child can have three of them, along with white frosted cookies—one per child.

2. The children can "glue" these together. They should begin by sticking the cookie bottom to a small paper plate to form a "snowy" base and then add the marshmallows one on top of the next with corn syrup by using this method: Place a small amount of corn syrup on a 2-by-2-inch square of aluminum foil for each child, and have the child dip a finger in it and then smear the corn syrup on his or her fingertip onto the white frosted cookie bottom and place the cookie on the plate flat side down. Now put corn syrup on the cookie top and place the flat side of a marshmallow on it. Next the child should "glue" a marshmallow on top of the marshmallow already on the cookie, then another marshmallow on top of that in similar fashion. This forms the snowman's body, and the corn syrup keeps him edible. (Corn syrup makes an edible "glue")

3. Use the paste form of food coloring to make the snowman's facial features and buttons. It works well to dip the end of a toothpick into the food coloring and then touch the marshmallow snowman to create a face and buttons down the front in black. The orange food coloring will be used to create a carrot nose. Remind the children to use a different toothpick for each color, to stick only the tip of the toothpick into the food coloring, and not to lick the toothpick while they are still decorating the snowman.

4. Next they can insert the two toothpicks they used to create the face and buttons food-coloring end first into the sides of the middle marshmallow to form the arms.

5. A large gumdrop candy can be "glued" with corn syrup, flat side down, to the top marshmallow to create a hat for the snowman.

6. This is a fun winter treat to eat for snack!

TEACHER NOTE

Corn syrup makes an efficient and safe edible "glue" whenever you wish to unite pieces of food that will (might) be eaten!

(continued)

FINE ARTS

Edible Art *(continued)*

TEACHER NOTE

Have each child create his or her own edible snack to avoid the transfer of germs.

CRITICAL THINKING CHALLENGE

Why do people create food sculptures or arrange foods in pleasing ways?

ACCOMMODATIONS

✔ Younger children may need help adding the facial features and buttons.

✔ You could also use tiny chocolate chips for the buttons and facial features by dipping the flat sides into the corn syrup and then attaching them to the marshmallows.

EXTENSIONS

✔ Edible snow sculpture creations could be made with fruits, etc. Small white marshmallows could be added to create different sized "snow" pieces.

✔ Have children select their own type of foods they enjoy to create food sculptures from.

Let's Create Scarecrows!

Let's Create Scarecrows allows the children to use fall leaves to make life-size scarecrows.

LEARNING

❋ Scarecrows can be used to actually keep crows away from gardens but are often used for fall decorating nowadays.

MATERIALS

An old long-sleeved shirt and a pair of pants of compatible size for each scarecrow to be made. (If you let parents know about this project, many will be willing to donate some items.)

A roll of somewhat heavy string cut into workable lengths (see directions)—six pieces per scarecrow

Two short pieces of wire (6 inches each should do) for each scarecrow

A sturdy stick an inch or two in diameter and as long as the length of the scarecrow from the pant seat bottom to a half-foot above the shirt neck

Several piles of leaves or straw to provide stuffing material

A plastic jack-o'-lantern head like that used to gather Halloween candy for each scarecrow with a hole the width of the stick cut into the middle of the bottom and the handle removed

An old hat of some type for each scarecrow

A strong piece of string to secure the scarecrow to a tree, or a "T"-shaped stand for the scarecrow and string to secure the scarecrow to that

STEPS

1. Decide how many scarecrows you wish to make, and divide the children into that number of groups.

2. For each scarecrow you wish to make, have the children close all fasteners on the pants and shirts and tie the leg bottoms and sleeve ends shut with string.

3. The bottom of the shirt also needs to be gathered together and tied shut.

4. Now the children are ready to stuff leaves or straw into the shirt through the neck hole and into the pants through the waist hole.

5. When these are stuffed full of leaves or straw, a stick, long enough to reach from the length of the pants seat to above the neckline of the shirt, needs to be pushed down through the shirt neckline, through the tied gathering at the bottom of the shirt, and into the seat part of the pants. This will require adult assistance. Tie a piece of string around the waistline of the pants to secure the pants to the shirt.

6. Add the hollow plastic pumpkin head by putting the hole in it over the stick.

7. A hat can be secured to the plastic pumpkin head by placing pieces of wires through the holes where the pumpkin handles have been removed and through the bottom edge of the hat rim and winding the ends together.

(continued)

Let's Create Scarecrows! *(continued)*

8. Now the scarecrow is ready to secure to a tree with more string or to a "T"-shaped wooden stand.

9. Place the scarecrows around the school grounds as fall decorations.

CRITICAL THINKING CHALLENGE

How can we find out if scarecrows really work to "scare crows"?

 ACCOMMODATIONS

✔ Depending on the ages of your children, this may be a project that requires an adult for each group of scarecrow makers. Older children will be able to do more of the complex steps, while younger children can easily help stuff the scarecrow with leaves or straw.

 EXTENSIONS

✔ Have the children name their scarecrows, and take pictures of the creators with their scarecrows.

✔ Read stories about scarecrows, such as a shortened version of *The Wizard of Oz*.

Animal Stamp

Animal Stamp involves creating realistic pictures of animals using a stamp painting technique.

LEARNING

* The body coverings of animals vary in texture.
* We can use textured materials to stamp paint realistic-looking animal pictures.

MATERIALS

* Real photos of animals or stuffed animals with realistic body coverings. (Use books and magazines such as *National Geographic* to find the pictures.)
* Several colors of liquid tempera paint
* Pie tins to hold the paint
* Fake fur, leather, feathers, etc. cut into small pieces to use for stamping
* Sturdy paper of several colors
* Drawing implements
* Scissors
* Paper towels

STEPS

1. Discuss the body coverings of several different and varied types of animals, such as elephants, parrots, horses, and snakes.

2. Explain that we can paint animals with realistic-looking body coverings by using materials similar to the real body coverings of these animals.

3. Demonstrate paint stamping techniques on paper using the various materials you've collected. You will get good results if you cut the materials into small (2-by-2-inch or less, depending on the size of the animal drawings) pieces and place the material right side down into the paint spread out in a pie tin. You need to blot out excess paint on a paper towel, as well.

4. Also demonstrate for the children how to mix different paint colors to get the shade of color they want for the animals. Having the children look at the photos of animals provided will be helpful for deciding what color is needed.

5. Have each child draw a picture of an animal on sturdy paper that is a similar color to the animal he or she chooses to draw.

6. Next have each child select the appropriate material (fake fur, leather, feathers, etc.) and use it to stamp paint on the animal drawing.

7. Having each child cut out the drawing when the paint is dry will make the stamp painting process easier, as this eliminates the need to stay inside the outline of the animal's body when stamping.

8. These animal paintings can then be displayed on a bulletin board with an outdoor motif.

(continued)

Animal Stamp *(continued)*

ACCOMMODATIONS

✔ An adult or older child could cut out the animal for a younger child.

EXTENSIONS

✔ Habitats for the different types of animals could be painted on larger sheets of paper, and the finished animals could be mounted on the appropriate habitats.

Chalk Mural

Chalk Mural calls for the children to work together on an artistic creation following a theme.

LEARNING

❋ A mural is a large picture or scene containing many different things related to a theme.

MATERIALS

❋ Enough sidewalk chalk of several colors for the group to share

❋ Real or pictured murals to observe

STEPS

1. If possible, take a field trip to a place in the area where a large outdoor mural can be viewed. Otherwise, you will need to find or take pictures of murals to show the children.

2. Point out how all the things pictured in the mural are related to a particular theme, such as our town, the ocean, etc.—whatever is the theme of the mural shown.

3. Tell the children that they are all going to work together to create a sidewalk chalk mural. Help them decide on a theme for their mural, and discuss how each person must draw something related to the theme and connected to the sidewalk squares of the people on each side of him or her.

4. Have the children line up each at a sidewalk square or, if the sidewalk is not laid out in squares, in a line facing the sidewalk separated from each other by an arm's length of room.

5. Remind the children that they are using their chalk to create one long and continuous picture and that what each one draws must go with the rest of the picture being jointly created.

ACCOMMODATIONS

✔ Adjust the length of the sidewalk you use to suit the learners.

✔ For younger children you may need to determine the theme to make this workable or allow them each to do a separate theme for their sidewalk square.

✔ It may be helpful to sketch out the mural on paper, incorporating the ideas of the children, to give the children a better visual idea of what they are creating.

✔ You may want to assign a specific scene to each child.

EXTENSIONS

✔ Each child could design a mural on paper and your group could vote on which one to create on the sidewalk with the others displayed on indoor walls, as often this is how a mural is decided on. Each child could be instructed to stick with the same theme for his or her mural.

✔ If it's possible to paint a real mural somewhere within your building, it would be a great beautification project for the children to be involved in!

Famous Artist Gallery

Famous Artist Gallery *introduces the children to the artworks of the masters.*

LEARNING

* There are many artists who created paintings and sculptures that are considered masterpieces.

* These artists used a variety of techniques that we can experiment with as well.

MATERIALS

* Prints of masterpiece works of art—these may be found over the Internet or in books and copied onto heavy paper to display in paper or cardboard frames on a bulletin board that can be used for this purpose throughout the year

* The art mediums and other supplies for the children to create their own masterpieces in the styles of the famous artists

* Art smocks and an easel or table to work on

STEPS

1. Collect the works of famous artists. Feature one artist at a time or a few who used the same medium to create their masterpieces—possibly one artist or technique a month. Display the prints of their works in paper frames on a bulletin board titled "The Works of (the artist's name)." On a table nearby, place the medium (for example, watercolors) that the artist used for his or her artwork and any other supplies necessary to try out the medium and technique used by the famous artist. An easel would work well for this.

2. Encourage the children to create their own masterpieces during free time using the materials supplied on the table.

3. Display their masterpieces on the bulletin board, as well, with the wording "Masterpiece by (the child's name)." Encourage them to name their works just as famous artists have done.

4. Ask the children what they like about their artwork and how they chose their subject. Have them consider that the famous artists probably did many paintings to develop the skills that they used in their masterpieces, and encourage them to continue in their artistic endeavors.

CRITICAL THINKING CHALLENGE

If you were an artist, what would you create, and why? Comparing two different artists' work, which do you like best, and why?

ACCOMMODATIONS

✔ Consider the ages and abilities of your children when considering appropriate artwork and mediums to use.

EXTENSIONS

✔ A visit to an art gallery or a local artist's studio would enhance the learning.

Chapter 3

Creative Dramatics

Activities in this chapter involve creative movement and developing plays and puppet shows, which can be used to introduce the children to theater and acting in a safe, nonthreatening environment that will boost their confidence in their abilities to express themselves in a variety of ways.

Here We Are at the Amusement Park

Here We Are at the Amusement Park calls for the children to imagine a trip to their favorite amusement park and to act out what they did there for the other children to guess.

LEARNING

✳ Real events can be acted out in pantomime form.

MATERIALS

✳ None needed

STEPS

1. Ask the children if they have ever been to an amusement park and what kinds of things they did there. Draw out that they may have gone on rides, stood in long lines, eaten food, played games to win prizes, etc.

2. Talk about how we usually go to these types of places with other people.

3. Then divide the children into groups of three or four, and have the groups get together to decide on some amusement park adventure to act out so the other children can guess what they are doing. Rotate around to the different groups to give hints and advice to help their pantomime be something that the other children will understand.

4. Give each group an opportunity to perform the pantomime they've developed for the other groups to see and guess what they are doing at the amusement park.

ACCOMMODATIONS

✔ This topic may be too difficult if the children are new at pantomime. You may wish to try something they may be better prepared to do, such as acting out different activities they do to get ready for school in the morning, games they play at recess, or sports they play.

EXTENSIONS

✔ Use pantomime to show children the directions for completing a project. Then ask them to orally state what the directions are.

✔ Invite a professional mime to your classroom to demonstrate his or her craft and to work with the children on learning how to do pantomime, or watch one on a video recording.

Give Me the Microphone

In Give Me the Microphone *the children pretend to sing (lip-synch) the songs sung by great singers using pretend microphones they have made.*

LEARNING

✳ Sometimes performers pretend to sing while the actual singer's voice is dubbed in.

MATERIALS

✳ Music to sing along to

✳ Samples of songs from good children's musicals to use with a TV and VCR like "Chitty, Chitty, Bang, Bang" or "Mary Poppins"

✳ A toilet paper roll and half Styrofoam™ ball to fit over one end, glue, black tempera paint, a paintbrush, and a 3-foot long piece of heavy black yarn per child

✳ Or a hair clip that opens at one end only, a small black Styrofoam™ ball painted black, and glue for each child

STEPS

1. Discuss the fact that a very good actor or actress may not always be a very good singer and a very good singer may not be able to act. The solution is to have the good actor pretend to sing the song in a movie and to add the good singer's voice.

This is called dubbing. When we do this live, or when we pretend we are singing when we listen to our favorite singer on the radio, it's called lip-synching.

2. Show the footage from the children's musical, pointing out how the singers move and act as they sing. You could also show a video of a singer performing on stage.

3. Have the children pretend to sing the songs themselves while you are playing the musical piece with the vocals.

4. Explain next that sometimes singers use microphones to enhance the volume of their voices.

5. An easy way to make an old-fashioned microphone is to use an empty toilet paper roll with a half Styrofoam™ ball of the right size fit over one end. Paint all this black, and attach a heavy piece of black yarn to it to look like the cord.

6. A clip-on microphone can also be made using a hair clip that opens on only one end and attaching a small Styrofoam™ ball painted black to it.

7. Let the children pretend to sing the songs you play with actions that singers use.

ACCOMMODATIONS

✔ Let the children get comfortable with the mouth movements before they try to add body movements.

EXTENSIONS

✔ Borrow a karaoke machine for a fun way to practice lip-synching. One of your students might have one.

Are You a Copycat?

In Are You a Copycat? *all the children try to move exactly as the leader is moving.*

LEARNING

✳ We can copy the movements made by others.

MATERIALS

✳ A large open floor space

STEPS

1. Have the children gather around you in a circle.

2. Begin to move your body a certain way in place, such as waving your arms over your head, touching your toes, or bending from side to side. Instruct the children to copy your motion exactly. Do each motion several times until the children have all caught on as to how to do it. Then switch to a different movement and repeat the process. Try to incorporate different parts of your body into your movements.

3. Now start another movement, but when you are ready to change the movement, point to a child and have him or her demonstrate the next movement. Then that child finishes his or her movement and points to another child to do a movement. A way to ensure that each child gets a chance to demonstrate a movement is to tell the children that no child can have a second turn until every child has had a turn. Also encourage the children to try to be creative and to think of movements no one else has demonstrated.

ACCOMMODATIONS

✔ Keep your movements at a level appropriate for your group's abilities.

✔ If one movement at a time isn't challenging enough for your group, do two movements to have the children mimic.

EXTENSIONS

✔ Consider movements to go with specific situations. For instance, pretend you are picking up tiny beads that have spilled on the floor. You could either tell the children what the movement is or have them guess as you demonstrate it.

✔ If space allows, the movements could incorporate actually changing where you are

I'm Walking on Clouds

For the activity I'm Walking on Clouds *the children will pretend they are walking on or through a variety of different materials.*

LEARNING

✳ Our walking motions change with what we are walking through or on as our bodies respond to what we encounter.

MATERIALS

✳ A large space for movement

STEPS

1. Have the children take their shoes off so they are in stocking feet and join you in a spot where there is room for movement.

2. Tell them that they are all invited to go on an imaginary walk with you. Begin by pretending to walk down the street in a normal fashion. Next tell them that there's a big puddle of mud that they can't walk around so everyone will have to just walk through it. Emphasize that it is sticky and thick and it's hard to move your feet through it. Demonstrate this by the way you move your feet in place. Have them attempt to do the same movements. Continue on with your story. Maybe the sidewalk is very hot or the gravel is really rough on the feet. Be as creative as you choose. Be very glad when you finally reach your imaginary destination and can take a load off your feet as you all sit down to rest. You may need to pretend to wash your feet in the cold water of the hose before you go inside! (If the children want to suggest the next thing to walk through or on as you go, let them add their creativity to your story.)

CRITICAL THINKING CHALLENGE

Why do we walk differently on different surfaces?

ACCOMMODATIONS

✓ Keep the length of your walk and the types of movements at a level your children can handle.

EXTENSIONS

✓ Discuss which material they enjoyed walking through or on the most and which one they least enjoyed walking through or on.

✓ Encourage the children to make up their own adventures and incorporate movement into telling about them. Praise their efforts no matter how small.

I Felt So Bad I Could Have Cried

In I Felt So Bad I Could Have Cried *the children demonstrate different emotions by the looks on their faces.*

LEARNING

✳ Our facial expressions often tell how we feel.

MATERIALS

✳ A story to tell that includes many different emotions

✳ A paper plate for each child and drawing implements

✳ A bulletin board for displaying the faces

STEPS

1. Tell the children that you have a story to tell them about an adventure you had, such as going shopping for school supplies at the beginning of the year, and that you experienced many different emotions or feelings during this adventure.

2. Tell them that when you talk about a feeling during the story of your adventure, they should try to show that feeling by using their faces.

3. Begin your story something like this: I was so happy to finally be going to get my new school supplies (big smile). We had to drive a long way to the store, which was boring (look bored). The store was very large and

I was a little confused (look confused) about where I should go. Finally I found the right aisle, which was pretty exciting (look excited). But then I noticed that all the cool folders were gone and I was very disappointed (look disappointed). I also got frustrated (look frustrated) trying to find the exact type of markers on my list. I got worried (look worried) when I left my list by the pencils and couldn't find it. But I was relieved (look relieved) when a boy also shopping for school supplies found my list and returned it to me. I gave him a big smile and left to pay for my supplies and go home to put my name on them. (Exaggerate your facial expressions and encourage the children to mimic you.)

4. Discuss all the different emotions you felt, and emphasize that your face showed how you felt. Give each child a large paper plate to draw a face on with a certain expression. Display these on a bulletin board with the title "Sometimes I feel . . ." and the paper plate faces with the expressions on them grouped with the name of the emotion they are expressing.

CRITICAL THINKING CHALLENGE

Is it always appropriate to show our emotions?

I Felt So Bad I Could Have Cried *(continued)*

ACCOMMODATIONS

✔ Keep the emotions you choose to emphasize ones that the children can comprehend.

EXTENSIONS

✔ Encourage the children to use words to describe their emotions, such as, "I am disappointed that we have indoor recess today," or "This worksheet is frustrating me because I don't understand how to do it."

I'm Changing

In the activity I'm Changing *the children will use movements to act out changes that take place in our world.*

LEARNING

✳ Things are always changing.

MATERIALS

✳ Space to move

STEPS

1. Talk about all the changes we go through as we grow. We start out as babies unable to walk or talk and we slowly grow up, changing every step of the way. Discuss how the children have changed since they were born and when they began to do certain things like walk, talk, skip, ride a bike, etc. Point out that this all takes time.

2. Now discuss how plants and animals change, too, as well as some inanimate things.

3. Have the children act out with their bodies how a seed changes to become a plant that slowly grows and blossoms and eventually sheds its seeds and dies.

4. Now act out as a group how a balloon changes. Start out close together in a group all holding hands and slowly spread out as the balloon is blown up bigger and bigger until it pops—the children all let go and twirl to the floor just like a real balloon would do.

5. Emphasize that we can act out the changes that occur in things.

CRITICAL THINKING CHALLENGE

How do you feel about change, and why?

ACCOMMODATIONS

✔ Stick to things that go through fairly obvious changes to begin wit[h ...]up to more subtle changes

EXTENSIONS

✔ As you study more things that change, ask the children to portray the changes with their body motions.

Now I'm a Statue, Now I'm Not

In Now I'm a Statue, Now I'm Not *the children will practice holding a pose.*

LEARNING

❊ We can stop an action at any point as we are doing the action.

❊ We can move in many unique ways.

MATERIALS

❊ Music that will encourage movement

❊ A tape recorder or CD player to play the music on

STEPS

1. This activity is fun to do with music. Call on the children to move to the music in a variety of different ways as long as it's playing and to stop wherever they are in the movement when the music stops, as if they have magically become statues.

2. When they are stopped have them look around to see all the forms their bodies are in. Remind them that statues cannot move.

3. Emphasize all the positions our versatile bodies can form.

4. Play the music and stop it several times to help them see that there truly are many ways to move our bodies.

ACCOMMODATIONS

✔ Keep the length of the song appropriate for your group's attention span.

EXTENSIONS

✔ Analyze movements we use to do different activities such as brush our teeth and tie our shoes. Go through the movements very slowly to see just how many changes our bodies go through to do even simple things.

Let's Picnic

A fun thing to do for a creative dramatics activity is to act out having a picnic. In Let's Picnic a few props spark the imaginations of the children, who pretend they are on a picnic.

LEARNING

✳ We can use our imaginations to pretend we are doing just about anything.

MATERIALS

✳ A large green blanket
✳ A picnic basket

STEPS

1. Bring in the large green blanket and lay it on the floor. Tell the children that this is the greenest grass you have ever seen and a perfect spot for a picnic on a beautiful day like today. Ask them what the weather is like that they are imagining.

2. Gather everyone on the blanket and open up a real picnic basket filled with imaginary food. Act out handing out the imaginary food as the children tell you what it is. Then have everyone act out eating it. Discuss how on a picnic you shouldn't leave a mess after you eat, and have the children act out cleaning up the picnic area.

3. Now tell them they will have lots of time to play in the great outdoors, but they must show us what they are doing using their bodies but not their voices. When someone guesses correctly what another child is doing, all the children may pretend to do that activity. Try out lots of different activities this way.

4. Now tell them that picnic time is coming to an end. Discuss what picnic activity they liked best, and ask them where they would like to go next in their imaginations. Then plan a new adventure for another day using a few simple props.

ACCOMMODATIONS

✔ Keep the activities at the appropriate level and of the appropriate length for your group.

EXTENSIONS

✔ Have children go on a real picnic.

Paper Plate Masks

The children will make Paper Plate Masks *to wear as they act out a familiar story as a play.*

LEARNING

✳ Paper plates can easily be made into masks to wear to portray characters in a play.

MATERIALS

- Paper plates
- Materials to decorate the masks: paper, cardboard, markers, glue, yarn
- Elastic and a stapler to make the masks wearable
- Play scripts, like "The Three Little Pigs."
- Props (optional)

STEPS

1. Decide on plays groups of children would like to perform.

2. Decide who will portray which character.

3. Then show the children how a paper plate can be made into a mask by cutting out holes for eyes, nose, and mouth, decorating it, and attaching a piece of elastic to the sides using a stapler so that it can be worn over the face. Make a mask of a character from a familiar story as you explain each step. Show the children how you can wear it.

4. Give each child a paper plate to make a mask for the character he or she will be portraying. You may wish to supply extra paper and cardboard to add features to the plates along with glue and markers.

5. Have the children practice their plays first without the masks to concentrate on the dialogue. Then have them add the masks. When they are comfortable with the dialogue, masks, and movement, have them perform the plays for others. Props can also be added for the plays.

ACCOMMODATIONS

✔ Keep the plays at a level manageable for your group.

✔ If children are not accustomed to performing in plays, they might feel more secure just doing the plays for the other children in your group rather than for others in the school.

EXTENSIONS

✔ The children could write original plays to perform and make the masks to use with these plays.

✔ The children may also have other ideas for materials to use to make masks, such as paper bags, etc.

Stories with Props

In Stories with Props the children will learn to act out familiar stories using props.

LEARNING

※ Props serve to add to the stories we act out.

MATERIALS

※ A familiar story, such as "Goldilocks and the Three Bears" or "Little Red Riding Hood"

※ Simple props to go with the story when it's acted out

STEPS

1. For this activity you will want to start with a story the children are quite familiar with.

2. Read or tell the story to the children.

3. Choose children to portray the characters as you read the story again. It will probably be difficult to do without any props. Hopefully, the children will come to this conclusion on their own when they watch the story being acted out or perform as actors in it.

4. Help them decide which simple props would be useful to make the play better.

5. Now try acting out the story again with the props. Ask the audience and the performers if the props helped to improve the acting out of the story.

ACCOMMODATIONS

✔ Keep the difficulty of the story and the number of props appropriate for your group.

EXTENSIONS

✔ Gradually work towards having the actors use the props and saying the dialogue for the characters in stories like a real play.

✔ The children may be interested in writing their own plays and acting them out complete with props they have located or made.

Shadow Shows

In Shadow Shows the children learn how to create a shadow puppet show.

LEARNING

﹡ Puppet shows can be done in many different ways.

MATERIALS

﹡ A white bed sheet and a method to hang it above a table

﹡ A light source such as a floor lamp with the lamp shade removed of the height to shine on the sheet

﹡ A table with the front covered with a sheet of paper to the floor so that one cannot see under the table

﹡ An idea for a puppet show

﹡ Puppets for the show cut as silhouettes from cardboard and mounted on tongue depressors

STEPS

1. Discuss what a puppet show is and that there are many different ways they can be done. One of these is a shadow show.

2. To do a shadow puppet show you will need to hang the white bed sheet above a table so that the bottom of the sheet just touches the back edge of the table top. Behind this you will need a light source. A floor lamp minus its shade will work well for this. You will also want to cover the area below the front of the table with a sheet of paper to block the audience from seeing underneath it.

3. Next you need to decide on a play that the children would like to perform as a puppet show.

4. The figures for the characters need to be cut from cardboard in silhouette form with tongue depressors attached to them so that a person can hold the figures up by the tongue depressors.

5. Now the children who will perform the puppet show can sit down on the floor with the light source behind them and at the height of the bed sheet. This way they can move the figures along the table edge behind the sheet while saying their lines. The figures' shapes will show through the sheet for the audience to see.

(continued)

Shadow Shows *(continued)*

ACCOMMODATIONS

✓ A puppet play involving just a few characters and puppeteers will be the easiest to do at first. With some practice the children will be able to handle two characters apiece. Children switching places behind the table will be difficult, too, so try to arrange the children and puppets to limit this.

EXTENSIONS

✓ Allow the children to write their own puppet plays to do their own shadow shows.

✓ The children may wish to perform their shows for parents or other classes to view. They could send out invitations with free tickets to the show included, and children could collect tickets and seat the attendees as they arrive. A child could also introduce the play and, at the end, the puppeteers.

Magnetic Puppet Theater

Using Magnetic Puppet Theater *the children will create a puppet theater in which the puppets are moved by magnets.*

LEARNING

❋ There are many ways to perform puppet shows.

MATERIALS

❋ A shoe box with a curtain (optional) attached (see steps for further instructions)

❋ Puppet figures made from lightweight cardboard that can stand up. A paper clip needs to be attached with clear tape to the bottom of each.

❋ A magnet strong enough to move the figures through the box bottom

❋ A puppet play to perform

❋ Thin Plexiglas™ to replace the bottom of the shoe box (optional)

STEPS

1. Lay the shoe box to serve as the puppet theater on its side so that the open rectangle can be viewed the long way. To add a curtain for the shoe box theater, attach a dowel inside the top long edge of the box. Sew small curtains with sleeves at the top for the dowel to go through so that the curtains can be pushed open and pulled shut from the middle. You may need to secure the curtains to each side of the theater (shoe box) so they will stay open when the puppet show is being performed in the theater.

2. The characters need to be drawn on lightweight cardboard and attached to cardboard bases so they can stand up. Then a paper clip needs to be taped under each base with clear tape. The character figures must be of a size to be used in the shoebox theater.

3. Now a magnet moved under the shoe box where the figure is will move the figure around the stage (the bottom of the box). You will need to raise the shoe box up so that the puppeteer can get his or her hands under it. One way to do this is to tape the bottom front edge of the shoe box firmly to the back edge of a table with the shoe box itself hanging out over the edge. Then the puppeteer has a lot of room to work below the box bottom. He or she must put the magnet directly under where the figure is in the box and not take the magnet off the shoe box bottom to keep it moving the figure around the box floor. Another idea would be to replace the bottom of the shoe box with Plexiglas™, which will allow the child to see from underneath the box where to move the puppets. Be sure the Plexiglas™ is thin enough for the magnet to work through it.

4. This is a small theater appropriate for one child only to perform the puppet show for a small group of two or three children. A bigger theater could be made in the same manner, but you would need to consider what metal to put under the larger figure bases and the size of magnet you will need to move the figures from under the floor of the theater.

(continued)

Magnetic Puppet Theater *(continued)*

ACCOMMODATIONS

✓ Keep the number of characters small and the lines simple at first and for younger children.

EXTENSIONS

✓ Have the children write their own plays.

✓ Have the children take their theaters to perform their plays for other small groups of children within the school.

Overhead Puppet Shows

Using an overhead projector the children will create Overhead Puppet Shows.

LEARNING

❋ There are many ways to perform puppet shows.

MATERIALS

❋ Overhead projector

❋ At least two sheets of overhead film per puppet show—more if you want to use more than one background or several puppets

❋ Permanent as well as dry-erase markers in a variety of colors

❋ Scissors

STEPS

1. Choose a story you'd like to tell using puppets. The children can make puppets for the overhead projector by drawing the characters on clear overhead projector film and coloring them in with the permanent markers before cutting them out. Each puppet will need a clear piece of the film extending from the bottom of the figure so it can be manipulated on the projector. They must be made the appropriate size to be manipulated on the projector glass.

2. The children can draw the background on a sheet of projector film as well. If they use the dry-erase markers, the background sheet can be erased after use to be used again for a different projector puppet show.

3. Then the background sheet can be laid on the projector glass and the puppets manipulated over the top of it. The clear plastic below the figure will be invisible on the surface you are projecting onto. When you do this on a wall or large screen you will be able to adjust the size of the puppet show by moving the projector closer or farther away from the wall or screen.

4. The children should practice saying their lines while manipulating the puppets before presenting the puppet show to an audience.

ACCOMMODATIONS

✔ Limit the puppet play to just a few characters and one background initially, and then work up to adding more backgrounds and puppet characters as the children get used to doing puppet shows on the overhead projector.

EXTENSIONS

✔ Plan an overhead puppet show to do for a large group of people. If it is projected on a large wall, many people can watch the show at once.

✔ Encourage the children to write their own plays to do as puppet shows, as well as using stories they already know.

Sock It to Me Puppet Show

In Sock It to Me Puppet Show the children create their own sock puppets to use in an original puppet show.

LEARNING

❋ There are many ways to make puppets to use in puppet shows.

MATERIALS

❋ One tube sock per child. It can be one that is missing a mate due to wear

❋ Materials to create the puppets: buttons, felt in a variety of colors, ribbon, pipe cleaners, lace, a variety of fabrics, beady eyes, etc.

❋ Craft glue and scissors

❋ Paper for drawing the puppet designs on and writing out the puppet show plays

❋ A table and a large sheet of roll paper or tablecloth to cover below the table so one can't see under it

STEPS

1. Have the children draw the puppets they want to create on paper before they begin so they can visualize what materials they will use and how they will use them.

2. Then use the socks as the puppet bodies and heads. Decorate them with ribbons, beady eyes, etc. By tucking the sock toe in around the fingers of the hand inside the sock, a mouth can be formed.

3. When the puppets are complete and dry, form small groups of two to four children to create a puppet show play that their particular puppets could all be a part of.

4. Once the puppet show plays are written, give the children time to practice their plays before presenting them to the other children. A table with the front below it blocked from view with a cloth or large sheet of roll paper will work well to perform the puppet show behind.

ACCOMMODATIONS

✔ Have each child show you his or her idea for the puppet design before beginning to create it to allow you to give suggestions and anticipate possible problems he or she may encounter while creating the puppet.

✔ Cutting cloth and felt can be difficult, especially with children's scissors, so the teacher may have to do some of that or an older child could help a younger one.

✔ Showing an example of a teacher-made puppet might help get the children started, but emphasize that they probably have lots of better ideas of their own for their puppets so that they won't all look like the teacher's puppet.

EXTENSIONS

✔ The children could make puppets to fit specific characters in stories they have heard or read and then write the dialogue to go with those stories for puppet shows.

✔ They could also memorize lines from a play to do a puppet show using sock puppets.

FINE ARTS RESOURCES

Ashliman, D. L. (2004). *Folk and fairy tales: A handbook*. Pittsburg, PA: Greenwood Press.

Bahti, Mark, and Baatsoslanii, Joe. (2000). *A guide to Navajo sandpaintings*. Tucson, AZ: Rio Nuevo Publishers.

Bisson, Lynn. (1989). *3-D art projects that teach*. Nashville, TN: Incentive Publications, Inc.

Boiko, Claire. (1997). *Children's plays for creative actors*. Plays, Inc.

Carle, Eric. (1966). *The grouchy ladybug*. New York: Harper Trophy.

Cole, Joanna. (1989). *Anna banana: 101 jump rope rhymes*. New York: Beech Tree Books.

Consortium of National Arts Education Associations. (1994). National standards for arts education. What every young American should know and be able to do in the arts. Washington, DC: Author.

Douglas, Kathy. (2001). *Open-ended art*. Torrance, CA: Totline Publications.

Hart, Avery, and Mantell, Paul. (1993). *Kids make music*. Charlotte, VT: Williamson Pub. Co.

Koehler-Pentacoff, Elizabeth. (1989). *Curtain call*. Nashville, TN: Incentive Publications, Inc.

Marx, Pamela. (1997). *Take a quick bow: 26 plays for the classroom*. Glenview, IL: Good Year Books.

Mecca, Judy Truesdell. (1992). *Plays that teach: Plays, activities and songs with a message*. Nashville, TN: Incentive Publications.

Meish, Goldish. (2001). *50 learning songs sung to your favorite tunes*. New York: Scholastic Professional Books.

Sanders, Sandra. (1970). *Creating plays with children*. New York: Citation Press.

Smolinski, Jill. (1998). *50 nifty super animal origami crafts*. Chicago: Contemporary Books.

Storm, Jerry. (1995). *101 music games for children*. Alemeda, CA: Hunter House.

Video recording. (1997). *Fun with puppets*. Two Bobs Productions.

Unit 2

Language Arts

The National Council of Teachers of English has established the Standards for the English Language Arts, emphasizing literacy education for grades K–12. Skills involving reading, writing, and associating the spoken word with graphic representations are emphasized throughout the following standard areas:

✳ Reading for Perspective

✳ Reading for Understanding

✳ Evaluation Strategies

✳ Communication Skills

✳ Communication Strategies

✳ Developing Research Skills

✳ Multicultural Understanding

✳ Applying Non-English Perspectives

✳ Participating in Society

✳ Applying Language Skills

With these standards and their purpose in mind, we have divided the language arts unit into three chapters. Please note that Multicultural Understanding, Applying Non-English Perspectives, and Participating in Society are dealt with more extensively in the Social Studies unit.

✳ **Reading Challenges:** The activities in this chapter are divided into four areas: 1) letter and sound recognition, 2) words and their meanings, 3) building sentences, and 4) oral reading and listening activities. These activities are intended not to teach children to read but to offer opportunities for the children to practice and strengthen their developing reading skills.

✳ **Writing Challenges:** This chapter provides the children with opportunities to use their emerging writing skills and abilities in a variety of ways and for a variety of purposes.

✳ **Speaking Challenges:** The activities in the speaking challenges chapter give the children authentic ways to practice the important skill of speaking to communicate effectively with others in a variety of situations and through a variety of methods.

All of the activities presented in the language arts unit are meant to provide practice in reading, writing, and speaking skills to add to the formal instruction provided in these areas. We want reading, writing, and speaking to be seen as enjoyable, albeit essential, activities to be involved in throughout life. The skills the children hone today will be an asset to them in the future.

Chapter *4*

Reading Challenges

Activities in this chapter center around several different aspects of reading, including letter/sound correspondence, words and their meanings, sentence structure, and oral reading and listening skills. These areas are dealt with through reading challenges that are fun and yet provide practice in the skills necessary to be a proficient reader.

Alphabet People

Alphabet People is a fun way to work on alphabetical order.

LEARNING

❋ The letters of the alphabet are organized in a specific order.

MATERIALS

❋ 1-foot-by-1-foot pieces of white cardboard, each with a capital letter of the alphabet on one side and the corresponding lowercase letter on the other

❋ A hole punch and string to make the letter cards able to be worn around the neck

STEPS

1. Punch two holes near the top of each cardboard piece, and tie a string through them so the card can be worn around the neck.

2. Use either the capital letters or the lowercase letters, and use as many sequential alphabet cards as there are children in your group. For instance, if there are 10 children, you will use cards A through J. You should first play the game starting with card A, but later on you can start the sequence with a different letter.

3. Hand out the letters you will use in random order, and tell the children to place the strings over their heads so that the letters can be worn around their necks. They should then find a spot in the room.

4. When you say, "ABC order," the children need to arrange themselves in alphabetical order as quickly as possible on a predetermined line.

5. It will be harder to do this when you start with a different letter than A, but it is a good learning experience.

6. Use the lowercase letters for some games and the capital letters for others to practice the recognition of both.

TEACHER NOTE

To avoid a choking hazard, tie the strings behind the neck in a single knotted bow that will easily pull apart if tugged on. This will also allow you to adjust the length so the strings don't hang too long in front.

(continued)

Alphabet People (continued)

✔ ACCOMMODATIONS

✔ Use only the capital letters or the lower-case letters at first—whichever the children are most familiar with.

✔ If you have older children who would find this activity too easy, try forming two teams and seeing which team can arrange themselves in alphabetical order first. Simply divide the set of letters in half for this activity. One team will have the first half of the alphabet, and the other team will have the second half.

✔ Another activity to try with a more advanced group is to divide the letters into groups of three, skipping some letters in between the groups. Pass out the letters, and challenge the children to find their two partners to make themselves a threesome of letters that follow one another as quickly as possible.

✔ EXTENSIONS

✔ If you add extra vowel cards, the children could try to make a word as quickly as possible.

✔ Another idea is to randomly select some of the letters and then let the children get in the right order even though letters are missing. You might have A, D, F, H, etc.

✔ You could also have two children with letters that are separated by a single other letter stand next to each other leaving just enough space between them for the child who has the letter that goes between their letters.

Alphabet Snake

Alphabet Snake calls for each child to lock an arm with another child so that letter cards the children are wearing around their necks form the alphabet.

LEARNING

✳ The letters of the alphabet are organized in a specific order.

MATERIALS

✳ The letter cards made for the "Alphabet People" activity

STEPS

1. Use the letters from the activity called "Alphabet People."

2. Use as many letters as there are children in the group. The letters used must be able to be lined up sequentially.

3. Give each child a letter to wear and have them scatter about the room.

4. The child wearing "A" or the first letter in the sequence being used slides quietly (like a snake) on his or her feet around the room. When he or she passes the child with the letter that follows his or hers sequentially, that child must take one hand of the first child and the two must slide around the room with the first child leading the way. When they pass the child who has the third letter in the sequence, that child takes the free hand of the second child and they continue on around the room, picking up a new child for each letter in the sequence until all the letters are hooked together and a long snake is formed.

ACCOMMODATIONS

✔ Let the child who is least familiar with alphabetical order be the "A" or first letter of the sequence as he or she does not have to decide when to latch on, or put a child who knows alphabetical order with one who isn't as sure of it and have them hold hands as partners with two letters that are sequential. They will both join on at the same time.

✔ You could also partner older and younger children. The younger child should wear the letter, and the older child can help him or her decide when to latch on.

EXTENSIONS

✔ Form a train instead of a snake by having each child hook on to the child with the letter that comes before his or hers by placing two hands around the child's waist and following behind him or her.

✔ For added difficulty, you could also have the children try to be a backward train and line up in that fashion.

Alphabet Dominoes

Alphabet Dominoes requires the children to look carefully at the letters of the alphabet to match up those that are the same.

LEARNING

✳ We can visually discriminate between letters. No two letters look just the same.

MATERIALS

✳ Alphabet domino cards made from cardboard (see "Steps" for directions to make these) (You will need a large quantity of cardboard, depending on each card's size and the total number of cards you make.)

✳ A large, flat playing surface

STEPS

1. Create a set of alphabet domino cards by cutting a large, sturdy piece of cardboard into the size domino cards you wish to have. Young children seem to love bigger sizes to play the game with.

2. Next draw a line down the middle of each rectangular card, and write one letter on each side of the line. Try to use each letter the same number of times to make the game work well. Make up a large number of these cards—if you make up 104 cards, each letter can be used eight times. You could put capital letters on one side of the cards and lowercase letters on the other. If you do this, make sure the cards are all turned to show either lowercase letters or capital letters at the start of the game.

3. Then the children can play the game the way dominoes is played. The cards need to be divided equally among the players. The first person to play lays down any card. Then the next player must match a section of one of his or her cards to a letter on the card already laid down. The game progresses in the same manner. If a child cannot match a letter he or she has in his or her cards with one on the board, the child passes his or her turn on to the next player. The object of the game is to see how many matches can be made, not to determine a winner or loser. So if one child matches up all his or her cards, that child should help the others to continue to make matches to add to the total number of matches made. The game keeps going until no more matches are possible.

(continued)

Alphabet Dominoes *(continued)*

ACCOMMODATIONS

✓ To make the game shorter, cut the deck in half.

✓ To make the game more challenging for older children, make up a set of domino cards with cursive letters on them.

EXTENSIONS

✓ Bring in commercial domino games for the children to play. There are many different sets available. Children may also have domino games at home that they might wish to bring in to share with the class.

✓ Older children might enjoy making their own sets of dominoes for games. Using stickers would cut down on the amount of writing needed to make a set and, of course, the sets do not need to be as large as the alphabet set. They could make sets and teach younger children how to play using their sets.

Fishing for Letter Sounds

Fishing for Letter Sounds reinforces connecting a sound with the letter it is associated with.

LEARNING

✱ Each letter has at least one sound associated with it.

MATERIALS

✱ A set of Fishing for Sounds cards as described below

STEPS

1. Make a set of playing cards that contains four of each letter that has just one sound associated with it (b, d, f, h, j, k, l, m, n, p, r, s, t, v, w, and z).

2. Shuffle the cards and deal them out to four children so that each child has six cards in his or her hand. Lay the rest down in the middle of the group of children.

3. The children should all be looking at their cards as the first child asks someone by name if he or she has a card by saying the sound of the letter on the card he or she hopes to find a match for. If the child does have a match, he or she gives that card to the child who asked for it. If he or she does not have the card, he or she says, "Sorry, go fish." If the child does not get a card when he or she asks for it, he or she must draw a card from the pile. The idea is to get sets of four cards with the same sound (letter) and to lay them down as a set. When no more matches can be made, the person with the most sets of same sound cards wins.

ACCOMMODATIONS

✔ Using fewer sounds (cards) for the game will make it easier to play.

✔ If the children are familiar with the letter names but not the sounds yet, they could say the letter name instead of the letter sound to play the game.

EXTENSIONS

✔ Sets of cards could be made with digraphs on them to identify by their sounds.

Letter Match Game

In Letter Match Game *the child matches a capital letter with its lowercase letter equivalent.*

LEARNING

✳ Each capital letter has a corresponding lowercase letter that may or may not look like it.

MATERIALS

✳ A bulletin board covered with paper you can write on

✳ A dark marker for writing on the bulletin board

✳ A tack for each letter included

✳ Different colored pieces of yarn that reach from each letter on one side of the board to a corresponding letter on the other side of the board

STEPS

1. Write several capital letters down one side of a large, easy-to-reach bulletin board, that has been covered with background paper.

ACCOMMODATIONS

✔ The number of letters to match can be increased or decreased depending on the needs and abilities of your group of children.

✔ Cursive letters could be used instead of manuscript letters.

2. Next, write the lowercase letters that go with the capital letters you just wrote, down the other side of the board but in a different order.

3. Next to each capital letter, place a tack with a piece of string long enough to reach the letters on the other side of the board attached to it. The idea is for the children to connect each capital letter with its lowercase letter using the string and another tack. If you use a different color of yarn for each letter, you can make a card showing the correct layout of the attached pieces of yarn for the child to use to self-correct his or her work. Keep the answer card in an envelope near the bulletin board.

CRITICAL THINKING CHALLENGE

Let the children come up with other matching activities that could work with this setup, such as words and their meanings, math problems and their answers, or shapes and their names.

Rhyming Words Ball Toss

Through the interactive game Rhyming Words Ball Toss, *children will demonstrate their knowledge of rhyming words.*

LEARNING

✳ Many words rhyme with other words.

MATERIALS

✳ A ball to toss

✳ A word that can be rhymed with many other words

STEPS

1. Form a large circle with the children.

2. Begin by stating a word that many other words rhyme with—such as "cat," "door," "sit," etc.

3. Toss the ball to a child, who must say a word that rhymes with your word before tossing the ball to another child, who must follow suit.

4. The fun is in seeing how many words can be given that rhyme with your word.

5. When a child cannot come up with a word to rhyme with yours, the game ends. (A variation that allows the game to continue longer is to allow the child to ask a friend to help him or her out.)

6. One child should be designated the counter, to tally how many times the ball was thrown, or the recorder, to list the words stated on the chalkboard.

7. Keeping a chart to record the number of rhyming words tallied or recorded each time the game is played will allow comparisons from game to game over time. This will also challenge the children to think hard each game to surpass the totals from previous games.

CRITICAL THINKING CHALLENGE

Once they are familiar with how the game works, have the children try to make up their own variations for the game.

ACCOMMODATIONS

✔ The difficulty or ease with which the word can be rhymed can be adjusted to the group's abilities.

EXTENSIONS

✔ The variations for this game are nearly endless. You could use types of fruits, farm animals, words starting with a specific letter, etc. Then play the game in a similar fashion.

Categories Race

Categories Race allows children to work on classification skills.

LEARNING

✳ A category can include many related things.

MATERIALS

✳ A category that has many words that fit it, such as color words, vegetables, types of cookies, etc.

STEPS

1. Give the children the category word.

2. Divide your group up into smaller groups of equal size.

3. Then have the children in each group come up with as many words as possible that fit that category. One child will need to record these. In a multi-age group, that would be a good job for an older child, or in similar-age groups, choose a child with the ability to handle this challenge.

4. See which group comes up with the most words that fit that category in a specified amount of time. Going through the activity once as an entire large group first, will help the children understand what they are to do in their small groups.

5. Allow the group with the most words to take turns reading off their words while a checker from each other group checks off the words they have that match.

6. Then the other small groups should say any other words they have that were not already mentioned.

7. Count up how many different words were recorded altogether.

ACCOMMODATIONS

✔ Categories can vary to fit the abilities of your group. An idea for a multi-age group is to divide the children by age and give each group a category suitable for the level of abilities within that group.

EXTENSIONS

✔ Allow the children to suggest categories to work with, or base them on things specific to the season (winter fun), area (stores in our neighborhood), children's interests (dinosaurs), etc.

Categories

In Categories the children select an item and determine in which category it belongs.

LEARNING

✳ Items with similar characteristics belong together in a category.

MATERIALS

✳ Items that can be categorized—enough for each child to have an item such as clothes from the four seasons; fruits, vegetables, meat, and breads (use plastic foods or pictures); pets; farm animals; and wild animals (use stuffed or plastic animals or pictures), etc.

✳ A box large enough to hold all the items you have for each category

✳ A method to label the boxes—if you tape a piece of clear plastic to each box, leaving an opening at the top, the category can be written on a card and placed in the plastic pocket. Then the categories can be easily changed and the boxes used over and over again for different categories.

STEPS

1. Collect the items to be categorized.

2. Label a box for each category you will use.

3. Give each child one of the items and have him or her place it in the box that tells its category.

CRITICAL THINKING CHALLENGE

Encourage the children to come up with the categories and items to use for this activity.

ACCOMMODATIONS

✔ Increase the number of categories to make this activity more challenging, and decrease it to make it easier.

✔ The things you choose to sort into categories can vary in complexity, as well. For example, you could use the parts of speech with words such as "noun," "verb," etc. included as the categories and cards with pictures to depict "run," "boy," etc. on them to sort. Types of inclined planes we use daily (wedge, screw, etc.) would be another more difficult idea—many household items could be brought in to place in the correct category boxes.

✔ Pictures of the items (like in the parts of speech example above) rather than the actual items will work but generally aren't as interesting as the real things for these tactile learners!

EXTENSIONS

✔ Adding more items to those you have brought in that fit the categories would be a good experience for the children, as well.

Words of the Season

In Words of the Season children create a different word wall each season with the words that remind us of that season. This will lessen the amount of time you spend helping children spell words that they will be using regularly in their writing during that season.

LEARNING

* Certain words are associated with each season of the year.
* Words tell us about events and characteristics of the season.

MATERIALS

* Long sheet of light colored paper to create a chart
* Dark, thick marker for recording words. Attach it by a long string to the wall by the chart so you can easily add words as they come up

STEPS

1. Begin by discussing the current season and its characteristics.

2. As words come up that are generally seasonal, write them on a long sheet of paper on which you have written the season's name. For summer you would have such words as swimming, hot, sunny, vacation, camp, county fair, water park, Fourth of July, etc.

3. Then, when the children are doing their writing, remind them to look for needed words on the chart on the wall.

4. As new words come up, they can be added to those already there.

 ## ACCOMMODATIONS

✔ The difficulty of the words will vary with your group's abilities, but you may be surprised at the big words children will want on the list!

 ## EXTENSIONS

✔ Use this method for topics you will be covering that have new vocabulary words for the children to learn.

Go Together Race

In Go Together Race children who are familiar with compound words race to see who can make the most compound words in a designated amount of time.

LEARNING

* Sometimes two words can be combined to make a new word.

MATERIALS

* Heavy construction paper for sheets of words that can be combined to make compound words
* Plastic sandwich bags with zipper-type closures (one bag for each child)
* A minute timer
* Paper cutter

STEPS

1. Consider many compound words the children should be familiar with.

2. On a sheet of paper, list the words so that their two parts are separated into two columns.

3. Copy this sheet on heavy construction paper for each child.

4. Use the paper cutter to separate the sheets into the individual words, one sheet at a time so the words from one sheet stay together in a group. Place all the separate words from a single sheet into their own plastic sandwich bag.

5. Repeat this procedure until each sheet has been cut into separate words and those words put into sandwich bags.

6. Give the children each a bag of words and explain that they are to use the words in the bag to make as many compound words as they can in a specified amount of time.

7. When you say, "Go," they should dump out the words and begin finding combinations that make compound words. When you say, "Stop," they should count how many pairs they have.

8. Go over the compound words that can be made and discuss the fact that some people may have come up with different combinations of words to make the compounds and that as long as they are true words, that is fine.

9. Give the child who has the most actual compound words a round of applause.

(continued)

Go Together Race *(continued)*

ACCOMMODATIONS

✓ Keep the number of words to use to make the compound words appropriate for your group's ability level, and keep the words at their reading level.

✓ Working with a partner might be less stressful in this beat-the-clock-type activity!

EXTENSIONS

✓ Have the children come up with as many compound words as they can that incorporate a certain word such as "any" or "some."

✓ Write compound words on the board for the children to draw lines through to show where to separate them into two words.

Personal Word Finds

In Personal Word Finds the children create their own word find puzzles based on a specific category of things.

LEARNING

* Words can be hidden in a puzzle format.
* Things in categories have characteristics that in some way make them similar.

MATERIALS

* Grid paper with large-enough squares for children to write a letter in each square
* Blank sheet of paper

STEPS

1. Discuss things that are a part of a category. For example, cows are a part of the category "farm animals," and pumpkins are a part of the category "vegetables."

2. Have each child decide on a category he or she can name members of.

3. Have each child then list as many words as he or she can think of that name things in that category.

4. Next, explain how a word find works. Words that belong to a category are hidden within the grid of letters, and the person doing the puzzle must figure out where they are—they may be written vertically, horizontally, diagonally, and frontward or backward. The person circles the words as he or she finds them and then crosses them off the list of words to look for.

5. Give each child a sheet of grid paper with squares large enough for the child to write one letter in each.

6. Tell each child to fill in the letters for the words in his or her chosen category going in all the directions given above. The words may intersect, but they don't have to do so.

7. When a word is placed in the grid, it should also be recorded on the blank sheet of paper.

8. When all the words of the category have been recorded on the grid and the blank sheet, then all the other blank spaces on the grid should be filled in with any letters the child chooses.

9. When all the word finds are finished, gather them up and redistribute them so that each child has a word find to do other than his or her own.

ACCOMMODATIONS

✔ The number of squares to fill in on the grid paper, as well as the number of words to find, can be altered to fit your group's abilities.

EXTENSIONS

✔ You could require words from specific categories, such as travel or names of states.

✔ If you have access to a computer, there are puzzle maker programs to use for activities such as this one.

Describing Words

In Describing Words children use as many adjectives as they can think of to describe something.

LEARNING

❋ Adjectives are words that we use to describe something.

MATERIALS

❋ A large old-fashioned schoolhouse shape cut out of red paper

❋ A dark marker

❋ Paper of several different colors for the children to make their shapes on

❋ A vacant space to display the children's work

STEPS

1. On a schoolhouse-shaped piece of paper, write "My school is" on the bell tower and ask the children to tell you words that describe their school—big, brown, decorated, friendly, crowded, safe, wide, confusing, bright, loud, etc. Tell them that all these describing words are called adjectives.

2. Now have them think of something they'd like to describe and to draw that something on a piece of paper with room inside to write adjectives that describe it. Some examples are their house, bedroom, pet, favorite toy, favorite sport (a football shape, baseball shape, ice skate, etc.), friend, etc. It is helpful to brainstorm ideas before they begin to help those who have trouble coming up with an idea to get started.

3. Be sure to emphasize that the words they are writing down are adjectives.

4. Display these with the words "Adjectives are describing words."

ACCOMMODATIONS

✔ Some children may require some suggestions from you about words to describe their item.

✔ If writing is an issue, an older child or adult can write the words a younger child dictates.

EXTENSIONS

✔ The children could use the adjectives they've compiled to write a story about their item (room, pet, etc.).

✔ They could also add words to an adjective word bank you could create on a vacant wall.

I Am So Lucky

In the activity I Am So Lucky *the children each act out a word that fits a specific category.*

LEARNING

❋ A category contains things that are all related in some way.

MATERIALS

❋ Ideas for categories that will work for this activity

❋ Your imagination

STEPS

1. Start out with an easy category, such as pets. Then say, "I am so lucky to have a pet ____," and act like the pet you are thinking of while the children guess what it is.

2. Next give the children who have an idea in mind of what pet they might act like a turn to say the sentence and act like the pet for the children to guess.

3. Now tell them that since they did such a good job on this, tomorrow you will try something harder.

4. The next day say, "I am so lucky. I got to go to the circus and this was my favorite act." Pretend to be a tightrope walker, lion tamer, etc., and have the children guess what act you liked best. Again, let the children take turns saying the sentence and acting out what they liked best at the circus.

CRITICAL THINKING CHALLENGE

Have the children come up with the categories they wish to consider and then act out things that fit those categories.

ACCOMMODATIONS

✔ Keep the categories at a level the children can grasp.

✔ Don't call on a child unless he or she raises a hand to volunteer to act out an idea for the group.

Sentence Challenge

In Sentence Challenge children collect word cards to make complete sentences.

LEARNING

＊ A sentence is formed when specific words are placed in a specific order that makes sense.

MATERIALS

＊ Word cards that depict all parts of speech and can be combined to form sentences. Erasable cards would work great for this so that the "game" can be played over and over again.

STEPS

1. Place several word cards around the room. Be sure that these cards can be arranged to make logical and complete sentences.

2. Allow the children to roam the room collecting cards that will make a real sentence.

3. When they have a sentence, they should lay it out in a specified area.

4. Then gather all the children together to read the groups of words to see if they actually make real sentences, and explain why they do or don't.

ACCOMMODATIONS

✔ The ability level needed to complete this activity can easily be adjusted by the difficulty of the words you choose and the sentence length you require.

EXTENSIONS

✔ You can change the activity by specifying what the sentence must be about (an example might be "true facts about animals") and including words that could be used to accomplish this.

✔ You could also include punctuation marks.

✔ The sentences made could also serve as story starters.

Silly Sound Sentences

In Silly Sound Sentences the children are challenged to create complete sentences in which each word starts with the same letter sound.

LEARNING

✳ A specific sound can be repeated at the start of each word to create a sound sentence. It is a way to practice saying words that begin with specific sounds.

MATERIALS

✳ Letter cards for letters of the alphabet (Avoid all vowels, "x," or letters that have more than one sound.)

✳ Writing utensils

✳ Scratch paper for each child

✳ Drawing paper for each child

STEPS

1. Lay the letter cards facedown on a table.

2. You, the teacher, should pick one and demonstrate what needs to be done.

3. As a group, formulate a sentence in which every word begins with your letter's sound.

4. For example, if you picked an "s," the sentence could be, "Suzy Seal says several sentences." Then draw a picture on the board of the seal with comic book word clouds all around her with sentences in them.

5. Now have each child pick a letter and tell the sound it has before beginning to compose a sentence to go with the sound on a piece of scratch paper.

6. After a child has formed a sentence, have him or her read it to you, and help him or her consider whether it makes sense even in a silly way. If it does, have the child rewrite the sentence on the top of a sheet of drawing paper.

7. Then have the child draw a picture to go with the sentence created.

8. When all the sentences are finished, it will be fun to share the sentences and pictures with the group.

CRITICAL THINKING CHALLENGE

Allow the children to try to write short stories in which each sentence features a different beginning letter sound.

ACCOMMODATIONS

✔ For multi-age groups, pairing a younger child with an older child might work well.

✔ All children could do the same letter sound if you are working on a specific letter sound.

Answer in a Sentence

Through the activity Answer in a Sentence *the children learn to answer questions in complete sentences.*

LEARNING

❋ Questions need complete answers.

MATERIALS

❋ A question to ask each child (Some examples of questions to ask are: How old are you? When is your birthday? What did you do this past weekend? and What is your favorite show?)

STEPS

1. Talk about what a sentence is. Make some statements that are sentences and some that are not. Have the children show you which is which with a thumbs up if it is a sentence and a thumbs down if it is not.

2. Now ask each child the question that he or she is to answer in a complete sentence.

3. Then allow each child to ask you a question in a complete sentence, which you will answer in a complete sentence.

ACCOMMODATIONS

✔ If a child is having difficulty answering in a sentence, provide assistance.

EXTENSIONS

✔ Start with the children answering orally in sentences, and eventually work up to them answering written questions with written answers in sentence form including correct punctuation.

Listen to Me Read

Through Listen to Me Read, *children will learn to evaluate their own reading abilities.*

LEARNING

✴ When we know what mistakes we make when reading, we can work to overcome them.

MATERIALS

✴ Reading materials or books of different ability levels

✴ A tape recorder

✴ A blank cassette tape for each child

✴ A private place to read orally

STEPS

1. Allow each child to choose something to read that is at his or her ability level and to practice reading it through.

2. Next give each child a turn to privately tape himself or herself reading the chosen material orally. A large appliance box cut so it is three sided will make a private area for the child to read behind within the classroom. Provide a place to put the tape recorder and a comfortable chair for the reader to sit on.

Each child will need his or her own cassette tape so that he or she can tape himself or herself rereading the same material at a different time and/or tape himself or herself reading other material later.

3. After the child has had the opportunity to tape himself or herself reading the material, the teacher should take time to listen to the tape while the child and the teacher look at the written material that was read. This is the teacher's opportunity to praise the child for his or her accomplishments and to help the child determine what mistakes have been made and consider ways to overcome the mistakes. Give the child an opportunity to tape the same material again after some practice with attention to correcting any mistakes.

4. Once a month have the child record himself or herself reading something else. Give the child an opportunity to hear himself or herself reading again and to hear again what he or she is doing well and what he or she needs to work on. The goal is for the child to hear the progress he or she is making as a reader.

(continued)

Listen to Me Read *(continued)*

ACCOMMODATIONS

✓ At first you may need to point out the positives about the child's reading and the areas in which improvement is needed, but through your example the child should learn to do some self-evaluating of his or her reading.

EXTENSIONS

✓ The children could tape-record themselves reading stories to share with younger children who could follow along in the books as they listen to the tape-recorded stories. In this manner the children will see the importance of reading the stories without error.

✓ Listening to a commercial tape-recorded story and following along in the book is a good way for children to enjoy stories being read to them by good readers they can emulate.

✓ Read stories to the children yourself, as well, no matter what age the listeners. Everyone enjoys hearing a story read well!

What's Your Favorite Book?

In the activity What's Your Favorite Book? *the children bring their favorite book to share with a partner during National Children's Book Week, which is the third full week of November.*

LEARNING

* ❋ There are many good books to share with others.
* ❋ Reading books and listening to books being read is fun.

MATERIALS

* A favorite children's book of the teacher to share with the group
* Favorite books for the children to share
* Space for the children to spread out and read

STEPS

1. At the beginning of National Children's Book Week, bring your favorite book from your childhood to share with the children or a favorite children's book of yours now.

2. Ask each child to select a favorite book from home or the library to share with a partner on a specific day.

3. On the day when all the books are brought in, ask each child to show the book he or she brought and to tell why he or she chose that particular book to share.

4. Then allow the children partner up and find a comfortable spot in the room to share their books.

ACCOMMODATIONS

✔ In a multi-age group, older children could read the younger children's books to them.

✔ If the children are bringing in chapter books, have them share one chapter with a partner.

EXTENSIONS

✔ Encourage the children to bring in good books that they wish to share with others, and provide time for the sheer joy of reading just for fun.

Two Very Different Mice

In Two Very Different Mice *the children compare the lives and viewpoints of the two mice in the story "The Country Mouse and the City Mouse."*

LANGUAGE ARTS

LEARNING

❊ We do not all live or think the same.

❊ We can make comparisons between two things.

MATERIALS

❊ A copy of the story "The Country Mouse and the City Mouse"

❊ A chalkboard

STEPS

1. Read the story "The Country Mouse and the City Mouse" to the children.

2. After you have finished, write "Life in the Country" on one side of the chalkboard and "Life in the City" on the other side. Have the children think of the differences between the mice as stated in the story, and write them under the correct heading.

3. Ask them which life each mouse preferred and why and which place they'd prefer to live and why.

ACCOMMODATIONS

✔ You may need to direct the discussion to get the responses you are looking for. Give the children your reason first for where you'd like to live to get them thinking of their reasons.

EXTENSIONS

✔ Discuss other living situations with the children, such as living in a house or an apartment, having house pets versus having no pets, riding the bus versus walking to school, etc., and encourage the children to give their reasons for how they feel as well as to accept others' rights to their feelings.

5

Writing Challenges

Activities in chapter 5 are meant to foster the children's writing abilities through authentic writing situations that promote writing for a variety of purposes. The hope is that children will see the usefulness and value of writing as they acquire the ability to communicate more effectively through it.

What a Picture! What a Story!

What a Picture! What a Story! encourages children to use their imaginations to create interesting stories.

LEARNING

❋ A picture can add detail and excitement to a story.

MATERIALS

❋ Colorful and interesting pictures that show action cut from magazines

❋ Writing paper suitable for the age and ability of the writers

STEPS

1. Lay out the magazine pictures.

2. Have each child choose a picture that catches his or her interest.

3. Start by having each child tell a little bit about the picture he or she chose, including what he or she thinks might be happening in the picture. Comment on things that the child may not have considered or noticed in the picture, and encourage the other children to do the same. This will help each child to garner ideas about his or her picture.

4. Now have each child write an imaginative story about what is happening in the picture he or she chose. Encourage creativity but remind the children that the picture and story are partners! (They go together—the picture adds to the story and the story explains the picture.)

5. When the stories are completed, they can be shared with the group.

ACCOMMODATIONS

✓ Story length and depth can be varied to suit the individual children in the group.

✓ With multi-age groups, pair a younger child with an older one. Have them share story ideas, which the older child can write down.

✓ Tape-recording the stories will allow even the youngest children who may have limited reading abilities or are nonreaders to enjoy the stories on their own.

EXTENSIONS

✓ Pictures could be chosen to relate to a specific theme (the Fourth of July, school days, bad weather, etc.) and combined to form a book of stories about that topic to add to your library of reading materials.

How Many? Who? How?

How Many? Who? How? encourages the children to write their own stories similar to the familiar folktale "The Three Billy Goats Gruff."

LANGUAGE ARTS

LEARNING

✳ We can develop our own stories following the format of familiar stories.

MATERIALS

✳ The story "The Three Billy Goats Gruff"

✳ Writing paper

✳ Cardboard to make the book covers and a method to attach them to the pages to form a book

STEPS

1. Read or tell the story of "The Three Billy Goats Gruff"

2. Discuss that the story has a number of animals who have a certain characteristic. Gruff is an unfamiliar term to many children. Explain it.

3. Make up other titles that follow this pattern such as "The Five Cows Lazy" or "The Two Frogs Hoppy."

4. Choose a title to use, and write a story together on a story chart.

5. Then allow the children to create their own titles that follow the pattern and write their own stories.

6. Creating a list of adjectives together on the chalkboard will help the children handle this more difficult part of the activity.

7. Allow the children to share their stories in the form of a class book.

ACCOMMODATIONS

✔ For children who have limited handwriting abilities, the teacher could write down the stories as they are dictated.

✔ For children who have difficulty coming up with ideas, working with another child to write a joint story might work.

EXTENSIONS

✔ Stories could be acted out as plays.

✔ Children could read their stories to the class or to another child.

ABC Story

In ABC Story upper elementary children will tell a story one sentence at a time with the first sentence starting with the letter "A," the second sentence with the letter "B," and so on.

LANGUAGE ARTS

LEARNING

✳ In a story one sentence relates to the next so that the story makes sense.

MATERIALS

✳ A long sheet of chart paper or a flip chart
✳ A dark marker

STEPS

1. Make a chart with the letter "A" followed by a long blank line to write on.

2. Directly below the "A," place a "B" followed by a long blank line to write on.

3. Do this for each letter of the alphabet.

4. Now begin to tell a story, starting with the word "A" and making up a sentence to follow, such as "A boy went to the store."

5. The next sentence must start with a word that begins with a "B" and makes sense with the first sentence, such as "But he forgot his money."

6. Now go to the "C" row and fill in that line following the same procedure, such as "Could he call his mom to bring him the money?"

7. The challenge is to complete the story from A to Z in a way that makes sense or sticks to the topic of the story and follows the pattern set—A to Z.

8. Have the children give you the sentences to record on the story chart.

ACCOMMODATIONS

✔ This is an activity for children with fairly well defined reading skills, such as ABC order, letter/sound correspondence, and story sense.

✔ It might be easier if the sentence did not have to start with the next alphabet letter but could be a part of the preceding sentence, such as " 'A' girl went to the zoo 'B'ecause she wanted to see a 'C'amel 'D'ancing with an 'E'agle." In this case, the lines might be very different lengths.

EXTENSIONS

✔ Give each child a sheet of paper with the alphabet written down the left side, and let him or her create his or her own ABC story.

My Me Book

My Me Book has the children create their own books about themselves.

LEARNING

❋ Autobiographies are books written about us by us.

MATERIALS

❋ Paper, cardboard, yarn, a hole punch, stapler, and contact paper to make books

❋ A camera and film for picture taking

❋ White glue or glue sticks

❋ Writing utensils (markers or dark crayons would work well for this project)

❋ Catalogs and magazines

STEPS

1. Create a book by stapling together enough sheets of paper for the length of the book you wish each child to create. A sturdy book cover could be added by using a piece of cardboard for the front and the back, punching holes along the edges, and binding with yarn or string. Covering these with decorative contact paper will improve the appearance.

2. Take a picture of each child in your group, or have them each draw a self-portrait.

3. Have each child glue his or her picture to the front cover of a book.

4. Have each child add the title "My Me Book" to the cover.

5. Then allow the children to choose things that tell about them to write in the books, such as "I like pizza." or "I have a dog named Rusty." A different sentence should be written on each page.

6. Have them add pictures to go with their sentences. These could be drawn or cut from catalogs and magazines. Completing one page before going to the next will work well for this project. Also, this book should be done over a period of time and definitely not in one sitting!

7. Sharing their books with each other will help the children get to know each other more personally.

ACCOMMODATIONS

✔ The length of the book will be dictated by the ages and the abilities of the group.

✔ Sentences can be written by the children or dictated to an adult who can write them down.

EXTENSIONS

✔ Children could add to their books as important events happen to them. Using rings that can be opened and shut or tying the yarn of the binding in bows would allow the addition of extra pages.

✔ These books could be used as gifts (keepsakes) for their parents.

Sound Rebus Story

Sound Rebus Story works like a traditional rebus story, except instead of replacing words with pictures, you will be replacing words with sounds.

LEARNING

❋ We can use sounds to depict words.

MATERIALS

❋ A children's story involving a variety of animals in a format that lets the children visually follow along as the teacher reads it. Such stories as "The Sky is Falling" or "Brown Bear, Brown Bear, What Do You See?" incorporate several different animals.

STEPS

1. Write out the short story involving different animals on chart paper so that the children can follow along as you read the story to them. Or, if it's a well-known story, you may be able to find it in "big book" format, which would work well here.

2. Read the story to the children.

3. Now, with the children, decide on a sound that could vocally be made to depict each animal. For example, "moo" for a cow and "buzzzz" for a bee.

4. This time, as you read the story, you will point to the animal's name rather than saying it while the children make the sound for that animal.

CRITICAL THINKING CHALLENGE

Children could add sounds to their own stories to make sound rebus stories to share with the group.

ACCOMMODATIONS

✔ Consider the length of the story and the number of different animal sounds to remember for your group's ability level.

EXTENSIONS

✔ Sounds could be used to represent actions in stories as well, such as very fast clapping for running and a tongue clicking sound for trotting.

Resolutions

Resolutions encourages the children to consider something they could do better or a positive thing they could do that they don't do now.

MATERIALS

❋ Official-looking documents copied onto sturdy paper with the wording as stated in the steps below (one for each child and yourself!)

❋ 12-by-18-inch sheets of construction paper to make a folder the document can be stapled to so that it is covered up but can be peeked at

STEPS

1. To celebrate the new year and start it off on a positive note, discuss the things that happened over the past year.

2. Then discuss how a new year is a time to decide how we could change something for the better over the next year. Often people resolve to change something about themselves. Suggest several changes that would be appropriate for the children in the group. Some examples are: to fight less with my brother, to put away my toys without being told, to practice my violin regularly, etc. This will give them the idea of what you are looking for in a resolution they might make.

You may wish to share one you are making with them and then use it to show them how to do the rest of the project.

3. Have the children consider something they would like to do differently over the next year.

4. Tell them that this is a private matter and they don't have to share it with others unless they wish to.

5. Then hand out to each child the very official looking document you have made stating, "In the year 2005 (or whatever year it is) I, (name), do solemnly resolve to," and have them complete the sentence, ending it with a period. Have them place this document in a folder made from the construction paper folded in half, and staple it in so it is covered by the upper flap of the folder. (The fold should be across the top of the folder.) Have them each write "My New Year's Resolution for (the year)" on the front flap of the folder.

6. Have them take their resolution home and keep it in a safe place where it won't get lost but where they can reread it often and think about how they are doing with that resolution. Remind them that making a change is often difficult and they shouldn't give up if they don't always keep their resolutions but should just keep trying. Every now and then remind them to check and see how they are coming along on that resolution they made.

(continued)

Resolutions *(continued)*

ACCOMMODATIONS

✓ You may need to do the writing for less capable children.

✓ Some children may require some personal suggestions for resolutions that you whisper in their ears.

EXTENSIONS

✓ You may wish to come up with a class resolution or two that you will write on a much larger document and place in a much larger folder since it is a big resolution for the whole class to follow.

✓ You could also do a different class resolution for each month tied to a behavior you would like to see more of.

My Favorite Treat Recipe

For My Favorite Treat Recipe *the children compile a recipe booklet that they have all contributed to.*

LEARNING

✳ It is important to write clear directions to tell others how to do something so that they get the same results we did.

MATERIALS

✳ Notes to the children's families to explain the project (one for each child)

✳ Recipe-type cards that are large enough for your children to write on clearly. Send an extra with each child in case the information won't fit on the front of just one card. Remind the children to write on only one side of the card.

✳ Materials to compile the recipes into a book

✳ Recipe books

STEPS

1. Send home a note to each child's family asking them to come up with a simple snack recipe and to help the child write down the steps to make the snack. They should be sure to include the ingredients and the amounts of each necessary to make the snack for the number of children in the class. Give the families a week or so to complete this task, and provide a recipe-type card in a size appropriate for your children to write on. It is helpful to set a specific date by which the cards must be returned.

2. When you have received all the recipe cards, provide each child with his or her card and a sheet of paper divided in equal halves so that the child can glue the recipe on the bottom half and draw a picture of the finished snack on the top half. Show the children the recipe books you have that include pictures and tell them that this helps the person making the recipe know what the snack will look like when it is ready to eat.

3. Bind these finished sheets together into a book format, and add a table of contents listing each recipe name and its contributor.

4. Give the recipe book a title such as "Our Favorite Snacks."

5. Then once a week try out one of the recipes for a snack. Have the children help to read the recipe and do the mixing and fixing until all the recipes have been tried.

6. If your budget permits, send home copies of the recipe books with all the children at the end of the school year.

CRITICAL THINKING CHALLENGE

Discuss what would happen if an ingredient were left out or if the wrong amount were used, and emphasize that recipes must be carefully written down.

(continued)

My Favorite Treat Recipe *(continued)*

ACCOMMODATIONS

✔ If a child will be unable to write the recipe down for himself or herself, allow an adult to write it down while sharing the information with the child.

✔ Remind the families to keep the recipes simple, and let them know whether cooking can be involved. This will depend on your classroom and school facilities.

✔ Decide ahead of time whether the recipes must meet certain healthy eating guidelines and, if so, include these in the note sent home.

EXTENSIONS

✔ Add recipes if you use others during the year that the children like.

Picture This!

Picture This! involves the children in writing their own rebus stories.

LEARNING

❋ In rebus stories pictures are used to take the place of words.

MATERIALS

❋ A rebus story written on large chart paper

❋ A copy of a story that has many words that could be replaced with pictures, written with space between the lines of words so the children can draw pictures where appropriate (one for each child)

❋ A copy of a rebus story that has spaces in the places where pictures can go instead of words (one for each child)

❋ Writing paper that has space between the lines so that there is room to draw in pictures to replace words (one for each child)

STEPS

1. Select and copy a rebus story or write your own on a large sheet of chart paper.

2. Involve the children in reading the story—the teacher can read the words and the children can "read" the pictures that are in place of some of the words.

3. Now give each child a copy of the short story with space between the lines of text. Have the children draw pictures above the words that pictures could depict.

4. Next give each child a story in which words that could be depicted with a picture have been left out, and let them fill in pictures they choose that will make sense. Have them read the stories to each other to see how differently they may turn out using different "picture words."

5. Last, encourage the children to write their own rebus stories.

6. These steps are best spread out over the course of a few days.

ACCOMMODATIONS

✓ The level of difficulty of their stories and their length will depend on your group of children.

✓ You can also provide stories at different reading levels to match the abilities of different children.

✓ Rebus stories allow even children with minimal spelling abilities to write stories containing words that are difficult to spell because they use pictures to replace some of the hard words. They can also read rebus stories written by others because the pictures help them read some of the words that may be difficult for them to figure out.

EXTENSIONS

✓ Allow the children to use this rebus method in their writing to encourage more difficult language in the stories they write, and use it yourself to help them read notes on the board, written directions, etc.

Let's Be "Reason-a-Full"

In Let's Be Reason-a-Full the children must give their opinion on an issue and then support that opinion with the reasons they feel as they do.

LEARNING

* In order for our opinions to be taken seriously, we must be able to support them with reasons why we feel as we do.

MATERIALS

* An issue that the children are interested in and might have definite opinions about to discuss as a group (For example, do they think it is right that elephants are trained to perform in circuses, or do they feel that hot lunches at school should include soda to drink?)

* Another issue that fits the above description written on the board for the children to copy on writing paper

STEPS

1. Discuss the issue as a group with each child stating his or her opinion and why he or she feels that way. Tell the children that in order to convince people to feel as you do, you need to give them good reasons for your opinions.

2. Now give them a sheet of paper to copy down another issue written on the board and have them write down as many reasons as they can for why they feel as they do. Their sentence should begin "It is my opinion that" and state their position, followed by "because" and a numbered list of reasons. Encourage them to include at least two reasons and maybe more—the more the better, if they are good reasons!

3. Allow them to share their reasons with a small group of classmates.

4. As a large group, discuss which reasons came up the most often and that everyone has a right to his or her own opinion and we don't always agree on how things should be done.

CRITICAL THINKING CHALLENGE

Help the children form a compromise by using their opinions and reasons. For example, maybe hot lunch could include soda on special occasions or once a week, which allows those who like soda to have it once in a while, but children wouldn't drink soda every day, which isn't healthful.

ACCOMMODATIONS

✓ If writing is an issue for your group, allow the children to state their reasons as you record them either in writing or with a tape recorder.

✓ Keep the issues you discuss appropriate for your group of children.

Letters to the Stars

In Letters to the Stars *the children write friendly letters in the proper format to famous people they would like to hear from.*

LEARNING

✳ A friendly letter has a specific format as does the envelope address.

✳ Letter writing can be an enjoyable method of communication.

MATERIALS

✳ Chart paper displaying the format for writing a friendly letter and addressing the envelope

✳ Addresses of famous people the children might be interested in writing to

✳ Letter writing paper and envelopes

✳ A stamp for each child's envelope

✳ A loose-leaf binder with enough clear loose-leaf sleeves for each letter and picture to go in. Each sleeve will hold one letter and one picture.

STEPS

1. On the large sheet of chart paper diagram the proper format for writing a friendly letter.

2. As a class, choose a famous person you would like to know more about and write that person a friendly letter including information about the class and questions you would like the person to answer about himself or herself.

3. Now show the children the diagram of the proper way to address the envelope and address the large envelope for the class letter

to be sent in. Libraries might carry books with addresses of famous people or you may be able to locate them on the Internet. Magazines that feature sports figures, movie stars, or musical performers also often contain addresses for writing to these people. The children may have some of these materials to share with the class. Compile a list of addresses of famous people.

4. When the class gets its reply from the person you wrote to, share it with the class.

5. This experience will motivate the children to want to write their own letters to famous people.

6. Have each child choose a person on the address list who he or she would like to write to following the format you've shown the class.

7. Give them time to write the letters and provide guidance to help them come up with things to write about themselves and questions to ask. Also provide envelopes for them to address. Ask each child to contribute a stamp to place on his or her envelope. The letters can all be mailed from school or brought to a nearby public mailbox, but each child's return addresses should be his or her home.

8. The children should bring their letters to school to share with the class once they receive them. Remind them that not everyone will receive a letter on the same day and that they must patiently wait for their replies.

(continued)

LANGUAGE ARTS

Letters to the Stars *(continued)*

9. The children could request autographed pictures of the stars or they could cut out pictures of them from magazines or newspapers. Using clear loose-leaf paper sleeves, the letters and pictures could be compiled in a loose-leaf binder that the children could look at during their free time.

 ACCOMMODATIONS

✓ Children will write the letters at their ability levels. If writing is difficult for some of the children, letters could be dictated to be written down by an adult.

 EXTENSIONS

✓ You might wish to look at all the return addresses on the envelopes when the replies come to see how many places the stars sent letters from. The children can also look at the postmarks to find out when and from where the letters were sent.

Be My Valentine

Be My Valentine encourages the children to write clever phrases for valentines using plays on words.

LEARNING

✳ We can use words in clever ways to create valentine messages.

MATERIALS

✳ A variety of valentines that incorporate the clever use of words to make their point

✳ Materials for making the valentines, such as red, pink, and white paper, markers, glue, stickers, doilies, ribbon, etc.

STEPS

1. As soon as packages of valentines and Valentine's Day cards appear in the stores, begin looking for samples to show the children that use words in unique ways to get their points across. Some examples might be "I'm not lion, I want you for my valentine!" with a picture of a friendly lion, "Whooo'll be my valentine?" with an owl pictured on the card, or "I'll never leaf you!" with a picture of a leaf on the card.

2. Have the children think about other phrases like these that would work. Make a list of their ideas on the board over the next few days. Encourage them to get their families involved in coming up with ideas as well.

3. When your list has several examples, provide supplies for each child to create a valentine for someone special using one of the phrases on the board and adding a picture to suit it.

ACCOMMODATIONS

✔ If writing is an issue for some children, the teacher could write the phrase on the card the child has created.

EXTENSIONS

✔ The children could work together to create large valentine posters with the phrases to decorate the walls and halls.

✔ It would be interesting to compare valentines from different eras. There are books and Internet sources to use for this activity.

✔ The children could research how and when Valentine's Day got started.

Speaking Challenges

Activities in this chapter provide the children with practice in speaking before others in interesting and nonthreatening situations so that pubic speaking is not seen as intimidating but becomes second nature to them. The hope is that successful speaking experiences early on will lead to children feeling comfortable in public speaking.

What's the News? What's the Weather?

In What's the News? What's the Weather? *the children get to be television reporters.*

LEARNING

* We can learn to be comfortable speaking publicly through practice.

MATERIALS

* One large appliance box (Stores that sell such appliances are often willing to donate one to a good cause.)
* A cutting utensil that will cut through the cardboard
* Brass fasteners
* News sources such as newspapers, television and radio news programs, etc.
* Optional: a video camera and a television and VCR
* A map to use for reporting the weather

STEPS

1. Using a large appliance box, create a television set that allows a child to sit in it with a desk in front of him or her. Buttons to turn the television on and change channels can be added using cardboard cutouts and brass fasteners.

2. Then allow the children to take turns reporting the weather and the news each day. Information can be collected from city newspapers, actual reporting on television or radio, or children's newspapers.

3. The children can write down brief notes about what they want to report. This will give them the opportunity to look at the audience while they speak rather than just reading a report to the audience.

4. Watching real reporters on television will give the children an idea of how reporters give us the news and weather. They can also show pictures or video clips if you have access to a video camera. Roving reporters could actually tape the news happening around the school and show it on a real television with a VCR. The use of a weather map would add to the weather reports.

 ## ACCOMMODATIONS

✔ The content of the news reported should be geared to the children you are working with.

 ## EXTENSIONS

✔ If you use a children's newspaper in your classroom, the news from it could be shared using this method.

✔ A reporter who works for the local television station would make a great guest speaker, or, better yet, actually visit the television station.

Introductions

Introductions teaches children how to introduce people properly and gives them practice doing so in authentic situations.

LANGUAGE ARTS

LEARNING

✳ There are proper methods for introducing people to others.

MATERIALS

✳ Someone to introduce

STEPS

1. Demonstrate the proper method to use to introduce someone by having one child pretend to be brand new to the class and in need of being introduced to the other classmates.

2. Then have the children partner up and practice introducing each other to you.

3. Whenever you have a guest to your classroom, have a child in the class introduce him or her to the other children.

4. Children could also properly introduce the members of a group they have worked with on a presentation.

5. Use every opportunity you get for the children to practice this important social skill.

ACCOMMODATIONS

✔ Keep the introductions short—"Mrs. Jones, this is Sally. Sally, this is Mrs. Jones."—at first. Gradually work up to including more details in the introductions—"Class, this is my cousin Marcus from Atlanta. He is visiting me for a week while his parents are on a trip."

EXTENSIONS

✔ Have the children demonstrate their abilities to introduce people properly by introducing their parents to you at open house or conferences.

Interviews

In Interviews the children obtain information from a person by interviewing him or her.

LEARNING

✳ Interviewing allows us to obtain specific information from a person.

MATERIALS

✳ A chalkboard and chalk
✳ Paper to write the children's questions on
✳ A copy machine

STEPS

1. Pretend you are a reporter and you wish to obtain information about an event at school. Have the children help decide what questions people interested in the event would like answered. Write these down on the chalkboard with room underneath each question to fill in the answer to it. Then choose a child to interview. As he or she answers your questions, fill in the answers under the questions asked.

2. Tell the children that they can now take turns interviewing each other.

3. Devise a list of questions that they could ask their classmates to find out more about them. As they give you their suggestions for questions, write them down on a sheet of paper with space after each for writing the answers. Once you have 10 questions, make copies of them for each child. Then pair the children up to interview each other and record the answers. Remind them to add the name of the person they are interviewing to the sheet of questions before they begin.

4. After the interviews, have each child tell one thing he or she found out about the person he or she interviewed.

5. Place the interview sheets on a bulletin board for the children to read during free time.

CRITICAL THINKING CHALLENGE

Use this interview method when a new child joins the class to find out a little about that child. Have the children think of the questions to ask.

ACCOMMODATIONS

✔ Use fewer questions with younger children and help the children write the questions in a manner that will get more than just yes or no responses.

I Hear You Loud and Clear

Many people appear self-conscious speaking over a microphone. I Hear You Loud and Clear *helps children to feel comfortable in this situation.*

LEARNING

✳ A microphone is a useful tool when we want to make sure our voices will be heard by all listeners. We can become comfortable using it with practice in nonthreatening situations.

MATERIALS

✳ A microphone
✳ Material for each child to read that he or she is very familiar and comfortable with

STEPS

1. Set up a microphone in one area of the room.

2. Allow the children to play around with it a bit for a day or two at break times just to get used to how their voices sound over it, how close they need to be to it, and at what volume their voices need to be to be clearly heard.

3. Then give each child the opportunity to read something he or she is very familiar with over the microphone for the others to hear. Work on raising and lowering the microphone and speaking slowly and clearly with each child as his or her turn comes around. Let a few children read each day until everyone has had an opportunity to read something over the microphone.

4. As the weeks go by, offer opportunities to speak using the microphone whenever appropriate.

 ACCOMMODATIONS

✔ Raise or lower the microphone to suit the reader.

 EXTENSIONS

✔ Have the children take turns doing the announcements over the school public address system.

✔ If your school or classroom is doing a play or musical production for the children's families, have the children use the microphone when speaking and singing or when announcing for it.

Say Hello to My Pet

In Say Hello to My Pet the children each bring in a stuffed animal and pretend that it is a real pet. They will tell information about the pets and answer questions about them, as well.

LEARNING

❋ Speaking in front of a group can be an enjoyable experience.

MATERIALS

❋ A stuffed animal for each child

❋ An answer sheet for each child to fill out

❋ Questions that call for information on the answer sheets written out on index cards

STEPS

1. During National Pet Week, which is the first full week in May, have the children bring in a stuffed animal that they will pretend is a real pet.

2. Give them a copy of a sheet to fill out with the following information about their "pets."

   My pet is a _____.
   Its name is _____.
   My pet is _____ years old.
   I got my pet from _____.
   My pet eats _____.

   My pet likes to _____.
   The best thing about my pet is
   _____.

3. Each child should fill this out either at home or at school sometime before he or she introduces his or her pet to the class.

4. When the child talks about the pet brought to school, he or she can look at the sheet of information, if necessary, to answer the questions that children ask. The teacher will write these questions out on cards and pass them out to children in the audience who will ask the speaker their questions. The teacher will also allow children to ask other questions of the speaker to see if the child can think of answers for those questions, as well.

5. The idea is that the child will feel more comfortable speaking with the stuffed animal to hold and the answer sheet available. With this comfort established, the child may be able to use his or her imagination to answer spontaneous questions, as well. Plus, the teacher will have the opportunity to see if the children can formulate questions that stick to the subject of pets.

ACCOMMODATIONS

✔ Be prepared to supply a choice of stuffed animals to any child who does not bring one in.

✔ Help the children to fill out the information, if needed.

EXTENSIONS

✔ Have the children write stories about adventures they have with their "pets."

How Do You Do It?

In the activity How Do You Do It? *the children tell how to do something while they are demonstrating it.*

LEARNING

❋ We communicate through both words and actions.

MATERIALS

❋ Each child will need something to demonstrate and the equipment or materials to do this

❋ Chart paper (one sheet for each child)

STEPS

1. Demonstrate for the children how to do something while explaining what it is you are doing, such as setting the table, making a birthday card, arranging some pretty flowers, etc. Use a chart with the steps written on it. Keep the number of steps appropriate for the level of children you teach.

2. Now tell the children that they also have the opportunity to demonstrate something to the rest of the class. Brainstorm some ideas with them to get them thinking about what they might demonstrate. Some examples might be: how to make an easy snack, how to play an instrument, how to play a game, etc.

3. Have them go home and discuss this with their families. A note explaining the project might be necessary.

4. Tell the children to decide what they will demonstrate and to bring any needed materials to school to do the demonstration. Once the materials are all there, the children can be given chart paper to write down the steps that they will share with the class. Doing this at school will help you monitor the difficulty of the activities the children will demonstrate and adjust them if necessary. You will also be able to assist the children in writing the steps down clearly and in order.

5. When a child has the steps written down and has practiced the demonstration by himself or herself a few times in a somewhat private area, then he or she is ready to do the demonstration for the class.

ACCOMMODATIONS

✔ Encourage younger children to demonstrate something with few steps.

EXTENSIONS

✔ The children could do their demonstrations for other children in the school.

✔ Give the children more opportunities to explain and show how to do things whenever appropriate.

Haven't I Said That Before?

Haven't I Said That Before? *calls for the children to tape-record dialogue and sound effects for a play and then to act out the play using the taped recording for the dialogue and sound effects.*

LEARNING

❊ We can tape-record our voices and sound effects in advance to be used when acting out a play later.

MATERIALS

❊ Short plays for the children to perform, such as in "How to Do Plays with Children"

❊ Tape recorders and blank tapes

❊ Materials to use to make sound effects

STEPS

1. Have small groups of children choose short plays they would like to perform. These could be chosen from a children's play book, or the children could write out dialogue for a story they would like to make into a play with the teacher's guidance.

2. Now have them decide on the sound effects they might wish to have for the play and

how they might create those effects. Once they have decided on the methods and the materials to use to create them, they are ready to add notations on where to do the sound effects to the dialogue script.

3. The next task is to tape-record the dialogue with the sound effects. Remind the children to make the dialogue sound natural and not like it's being read and to use good expression in their voices without talking too fast. Play back the tape when they have finished recording to be sure it sounds the way they want it to. You can erase the parts they wish to redo.

4. Then using this tape the children will practice the actions for the plays so that everything will go together smoothly. They do not have to worry about remembering their lines—only about doing the actions at the right times—and their play will have sound effects too!

5. Now it is time to perform the plays using the prerecorded dialogue and sound effects.

ACCOMMODATIONS

✓ If a child is reluctant to read the dialogue on the tape recorder, he or she might feel more comfortable doing the sound effects.

✓ Consider the ages and abilities of your group of children when considering which plays to perform.

EXTENSIONS

✓ Offer the children many opportunities to tape-record their voices, such as to read stories for others to listen to or to record their singing.

LANGUAGE ARTS RESOURCES

Brenner, R. (1997). *Valentine treasury: A century of valentine cards.* Atglen, PA: Schiffer Publishing.

Love, Marla. (1977). *20 reading comprehension games.* Belmont, CA: Fearon.

Moore, Joe, Moore, Jo E., Tryon, Leslie, and Franco, Betsy. (1994). *How to do plays with children.* Monterey, CA: Evan-Moor, Corp.

Novelli, Joan. (2002). *40 sensational sight word games.* New York: Scholastic Professional Books.

Potts, Cheryl. (1999). *Poetry play any day with Jane Yolen.* Fort Atkinson, WI: Alleyside Press.

Prelutsky, Jack A. (selected by). (1993). *Nonny mouse writes again: Poems.* New York: Knopf: Distributed by Random House.

Roeber, Jane A. (1990–1999). *1990 through 1999 summer library program manuals (each based on a different theme).* Madison, WI: Wisconsin Department of Public Instruction.

Silverstein, Shel. (1974).*Where the sidewalk ends.* New York: Harper Collins Publishers.

Unit 3

Mathematics

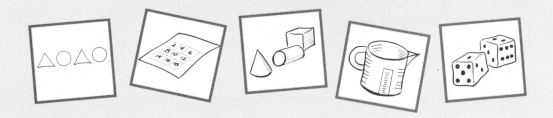

$\mathbf{F}$ ive chapters are contained in Unit Three. Each chapter reflects a major strand in mathematics as recommended by the National Council of Teachers of Mathematics (NCTM). The five strand areas are: number and operations, algebra, geometry, measurement, and data analysis and probability. Incorporated into many of the activities are the five processes of mathematics recommended by the NCTM: problem solving, reasoning, communicating, making connections, and representing. Each activity in the chapters can be used independently when planning activities for children. The chapters are set up to permit a teacher to group together several activities to provide for a continued learning experience. Listed below are the learning skills for each of the five chapters.

* **Algebra:** These activities help children understand classification, patterning, and properties and change with number.

* **Data Analysis and Probability:** Activities include collection, organization, display of data, and analysis of data, as well as concepts of probability.

* **Geometry:** Activities reinforce understanding of properties of spatial sense, two-dimensional and three-dimensional shapes and patterns.

✳ **Measurement:** This chapter's activities help students understand measurement units of length, capacity and volume, weight, time, and area and perimeter.

✳ **Number and Operations:** Skills reinforced by these activities include understanding numbers; number operations of addition, subtraction, multiplication, division; and making reasonable estimations.

As indicated above, when designing activities for each of the five areas in mathematics, attention is given to NCTM's recommended processes. As children work through activities that emphasize the processes of *problem solving* and *reasoning* they are provided the opportunity to think and draw conclusions. By including the mathematical process skill of *communication* children are provided the opportunity to explain and share how they worked through the activity, increasing their involvement in the experience. The inclusion of the process skills of *making connections* and *representing* allows for the development of activities that help children connect their experience to daily living events and to solve daily mathematical situations.

Chapter 7

Algebra

Activities involving algebra help children to classify properties, understand patterns, and see relationships and observe change among numbers. Through activities related to algebra, students begin to identify and work with commutative, associative, and distributive properties of whole numbers.

Sort Our Shoes

Sort Our Shoes is a fun activity for younger children that helps them form relationships among objects. The activity gives them experiences that will be helpful as they begin to form relationships among numeric patterns later.

LEARNING

* Classifying objects with common properties
* Problem solving
* Communicating results

MATERIALS

* Children's shoes or sandals
* Recording paper and marker

STEPS

1. Have the children sit in a circle. Tell them that eight of them at a time will be asked to place one of their shoes (or sandals, boots, etc.) in the middle of the circle. After the first set of shoes has been put in the circle, have the children identify ways in which the shoes in the pile are the same. As children communicate how they would put shoes into a pile, ask them if they understand the classification pattern(s) being shared.

2. Record the classification ideas on a chart to be reviewed later.

3. After several children share their classification ideas, return the shoes in the pile to the children and have eight different children place their shoes in the middle of the circle. Follow the same procedures as before, allowing different children to share their classification patterns.

4. Repeat the activity until all children have had a chance to place a shoe in the pile.

CRITICAL THINKING CHALLENGE

Slightly older students could be asked to put the shoes into two or three piles so that each pile is the same in some way. Since the mix of shoes may be very diverse, they may need to look for such characteristics as having white, not having any white, having ties versus Velcro, etc.

ACCOMMODATIONS

✔ Younger children could be asked to first sort out the shoes from the pile and then tell how they are the same.

✔ Fewer shoes could be used if children struggle with eight at a time.

Can the Objects

Can the Objects can be used to teach children to classify a set of objects in multiple ways using different attributes. The activity can be used by children of different ages depending on the objects selected.

MATERIALS

* Three or four cans of sufficient size to hold objects used for classifying
* Different sets of objects with common attributes for each set—the objects should have various attributes such as color, shape, size, texture, function, and so forth
* Paper to record attributes

STEPS

1. Set up a learning area in the classroom that includes the three or four empty cans and a container with a variety of objects to be classified.

2. Tell the children that they should place the objects into the different containers so that the objects in each container are the same in some way.

3. As the children place the objects into the different containers they can record one or more attributes that are the same for the objects in each can. A list of the ways the objects were classified can be attached to the can.

4. At the end of each day or at some other interval the teacher may bring the children together to review the different properties that they used to classify the objects.

ACCOMMODATIONS

✔ For younger children objects with clearly identifiable attributes, such as color, texture (wood, cloth, metal, etc.), simple shapes, and size, might be used. Simple attribute blocks could be used.

✔ For older children select less identifiable or random objects with no predetermined attributes. Children may come up with such attributes as partly white, having holes, etc.

✔ To make the task more challenging children could be required to put *all* the objects into three cans, forcing them to identify three distinct attributes that would be used, one for each can.

EXTENSIONS

✔ The teacher can select objects that relate to other curriculum subjects being discussed. Children could classify pictures of different classes of animals, or separate pictures by small towns, capital cities, states, and so forth.

✔ Teams of children can take turns on a weekly basis selecting objects to be classified into the cans.

Which Numbers Belong Together?

Which Numbers Belong Together? helps children to look at a set of numbers and identify how the numbers can be grouped together based on different number attributes.

LEARNING

* Classifying number attributes
* Reasoning
* Communicating number classifications

MATERIALS

* Number cards for each child or group of children
* Sheet of paper with boxes for classifying the numbers

STEPS

1. Pass out cards to children that contain sets of numerals for kids to classify. Children could be put into teams to accomplish the task.

2. On the back side of the number card or on a separate sheet of paper have a set of blank boxes to record number patterns.

3. Tell children they are to write numbers in each box that are the same somehow, for example, all the numbers have two digits, all the numbers in the ones column are 6, all digits in the number add up to a certain number (345 [3 + 4 + 5], 237 [2 + 3 + 7], add up to 12), and so forth. Tell them they need to explain how the numbers are the same.

4. Allow children a certain amount of time to complete the task.

5. Once the time period is up have children share the different ways they classified the numbers in the boxes.

CRITICAL THINKING CHALLENGE

Children could be shown just two or three numerals and be asked to tell if there is any way they are the same.

(continued)

Number Card (Sample)			
345	435	47	747
61.6	85	2382	9
72	66	18	22
171	466	8	9191
333	74	474	901.3

Boxes for Classifying Numbers				

ACCOMMODATIONS

✔ The numbers used can be modified for children: smaller or larger whole numbers or rational (fractions, decimals) numbers.

✔ The quantity of numerals on each card can also vary.

EXTENSIONS

✔ Children could be given a number and asked to write down different numbers that are the same in some way. For example, if given 356 children could write down 563 or 635 because all have the same three digits, or they could write down 746 because both 356 and 746 have a 6 in the ones column.

MATHEMATICS

Number Hunt

Number Hunt is an outdoor adventure that requires younger children to find sets of numbers that have been classified into groupings.

LEARNING

✳ Classifying numerals by magnitude

MATERIALS

✳ Number sheets with numbers listed in categories

✳ Large recording sheet for numbers collected by all children

✳ A walking area containing a variety of signs, etc. that include numbers

STEPS

1. Tell children they are going on a walk outdoors. As they go on the walk they will write down numbers that belong to certain number groups on a list provided. They should try to find two or three numbers that belong to each group. Children can be grouped for the activity.

2. After the walk, show the children a large sheet that contains the same number categories as on the sheet they received. Have the children record their numbers in the appropriate spaces.

3. After all numbers have been recorded on the sheet, children can review the numbers to see if they were placed in the appropriate categories.

Number Categories		
0	to	49
50	to	99
100	to	150
151	to	250
251	to	700
701	to	1000

ACCOMMODATIONS

✔ The size of numbers for the categories can be adjusted for the ability level of the children.

✔ Trips to stores may be used to ensure that plenty of numbers are available, or the teacher may ask parents to post numbers on colored cards in an area (such as a park) after receiving the appropriate permission.

EXTENSIONS

✔ Rational numbers (fractions, decimals) could be used for the categories in place of whole numbers.

✔ Money values could also be substituted for the activity.

Group These Fractions

Group These Fractions is a good review activity to help children deepen their understanding of fractions.

LEARNING

✳ Grouping together fractions that are alike

MATERIALS

✳ Sheet containing a number of fractions to be grouped (one for each child)

✳ Scissors

STEPS

1. Pass out to each child a sheet of paper that contains a variety of fractions.

2. Have children cut out each fraction on the appropriate lines to form a set of fraction cards.

3. Tell children they are to group the fractions so that each set of fractions represents the same amount of a whole quantity. For example, one-half and two-fourths equal the same amount of a whole quantity.

4. After children have finished grouping the cards, have them pair up with a partner and share their groupings with one another.

5. If children partnered together cannot come to a consensus about which cards belong together, they can later ask the class for input when all groups share their work.

Fraction Sheet (Sample)

1/4	2/12	8/10	10/20	2/3	4/8
18/24	1/5	4/16	3/6	4/8	1/7
6/9	1/3	7/21	2/18	2/6	8/12
2/14	4/5	3/15	1/2	4/32	2/10
5/10	3/6	6/12	12/16	2/8	1/6

ACCOMMODATIONS

✓ The sheet containing the fractions could be cut apart and put into packets for the children beforehand to save class time.

✓ The level of fractions used could be adjusted to the learning levels of children.

EXTENSIONS

✓ Pockets can be set up in the room with a fraction written on each pocket. Kids could be given a number of blank cards (sheets of paper cut up) and write other like fractions that represent the same amount of a whole quantity and put them in the corresponding pockets.

✓ Children can create their own set of cards with fraction groupings and exchange them with peers to solve.

Animals in a Row

Animals in a Row helps young children begin to understand and experience the concept of patterns as they prepare to work with numbers. In working with patterns, children become aware of what has come before and what might possibly come next.

LEARNING

* Identifying patterns
* Problem solving
* Communicating understanding

MATERIALS

* A number of different types of toy animals of different colors, sizes, etc.

STEPS

1. Present a row of five to seven toy animals including several different types of animals that create patterns:

   Sample A: three cows, three dinosaurs, two cows, two dinosaurs, and one cow _____.

   Sample B: one cow, one horse, one dinosaur, one cow, one horse, and _____.

2. Ask the children what animal or animals they think would come next to continue the pattern. Ask the children to tell why they selected that particular animal. Other children can be asked if they agree or if they had another animal in mind that might come next.

3. After the answers and discussions take place, reset the animals with a different pattern and have children again identify and explain which animal or animals comes next.

4. Children could work with patterns by asking which animal would come *before* the row of animals. The animals could also be set up with an animal missing in the middle, and children could be asked to tell what animal would go in the middle spot.

   Sample C: _____, big cow, little dog, big dog, little dog, big dog

   Sample D: two black cats, two grey cats, one black cat _____.

5. Once the activity is over children can be informed that the animals will be placed in an area of the classroom and they can make up their own patterns.

(continued

Animals in a Row *(continued)*

ACCOMMODATIONS

✔ A set of extra animals could be put off to the side, and children could be asked to pick out the one that fits in the blank space.

✔ If children are being introduced to animals they are unfamiliar with, those animals could be used in this activity to enhance their learning about the new animals.

✔ Pictures of animals could be substituted if toy animals are not available.

✔ More abstract symbols (circles, ovals, hexagons, octagons) could be used for slightly older children.

EXTENSIONS

✔ Children could be shown a series of four to six toy animals, be told to look for the pattern, and then be asked to explain the pattern.

✔ Children could be asked to look at a patterned set of toy animals for several seconds, have the set covered or taken apart, and then be asked to rebuild the pattern they just saw.

MATHEMATICS

△○△○...

Bolt It Right

Bolt It Right is an activity for young children that can help them begin to develop an understanding of patterning. Children have the opportunity to see a pattern and then reproduce it.

LEARNING

* ❋ Working with patterns
* ❋ Producing patterns presented
* ❋ Developing fine motor skills

MATERIALS

* ❋ A tub containing bolts, nuts, and washers (Colored bolts, nuts, and washers could also be used to add another attribute.)
* ❋ A container with premade bolt, nut, and washer patterns

STEPS

1. Show children the tub containing different-size bolts, nuts, and washers. In a separate container show children sets of bolts that have different patterns of nuts and washers already placed on a bolt (for example, a bolt with the following pattern: large washer, small nut, medium nut, small washer, medium washer, large washer). The tub and container with the patterned sets of bolts can be placed at a work station. Children are to pick out a bolted patterned set from the container and build another set just like it using the bolts, nuts, and washers from the larger tub.

2. Children can be assigned to work in pairs or small groups and they can share their finished patterns with one another or leave their completed patterns next to the premade set for the teacher to view.

3. After the work station time has ended, children could be asked to show a premade pattern they selected along with the bolt pattern they made.

CRITICAL THINKING CHALLENGE

Children could be shown a partially completed bolted pattern and be asked to complete the pattern.

(continued)

ACCOMMODATIONS

✔ The teacher should check to make sure the nuts and washers fit easily onto the bolts. Children could practice using a wrench to get the nuts on.

EXTENSIONS

✔ Children could create different patterns on bolts for peers to copy.

✔ The teacher could present to children two different patterns on bolts and ask the children to explain how the two are the same and how they are different.

△○△○...

Number Decoder

Number Decoder is an activity that provides children the opportunity to use reasoning to uncover different number patterns.

LEARNING

✳ Identifying number patterns
✳ Reasoning with numbers

MATERIALS

✳ Secret Code Sheets for each child or group
✳ Pencils

STEPS

1. Inform children they are going to complete a sheet that contains numbers that have to be decoded. They will be like government agents trying to decipher a secret number message. The number codes they have are incomplete and they need to determine what the remaining or missing numbers are.

2. Provide the Secret Code Sheet to children and have them fill in the missing numbers. Tell children that each set of numbers to be decoded fits a pattern. If they figure out the pattern, they can break the code.

ACCOMMODATIONS

✔ The Secret Code Sheets can be modified for younger children who may not have knowledge of skip counting.

EXTENSIONS

✔ Teachers could redesign the Secret Code Sheets so that the number answers could be converted into a secret message.

✔ After completing the Secret Code Sheets, children could be asked to make up their own code sheets for peers to solve.

(continued)

Number Decoder *(continued)*

Secret Code Sheet

For each row of numbers below you need to fill in the missing secret code number. The solution to the code is based on a pattern.

Sample:　2　4　6　8　____　12　14　16　____

The two missing numbers would be 10 and 18. The pattern would be counting by 2s.

Normandy Code	3	7	11	15	____	23	27	31	____
Kiel Code	2	4	8	16	32	____	128		
New York Code	49	____	35	28	21	14	7		
China Code	3	6	9	12	____	12	9	6	3
Russian Code	97	147	197	237	377	407	437	457	____
Washington Code	16	96	15	95	14	____	13	93	
Disneyland Code	1001	1	101	01	____	101	1	1001	
My Code (make your code)	____	____	____	____	____	____			

100s Board Skip Counting

100s Board Skip Counting can be used to help children learn to skip count. Children can learn skip counting with small numbers such as 2s or 5s or larger numbers such as 11s or 12s.

LEARNING

✳ Skip counting with numbers

MATERIALS

✳ 100s board for each child
✳ A set of markers for each child (coins, beans, etc.)

STEPS

1. Provide children with a number card that contains the numbers 1 to 100. Also provide children with a set of markers. Tell children they are going to mark off different number patterns.

2. Identify an appropriate number to start with. For instance, tell children they are to put their first marker on 2 and then begin to count by 2s.

3. When children are finished they can share where the markers were placed on the board. Then have children clear their boards and get ready for the next task.

4. After they complete the task tell children to put their markers on 28 and tell them to count by 2s and place markers on the appropriate spaces from 28 to 54. Check responses and have children clear their boards.

5. Have children place a markers on 66. Ask them to count *back* by 2s from 66 to 36, placing markers on the appropriate numbers.

ACCOMMODATIONS

✔ When counting by smaller numbers (2s, 3s) you could have children skip count and place markers to certain levels. For example, they could first place markers from numbers 2 to 40 if they were counting by 2s.

EXTENSIONS

✔ For older children number cards beyond 100 could be created. For example, a number board to 1000 could be set up with base ten increments. The board would have ten numbers per row all the way up to 1000.

✔ Decimal or fraction boards could also be created.

(continued)

100s Board Skip Counting (continued)

100s Board									
1	2	3	4	5	6	7	8	9	10
11	12	13	14	15	16	17	18	19	20
21	22	23	24	25	26	27	28	29	30
31	32	33	34	35	36	37	38	39	40
41	42	43	44	45	46	47	48	49	50
51	52	53	54	55	56	57	58	59	60
61	62	63	64	65	66	67	68	69	70
71	72	73	74	75	76	77	78	79	80
81	82	83	84	85	86	87	88	89	90
91	92	93	94	95	96	97	98	99	100

MATHEMATICS

Ordering Shapes Memory Game

Ordering Shapes Memory Game requires children to use their knowledge of shapes while reinforcing the concept of order. Children also have an opportunity to work on short–term memory.

LEARNING

* Ordering
* Teach shape identification
* Developing memory

MATERIALS

* Sets of paper shapes of different color and size for each child
* Paper clips for each child
* A set of shape sequence cards (teacher made)
* Blank strips of paper

STEPS

1. Provide children with a set of pieces of paper that are of different colors, shapes, and sizes. Show the children a card that has a number of shapes in a specific order.

2. After five seconds turn down the card and tell the children to reconstruct the order of shapes they just saw.

3. After several patterns have been shown, pass out a strip of paper and paper clips to each child.

4. Tell the children they will take turns setting up patterns for the rest of the class to recon-struct. Children are to use the paper clips to attach each shape to the strip of paper.

ACCOMMODATIONS

✔ The number and type of shapes used in the sequences can be adjusted for younger or older children. Younger children could be shown four or five shapes with few variables while older children might have five to seven shapes with more variables in terms of color and size.

✔ The amount of time allocated for children to study the shape pattern can be increased or decreased.

EXTENSIONS

✔ Additional attributes can be added to the activity. Rather then have children use color and size, the shapes could be oriented in different directions or contain dots or no dots on the shape pattern.

✔ Other objects than shapes could be used, such as different buttons, straws, and so forth.

It Will Not Work That Way

It Will Not Work That Way is a problem-solving activity that has children discover why a way of solving one problem with numbers may not work for another number problem.

LEARNING

✳ Problem solving with numbers
✳ Reasoning with multiplication

MATERIALS

✳ Sheets of paper to work out answers

STEPS

1. Give children the problem 12×6, and ask them if the problem can be solved by using the following method:

   $$10 \times 6 =$$
   $$2 \times 6 =$$

2. Is 12×6 the same as $(10 \times 6) + (2 \times 6)$? Have children illustrate or explain how both approaches end with the same answers.

3. Next give children the problem of 12×12, and ask them if they can solve the problem using the following method:

   $$12 \times 10 =$$
   $$12 \times 2 =$$

4. Is 12×12 the same as $(12 \times 10) + (12 \times 2)$? Have children show their answers.

5. Last, ask the children if 12×12 is the same as $(10 \times 10) + (2 \times 2)$. Do children get the same answer for both problems? Have children illustrate or explain their answer.

ACCOMMODATIONS

✔ Some children may use unifix cubes, blocks, or other materials to illustrate their answers.

EXTENSIONS

✔ Have children use the same number combinations with addition.

MATHEMATICS

Block Building

Block Building is a good activity for children to gain experiences with the associative property of numbers.

LEARNING

* Experiencing the associative property of mathematics
* Reasoning with numbers
* Working with multiplication combinations (facts)

MATERIALS

* Blocks or 1-inch-square pieces of paper

STEPS

1. Give the children a set of blocks. Tell them they are going to be shown multiplication combinations (facts) and are to use the blocks to show how the problem could appear using the associative property of mathematics.

2. Give the children the following multiplication problems: 2 × 4 and 4 × 2. Then ask them to illustrate both problems using their blocks. The first number could be represented by columns and the second by rows.

3. Give students a variety of problems to solve at their level.

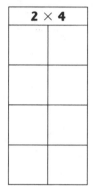

ACCOMMODATIONS

✔ Older children could be given 1/2-inch graph paper and be asked to trace block patterns that would represent different combinations asked for.

EXTENSIONS

✔ A similar activity could be used for addition by having children show 2 + 3 and 3 + 2.

✔ Students could also work with other number properties by working through examples such as (2 + 3) + 4 = 2 + (3 + 4).

Chapter 8

Data Analysis and Probability

Data analysis and probability in mathematics require children to learn how to collect, organize, report, and analyze numerical information they gather. Children learn how to use tally marks, charts, and graphs to represent their findings. They learn how to compare data and to present simple statistical information such as frequency, range, and norms.

Activities in this chapter also include work with probability. What are the chances that something might happen? What is the likelihood that they will draw a particular color of gum?

Mini Muffins Are the Best

Mini Muffins Are the Best can be used to help children compare different units of data from meaningful classroom activities.

LEARNING

✳ Comparing different sets of data

✳ Identifying the range for a set of data

✳ Representing different units of data

✳ Reinforcing the money concept of making change

MATERIALS

✳ Bakery items for the breakfast bakery sale

✳ Flyers announcing the bake sale

✳ Tables and chairs

✳ Record sheet to tally items sold

✳ Graph or chart paper

STEPS

1. Organize a breakfast bakery sale for your class. Have children select three or four different types of bakery items for the sale, such as mini muffins, doughnuts, and breakfast bars. Some of the bakery items could be made by the children or parents.

CRITICAL THINKING CHALLENGE

Items could be packaged differently: one to a wrapper, two to a wrapper, etc. to have children also determine if items sell better if they are sold one or two to a package.

2. Have kids make up a flyer announcing the breakfast bake sale for other classrooms, parents, and other school or community groups.

3. Set up three or four different tables, one for each of the bakery items to be sold. For each table identify tasks for the children: acting as cashier, wrapping the items, keeping the table full of bakery items, etc. Two of the children at each table can be accountants who keep track of how many bakery items are sold and how much money is taken in.

Sample Bakery Items Sold	
Mini Muffins	32
Doughnuts	21
Breakfast Bars	18

4. At the end of the breakfast bake sale the accountants can report the sales to their group and each group can plot the number of bakery items sold and the amount of money made on a graph.

5. A simple bar graph can be used. Children can compare the different number of bakery items sold, they can discuss the range (difference between most and least), and they can identify how many more of one item would be needed to equal the amount sold of another.

(continued)

Mini Muffins Are the Best *(continued)*

✔ ACCOMMODATIONS

✔ The bakery sale could be for a smaller group or contain items that are easier to get.

✔ The cost of items could be scaled down for younger children or increased for older children.

✔ The graphs used could be made simpler with the use of tally marks (*/////   ///*) or strips of paper in 1-inch lengths, 1 inch per unit sold. These could be put horizontally or vertically on a board or chart.

✔ EXTENSIONS

✔ Children could plan to have a second sale and identify which breakfast items they might add or drop based on the number of items sold during the first sale.

✔ In place of a breakfast sale, popcorn sales or pizza sales with different items on the pizzas could also take place.

Data Analysis and Probability · **151**

Making Bar Graphs

Making Bar Graphs can help children learn how to represent data they collect from different classroom activities. After children learn to make simple bar graphs, they can get more creative and establish their own types of graphs.

MATERIALS

❋ Different sets of colored objects such as, buttons, beans, candy, pasta, blocks, etc. (no more than 12 of any one color)

❋ 1-by-12-inch strips of colored paper matching the colors of the objects

❋ Glue

❋ White sheets of paper, 8½ by 11 inches

❋ Rulers

STEPS

1. Give the children a random set of colored objects to sort into groups based on their color. Once the objects are sorted, have children count the number in each colored group. After the number of objects for each group is counted, have the children write the number for each color on a piece of paper which will be used later as data for bar graphs.

2. Tell children they are going to illustrate the information they collected on a chart called a bar graph. To make the bar graph they will be given 1-by-12-inch pieces of paper matching the colors of the objects they just sorted. Also provide children with an 8½-by-11-inch piece of white paper.

3. Tell children to look at the number they recorded for each set of colored objects. They are to measure and cut each colored strip so that the length of each strip in inches is equal to the number of objects recorded. For example, if there were five red objects the red strip would be 5 inches long.

4. After each colored strip is measured and cut, have the children place the 8½-by-11-inch piece of paper in front of them in a vertical orientation.

5. Tell the children they can glue the colored strips of paper to the white sheet of paper vertically so that all the strips are even with the bottom of the white sheet of paper.

6. After the colored strips are glued to the white sheet of paper, have the children write the number of objects on the bottom of each colored strip of paper.

7. Have children explain their graphs once they are completed.

(continued)

MATHEMATICS

Making Bar Graphs *(continued)*

ACCOMMODATIONS

✔ With older children a larger number of objects could be used or the data could be provided in written form.

✔ Older students could use larger numbers and cut the strips of paper to represent ¼ inch for each colored object sorted.

✔ Younger children who have little experience in working with measurement could be given colored paper with 1-inch squares already printed on them. They would only need to count the number of inches corresponding to each colored set of objects before they cut them.

EXTENSIONS

✔ After children complete their graphs, they could fill out a data summary sheet to answer such questions as:

- Which color of objects was there the most of?
- Which color of objects was there the least of?
- What was the range for the colored sets of objects?
- What was the number difference between the most and least colored objects?
- How many more of the middle number of colored objects would be needed to have as many as the most colored objects?
- What was the mean number of colored objects for the sets?

✔ Children could set up their graphs as different stations and explain them to invited guests.

Data Analysis and Probability · **153**

MATHEMATICS

More Zippers or Buttons

More Zippers or Buttons is an activity for younger students that allows them to experience the concept of representation of quantity. Children learn how to show different quantities of objects.

LEARNING

❋ Representing quantity of objects

❋ Comparing quantity of objects

❋ Reinforcing counting and computation skills

MATERIALS

❋ Same-size pictures of zippers and buttons

❋ Scissors

STEPS

1. Divide the class in half. Tell children that each group is to identify how many zippers they have on their clothing and how many buttons they have on their clothing.

2. Once each group has identified their number of zippers and buttons, tell the children they will make a simple chart on the floor to show how many of each they have.

3. Pass out a data sheet that has 1-inch pictures of buttons and 1-inch pictures of zippers for both groups of children. Tell children they are to cut out the pictures of the zippers and buttons so they have the same numbers of each that they counted on their clothes.

4. Once the pieces are cut out, assign each team a section of the floor to line their pictures up, one row with the zipper pictures end-to-end and one row with button pictures end-to-end.

5. Ask questions about both sets of pictured data once children finish.

ACCOMMODATIONS

✔ Larger pictures of zippers and buttons could be used.

EXTENSIONS

✔ Both groups could add their zippers and buttons together.

Analyze This

Analyze This is an activity that requires children to answer a set of questions about data collected through some investigation done at school. The activity requires children to demonstrate their understanding of proportion, range, and median.

LEARNING

* Identifying what the range is for a set of data
* Identifying what the median is for a set of data
* Problem solving using data
* Estimation
* Data report writing

MATERIALS

* Paper for report writing
* Survey form for each child (see sample)

STEPS

1. Tell the children they are going to complete a survey of the preferences children from different classrooms have or their family members have regarding food. They will ask individuals which one of the following foods they like best: hamburgers, tacos, chicken fried rice, hot dogs, or spaghetti. They will record the answers and make up a report answering a number of questions regarding the food preferences of others.

2. Before they complete the survey all students will make guesses as to which food the people surveyed will indicate they like the best, second best, etc. and which food will be liked the least.

3. Provide each child with a simple survey form listing the foods, and ask him/her to place a tally mark next to the food item that is identified as the food liked best by each person surveyed.

4. Once the surveys have been completed, inform children they are to write a report on foods liked best by their classmates or families. In their report they are to provide the following information:

   The total number of people surveyed

   The food that was liked the best and by how many, the least, etc.

   The food choice that was the median (middle) choice

   The range between the best-liked food and the least-liked food

(continued)

Analyze This *(continued)*

✔ ACCOMMODATIONS

✔ Children can work in teams to collect the data and write the reports.

✔ Sample report forms could be made up with or without the types of food filled in.

✔ Other regional foods can be selected that better represent the local taste of individuals being surveyed or the age of the individuals being surveyed.

EXTENSIONS

✔ Children could also report data by percentages or create pie or bar graphs as part of their reports to illustrate the proportions of best-liked and least-liked foods.

✔ Children could be asked to give a copies of their reports to the individuals they surveyed.

Sample of Survey Form

Directions: Ask each individual you survey to select the *one* food he or she likes the best. After each individual makes the selection, put a tally mark in the right column next to the food type selected. Use only one tally mark for each person surveyed.

Type of Food	Tally Marks for Each Best–Liked Food
Hamburgers	
Tacos	
Chicken Fried Rice	
Hot Dogs	
Spaghetti	

The Red, White, or Blue Gumball

The Red, White, or Blue Gumball *activity is a fun task for younger children who are being introduced to the concept of probability. Children will experience what their chances are of picking a certain color of gumball.*

LEARNING

* The chances (probability) of selecting a particular object from a group of many
* Terms that reflect chance
* Making appropriate guesses of chance

MATERIALS

* Gumball machine (a clear jar with a lid can be substituted—a hole slightly bigger than the size of the gumballs should be made in the lid)
* A number of gumballs perhaps twice the size of the class (See the Steps for suggested colors and numbers.)

STEPS

1. Show children a gumball machine containing red, white, and blue gumballs. Tell children that each of them will get a chance to draw a gumball from the machine. There are 5 red gumballs, 20 white gumballs, and 10 blue gumballs in the machine.

2. Before the children draw a gumball ask them the following two questions: (1) What color gumball would they like to draw? and (2) Do they think their chance of drawing that color gumball is *really good, somewhat good,* or *not really good?*

3. After each child makes a guess he or she draws a gumball. Children will then state whether or not they got the color they wanted and whether or not their stated chance of getting it was a good choice.

4. At the end of the activity review the concept: the fewer the number of gumballs of a color in a machine, the less chance there is to get that color gumball. The terms *really good, somewhat good,* and *not really good* can be discussed.

CRITICAL THINKING CHALLENGE

Older students could be asked to set up the container of objects to contain objects that had a *really good, somewhat good,* or *not really good* chance of being drawn.

(continued)

The Red, White, or Blue Gumball *(continued)*

ACCOMMODATIONS

✔ Cards with the words *really good*, *somewhat good*, and *not really good* could be shown to the children and they can pick out the one that represents their chance of getting the color they selected.

✔ If gum balls are not appropriate other objects could be used, with the same proportions of objects being made available.

EXTENSIONS

✔ A chart might be made up or the teacher might record all the color choices along with children's guesses of their chances. The color preferences could be grouped along with their chances.

Chances Are It Will Be a 1980s

Chances Are It Will Be a 1980s *is a good activity to use when teaching children how to determine the probability of getting something if certain frequency information is known about that thing.*

LEARNING

* Determining chance based on past experiences
* Problem solving with chance

MATERIALS

* Two rolls of coins (pennies) for each team
* Chalkboard or flip chart and marker to record data

STEPS

1. Divide children into pairs or small teams. Give each team a roll of 50 coins and tell them they are to go through the coins and identify how many of the coins were minted in the 2000s, 1990s, 1980s, 1970s, and before 1970. Children can stack the coins up for each of the decades identified.

2. All groups will report their findings when finished and the teacher can record the data on the board. When all groups have reported, the class can add up the total number of coins the class found for the 2000s, 1990s, etc.

3. Pass out a second roll of coins to students. Ask them to write down about how many coins they expect to find for each of the decades based on the information they learned from the first set of coins.

4. Groups should report their predictions along with their findings while the teacher again records the information on the board. All the totals will be added up to see if the probability of getting a certain decade coin was the same this time as in the first experience.

5. A final discussion can take place to discuss how previous experiences or information can be helpful when dealing with probability.

 ACCOMMODATIONS

✔ A smaller number of coins could be used by placing fewer in small containers.

✔ If coins are not available, a number of different decade dates could be put on sheets of paper, copied, cut up into small slips, and used.

 EXTENSIONS

✔ Older students who are working with percentages could determine the percent of coins found belonging to one decade.

✔ The activity could be used with two different coin values (pennies, nickels) to determine whether the probabilities are similar for each coin.

✔ Individual years could be recorded to determine which year in which decade might have the highest probability of being found in a set of coins.

MATHEMATICS

Data Analysis and Probability • **159**

My Forecast

My Forecast is a task for children that has them use data to make predictions regarding the chances of having a specific kind of weather over the course of a week.

LEARNING

* ✳ Using data to identify the chance of certain phenomena happening
* ✳ Using chance with problem solving

MATERIALS

* ✳ Weather recording charts
* ✳ Thermometer

STEPS

1. Have children record the weather for a two-week period. Have them record on a sheet of paper each day around noon the (1) temperature, (2) precipitation (use a symbol to identify whether it is raining, snowing, dry, or other), and (3) sky appearance, whether it is sunny, partly sunny, or cloudy.

2. After the two-week period, have students list the data for the three conditions above. Place children into forecast groups and tell them to predict the chances for certain temperatures, precipitation, or sunny/cloudy days for the coming week based on the weather patterns they recorded over the last two weeks. For example, they may predict there will be two days with temperatures in the low 80s, no days of precipitation, and only one cloudy day.

3. After the predictions are made, have the children record the actual weather patterns for the week and add the data to the third column.

4. Compare the predictions and results.

 ACCOMMODATIONS

✔ The type of weather components picked can be matched up with where you live and the type of weather patterns you normally have. Colder regions could have a category for snow, windy regions could include wind speed, etc.

✔ Younger children could record more basic weather components such as temperature while older students could include such things as barometric pressure.

 EXTENSIONS

✔ The activity could take place two or three times. Children could then compare predictions with actual weather happenings and try to determine the extent to which weather could be predicted.

✔ Different forecast teams could report the weather schoolwide as they are collecting the data. The teams could also make a forecast based on their predictions.

(continued)

MATHEMATICS

My Forecast (continued)

Sample Recording Sheet for Weather Patterns and Predictions*		
Predicted Weather	Predicted Number of Days	Actual Number of Days
Temperature		
79 or below	3	
80 to 84	2	
85 or above	0	
Precipitation		
No rain	4	
Rain	1	
Sky		
Sunny	2	
Partly Sunny	2	
Cloudy	1	

*This same chart could be used to record the weather by placing tally marks in the Actual Number of Days column.

Drop Those Beans

Drop Those Beans is a game for young children that gives them an experience with concepts of probability and chance.

LEARNING

✳ The concept of chance

✳ Making predictions based on past trials

✳ Reasoning about chance

MATERIALS

✳ Cups

✳ Sets of six bean or watermelon seeds with two different colored sides (red and white)

✳ Sheets of lined paper

STEPS

1. Provide each child or small group of children with a cup and six beans or watermelon seeds that have different colors on their two sides, red on one side and white on the other side, for example.

2. Give the children a piece of lined paper and tell them to write "red" on the left side of the paper on one line and "white" on the left side of the paper one line below that.

3. Tell children they are to put the beans in the cup and pour them out on their table, then put a tally mark on the line next to the word "red" for every red side that shows on their beans and a tally mark on the line next to the word "white" for each white side of the bean that appears. The child should complete five trials.

4. After the five trials are completed, have the children total up their marks and share their outcomes. Results from all children or groups can be shared and added up.

5. Based on what they found, ask the children what they think would happen if they repeated the activity. Ask them if they think they would have the *same results*, *close to the same results*, or *completely different results*.

6. Have the children repeat the activity, recording their results on two new lines marked "red" and "white".

7. Discuss the results and ask how many red sides or white sides would show if they did the activity 100 more times.

ACCOMMODATIONS

✔ If beans are unavailable or impractical to color, two-sided chips or coins with heads and tails could be used.

✔ Tally sheets could be made up and given to the children.

EXTENSIONS

✔ Dice could be used to have children work with more than two variables.

✔ The teacher could put up a chart for children to record their responses over time as an extra credit project, learning center, or free time option. The chart could record the responses of all children over a week, a month, etc.

Chapter 9

Geometry

The activities presented in this chapter on geometry help children develop spatial sense and help them learn to explore two- and three-dimensional shapes and structures. In working with spatial sense they will work on activities that include directionality, positioning, and space. Activities with two-dimensional shapes focus on identification of, combining, and subdividing shapes. Activities for three-dimensional structures have children identify how structures look from different positions.

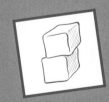

Shape Find

Shape Find is an activity that can be used over and over again to help children identify, name, and develop a fuller understanding of basic shapes.

LEARNING

✷ Identifying different basic shapes (triangle, square, rectangle, oval, hexagon, octagon)

✷ Naming different shapes

✷ Identifying shapes positioned differently

MATERIALS

✷ A set of attribute blocks, geoblocks, or paper shapes of different types and sizes

STEPS

1. Place in front of children, a set of geoblocks or shape cutouts that are of different sizes and are positioned in different directions.

2. Ask children to name the different shapes until all the shapes have been identified by the children. Ask children to look at the triangles and identify how they are different in terms of their size and positions.

3. After children are finished with the first set of shapes, a new set of shapes can be shown to the children. With each set a different shape could be looked at more closely after all shapes are named to see how instances of that shape are different in size and position.

Sample

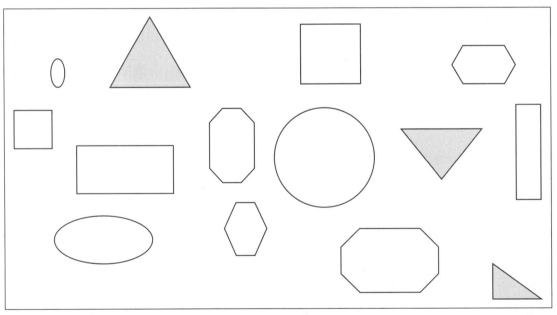

(continued)

Shape Find *(continued)*

✔ ACCOMMODATIONS

✔ The type of shapes selected can be adjusted based on the age level of the children. Older children may be asked to identify all quadrilaterals, pentagons, and so forth.

EXTENSIONS

✔ Children can take turns presenting sets of shapes to other children to see if all the shapes selected can be identified or named.

✔ After naming each shape children could be asked to look for all objects in the classroom that are that shape.

MATHEMATICS

Shape Designers

Shape Designers is an activity that can be used with younger or older children depending upon the types of shapes selected. Younger children can use more basic shapes, while older children can work with more advanced or irregular shapes.

LEARNING

✳ Identifying and naming shapes
✳ Exploring shapes in greater depth
✳ Representations with shapes

MATERIALS

✳ Sets of paper shapes

STEPS

1. Provide children individually or in small groups with a set of paper shapes. Tell children they are going to design patterns using a variety of shapes.

2. Once children complete their designs they are to explain their designs to the rest of the class.

3. Their explanations should include information on the types of shapes used, how they positioned the shapes, and other designing techniques they used.

ACCOMMODATIONS

✔ Children should be given sets of shapes that they are to learn.

✔ Geoblocks or other shaped materials could also be used.

EXTENSIONS

✔ Children could be asked to create a piece of art by using shapes made out of different materials.

✔ Children could work as a class and fill up a board with a variety of different shapes as a classroom art project.

It's My Puzzle

It's My Puzzle is a good activity for younger and older children. The activity helps children to increase their understanding of positioning when working with known or unknown shapes.

LEARNING

❋ Experiencing positioning of shapes

❋ Problem solving with shapes

❋ Representing patterns

MATERIALS

❋ Sheets of paper 8-by-8 inches (size can be modified)

❋ Scissors

STEPS

1. Using a number of 8-by-8-inch sheets of paper, teachers should cut off parts of the sheets to make shape templates for shapes the children are learning about (triangles, for example).

2. Next the teacher should cut the shape templates into other shaped pieces (puzzle pieces) to form a shape puzzle.

3. Pass out the puzzle sets to the children or teams of children. Tell the children that each set of paper pieces will form a particular shape when put together. Their task is to put the pieces together so that all pieces are used and connected together to form a known shape.

 ACCOMMODATIONS

✓ The shapes used for the puzzle can be adjusted to the level of the children.

✓ The number of pieces used for each puzzle can be modified to make the task appropriate for the level of the child.

✓ The puzzles could have pieces that are similar in appearance to make the puzzle more challenging.

 EXTENSIONS

✓ Tangrams or other commercial materials could be used.

✓ Children could be given sheets of paper to cut out their own shape puzzles.

✓ Children could work with puzzles that include pieces of all one shape. For example, they could be asked to make a parallelogram with all triangle pieces.

(continued)

MATHEMATICS

It's My Puzzle (continued)

Sample Puzzle to Cut for a Rectangle

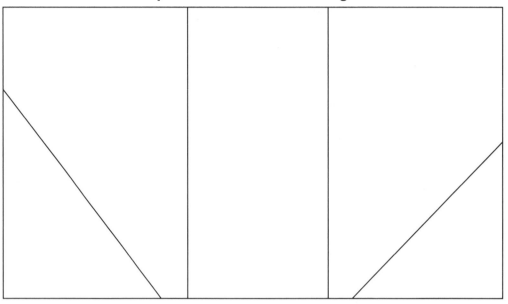

Pack It Tight

Pack It Tight is a good problem-solving activity to use with children to help them work with positioning and directionality.

LEARNING

* Problem solving with positioning of shapes
* Experiences with combining shapes
* Communicating problem-solving strategies

MATERIALS

* Boxes that are the same size (shoe boxes, envelope boxes, wet-wipe tubs, etc.)
* Sets of objects of different sizes and shapes (geoblocks, lids, marbles, wooden blocks, bottle caps, sugar cubes, etc.)

STEPS

1. Inform students that they are going to play the role of packers. Their challenge will be to see how many objects their group can fit into a box.

2. Pass out boxes to the groups. Also pass out a set of geoblocks or other objects to the groups. Each set should be the same.

3. Identify a certain amount of time the children have to pack their boxes.

4. After the time period has ended, each group will identify the number of objects they got into the box and show the box.

CRITICAL THINKING CHALLENGE

Children could be given a number of paper shapes and be asked to fit as many as possible onto a sheet of paper.

ACCOMMODATIONS

✓ The number of objects that could possibly fit into a box could vary. Older children may work with boxes and objects involving higher amounts.

✓ More basic shapes could be used to make the task easier.

✓ Time limitations may be adjusted to the level and interest of the children.

Rope It Square

Rope It Square is a motor activity that can be used to help children demonstrate different shapes and how different shapes can be made into other shapes.

LEARNING

❋ Making shapes

❋ Converting shapes into other shapes

❋ Reasoning with shapes

MATERIALS

❋ A tied rope for each group of children (yarn or string could also be used)

STEPS

1. Show children a large rope that is tied together to form a polygon (closed shape). Tell the children that the rope is special because it can form many of the shapes they have been learning about.

2. Invite two children to come to the front, and ask the children to make a shape (triangle). Another set of children can be invited up to make another shape.

3. After children have been given these demonstrations of how to make a shape, group the children by threes and give each group a rope.

4. Ask the children to make the following shapes one at a time and hold them up for review:

   a square

   a hexagon

   an octagon

   two connecting triangles

   two connecting rectangles

   a parallelogram

5. If time is left over, each team can be asked to create a shape or a set of connecting shapes not asked for by the teacher.

CRITICAL THINKING CHALLENGE

Children could be asked to show how one shape could be turned into two shapes. For example, show how your square could be changed into two triangles.

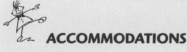

ACCOMMODATIONS

✔ Older children can be asked to make more difficult shapes or connecting shapes.

EXTENSIONS

✔ Children could be given clay and be asked to demonstrate a variety of shapes.

Square to Triangle

Square to Triangle *is an activity that helps children learn to convert one shape to another by folding a piece of paper. This easy-to-use activity has many applications.*

MATERIALS

✳ 8-by-8-inch sheets of paper (cloth or other material could be used)

✳ A display board to use for displaying various shapes formed by the square

STEPS

1. Present an 8-by-8-inch piece of paper to the children. Tell them they are going to fold the paper in different ways to form new shapes. Ask all children what shape the piece of paper is.

2. Pass out paper to each child and ask the children to set the paper in front of them and wait for further instructions before trying to fold it.

3. Have children watch you as you show them how to fold the piece of paper to make a rectangle. Ask the children to change their square sheet of paper into a rectangle by folding it once. Have children show their rectangles to the class and discuss how they made their rectangles. Some children might fold it edge to edge, while some children may fold the square part way down to form a bigger rectangle.

4. Have children spread the paper back out to its square shape and begin to give them different shapes to fold. (Tell them they can make more than one fold if they choose to do so.)

triangle	smaller square
hexagon (six sides)	octagon (eight sides)
parallelogram	create your own

5. Tell the children to unfold their paper after each shape is made. At the end of the session children can create and display their own special shapes.

ACCOMMODATIONS

✔ The types of shapes to be folded can be modified based on the learning level of the children.

EXTENSIONS

✔ Students can be given a set of toothpicks and be asked to make different shapes with four toothpicks, then five toothpicks, six toothpicks, etc. They can show multiple ways of using four, five, six, etc. to form shapes.

MATHEMATICS

Arrange Eight

Arrange Eight is an activity that helps children learn how they can combine or join shapes together to make new shapes. The activity helps children to see relationships among shapes.

MATHEMATICS

LEARNING

❋ Combining shapes to form new shapes

❋ Working with positioning of shapes

❋ Reasoning with shapes

❋ Estimation

MATERIALS

❋ Provide children with eight triangles cut from an 8-by-8-inch piece of paper (Cut the piece of paper in half and then cut each half in half again to make four 4-by-4-inch sheets. Cut each of the 4-by-4-inch sheets corner to corner to form two triangles

STEPS

1. Inform children that they will be combining triangles to form new shapes.

2. Pass out the packets of triangles to each small group of students. Tell children to spread the eight triangles out in front of them.

3. Ask children to make the following shapes with the eight triangles by using *all* of the triangles:

   a square   a triangle

   a rectangle   a parallelogram

4. Ask the children to set two triangles off to the side and tell them they are to make as many shapes as possible with the six triangles they have. Before they start to make shapes they are to make a guess as to how many different shapes they might be able to make.

5. Give the children a time limit. After they are finished they can tell how many shapes they made and show how they made each one.

CRITICAL THINKING CHALLENGE

Children could be asked to identify how many different numbers of pieces can be used to make a square. Can a square be made with four pieces? six pieces? eight pieces? and so forth.

ACCOMMODATIONS

✔ The types of shapes to be asked for will depend on the children's understanding of shapes.

✔ Older students could be given more shapes to combine.

EXTENSIONS

✔ Two groups of students could be asked to combine their eight pieces for a total of 16 pieces. They could be asked to reason whether the same shapes could be produced with 16 triangles that were produced with eight triangles.

Count My Sides and Points

Count My Sides and Points is used to help children begin to understand the characteristics of three-dimensional shapes and structures. By counting the sides and points on three-dimensional objects children can begin to make comparisons among objects.

LEARNING

✳ Identifying and counting sides and points of three-dimensional objects

✳ Comparing three-dimensional objects

MATERIALS

✳ A collection of three-dimensional objects (cubes, cones, prisms, etc.)

✳ A data collection chart (see sample below)

✳ A red pen or marker

STEPS

1. Show the children a cube. Ask them how many sides the cube has. After a number of children respond, have the children count the sides by writing numbers in sequence as each side is counted. Record the responses on a chart for the cube.

2. Ask children how many points they see on the object. You may wish to show them a point. After children share their responses, count each point on the cube by making a mark on each point (corner) with a red pen or marker. Record the number on the board.

3. Show the children a rectangular prism and again ask them to identify the number of sides and points they see. Then count each side and point and record the answers on the chart.

4. Time permitting, you may also review a hexagonal prism and others.

Three-Dimensional Objects Sides and Points		
Object	Number of Sides	Number of Points
Cube		
Rectangular Prism		
Cylinder		
Cone		
Hexagonal Prism		

(continued)

Count My Sides and Points (continued)

5. After the data collection chart has been filled in, a discussion can take place about the sides and points of the three-dimensional objects.

CRITICAL THINKING CHALLENGES

1. Children could be given paper and asked to form different three-dimensional objects by folding it different ways.

2. Children could be asked to find in the classroom the different types of three dimensional objects they studied.

ACCOMMODATIONS

✔ More basic shapes would be used by younger children.

✔ The objects could be passed around to children or, if there were enough, each child might receive his or her own to gain a better understanding of the feel of the different three-dimensional objects.

EXTENSIONS

✔ After children have a chance to experience the three-dimensional objects with regard to sides and points, children could be blindfolded, given an object, and then asked to identify what type of three-dimensional object it is based on the number of sides and points they feel.

MATHEMATICS

It Looks Different from Here

It Looks Different from Here *is an activity used to have children begin to reason how three-dimensional objects look from different positions. They begin to understand how location may provide different perspectives.*

LEARNING

✳ Perspectives of three-dimensional objects
✳ Reasoning about objects from different locations

MATERIALS

✳ A number of 1-inch blocks

STEPS

1. Set up a structure using a set of four or five blocks:

2. Ask children to look at the set of blocks from where they are sitting. Then ask the children to take a set of blocks and make the same design.

3. Ask the children to think about what the set of blocks they made might look like if the children were on the ceiling and the blocks were on a table directly below them. Have the children then lean over the blocks they set up and look straight down. Have them take another set of blocks and set them up so they show what the first set looks like from a top view.

4. Next, ask the children to move to one side of the blocks so they are looking at them from the side rather than straight on. Ask them what they see. Then have them use blocks to show what a side view is like.

5. Once children begin to demonstrate how a set of three-dimensional objects looks straight on, from the top, and from the side, you can rearrange the blocks to form more difficult patterns.

ACCOMMODATIONS

✔ The patterns to be looked at can be made simpler with three or four blocks for younger children.

✔ Older children may be asked to draw rather then rearrange the blocks to show what they look like from the different positions.

EXTENSIONS

✔ Use a variety of different three-dimensional objects for children to draw perspectives from. A mixture of cubes, rectangular prisms, triangles, etc. could be mixed together.

✔ Have children set up their own three-dimensional structure for other kids to examine from different perspectives.

✔ Show children a structure as it is viewed from the top, and have them construct the view or possible views from the front and side.

MATHEMATICS

Drawing Sides

Drawing Sides provides children with an opportunity to deepen their understanding of three-dimensional objects.

LEARNING

✳ Understanding different perspectives of three-dimensional objects

✳ Representing sides of three-dimensional objects

MATERIALS

✳ A number of three-dimensional objects: cubes, cylinders, prisms, cones, etc.

✳ Paper and pencils

STEPS

1. Provide each child with a piece of paper and a three-dimensional object. Tell the children they are to trace each side of the three-dimensional object on the paper.

2. Have three or four different children make drawings of the same three-dimensional object.

3. After children are finished with their drawings they should place the three-dimensional object back onto the sheets over each drawing to check to see if all drawings are correct and to see if they made the drawings from each side.

4. When individual children are finished checking their own drawings, ask that all children who drew the same object get together to compare their drawings. If children have different drawings they can discuss the differences and ask the teacher for an outside opinion.

Sample

3-D Object to Be Drawn	Drawings

ACCOMMODATIONS

✔ The teacher may choose to have younger children work on one three-dimensional object at a time.

✔ Children could be paired together if some children have difficulty making drawings.

EXTENSIONS

✔ Once a number of different three-dimensional objects have been drawn by children, the drawings could be placed at a workstation for other children to work with. They can pick out a set of three-dimensional objects along with a set of drawings and try to match the drawings with the objects.

✔ Children can trace sides of other structures and have other children look at the drawings and attempt to identify what the objects are.

Chapter 10

Measurement

This chapter on measurement provides activities to use in teaching the measurement systems of length, capacity and volume, weight, area and perimeter, and time. The activities provide students with the opportunity to learn how to measure using nonstandard and standard units, make comparisons of units measured, and make estimates based on nonstandard and standard measuring tools.

X Toothpicks Long

X Toothpicks Long is an activity to help younger children learn the importance of starting and ending points, proper spacing, and counting each unit when learning to measure the length of different objects.

LEARNING

❋ Using starting and ending points when measuring

❋ Using appropriate spacing

❋ Counting units

❋ Measuring with nonstandard measures

MATERIALS

❋ Toothpicks

❋ String or tape

STEPS

1. Team up children for the measurement activity. Have one child lie down on the floor. Have a second child place a piece of tape along the end of the feet and along the top of the head.

2. Have the child who is measuring the other child place the first toothpick so it is touching the top of the tape at the feet. Then have the child place toothpicks one above the other along the side of the other child until the last toothpick touches or crosses the head of the child.

3. Once the toothpicks are laid out have the child check to see if there are any spaces between the toothpicks or if any toothpicks overlap. If so, have the child slide the toothpicks together more or spread them apart further so the spacing is right.

4. Have the child then count the number of toothpicks it took to measure the other child.

5. Have the children change positions so each one has a chance to measure and be measured.

(continued)

X Toothpicks Long *(continued)*

ACCOMMODATIONS

✔ Younger children can use longer nonstandard measuring tools to keep the number of units to count smaller. Straws, slips of paper, or sticks could be used.

EXTENSIONS

✔ Children could be asked to guess how many toothpicks long they think they are before being measured.

✔ Skip counting (by 2s, 5s, 10s) could be practiced if nonstandard measuring tools with different colors were used when measuring children. Measure using alternating colored toothpicks, for example, two blues, two yellows, two blues, etc. Children could count the units by 2s.

✔ After a child has been measured with one nonstandard measuring tool, a different measuring tool of a different length could be used. Children could measure each other first with toothpicks and later with 8-inch straws.

✔ All children to be measured could lie down with their feet at the same spot. After each is measured the toothpicks could be left until all children are finished. Children could make comparisons of the toothpick lengths. Whose measurements are the longest and the shortest? How many more toothpicks would be needed to make the shortest equal to the longest? etc.

MATHEMATICS

The Measurement Hunt

The Measurement Hunt is an activity to be used when teaching children to measure the length of different objects in inches and feet. The objects to be measured can have straight or curved lines.

LEARNING

* ❋ How to use a tape measure
* ❋ Measuring lengths in inches and feet
* ❋ Measuring straight and curved lines

MATERIALS

* ❋ Tape measure 6 feet or longer (If tape measures are not available, children could use rulers to measure objects with straight lines. Curved objects could be measured by lining up a string along each object and then straightening the string and measuring it with a ruler.)
* ❋ The Measurement Hunt record sheet
* ❋ Pencil

STEPS

1. Children can work individually, with a partner, or as part of a small team. Give each child, pair, or team a tape measure along with a Measurement Hunt record sheet as illustrated below.

2. Tell children they are going on a measurement hunt (in the classroom, in the school building, outside, in a park area, etc.). On the hunt they are to find objects of different lengths, as listed on the Measurement Hunt record sheet. A time limit can be set.

3. Have the children go on the hunt, identify objects that fit the categories listed on the record sheet, and record their findings.

4. Once the hunt is completed, have children report their findings.

CRITICAL THINKING CHALLENGE

A "Guess" column could be added to the Measurement Hunt record sheet. Children can make estimates of the length of objects before measuring them. The differences between guesses and actual measurements can be compared.

(continued)

The Measurement Hunt *(continued)*

ACCOMMODATIONS

✔ Younger students can use nonstandard measures when measuring the objects, while older students can make measurements in yards or report their measurements with fractional parts, such as 34 and 3/4 inches.

EXTENSIONS

✔ Children could measure objects using the metric system or convert the standard measurements to metric measurements.

MATHEMATICS

**The Measurement Hunt
Record Sheet**

Your Challenge: Today you will hunt in an area (classroom, playground, or gym) to find objects that are the lengths listed in column 1. In column 2 you need to name or describe/illustrate the object that is the length listed in column 1.

Length	Objects Found in the Hunt*
3 inches	
1 foot	
16 inches	
2 feet 6 inches	
5 feet	
10 feet	
1 inch	
15 feet	

* If objects cannot be found that have the exact measurements, find one that comes close to the measurement being asked for.

How Many Birds Will It Take?

How Many Birds Will It Take? *is a problem–solving measurement activity for older students. Students need to determine how many birds of each type it would take to cover the railing of a deck. Each bird type is of a different size.*

LEARNING

* Applying knowledge of measurement of inches and feet
* Using problem solving with measurement
* Reasoning with measurement
* Conversions of inches and feet

MATERIALS

* Pencil and paper

STEPS

1. Give children the problem below to solve.

How Many Birds Will It Take?

The deck on the back of a house is 12 feet long. You decide to figure out how many birds it might take to fill a railing running the length of the deck. Using the information on the length of the birds listed below, you need to find out how many of each type of bird it will take to fill the 12-foot length of the deck. How many different answers can you find?

Birds

Blue jay	10 inches
Bald eagle	2 feet 8 inches
Finch	4 inches

Answers

Number of blue jays	_____ = + _____ feet/inches
Number of bald eagles	_____ = + _____ feet/inches
Number of finches	_____ = + _____ feet/inches

Total = _____ (should equal 12 feet)

(continued)

ACCOMMODATIONS

✔ A number of paper cutouts of birds or strips of paper to represent the lengths of the different birds could be given to children to manipulate to help figure out possible answers.

✔ Different measurements for birds could be used to represent larger or smaller measurement amounts.

EXTENSIONS

✔ The problem could be changed by providing students with a list of some birds that are already on the deck (for instance, four finches and one bald eagle) and asking them to figure out only the remaining number and type of birds that would be needed.

✔ Children could create a second problem for other children to solve.

✔ Other animals or objects could be selected that would relate to another topic currently being covered in class (for example, in fall colored leaves from different trees could be used).

MATHEMATICS

Build the Iguana Cage

Build the Iguana Cage provides children with the opportunity to use metric or standard measurement to construct a three-dimensional object.

MATERIALS

* Long sheets of paper (wire would be used if an iguana were to live in the cage)
* Rulers
* Glue
* Scissors

STEPS

1. Inform the children that they will be building a cage to house an iguana. An appropriate size for an iguana cage could be 36 inches long, 28 inches wide, and 15 inches high. Children could be grouped into teams.

2. Give children rulers and long sheets of paper to be cut and glued to build the cage. The cage should be built to the size of the measurements mentioned.

3. Once the cages have been constructed have children share the steps they took to construct their cage.

CRITICAL THINKING CHALLENGE

The dimensions of the cage could be given in standard measures and students could be asked to construct the cage based on metric measures.

ACCOMMODATIONS

✓ Different-size cages for different animals could be used to increase or decrease the amounts to be measured. Refrigerator boxes could be cut down to a smaller size for a doghouse, etc.

✓ To challenge children use sheets of paper that are not the exact sizes to be used for the cages. (Have sheets that are longer or shorter than the 36 inches asked for.)

EXTENSIONS

✓ Children could also construct objects to be placed inside the cage so more children can be involved. Make food or water trays in certain sizes.

Which Stuff Is Longer?

Which Stuff Is Longer? helps children to add objects of different lengths to find sums. Reasoning can also be used to determine which set of objects is longer.

LEARNING

❋ Adding the lengths of objects
❋ Reasoning with measurement

MATERIALS

❋ Ruler or nonstandard measurement tool
❋ Bag to collect objects in

STEPS

1. Take a hike and ask children to pick up eight to ten objects of different lengths, such as sticks, leaves, stones, etc.

2. After the objects are collected, have the children spread their objects out and provide each child or group with a ruler or nonstandard measurement tool. Ask the children to solve the following:

   Which three objects put end-to-end would form the longest length?

   How long are they when put together?

   Which three objects put end-to-end would form the shortest length?

   How short are they when put together?

   Can you find two objects that put together are the same as one longer one?

   Can you find two sets of three objects that are about the same length?

   Can you find two objects that are about the same size as three objects?

   Which four objects are as long as two objects?

   If you put all the objects end-to-end how long would they be?

ACCOMMODATIONS

✔ Smaller or larger numbers of objects could be collected.

✔ Instead of taking a hike children could be provided a set of objects and respond to the same set of questions.

EXTENSIONS

✔ Metric measures could be used.

✔ Children could create additional questions with their answers.

MATHEMATICS

How Long Are My Body Parts?

How Long Are My Body Parts? can be used to assess children's ability to measure objects using a standard ruler. The activity can also encourage children to think about how long body parts are.

LEARNING

✳ Ability to use a standard ruler
✳ Knowledge of the lengths of different body parts

MATERIALS

✳ Standard rulers
✳ Paper and pencils

STEPS

1. Provide the children with rulers and pieces of paper.

2. Tell them they are going to measure different body parts.

3. On the board list the body parts to be measured:

4. Have children write down each body part and how long it is in inches.

5. When all children are finished, their different lengths can be compared.

6. Suggest that children might try to remember how long a body part is so they can use it to measure things when a ruler is not available.

Length of My Body Parts	
Body Part	Length in Inches
Foot	
Pinkie Finger	
Knee to Ankle	
Right to Left Hip	
Elbow to Thumb	
Head to Foot	
Choose Your Own	

ACCOMMODATIONS

✓ Children could be paired up if some children are still learning how to use and read standard measurements.

EXTENSIONS

✓ After children record the measurements in inches they could be asked to convert inches to feet.

✓ Children could complete the same activity using metric rulers.

✓ Children could be asked to measure different body parts that might approximate an inch, a foot, and a yard.

Cup to Cup

Cup to Cup is a volume measurement activity for younger children. Children use perceptions to determine more, less, and the same quantities of liquid in a cup.

LEARNING

✳ Comparing different volumes

✳ Concepts of more, less, the same

MATERIALS

✳ Eight clear plastic cups

✳ A tray for the cups to avoid messy spills

✳ Liquid (water colored with dye or other colored liquid)

✳ A container with liquid for pouring activities

STEPS

1. Set about six cups filled with different amounts of a liquid in front of the children. Set a seventh cup off to the side. Ask children to look at the cup off to the side and make comparisons with the six cups in front.

Which of the six cups has the same amount of liquid as the one to the side?

Which of the six cups have more liquid?

Which of the six cups have less liquid?

Do any of the six cups have about the same amount of liquid?

2. Show the children an empty cup and ask different children to complete the following pouring tasks:

Pour liquid into this cup so it has as much liquid as the cup off to the side.

Pour liquid into this cup so it has more liquid than any other cup.

Pour liquid into this cup so it has less liquid than any other cup.

Pour liquid into this cup so it has more liquid than two of the cups.

Pour liquid into this cup so it has less liquid than three of the cups.

ACCOMMODATIONS

✔ A pouring cup with a handle could be used to help children whose fine motor development may call for this adaptation.

✔ Different-size containers could be used.

EXTENSIONS

✔ Cups could be filled with sand rather than a liquid.

✔ Children could be asked to point to a level of the cup to ask "how much more?" questions. (How much more liquid would be needed in the glass off to the side to equal the amount of liquid in this cup? Point on the cup where it would need to be filled to.)

Fill My Pail

Fill My Pail can be used to help children measure and record measurements using nonstandard capacity and volume measures. Children will also estimate how much it will take to fill pails of different sizes.

LEARNING

✳ Concepts of capacity and volume
✳ Making capacity and volume estimates

MATERIALS

✳ Three or four different-size pails (other containers may be used)
✳ A number of balls (ping-pong balls, golf balls, or tennis balls, etc. could be used)
✳ Cards to record the number of balls

STEPS

1. Show children a small pail that might hold 10 to 12 balls that are 1 to 2 inches in diameter. Ask the children to guess how many balls might fill the pail so it is level on top. Record children's guesses on the board or on a chart.

2. Have one or two children place the balls into the pail. As they are putting the balls into the pail, have the rest of the children count the number of balls that are going into the pail.

3. After the balls have been put into the pail so they are level with the top of the pail, have the children record the number of balls on a card and place it in front of the pail. Have them compare their guesses with the actual number.

4. Bring out a second pail of greater capacity. Before guesses are made, have children talk about the difference in size between the two pails. Again record the guesses on the board or chart.

5. Have one or two different children fill the pail with balls while the rest of the children count. When the pail is filled to the top, record the number of balls it took to fill the pail on a card and place it in front of the bigger pail. Compare the two pails.

6. The activity can continue using different-sized pails.

CRITICAL THINKING CHALLENGE

Children could also do computations by determining how many balls of a different size would be needed. For example, if the tennis ball is two-and-a-half times bigger than the golf ball, how many golf balls would fill a pail if it took 12 tennis balls to fill the pail?

(continued)

Fill My Pail *(continued)*

ACCOMMODATIONS

✔ Clear containers can be used with children who are still learning number quantities.

✔ Larger objects and containers such as volleyballs and boxes could be used with young children.

EXTENSIONS

✔ Instead of using different sized containers, different sized balls could be used following the same steps.

✔ Older children could use other shaped containers that may add difficulty to estimating. Funnel-type containers could be constructed.

Supersize Drink

Supersize Drink provides students with the opportunity to make capacity measurement conversions.

MATHEMATICS

MATERIALS

* Water
* Construction paper or other sturdy paper
* Tape and rubber bands
* Standard liquid measuring device(s)
* Plastic food bags

STEPS

1. Tell children they are going to work for a new supersize fast food restaurant. The owner asked them to create new supersize containers for their drinks. The new size drinks are identified in ounces and the owner wants the children to make labels that convert the ounces to pints and ounces for the new labels.

2. Have the children complete the following chart:

Supersize Drink Labels Converted		
Size of Drink	Size of Drink Converted to Pints and Ounces	
(sample) 16 Ounces	__1__ Pints	__0__ Ounces
24 Ounces	_____ Pints	_____ Ounces
30 Ounces	_____ Pints	_____ Ounces
36 Ounces	_____ Pints	_____ Ounces

(continued)

Supersize Drink *(continued)*

3. The owner also asked the children to make containers that will hold the different-size drinks. Have groups of children use construction paper to form the cups they think will hold the right amount of liquid, water in this case. Make sure children fortify the cups (using rubber bands or extra tape) to hold water. Insert a plastic food bag inside each cup.

4. Have children measure out the quantity of water for each size cup using a standard measuring container. Place the cup on a tray and then pour the water into the plastic bag inserted into the cups to determine if the cup is the right size.

5. Time permitting, have children remake cups to hold the right capacities if capacities were not correct.

CRITICAL THINKING CHALLENGE

Children could be asked to determine how many of each supersize drink could be made from large tubs. For example, if the owner were to make drinks in tubs that hold 9 gallons, about how many 30-ounce drinks could be made?

 ACCOMMODATIONS

✔ Larger or smaller containers could be used. Older students could be asked to determine conversions for ounces, pints, quarts, and gallons for large tubs.

✔ Teachers could make the four cups with input from the children rather than having the children make the cups if this would be more manageable or appropriate.

 EXTENSIONS

✔ Children could use metric measures for the same activity or be asked to make conversions from standard to metric measures.

MATHEMATICS

Storing My CDs

Storing My CDs is a volume problem-solving activity for older students. Students need to compute volume measurements to determine appropriate space needed for CDs.

LEARNING

❋ Computing volume measures

❋ Problem solving with volume measures

❋ Representing responses

MATERIALS

❋ Large cardboard boxes to be cut up into strips

❋ 25 empty CD cases

❋ Scissors

❋ Tape

STEPS

1. Tell the children they will be making CD boxes to hold different numbers of CD cases. If appropriate, they could actually bring in CD cases from home. They will use parts of cardboard boxes to build the CD cases.

2. The standard size of a CD case is approximately 5½ inches wide, 5 inches long (deep), and ½ inch high. Put children into teams and ask them to build a cardboard case out of strips of cardboard from larger boxes. Ask them to build boxes that will hold 10, 15, and 25 CD cases.

3. Once the CD boxes are made ask the children to fill them to see if the appropriate number of CDs fit.

4. The students should make adjustments if the CDs do not fit.

ACCOMMODATIONS

✔ If enough CD cases for the activity are not available, teachers can make blocks of the appropriate size to fit into the CD containers made by the children.

✔ Teachers could precut some of the cardboard strips to be the approximate height, etc. to save time for students.

✔ Younger students could be asked to identify how many 1-inch-cube blocks would fit into boxes or be asked to select premade boxes that a certain number of blocks might fit into.

EXTENSIONS

✔ Children could be asked to make containers for CDs that come in two different specified sizes.

MATHEMATICS

Everything Is a Pound

Everything Is a Pound is an activity that helps younger children understand what a pound is. Children practice adding a variety of objects onto a scale until they equal a pound.

LEARNING

* Demonstrating how to weigh a pound
* Understanding what a pound looks and feels like
* Making estimates

MATERIALS

* One to five small scales
* A pail of sand weighing over 1 pound
* A number of pencils that weigh over 1 pound
* A number of scissors that weigh over 1 pound
* A number of 3-by-5-inch cards that weigh over 1 pound

STEPS

1. Show the children a scale and review how a pound is read on the scale. Tell them they are going to see how many units of different objects it takes to equal a pound.

2. Show the children a set of materials: sand from a pail, a pencil, scissors, and a 3-by-5-inch card. Other materials can be selected.

3. Have the children get into teams. Give each team one set of the materials mentioned above.

4. First ask each team to guess how many or how much of the material will be needed to make a pound.

5. Each team then puts the number or amount of the material on the scale to see how close it comes to a pound.

6. Teams add or subtract a number or amount of the material until it equals a pound.

7. After all the materials have been measured to equal a pound, they will be set on a table for children to look at and compare.

ACCOMMODATIONS

✔ For younger children you may want to use objects or materials that are a little heavier so that the estimates may be smaller. For older children you can use objects or materials that are a little lighter so larger estimates can be used.

✔ Larger balance scales can also be used with a 1-pound weight being added to one side.

EXTENSIONS

✔ Metric measures could be used rather than standard measures. How much is needed to equal 450 grams, etc.?

✔ Children could be given a bag and asked to fill it with things from a nature walk that they estimate would equal a pound.

MATHEMATICS

Buttered Lite Weights

Buttered Lite Weights is a weight comparison activity for young children. The activity asks children to order and compare butter or margarine containers of different weights.

LEARNING

* Ordering objects of different weights
* Making comparisons by weight

MATERIALS

* 10 to 12 small margarine containers (film canisters can also be used)
* A picture of a different animal or object to label containers
* Materials of different weights to be put in the containers

STEPS

1. Show children four butter or margarine containers of the same size. Tell the children that they are filled with some secret stuff. Some are heavier than others. Label each with a picture of a different animal or object.

2. Tell the children they will be asked to hold each container and then put them in order from those that feel lighter to those that feel heavier. While only four containers will be given to a child each time, a number of different containers will be used so that not all children will be ordering the same containers.

3. After one child orders the four containers based on weight, another child will check the first child's order. If necessary, the second child can change the order. Additional children can check the order, if needed.

4. After all children get a chance to order a set of containers or check another child's order, a second activity can take place in which the children place a new container into an existing row of containers that are already ordered from lightest to heaviest. Again, a second child or several children can share where they would put the new container.

ACCOMMODATIONS

✓ For younger children the differences among the containers should be more noticeable.

✓ Larger containers could be used for younger children.

EXTENSIONS

✓ Children can be given a container that is filled with a material or substance along with a second container that is empty. Ask children to put a similar amount of material or substance into the unfilled container to equal the weight of the filled container.

✓ Extra containers can be put in an area for children to practice ordering of weights.

✓ Children could be asked to fill up several bags with sand or small stones so they could be ordered from lightest to heaviest.

Sort This Junk

Sort This Junk helps children to understand the difference between different weights. Children are asked to place things into different containers by the weight of the objects.

LEARNING

* Discriminating between weights measured in ounces and pounds
* Problem solving with weights
* Making judgments about weights

MATERIALS

* Four marked tubs or boxes
* A collection of things that fit the approximate weight categories—1 ounce, 8 ounces, 1 pound, and 2 pounds

STEPS

1. Place four tubs or boxes in an area of the classroom. The boxes should be labeled as shown below:

2. Every day each child should pick one object from a separate box of junk that contains objects weighing about 1 ounce, 8 ounces, etc. and place it in the appropriate marked box.

3. At a specific time each day the class can check to see which objects have been put into the different boxes. An object could be moved into a different box if a majority of children agree.

4. The weights listed on the boxes can be changed as children become more accurate with their judgments about the weights.

1–Ounce Stuff	8–Ounce Stuff	1–Pound Stuff	2–Pound Stuff

 ACCOMMODATIONS

✔ For younger children it is usually helpful to start with objects that weigh at least a pound.

✔ Having open-faced boxes or transparent tubs is helpful for children as they can see into them.

 EXTENSIONS

✔ Have children find objects at home, and then bring them to school to be sorted into the boxes by weight.

✔ Empty containers that have weight information on labels could be collected, and children could sort cans into boxes based on the weights identified on the labels.

✔ Over a longer time period children could make a list of materials that weigh different amounts.

MATHEMATICS

How Many to Sink Me

The How Many to Sink Me activity can be used to help children learn to compare objects of different weights using two tins on water. Children can also estimate how many of an object it might take to sink one tin versus how many of the other object it might take to sink the second tin.

MATHEMATICS

LEARNING

✳ Making weight comparisons between different objects

✳ Making estimates

MATERIALS

✳ Two 3-by-3-inch tins made of aluminum foil with a lip around the tin about ½-inch high

✳ Quantities of pennies, nickels, and quarters

✳ Chalkboard or chart paper and marker

STEPS

1. Show children a tub of water with two flat 3-by-3-inch tins made from aluminum foil sitting on top of the water. Pass a quarter around to children, and ask them to think about how heavy it is. Place the quarter on one tin and ask children to guess how many quarters they think it will take to sink the tin. Record responses on the board or a chart. Place quarters, one at a time, on the tin until it sinks below the water level.

2. Next pass around a quarter and penny to the children. Ask them to put the penny in one hand and the quarter in the other hand. Ask them if they think the penny feels heavier, lighter, or the same weight as the quarter. Have them guess how many of the pennies they think it would take to sink the second tin, and record responses.

3. Place one penny at a time on the tin until it sinks. Record the number of pennies it took to sink the tin.

4. Compare the different numbers of quarters and pennies it took to sink the tins.

5. Pass around a nickel and ask the children to guess how many nickels it will take to sink the tin based on what they know about quarters and pennies.

(continued)

How Many to Sink Me *(continued)*

ACCOMMODATIONS

✓ For younger children heavier objects could be used along with bigger tins.

✓ If sufficient materials are available, children, in pairs or small groups, could carry out the measuring activity on their own.

EXTENSIONS

✓ Older children could be asked to record the results for the penny, nickel, and quarter and to state the proportions or ratios for the three. They could also be asked the question, "If the tins were 6 by 6 inches, what might you expect the numbers of pennies, nickels, and quarters to be?"

✓ The type of tins to be used could be different. Would it take more quarters to sink the 3-by-3-inch aluminum foil tin or a 3-by-3-inch plastic plate?

✓ To add appeal, small toy boats could also be used.

MATHEMATICS

My Balancing Act

My Balancing Act is designed to help children make comparisons among objects of different weights. The task also instructs children in the use of a balance board.

LEARNING

* Balancing objects that have different weights
* Making comparisons between two objects of different weights
* Reasoning about weight differences
* Representing results

MATERIALS

* Two tins
* A balance board 4 inches wide by 2 feet long by 1 inch thick
* A fulcrum board for balancing 4 inches long by 2 inches wide by 2 inches high
* A cup of water
* A cup of sand (may have some extra sand available)
* A cup of marbles (may have a few extra marbles available)
* An illustrated chart of the balance board for recording (created by the teacher)

STEPS

1. Show the children the balance board sitting on top of the smaller board. Tell them that they are going to use the balance board to: (1) determine if objects weigh the same and (2) determine how many of one object it might take to balance the board with a single heavier object. Note: tubs could be nailed on at both ends to keep objects from falling off the board.

2. Pour a cup of water into a tin on one side of the balance board and ask children to explain what happened. Show them a tablespoon of sand and place it in the tin on the other side. Ask children what happened. Does the water in the tin weigh more or less than the sand? Ask children how they might be made the same.

3. Have children take turns adding one tablespoon of sand to the tin until the two tins are balanced. Record on the illustrated chart of the balance board how many tablespoons of sand it took to equal the cup of water. Pour the sand into a cup to show the amount of sand used. Was the cup full? Ask if the amounts of water and sand were the same or different. Also ask them to explain which is heavier, water or sand.

4. Keep the water on one side of the balance board and dump out the sand on the other side. Bring out a cup of marbles. Ask children if they think a cup of marbles will weigh the same as the water. Place several marbles at a time on the balance board until the cup of marbles is gone or until the board is balanced. Once the board is balanced, discuss the results and record them on the chart next to the sand. Ask children if it took more or less than a cup of marbles to balance the cup of water. Ask which is heavier.

(continued)

My Balancing Act (continued)

5. Based on what they found out about the relative weights of water and sand and water and marbles, ask what they think is heavier, sand or marbles.

6. Have children carry out the same activity to determine whether sand or marbles is heavier.

CRITICAL THINKING CHALLENGE

Children could be given the opportunity to move the fulcrum closer to one end of the board and be asked to determine how many more or fewer objects of one kind it would take to balance the object on the other end.

ACCOMMODATIONS

✓ Commercially made balance scales or boards could be used if available.

✓ Adjustments can be made to the size of the fulcrum and length and thickness of the boards for weighing lighter or heavier objects.

EXTENSIONS

✓ The teacher could work with the concept of "distance from the fulcrum" to balance objects of different weights. For example, if we moved the tub of marbles closer to the fulcrum and kept the water tub at the other end of the balance board, would we still need as many marbles or more marbles to lift the water?

MATHEMATICS

Squared Up

Squared Up is an activity designed to help children understand the measurement concept of area. Children begin to learn the concept of area by filling in spaces with arbitrary measures.

LEARNING

✳ What area is

✳ Measuring the area of spaces with arbitrary measures

✳ Making estimates based on previous experience

MATERIALS

✳ 4-by-4-inch sheet of paper for each child (partners could be used to reduce the number of sheets)

✳ 3-by-6-inch sheet of paper for each child

✳ 25 1-inch-square tiles for each child (or set of partners)

✳ Other sheets with different designs for extra practice

STEPS

1. Provide each child with a 4-by-4-inch sheet of paper. Give children a number of 1-inch-square tiles (or cut strips of construction paper into 1-inch squares). Ask the children to think about how many tiles it might take to fill up the sheet of paper.

2. Fill the top part of the paper with tiles to show children how to fill up the paper.

3. Have the children fill their sheets of paper and then have them count up the number of tiles it takes.

4. Next give children a 3-by-6-inch sheet of paper and ask them to guess how many tiles it would take to fill this shape. Have them fill the sheet with their tiles and share their numbers. A discussion could take place regarding the number of squares needed to fill the two different sizes of paper.

5. Give children a variety of different-shaped designs and have them make guesses and then record the actual results (see sample).

(continued)

Squared Up (continued)

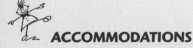

ACCOMMODATIONS

✔ The size of the paper and arbitrary measures can vary depending on the age of the children, with bigger pieces for younger children and smaller pieces for older students. For example, very young children could use 1-foot-square tiles to measure floor spaces while ¼-inch squares could be used by older children.

EXTENSIONS

✔ Older children could make estimates based on known quantities of different-size shapes. If a 4-by-6-inch shape has 24 tiles and a 5-by-6-inch shape has 30 tiles, how many tiles might a 6-by-6-inch shape have?

✔ Fractional parts could also be used for problem solving for older students. If the shape contains 18 1-inch-square tiles, how many ¼-inch tiles would it take to fill the same shape?

MATHEMATICS

Samples of Other Designs

My Guess _____
Actual Number of Tiles _____

L

My Guess _____
Actual Number of Tiles _____

H

My Guess _____
Actual Number of Tiles _____

E

My Guess _____
Actual number of Tiles _____

T

Measure It Around

Measure It Around is a task that will help children begin to understand the perimeter of objects. The task will further help children learn how to measure perimeters of simple shaped objects.

LEARNING

* ❊ The concept of perimeter
* ❊ Measuring the perimeters of objects
* ❊ How to measure length

MATERIALS

* ❊ 1-by-1-foot pieces of cardboard for each child or set of partners
* ❊ Set of 1-inch strips of paper for each child or set of partners (bolts, nails, etc. could also be used)
* ❊ Large sheet of paper to identify objects and their corresponding perimeters
* ❊ Marker

STEPS

1. Show the children a piece of cardboard that is 1 foot by 1 foot. Tell them that today they will learn to measure the outside edge, or what is called the *perimeter,* of the piece of cardboard.

2. Bring out 1-inch strips of paper and show children how to measure one side of the piece of cardboard.

3. Pass out a piece of cardboard to each child (or set of partners) and ask children to count the number of strips of paper it takes to measure all around the piece of cardboard (all four sides).

4. Have children compare answers once they are finished. Review with them that when they measured around the piece of cardboard they were measuring its perimeter.

5. Have children, as a group, identify appropriate objects in the classroom for which a perimeter could be measured. Write the list on a large sheet of paper taped to a wall. One by one have the children select an object in the classroom and measure its perimeter.

6. After children have measured the perimeters of the objects, record the measurements on the large sheet of paper. Comparisons and a discussion of the perimeters can follow.

7. Children can be told that the large sheet of paper will stay on the wall for awhile and that they can add objects and their corresponding perimeter measurements to it.

(continued)

ACCOMMODATIONS

✓ Older students may be asked to make estimates of larger objects such as a tennis court and measure perimeters using tools such as 6-to-10-foot boards.

✓ Older students could use standard measures such as yard sticks to measure the perimeter of a room and then convert the measures to feet, meters, etc.

EXTENSIONS

✓ Children might be asked to measure the perimeters of curved objects by using string, yarn, or other flexible measuring tools. Older students could convert these arbitrary measuring tools to standard measures and measure the perimeters of larger objects.

✓ If magnifying glasses are available, older students could practice measuring really small objects to ½₂ of an inch, etc.

MATHEMATICS

Area to Perimeter

Area to Perimeter is a set of activities to be used to help children discover relationships between area and perimeter. Children should already have a basic understanding of the concepts of area and perimeter and be able to measure the area and perimeter of objects with nonstandard or standard measures before starting these activities.

LEARNING

❋ Discovering relationships between area and perimeter

❋ Using reasoning to make estimates

❋ Representing relationships between area and perimeter

MATERIALS

❋ Colored pencils or pens for each child

❋ 8½-by-11-inch sheets of graph paper for each child

❋ Board to create a chart and record responses

STEPS

1. Provide each child with an 8½-by-11-inch piece of graph paper. Younger children can be provided with graph paper with 1-inch squares, while older children can be given graph paper with ¼-to-½-inch squares.

2. Tell the children they are to draw a square with a colored pencil or pen on the top part of their paper that has an area of four graph squares. Illustrate, if necessary.

3. After the square with an area of 4 is drawn, ask the children to use the top half of the paper to make as many different shapes as possible that have an area of 4.

4. After an appropriate amount of time, have the children stop and share the different patterns they came up with.

5. After the patterns are shared, ask the children to go back and identify the perimeters for each of the 4-area patterns created.

6. On the board make the following chart:

Area to Perimeter	
An Area of	Has the Following Perimeters
4	Smallest Perimeter Found ____ Largest Perimeter Found ____
5	Smallest Perimeter Found ____ Largest Perimeter Found ____
6	Smallest Perimeter Found ____ Largest Perimeter Found ____

(continued)

Area to Perimeter (continued)

7. Once the perimeters have been recorded, ask children to identify what perimeters they found for the patterns with an area of 4. Record answers on the chart.

8. Ask children to reason what perimeters they might find for patterns with an area of five squares based on what they learned about the patterns created with areas of four squares.

9. Have children create area patterns with five squares on the lower half of the graph paper, record answers, and report them to the class. Again fill in the responses on the chart. Following the discussion children could go through the same steps using patterns with areas of six squares.

10. At the end of the activity ask children what they learned about the relationship between area and perimeter.

ACCOMMODATIONS

✔ As mentioned in the set of activities above, the size of the squares on the graph paper can be made bigger for younger children.

✔ Children could use geoboards and rubber bands to form the areas.

EXTENSIONS

✔ In schools with 1-foot tile floors, children could be asked to carry out the activities using 1-foot sheets of paper or tape to form the different patterns.

✔ Students could do the same activity using half squares to form the areas and see if this changes the perimeters.

MATHEMATICS

The Wall Mural

The Wall Mural is an exciting activity for children who have an understanding of how to work with perimeters. Groups of children are given a small part of a picture on small graph paper and then transfer the image to large graph paper.

LEARNING

* Transfering the perimeter of a picture on small graph paper to large graph paper
* Reinforcing the knowledge of perimeter

MATERIALS

* A large sheet of paper 8 feet tall and 3 feet wide ruled with 1-foot squares for each team (Long boards can be used to draw the squares on the large sheets—smaller sheets could be used if you adjust the graph squares to ½ foot rather than 1 foot.)
* A small sheet of graph paper with 1-inch squares containing a piece of a picture for each team (Start with a picture on graph paper 8 squares tall and 15 squares long and cut it into pieces that are 8 squares tall and 3 squares long.)
* Pencils
* Markers
* Tape

STEPS

1. Divide the class into five groups. Provide each group of children with a piece of graph paper with 1-inch squares with part of a picture on it. The graph sheet should have three horizontal rows of squares and eight vertical columns of squares. Also provide each group with a large sheet of paper with 1-foot squares in three rows and eight columns.

2. Ask each group to transfer their drawing from the small graph paper onto the large graph paper.

3. Each group will have a number on the back of their large graph paper that will indicate the position their transferred picture should be put in on the wall.

4. Once each team completes its section of the wall mural, the groups will hang them based on the position order written on the back of each sheet. If all groups successfully transfer the image from the small graph paper to the large paper, the classroom will have a mural 8 feet tall and 15 feet long!

5. Team members can then color the mural.

(continued)

The Wall Mural *(continued)*

ACCOMMODATIONS

✔ As indicated above, the size of the squares can be adjusted to meet the needs of the classroom space or size of paper available to the teacher.

✔ If large boards (1-by-12-inch boards about 8 feet long) are available children could be asked to make their own large graph.

✔ The level of difficulty of the images can be adjusted for younger children.

EXTENSIONS

✔ Rather than using large graph paper, groups of children could tape the appropriate number of 1-foot-square pieces of paper together and transfer the image to that.

✔ Older children might use the same size graph paper but be asked to increase the size of the picture by doubling or tripling the sides (perimeter) of the picture.

MATHEMATICS

My School Day

My School Day can be used by children who are learning to tell or write time. They can tell or write the time of different events throughout the school day or after the school day.

LEARNING

* Telling time
* Writing time

MATERIALS

* A classroom clock (digital, standard, or both)
* Time Sheets for recording time (one for each child)

STEPS

1. Pass out a Time Sheet (see attached sample) to each child and inform them that they will be identifying or recording the different times at which certain things happen at school or home. (If at home, parents can be informed as to how they can assist with the activity.)

2. As different events start, have children tell or write down the time.

3. At the start of the next day, review what happened the day before. Children can compare the times they recorded.

Time Sheet	
What Happened	What Time It Was
Went into the classroom to start school	
Had reading	
Morning recess	
Had math	
Had lunch	
Had science	
Left the classroom to go home	

(continued)

My School Day (continued)

ACCOMMODATIONS

✓ The number of events to be recorded can be limited based on how far along children are into telling time.

✓ The type of clocks to be used can be selected based on how much assistance children may need (minute markings, etc.).

EXTENSIONS

✓ A Time Sheet could be made up for after-school events with the teacher informing parents how they can be involved in the activity.

MATHEMATICS

How Much Time

How Much Time is an activity to help children estimate time. The activity provides an opportunity for children to estimate number of seconds, minutes, and hours.

LEARNING

✳ Estimating time in seconds, minutes, and hours

MATERIALS

✳ Recording sheets for the timed activities
✳ Stopwatches
✳ Different materials depending on the timed activities selected.

STEPS

1. Tell the children that over the next several days they will be involved in a number of activities for which they will guess the amount of time it will take to complete each activity. For some activities they will make their guesses first and then record the actual amount of time the activities took.

2. Before each timed activity takes place, record how long the children guess the activity will take.

3. Time the activity and make comparisons with their guesses.

4. Possible timed activities to be used are

   finding a specific page in a book

   erasing the board

   walking around the school building

   brushing your teeth

   waiting for an ice cube to melt

   waiting for painted pictures to dry

   completing five problems

   listening to a specific musical piece

   cleaning up your work area

 ACCOMMODATIONS

✔ When planning the week's curriculum, think about certain teaching activities that could be integrated into these timed activities.

✔ The length of the timed activities should be aligned with the time concepts being taught to children.

✔ Longer timed events such as days, weeks, and months may be appropriate for older students. (How long will it take the clay pots to dry, the plants to grow, etc.?)

 EXTENSIONS

✔ Some of the timed activities could be extended to include computation or rational numbers. For a 30-minute TV program, how many minutes will be commercial time? How many minutes will it take to erase half the board? The whole board?

Convert My Time

Convert My Time can be used to help children convert seconds, minutes, and hours. The time periods selected to be converted can be based on real school events.

LEARNING

* Converting time measured in seconds, minutes, and hours
* Problem solving with time

MATERIALS

* Copies of the Time Conversion Task Sheet
* The times identified from the "How Much Time" activity in this book (optional)

STEPS

1. Identify different timed events that take place during the course of the week and have children convert time among seconds, minutes, and hours. You could also use the times recorded in the "How Much Time" activity in this book.

2. The time conversions can be recorded on the board and different converted times could be discussed and reviewed with the children.

3. The children can have extra practice on time conversions by using the sample Time Conversion Task Sheet included with this activity.

ACCOMMODATIONS

✓ For older students conversions could be made for days, weeks, months, and years.

✓ For children working with computation at lower levels, conversion sheets (i.e., 1 minute equals 60 seconds, 2 minutes equals 120 seconds, etc.) could be used.

EXTENSIONS

✓ To reinforce estimation, children could be asked to estimate the amount of time the conversion will be before they work through the conversion process.

(continued)

MATHEMATICS

Convert My Time (continued)

Time Conversion Task Sheet	
It took Sam 2 minutes and 37 seconds to ride on his skateboard from his home to the video store. How many seconds did it take him to ride his bike to the video store? Answer _____	Maria had basketball practice for 1 hour and 52 minutes. How many minutes of practice did she have? How many seconds did she practice? Answer _____
Tamara read the comics section of the paper in 420 seconds. How many minutes did it take her to read the comics section of the paper? Answer _____	Juan ran a mile in 4 minutes and 12 seconds. How many seconds did it take Juan to run the mile? Answer _____
It took Matty 3 hours and 17 minutes to paint a new dog house. How many minutes did it take Matty to paint the dog house? Answer _____	Jordan was on the Internet for 3 hours on Monday and 1 hour and 14 minutes on Tuesday. How many minutes was Jordan on the computer? Answer _____
Jess and Toni walked into the burger place. It took them 300 seconds to place their orders, 180 seconds to get their burger meals, and 11 minutes to eat their food before they left. How many minutes did Jess and Toni spend in the burger place? Answer _____	Cheryl entered the Swim, Run, and Bike Challenge. It took her 45 minutes to complete the swimming event, 78 minutes to complete the running event, and 57 minutes to complete the biking event. How many hours did it take her to complete all three events? Bonus question: How many seconds did it take her to complete all three events? Answer _____

Time Setting

In Time Setting children try to set a number of different clocks with different faces to the same time.

LEARNING

❋ Setting clocks to the same time

❋ Setting time using standard, digital, Roman numeral, and other clock formats

MATERIALS:

❋ Standard watch with hour and minute markings

❋ Digital clock

❋ Clock with Roman numeral markings

❋ Other clocks with no minute or hour markings

STEPS:

1. Have the children observe the time on a standard clock that has minute and hour markings.

2. Tell the children that some of them will be given a different type of clock and be asked to set the clock to the same time as the one being shown them.

3. Start out with the following example: show children the time of 1:40 on a standard clock. Pass out a digital clock and have one of the children set the digital clock to the same time.

4. Have other children discuss whether the time was set correctly.

5. Some other examples that could be tried include

    ❋ Show a digital time reading on a clock and have children set the same time using a clock with Roman numerals.

    ❋ Show children a clock with only hours identified and have them set a digital clock to the same time.

    ❋ Show children a clock with Roman numerals and have them set the same time on a standard clock.

6. Suggest a number of other times for the children to show on the clocks.

7. Children could also come up with different times.

 ACCOMMODATIONS

✔ Children should have some awareness of the different types of clocks discussed before they are introduced to this activity.

 EXTENSIONS

✔ Children could be asked to write down the time they are trying to set the new clock to. This activity could help children reinforce how to write time.

✔ Children could be asked to show military time. For example, have them show the time for 23 hundred hours.

MATHEMATICS

Chapter 11

Number and Operations

This chapter on number and operations includes activities grouped into three categories: understanding number, computation with number, and estimation with number. The level of number can be adjusted for in each activity. Younger children can work with two-digit numbers (24) in the activities, while older students can work with larger or varied numbers (396, 2680, 23, 459).

Number Scramble

Number Scramble is a fun activity that allows children to recognize numbers and see relationships among numbers. One or more children can play.

LEARNING

❋ Identifying numbers

❋ Making connections among numbers

❋ Problem solving with numbers

MATERIALS

❋ 3-by-5-inch index cards (or scraps of paper)

❋ Pencils for recording

❋ Grid paper or self-made grid sheets

❋ Three dice per child or group of children (spinners with numbers or playing cards could be substituted)

STEPS

1. Develop a set of number cards on 3-by-5-inch cards that are at the level the children are learning to identify.

   Example   547

2. Show a card and ask the children to say the number. Ask the children to rearrange the numbers individually or as a group so the number is smaller, then so it is larger. Have the children write the new number on a blank card and show the new higher or lower number.

3. After children have the chance to work through several cards, provide them with three dice. Have a child roll the three dice and ask the child to say what the number rolled is.

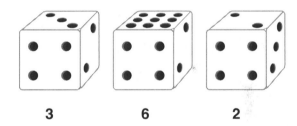

3   **6**   **2**

4. Have children record their answers on a simple grid and continue to play until time is up.

ACCOMMODATIONS

✔ The numbers selected could be two-digit numbers or four digits, etc. to meet the needs of children.

✔ Multi-ability groups could be used to provide peer support for children moving to higher levels with numbers.

EXTENSIONS

✔ Children could be shown a number card and be asked to say a lower or higher number.

✔ Children could be given three number cards and asked to place them in order from lowest to highest.

(continued)

MATHEMATICS

Number Scramble (continued)

Number Scramble Grid*		
Number Rolled	Larger Number	Smaller Number

*At times lower or higher numbers may not be recorded (e.g., if 555 is rolled no higher or lower number is possible). Children could either re-roll the dice or indicate a higher or lower is not possible (problem solving).

Guess My Number

Guess My Number *is a game used to reinforce number recognition through a problem-solving approach. Two children or two small groups play against each other trying to guess each other's secret number.*

LEARNING

✳ Number recognition
✳ Problem solving

MATERIALS

✳ Pieces of paper
✳ Coin
✳ Graph paper or self-made grid paper

STEPS

1. Match up players in pairs. Each player identifies a number appropriate to the level the children are working on. Two-digit or higher numbers [93, 479, 2248, 25, 783] can be used. Before play starts each player writes down his or her secret number on a piece of paper and turns the paper over so it cannot be seen by the other player. Players can flip a coin to see who goes first.

2. Each player needs a playing card with the numbers 0 to 9 written in each column. The number of columns needed is determined by the number of digits used in the opponent's number. For the number 5659 a player would need a card with four columns with 0 to 9 written in each column.

Card Sample			
0	0	0	0
1	1	1	1
2	2	2	2
3	3	3	3
4	4	4	4
5	5	5	5
6	6	6	6
7	7	7	7
8	8	8	8
9	9	9	9

3. The player who goes first asks if the secret number contains a specific number in a particular column. For example, the child may ask if the secret number has a 4 in the second column from the left. If the secret number is 5659 the player with the secret number would say no and the child would place a marker or x on the 4 in the second column to indicate the secret number does not have a 4 in that column. If the guess is correct the child may circle that number in the appropriate column.

4. Play continues until a player correctly determines the other player's secret number through the elimination of each number in each column.

(continued)

Guess My Number *(continued)*

ACCOMMODATIONS

✓ The number of digits used can be selected based on the number recognition level the players are working on.

✓ For children beginning to work on higher-level numbers, partners who have a greater knowledge with this level of number can be assigned.

✓ For players working on lower numbers for the different place value categories, numbers up to 5 can be used for each column.

EXTENSIONS

✓ Week-long competitions can be planned, allowing children to include a number of games.

✓ By using a decimal point, the same game could be used for teaching money ($47.45) or telling time (2:45).

MATHEMATICS

Move to the Number

Move to the Number helps children to see relationships among numbers. Move to the Number is an active game and permits children to make body movements as they learn relationships among numbers.

LEARNING

❋ Identifying numbers

❋ Understanding relationships between numbers

MATERIALS

❋ Masking tape

❋ Teacher-made player cards with numbers

❋ Teacher-made player cards with the words *a lower number* or *a higher number* written on them

STEPS

1. Use a floor space approximately 6-by-6 feet to make a 36-square grid with masking tape.

2. Inside each square have a number 0 to 9 written at random. If you have a tile floor you can simply place numbers inside each tile square being used.

3. Have a player draw a number from a set of cards, for example, 612. The player is to place three body parts on 6, 1, and 2 in the grid. Specific body parts can represent certain place values. The right hand may be hundreds, the left foot ones, and so forth. If higher numbers are used, two players could form the numbers.

4. After the correct number is formed, have the players draw a card from a second pile that includes cards with the words *a lower number* or the words *a higher number* on them. The player must then place three body parts on a number that is lower or higher than the first number.

ACCOMMODATIONS

✔ The level of numbers selected can be adjusted to the needs of the children.

✔ The size or number of squares can be increased or reduced to better accommodate players' needs.

EXTENSIONS

✔ Players could be asked to place their body parts on the answer to an addition or subtraction problem.

✔ Coin values could be used instead of numbers.

MATHEMATICS

Ad Inspector

Ad Inspector is an investigation activity that is used to develop number relationships. The activity requires players to find numbers that fall between two given numbers.

LEARNING

* Comparing quantities of numbers
* Identifying number order
* Understanding of dollar amounts

MATERIALS

* Ad sheets from newspapers
* Pencils
* Copies of Ad Price Sheet (one for each child)

STEPS

1. Pass out ad sections from newspapers to each child. Children could also work in small groups if too few ad sections are available. Along with the newspaper ad sections pass out the Ad Price Sheet (see sample), which includes two amounts, a higher amount in column A and a lower amount in column B.

2. Explain to the students that they are to look at each of the dollar amounts in columns A and B and find two dollar amounts in the newspaper ads that fall between the amounts in columns A and B.

3. Students should record each amount in column C and identify each type of item in column D.

4. After they complete the sheet children can share their findings.

CRITICAL THINKING CHALLENGE

When finished, children could classify the types of items found (clothes, cars, etc.).

ACCOMMODATIONS

✔ Teachers can make their own Ad Price Sheets that are at the level of their children.

✔ If newspaper ad sheets are not available, teachers could use supply catalogs or make up their own price sheets.

✔ For younger children, items from a model store set up in their classroom could be used.

EXTENSIONS

✔ Children could locate more than two items for each set of prices.

(continued)

Ad Price Sheet			
Column A Lower Price	Column B Higher Price	Column C Prices Found	Column D Items
$750	$1100	1. _____ 2. _____	1. _____ 2. _____
$50	$125	1. _____ 2. _____	1. _____ 2. _____
$11,000	$17,000	1. _____ 2. _____	1. _____ 2. _____
$76,000	$175,000	1. _____ 2. _____	1. _____ 2. _____
$10	$50	1. _____ 2. _____	1. _____ 2. _____
$120	$247	1. _____ 2. _____	1. _____ 2. _____
Free	$25	1. _____ 2. _____	1. _____ 2. _____

MATHEMATICS

Number Expansion

Number Expansion is a card game used to help children associate higher and lower values of numbers. Number Expansion helps children to recognize numbers and their relationship to other numbers.

LEARNING

* Understanding number values in relationship to other numbers
* Recognizing numerals

MATERIALS

* Number Expansion Board
* 49 teacher-made number sequence cards, 1-by-1 inch

STEPS

1. Two or four children can participate in this activity. Each player gets a Number Expansion Board and a deck of player number cards. The player number cards contain number sequences made up by the teacher that children are working on. Younger players may use cards with numbers below 50 or 100, while older children can use a set of cards numbered over 1000.

2. Children start by drawing a card to see which player goes first. The player who draws the highest numbered card starts play.

3. Each player is dealt five cards. Before the first player begins, the dealer turns over the top card and places it on the middle square labeled *Starting Space* on the Number Expansion Board.

4. Each player plays only one card at a time. A higher numbered card can only be played on top of or to the right of a card that has been played. Lower numbered cards can only be played below or to the left of a card that has been played.

5. The first player starts by playing one of his or her cards above or to the right of the starting space card if it is higher than the starting space card. A lower numbered card could be placed below or to the left of the starting space card. Each of the players continues to add cards. If a player does not have a card that can be appropriately placed adjacent to a card on the board, the player draws a card from the pile until one can be played. The game ends when a player has no cards left in his or her hand.

ACCOMMODATIONS

✓ As indicated in the activity, teachers should make up numbered cards that match the levels of the children. Cards could be numbered 0 to 20, 100 to 1000, etc.

✓ Larger boards or squares on the floor could be used for younger children.

EXTENSIONS

✓ Number patterns such as multiples of 2, 5, 25, etc. could be used.

✓ Decimals, money amounts, or times could be used in lieu of basic numbers.

(continued)

Number Expansion (continued)

Number Expansion Board

			Starting Space			

MATHEMATICS

Big Strips, Little Strips

Big Strips, Little Strips is used to work on computation asking the question "how many more?" In the activity children are given a number of stars in a box and need to determine how many more stars they will need to get to a higher number.

LEARNING

❋ Number recognition

❋ Addition (adding up) or subtraction

❋ Communicating a process

MATERIALS

❋ Unit strips of stars (at least 9 ones, 9 tens, 9 hundreds per individual or team)

❋ Big Strips, Little Strips Company Log Sheet (one for each child)

❋ Pencils

STEPS

1. Provide children with sets of stars in units of 1, 10, and 100. See the sample on next page.

2. Pass out the Big Strips, Little Strips Company Log Sheets. Tell the children that in column A is the number of stars in a box. In column C is the number of stars that needs to be in the box. In column B they are to fill in the number of unit strips that need to be added to the box to get to the number needed in column C.

3. As children complete each task they should show the strips they used and explain how they got their answer.

CRITICAL THINKING CHALLENGE

Another column could be added to require children to add up the boxes in columns A and B and then identify how many would need to go into the box in column C to meet the amount identified in column D.

ACCOMMODATIONS

✓ Having children use actual boxes to place their strips into may be helpful for children who benefit from using manipulatives.

✓ For older children thousands strips could be added.

EXTENSIONS

✓ Other unit items could be used such as sticks, straws, or toothpicks.

✓ The concept of money could be reinforced by using pennies, dimes, and dollars.

✓ The activity could be reversed so that you have an amount in column A and need to take so many out to get to a specific number in column C.

(continued)

Big Strips, Little Strips (continued)

Unit Strips

Ones

Tens

Hundreds

Big Strips, Little Strips Company Log Sheet		
Column A Number of Stars in the Box	**Column B** Number of Stars to Be Added to the Box	**Column C** Total Number of Stars Needed in the Box
239		562
114		347
873		926
42		795
555		831
93		312
884		903
615		888
29		656

Fewer Crops This Year

Fewer Crops This Year requires children to compute data using subtraction and multiplication and to make comparisons among quantities.

LEARNING

* Using subtraction
* Using multiplication
* Using division
* Making comparisons
* Reading data from charts
* Problem solving

MATERIALS

* Pencils
* Copies of Big J's Farm Report (one for each child)

STEPS

1. Read and review with the children the partially completed Big J's Farm Report included with this activity.

2. Have the children review the chart included in the Big J's Farm Report to ensure they understand the data being presented.

3. Have children complete the parts of the Big J's Farm Report that were not completed in the spaces provided.

4. Have children compare their answers and discuss how they arrived at the answers.

ACCOMMODATIONS

✔ For children at different levels you can use higher or lower numbers in the report.

✔ Younger children could be presented with an illustrated chart to help them read the data.

EXTENSIONS

✔ More farm crops could be added to the report.

✔ More years could be added for different types of comparisons.

(continued)

Fewer Crops This Year *(continued)*

Big J's Farm Report

The year 2004 was a poor year for the five crops grown on the Big J Farm. The Big J Farm grows potatoes, corn, peas, beans, and watermelons. The chart below shows the different amounts of each crop sold at market in the year 2003 and the year 2004. Overall this was a very bad year.

Chart of Crops Sold at Market for Years 2003 and 2004 In Tons			
Crop	Tons Sold in 2003	Tons Sold in 2004	Difference
Potatoes	990	495	
Corn	348	219	
Peas	649	326	
Beans	735	499	
Watermelons	1275	863	

[Students fill in]

Fill in these parts of the report:

The crop that produced the most in 2004 was _____.
The crop that lost the most between 2003 and 2004 was _____.
The crop that lost the least between 2003 and 2004 was _____.
The average amount per crop lost between 2003 and 2004 was _____.
There are 2000 pounds in a ton. _____ pounds of food were sold by the Big J Farm in 2004.

Problem Question for Students

Because of the loss of money from the low crop output in 2004, the Big J Farm has to stop producing one of its crops. The crop that should not be produced in 2005 is _____. Explain why this crop should not be produced.

MATHEMATICS

How Many Cartons of Milk

How Many Cartons of Milk provides children with the opportunity to read charts and work with the computations of addition and multiplication.

LEARNING

❈ Computing with addition
❈ Computing with multiplication
❈ Chart reading and interpreting
❈ Problem solving

MATERIALS

❈ Sheet of paper

STEPS

1. Inform children that the center director or principal has asked them to order the milk for the third, fourth, and fifth grades for the week.

2. The students should first review the chart below to determine how many cartons of milk are needed for a day.

Number of Children Who Drink Milk Each Day by Grade	
Grade Level	Number of Children
Third	22
Fourth	27
Fifth	23

3. Once the children have determined the number of children in all grades that need a carton of milk, they need to determine how many cartons must be ordered for the five-day week. They should record their answers on a sheet of paper.

CRITICAL THINKING CHALLENGE

The activity could include a follow-up statement from the principal that informs children that normally there is a total of six children absent each day from the third, fourth, and fifth grades. Students could attempt to figure out how many fewer cartons of milk might be ordered based on this information.

ACCOMMODATIONS

☑ Higher numbers or more grades could be used to challenge children at different levels.

Build My Cage

Build My Cage is a fun activity that requires children to use multiplication, problem solving, and reasoning to complete a project. Children also represent the solution to the problem.

LEARNING

* Applying multiplication
* Problem solving and reasoning
* Representation—model building

MATERIALS

* Cardboard or poster board
* Scissors
* Ruler
* Tape

STEPS

1. Inform children that they have a problem to solve. The situation is that they will be getting an iguana next week and they need to build a cage for the iguana. The iguana cage needs to be 3×6 inches high, 4×9 inches long, and 8×2 inches wide.

2. Have children in small groups figure out how many inches high, long, and wide the cage should be.

3. Once the children identify the dimensions of the cage, have them construct the cage using poster board, cardboard, or some other material, a ruler, scissors, and tape. If needed, you may have children think about the fact that they need two of each piece to make the top and bottom, the front and back, and both sides of the cage.

4. Once finished, the groups can share how they figured out the size of the cage and show their model.

ACCOMMODATIONS

✔ If children have difficulty making the cage they could look at several premade cages of different sizes and determine which box has the correct measurements.

✔ Other materials such as chicken wire, etc. could be used to form the cages.

EXTENSIONS

✔ Higher numbers could be used to build bigger boxes for bigger animals.

✔ Centimeters could be used in place of inches.

✔ Rather then providing measurements using multiplication, the number of inches for each dimension could be given as a sum and children could use addition only.

Snack Bags

Snack Bags provides children with the opportunity to use division to identify how snacks can be shared among a group of children.

LEARNING

❋ Applying division
❋ Problem solving

MATERIALS

❋ Snack Chart
❋ Paper
❋ Pencils

STEPS

1. Inform the children that they have been asked to put together snack bags for another class. They will need to make sure that each child has the same number of snacks. There are 24 children in the class so 24 bags will have to be filled.

2. Make up the chart below and show children the type of snacks that will be put into the bags. Explain to the children that next to each snack is the total number of pieces of that snack.

Snack Chart		
Snack	Number of Pieces	Pieces in Each Bag
Peanuts	432	
Bubble Gum	48	
Grapes	264	
Oreo Cookies	72	
Starburst	168	

3. Tell the children that they are to fill in the last column on the chart to indicate the number of pieces of each snack that should be placed into each of the 24 bags.

4. When all children finish they can share their answers and explain how they arrived at them.

CRITICAL THINKING CHALLENGE

Unequal quantities could exist to require children to determine how many more or fewer pieces would be needed so each child would have the same amount.

(continued)

230 · **Number and Operations**

Copyright © 2005, Thomson Delmar Learning

MATHEMATICS

ACCOMMODATIONS

✔ Higher or lower amounts of each snack can be used based on the level of children.

✔ A discussion of how they might determine the number of snacks for each bag could take place before children start the task.

✔ For young children simple sorting could be used in place of division to solve the problems.

EXTENSIONS

✔ Real snacks and bags could be used, and children could actually fill bags for an upcoming party.

MATHEMATICS

My Stars

My Stars is an estimation activity that can be used to improve younger children's ability to make estimates. The activity can also be used to determine to what number level children can estimate.

LEARNING

✳ Making number estimates

MATERIALS

✳ 8½-by-11-inch sheets of paper
✳ Star stickers or glued-on star figures (number depends on the level of your children)

STEPS

1. Tell the children they are going to look at several star charts and they are to try to estimate how many stars there are. Also tell the children that they will have a short time to look at the stars before they make their estimate.

2. Show children an 8½-by-11-inch sheet of paper with stars on it with an easy number (10) of stars to estimate. Show the sheet for only a few seconds so children cannot count the actual number of stars.

3. Have children share and compare their estimates and then show the star chart again so children can count the actual number of stars.

4. One at a time, show the children more sheets with increasing number of stars until you find children making estimates that become greatly different from the number of stars shown on the charts.

ACCOMMODATIONS

✓ Larger sheets and larger stars could be used with larger groups.

✓ Other objects such as smiley faces could also be selected.

EXTENSIONS

✓ The number of objects to be estimated can be adjusted to the level of the children.

✓ Estimates could be recorded on the board to compare the range of numbers being estimated.

Number in the Bundle

Number in the Bundle allows children to develop the ability to make estimates with number quantities and to use comparisons when making estimates.

LEARNING

* Making number estimates
* Reasoning
* Making comparisons with known numbers
* Communicating ideas

MATERIALS

* Toothpicks (the amount depends on the level of children)
* Rubber bands

STEPS

1. Tell the children that you will show them a bundle of toothpicks very briefly and they are to estimate how many they see.

2. Show the children a small number of toothpicks bundled up with a rubber band for two or three seconds. For younger children you could use 10 and for older children, 25 to 50. Have them make a quick estimate of how many toothpicks they see.

3. Have children share their estimates and compare the different answers and perhaps reasons why they made their estimates.

4. Let the children count the number of toothpicks, or tell them how many toothpicks were bundled up.

5. Set the bundle of toothpicks to the side, and tell children you are going to show them another bundle of toothpicks that is larger. They are to look at the first bundle and then look at the new bundle shown and estimate how many toothpicks there are.

6. Once estimates are made they can share why they made the estimates they did.

7. Count up or identify the number of toothpicks in the second bundle, and have children compare the number with their guesses.

8. You can continue with more bundles of larger or smaller amounts.

ACCOMMODATIONS

✔ For younger children you can use other materials (crayons, etc.) that are easier to see.

✔ The number of objects to be estimated can be adjusted depending on the level of the children's estimation ability.

EXTENSIONS

✔ The estimates made by children could be placed on the board and ranges of estimates could be discussed.

✔ Estimates and the actual number of toothpicks in the bundles could be used in a graphing activity.

Balls in a Jar

Balls in a Jar provides the opportunity for children to make estimates based on number and perception. The activity includes problem solving as well as understanding of number quantities.

LEARNING

* Estimation of number
* Problem solving
* Communicating ideas

MATERIALS

* Clear jar
* Ping-Pong balls (other types of small objects may be used)

STEPS

1. Show children a jar with a Ping-Pong ball in it. Have children get into groups, and tell them they are to estimate how many

Ping-Pong balls would fill the jar to the top so the lid could be put back on.

2. As each group makes their estimate, record the estimates on the board and ask children how they determined their answer.

3. After all teams make their estimates, place Ping-Pong balls into the jar until no more can be added, and put the lid back on. Have the children count the balls as they are being placed into the jar.

CRITICAL THINKING CHALLENGE

After you fill the jar halfway, you could have children review and modify their estimates based on what they know about how many Ping-Pong balls it takes to fill about half the jar.

ACCOMMODATIONS

✔ Larger or smaller balls or jars could be used depending on the ability levels of children with regard to number estimation.

How Many Now

How Many Now can be used to help children estimate numbers when some have been taken away from or added to a known value.

LEARNING

* Making number estimates
* Estimating values that are more or less

MATERIALS

* Clear bowls or other clear containers
* Small cups
* Large bag of colored objects (small colored candies, blocks, marbles, etc.)

STEPS

1. Show the children a number of colored objects in a bowl. Ask them to make a quick estimate of how many they think are in the bowl. After estimates are made tell the children how many colored objects are in the bowl. Children could also be asked to count the colored objects if the number is reasonable to count.

2. After the number of colored objects are counted, show the children a second bowl with a few colored objects and ask them to estimate how many colored objects there would be if you added the contents of the second bowl to the first bowl. Several different amounts could be added in sequence.

3. Remove the second bowl and remind children how many objects were in the original bowl. Pick up a handful of colored objects from the bowl and ask children to estimate how many colored objects are left in the bowl. Children could also estimate how many were taken out. Count the number taken out and the number left.

4. Place a number of small cups in front of the children. Take some colored objects from the original bowl and place them into the first cup. After children have the chance to see how many are in the first cup and how many are left in the bowl, have them estimate how many more cups of colored objects could be filled from the bowl. Fill the cups to find the answer.

ACCOMMODATIONS

✔ The amount of colored objects to be estimated can vary depending on the number understandings of the children.

✔ Larger objects could be used with younger children.

EXTENSIONS

✔ If children make estimates of how many were taken out of the bowl, they can use subtraction to figure out how many are left in the bowl.

Make Me a Guess

Make Me a Guess provides children the opportunity to use mental math to make estimates. In the activity children are given a number amount and asked to estimate what number might be added to the amount to reach a higher amount or subtracted to reach a lower amount.

LEARNING

* Making estimates
* Using mental math
* Making comparisons between numbers

MATERIALS

* A set of starter numbered cards (numbers at the understanding level of the children)
* A corresponding set of higher numbered cards.
* A corresponding set of lower numbered cards.

STEPS

1. Before starting the activity three sets of numbered cards should be made up at the children's level of understanding. The first set of number cards is the starter set. The starter set of cards will be shown first to children one at a time. The second set of numbered cards contains higher numbers than the starter set. The third set of cards has corresponding lower numbered cards.

2. Show a starter card to the children, for example 31, or 1245, etc. Ask the children to identify the number.

3. Next show the children a corresponding higher numbered card, for example 48 or 1834. Ask the children to estimate what they could add to the starter card to get the number on the higher card.

4. Set an amount of time for responses to force children to use estimation instead of adding on, etc. to determine the answer.

5. Show the same starter card to the children and ask them to again identify the number.

6. Then show children a corresponding lower numbered card, for example 17 or 800, and ask them to estimate about how much they could subtract from the starter card to get the number on the lower card.

7. After each task children should share how they quickly made their estimate.

(continued)

Make Me a Guess *(continued)*

ACCOMMODATIONS

✔ Start with decade (30, 40, 50, etc.) or other easy-to-estimate numbers.

EXTENSIONS

✔ Children in groups or individually could make up their own sets of starter, lower, and higher numbered cards. Check to make sure the numbers are higher and lower than the starter set. Kids could share the sets.

✔ The estimates could be recorded on the board so children can determine the range of estimates made.

MATHEMATICS

MATHEMATICS RESOURCES

Bacarella, Dawn H. (1997). *1–100 Activity book: Activities and worksheets for the hundred board.* Vernon Hills, IL: Learning Resources, Inc.

Bresser, Rusty, & Holtsman, C. (1999). *Developing number sense grades 3–6.* Sausalito, CA: Math Solutions Publications.

Carter, Rik. (1996). *Exploring measurement grades 5–6: Length, area, volume, mass, time.* Rowley, MA: Didax Educational Resources, Inc.

Charlesworth, R. (2000). *Experiences in math for young children* (4th ed.). Clifton Park, NY: Thomson Delmar Learning.

Copley, Juanita V. (2000). *The young child and mathematics.* Washington, DC: National Association for the Education of Young Children.

May, Lola J. & Frye, Shirley M. (1995). *Down to earth mathematics: Activities for building strong math foundations.* Rowley, MA: Didax Educational Resources, Inc.

Overholt, James L., White-Holtz, Jackie, & Dickson, Sydney. (1999). *Big math activities for young children.* Clifton Park, NY: Thomson Delmar Learning.

National Council of Teachers of Mathematics. (1999). *Mathematics for young children.* Reston, VA: Author.

National Council of Teachers of Mathematics. (2000). *Principles and* standards *for school mathematics.* Reston, VA: Author.

Reys, Robert E., Suydam, Marilyn N., & Lindquist, Mary M. (1995). *Helping children learn mathematics* (4th ed.). Needham Heights, MA: Allyn and Bacon.

Richardson, K. (1999). *Developing number concepts, Book 1: Counting, comparing, and pattern.* Parsippany, NJ: Dale Seymour Publications.

Richardson, K. (1999). *Developing number concepts, Book 2: Addition and subtraction.* Parsippany, NJ: Dale Seymour Publications.

Richardson, K. (1999). *Developing number concepts, Book 3: Place value, multiplication, and division.* Parsippany, NJ: Dale Seymour Publications.

Richardson, K. (1999). *Understanding geometry.* Bellingham, WA: Lummi Bay Publishing.

Silverman, Helene, & Oringel, Sandy. (2001). *Math activities with dominoes: Grades K–3.* Vernon Hills, IL: Learning Resources, Inc.

Smith, Nancy l., Lambdin, Diane V., Linquist, Mary M., & Reys, Robert E. (2001). *Teaching elementary mathematics: A resource for field experiences.* New York: John Wiley and Sons.

Smith, Susan S. (1997). *Early childhood mathematics.* Needham Heights, MA: Allyn and Bacon.

Wakefield, Alice P. (1997). *Early childhood number games: Teachers reinvent math instruction.* Needham Heights, MA: Allyn and Bacon.

Unit 4

Physical Activity

The National Association for Sport and Physical Education (NASPE) established standards to help identify what children should know and be able to do. An Outcomes Committee established by NASPE, developed a definition for the physically educated person. The definition included five major focus areas:

✳ Has learned skills necessary to perform a variety of physical activities

✳ Is physically fit

✳ Participates regularly in physical activity

✳ Knows the implications of and the benefits from involvement in physical activities

✳ Values physical activity and its contributions to a healthful lifestyle

The following three physical activity categories are included in Unit Four:

✳ **Movement Activities:** Movement activities help children develop the basic foundations for fitness, games, and other sport activities. Locomotor (hopping), nonlocomotor (balancing), and manipulative (throwing) activities are included in Unit Four under this category.

✳ **Fitness Activities:** Fitness activities include a combination of movement and gaming activities to help children develop higher levels of energy and better health. Activities for fitness include flexibility, exercise, and muscular development.

✳ **Games:** Gaming activities provide students with the opportunity to enhance their physical development for movement and fitness. Games also help children nurture social development and foster feelings of self-worth. Many games identified have noncompetitive options and include individual goal setting for improvement.

Chapter 12

Movement

Activities developed for this chapter can be categorized as locomotor, nonlocomotor, or manipulative. Locomotor activities for children include such activities as walking, jumping, skipping, hopping, and leaping. Nonlocomotor activities for children are stationary tasks that include balancing, twisting, and swaying. Manipulative activities presented deal with catching, tossing, throwing, kicking, and dribbling.

Hoop Jumping

Hoop Jumping is a fun activity for children that can be used to help improve eye–body coordination, balance, leg strength, and fitness.

LEARNING

* Jumping
* Coordinating eye-body movement
* Enhancing fitness

MATERIALS

* Set of hoops of different sizes (rope, taped together, can also be used in lieu of commercial hoops)
* Open space
* Numerals or alphabet letters to be placed next to hoops

STEPS

1. Set out a variety of hoops in the gym or any open area. The hoops can be of different sizes and can be spaced different distances apart.

2. Place a numeral or alphabet letter next to each hoop to identify the sequence in which children are to jump through the series of hoops.

3. Tell the children they are to try to jump into each hoop without touching the hoop.

4. Children can be timed (optional). Children can try to beat their own performance in subsequent attempts.

ACCOMMODATIONS

✔ The number sizes of the hoops and the distances between them can vary depending on the motor levels of children.

EXTENSIONS

✔ Children could be partnered up to try to jump through the hoop pattern.

✔ Some of the hoops for the sequence could be placed alongside or behind one another to help children add the dimension of direction to the activity.

✔ Different-shaped objects could be used from time to time, or children could jump *on* instead of *into* different objects.

PHYSICAL ACTIVITY

Skip on the Trail

Skip on the Trail is a good activity to use to help children develop the locomotor skill of skipping.

LEARNING

✳ Enhancing locomotor skill of skipping

MATERIALS

✳ Rope, boards, chalk, or other material to make a trail 20–25 feet long

✳ Sidewalks could also be used as a skipping area

STEPS

1. Line children up behind a starting line.

2. Show the children a trail (about 20 to 25 feet) made with rope, boards, or chalk lines. Sidewalks could also be used.

3. Tell them they are to skip on one foot until they reach the end.

4. Once children reach the end of the trail, ask them to skip about 5 feet backwards or to a particular marker.

ACCOMMODATIONS

✔ The distances and times set for children to skip forward or backward could be modified depending on children's endurance.

EXTENSIONS

✔ Objects could be placed along the trail for children to skip around to add flexibility to their movements.

✔ Children could be paired up and asked to skip in rhythm.

PHYSICAL ACTIVITY

Animal Walking

Animal Walking helps children explore different ways of walking around. The different walking movements help develop agility, strength, and balance.

LEARNING

* ❋ Developing different walking motions
* ❋ Developing agility, strength, and balance

MATERIALS

❋ Open play area

STEPS

1. Have the children stand on a line so they have space between them.

2. Tell them that they are going to be walking toward you until you say stop.

3. Explain that from time to time you will ask them to demonstrate how different animals walk.

4. To start, ask children to walk like a monkey might. After about 30 seconds say, "Stop."

5. Continue to have children walk like different animals toward you or away from you.

6. Other two- and four-legged animals to use could be a turtle, peacock, lion, cheetah, hippo, etc.

7. Select animals that may move faster or more slowly, have longer or shorter strides, sway back and forth, etc.

ACCOMMODATIONS

✔ The movement of certain animals could be modeled by the teacher if a number of children are not quite sure of how the animal moves.

EXTENSIONS

✔ Take children on a field trip to a zoo or around the neighborhood where a variety of animals might be found. Tell children to observe how they are walking and try to imitate them.

✔ Show an animal video and have children try to reproduce the movements of animals that are shown.

PHYSICAL ACTIVITY

Hop the Footprints

Hop the Footprints helps children to develop the locomotor movement skill of hopping.

LEARNING

* Developing hopping skill
* Developing fitness

MATERIALS

* Right and left foot patterns. The foot patterns could be made of paper that is laminated and taped to the flooring. Chalk outlines shaped like feet can also be used.

STEPS

1. Set out several courses of footprints (some right and some left) on a sidewalk or in a gym or other play area. Each course of footprints should have a different pattern, such as a straight line, a zigzag, etc.

2. Have children form teams, and position each team in front of one of the footprint courses.

3. Explain to children that each child in their team is to hop through the pattern twice.

4. Once all children hop through the pattern twice the team can move to the next course to their right when the other team has finished. The teams can switch until all courses are completed.

5. When all teams are finished the children can discuss which courses they liked the best and which courses were easier or harder.

ACCOMMODATIONS

✔ The number of foot patterns can be adjusted depending on the hopping abilities of children.

✔ If more children are right-foot dominant, more right-foot patterns could be included.

EXTENSIONS

✔ Foot patterns could be placed on a level surface, or some foot patterns could be slightly elevated by being placed on a square block of wood.

✔ Foot patterns could be placed going up or down a small incline.

✔ Stars or other types of patterns could be used instead of foot patterns.

PHYSICAL ACTIVITY

Leap the Log

Leap the Log helps children improve their leaping ability. Leg strength, agility, and balance can also be improved through the activity.

LEARNING

❋ Improving leaping ability
❋ Developing agility and balance

MATERIALS

❋ A smooth log or round cushion (start with a log with a diameter of about 3 inches)
❋ Safety pad
❋ Starting line marker

STEPS

1. Set a smooth, round log or round cushion in front of the children. Gym pads could be placed around the area. Place a marker in front of the log, about 5 inches away to start with.

2. Tell the children they are going to try to leap the log today.

3. Demonstrate how to leap. With both feet on the ground start a swinging motion with your arms while keeping your knees bent, and leap forward.

4. Have children take turns trying to leap over the log. If children are successful place the marker further from the log.

5. Tell children that the first several times they try to leap the log their feet can be as far apart or as close together as they want them to be so they feel comfortable.

6. Children can keep individual records on how far they leaped.

 ACCOMMODATIONS

✔ The diameter of the log can vary depending on the leaping ability of your children.

✔ For greater safety with younger children, cushions might be used in place of logs.

 EXTENSIONS

✔ Several logs could be placed in a row and children could practice making two leaps back-to-back, three leaps back-to-back, etc.

✔ Children could make the leaps with their feet wider apart or closer together.

✔ Children could practice leaping to the side or backward.

PHYSICAL ACTIVITY

Dodge the Balls

Dodge the Balls helps children to learn to make movements away from moving objects. The activity helps children to develop perception, timing, and movement.

LEARNING

* The ability to dodge moving objects
* Coordinating perception of moving objects and timing

MATERIALS

* Balls for the children to roll
* Stopwatch or watch to watch to time the children (optional)

STEPS

1. Have the children form two lines that are across from each other about 10 to 15 feet apart.

2. Have children in each line also stand about 6 feet from each other.

3. Give a ball to every second child in each line. Stagger the balls so the first, third, fifth, etc. child in one line has a ball while the second, fourth, sixth, etc. child in the other line has a ball to start with.

4. Tell the children that each child will have an opportunity to walk quickly between the two lines while the children roll the balls back and forth. The object is to dodge the crossing balls *and* to walk as quickly as possible.

5. When the teacher says "Start" a child should begin to walk quickly down the middle.

6. The teacher or a child judge can keep track of how long it takes the child to move through the middle of the lines and how many times the child was hit by a rolling ball (optional).

TEACHER NOTE

Caution the children to roll the ball and not throw it at children.

CRITICAL THINKING CHALLENGE

Different patterns could be set up so that the balls are not just being rolled across to an opposite child. The third child in one line could roll the ball to the third child in the other line while the first child in one line is rolling it to the sixth child in the other line.

(continued)

PHYSICAL ACTIVITY

Dodge the Balls *(continued)*

ACCOMMODATIONS

✔ Children can be spread out more or moved closer together to adjust the challenge of the task to the level of a child walking between the lines.

✔ Rather than have younger children be concerned about moving fast through the lines, the rule could be that they only need to keep moving at some pace.

EXTENSIONS

✔ Different-sized balls can be used.

✔ The size of the balls being used can be mixed up so some children are using small ones (tennis balls) while other children are rolling larger ones (soccer balls).

PHYSICAL ACTIVITY

Broomstick Race

Broomstick Race is an excellent activity to use to teach children how to run in unison. The activity helps children to adjust their running pace to another child's.

LEARNING

* Controlling the rate one runs at
* The concept of synchronization

MATERIALS

* Gym or outdoor running space
* One broomstick per team (other poles or rope about 5 feet long could also be used)

STEPS

1. Pair children up for a race.

2. Explain to the children that they and their partner are going to race as a team from one end of the gym to the other. An outdoor play space could also be used.

3. Pass out a broomstick or another type of pole about 5 feet long to each team. Tell children that when they run each of them has to hold onto the pole. If the pole falls, or if one of their hands lets go of the pole, they will need to restart the race.

4. Line up the teams for the race.

5. Tell the teams they will have two races.

6. Run the first race.

7. After the first race, tell the teams to discuss how things went and have them think about any adjustments they could make to improve their performance.

8. Run the second race.

9. After the two races are completed, partners can be reassigned and a new set of races can be run.

ACCOMMODATIONS

✔ The distance the children need to run can be adjusted.

✔ Shorter broomsticks could be used by younger children.

EXTENSIONS

✔ Children could race with a rope tied to each child's inside foot.

✔ Children could be asked to run backward while holding onto their broomstick.

✔ Three children might be assigned to a group with one child holding the middle of the broomstick.

PHYSICAL ACTIVITY

Obstacle Course Challenge

Obstacle Course Challenge *is a race in which children use a number of locomotor movements. The challenge can include running, skipping, leaping, and so on.*

MATERIALS

✳ A large outdoor or indoor space
✳ Small flags to be placed into or on top of the ground
✳ Bike or car tires for hopping into
✳ Piece of plywood to skip across
✳ Two pieces of rope
✳ Other appropriate materials for other obstacle course race modifications or additions
✳ Stopwatch

STEPS

1. Set up an obstacle course that includes several locomotor movement activities in a large open area. The obstacle course could include such events as:

   Run around a series of flags set in the ground, and then

   Hop through several bike tires, and then

   Skip across an 8-foot piece of plywood, and then

   Dodge the moving ropes (other children on both sides of an aisle weaving two ropes back and forth on the ground)

2. Children could be timed as they go through each event, and points could be assigned for going through each activity in the obstacle course without errors (hitting a flag, touching the rope, stopping skipping, etc.).

3. Children can be assigned to a team. Team times can be compared *or* each team's time can be compared with the team's own best time if the children have the opportunity to complete the obstacle course more than once.

(continued)

PHYSICAL ACTIVITY

ACCOMMODATIONS

✔ The length of the obstacle course could be adjusted depending on the endurance levels of children participating it the event.

✔ The type of activities selected for the obstacle course could be adjusted to make the course more or less challenging depending on the skill level of the children.

EXTENSIONS

✔ Relay teams could be formed for the event. As one child finishes the course or a part of the course, another team member could start or continue on.

✔ Children could be required to carry an object as they went through the course to create an additional type of experience. They could carry a bag of sand as they went through the course.

PHYSICAL ACTIVITY

Walk the Plank

Walk the Plank is an excellent activity for developing balance among children. A number of variations can be used that make appropriate for children at a variety of levels.

LEARNING

✳ Balancing when moving across narrow objects

MATERIALS

✳ A balance beam or elevated boards. A 2-by-6-inch or 2-by-9-inch board 6 to 8 feet long could be used if a balance beam is not available (Sidewalk curbs also could be tried out.)

STEPS

1. Set up the balance beam.

2. Have children practice going across the balance beam with their toe touching down on the board first with their heel to follow as they move across the beam. Children can also spread out their arms.

3. To help children develop their sense of balance further you may want to try a number of the following variations with the balance beam:

   Have children walk across backward.

   Have children walk across sideways, cross-stepping.

   Elevate one end of the beam and have children walk uphill, then downhill.

   Elevate the whole board off the ground.

4. A list of the different variations could be written on a balance beam chart, and children could mark their progress as they successfully complete each task.

ACCOMMODATIONS

✔ The width, the length, and the height of the board should be appropriate for the different ages of children involved with the activities. Wider and lower boards could be used for some children.

EXTENSIONS

✔ Setting objects on the balance beam gives children an opportunity to practice keeping their balance as they move along the balance beam and step over the objects.

Try One Limb

Try One Limb is a fun activity to use when trying to help children improve their balance. The activity can also allow children to be creative with their movements.

LEARNING

* Improving sense of balance
* Being creative with balance

MATERIALS

* Open floor space

STEPS

1. Explain to the children that they are going to practice balancing movements with their bodies.

2. Space children far enough apart that they will not fall into each other.

3. First tell children to stand on one leg until they are told to set their other leg down.

4. Have children stand on their opposite leg until they are told to set their other leg down.

5. After this warm-up activity, ask children to try the following:

   Balance with one hand and one foot on the floor.

   Balance with two hands and one foot on the floor.

   Balance with one hand and two feet on the floor.

   Balance with one hand, one knee, and one foot on the floor.

6. Children can suggest other ways to balance their bodies on the floor.

ACCOMMODATIONS

✔ Mats could be used if there is not a soft surface available for the activities.

EXTENSIONS

✔ Children could be asked to hold objects in one arm as they go through the activities.

✔ Children could be paired up and asked to complete similar tasks while connected to their partner. Each child can hold his or her partner's hand while balancing with one foot and one hand on the floor.

PHYSICAL ACTIVITY

The Leaning Body

The Leaning Body fosters balance with movement in children. The activity also helps children to develop agility in movement.

LEARNING

❋ Enhancing balance with movement
❋ Developing agility

MATERIALS

❋ Open area
❋ Floor mats (optional)

STEPS

1. Have the children stand far enough apart that they can make body movements without touching one another.

2. Have them stand with two feet on the ground and their arms extended over their heads. Tell them to reach for the sky.

3. With their arms over their heads, ask the children to slowly start to move their arms to the left as far as they can with their feet still touching the ground. Then have them try to move their arms to the right and then try to sway back and forward.

4. Next ask children to stand with one foot on the ground and go through the same movements.

5. Have children also try the following:

   Arms at your side, lift one leg up and try to bend your other leg so your body moves towards the ground.

   Move two arms and one leg around while standing on just one leg.

   Try to twist your body while on one or two legs.

ACCOMMODATIONS

✔ Vary the amount of time children are to cycle through each activity. Younger children should be involved in some movements for less time than older students.

✔ Not all of the balancing with movement activities may be appropriate for children with low muscular strength.

EXTENSIONS

✔ Children could match up with a partner and try to complete some of the same movement activities as a pair.

✔ Children could stand on square blocks or curbs to complete some of the activities.

Bear Stand

Bear Stand is a fun activity that helps children practice shifting weight through movement.

LEARNING

✳ Shifting weight

MATERIALS

✳ Open floor space
✳ Floor mats (optional)

STEPS

1. Have the children kneel down and put their hands on the floor.

2. Have them keep their hands on the floor and lift one knee off the floor.

3. Have the children keep their knees on the ground and lift one hand off the floor.

4. Have them place both hands on the floor while they lift their knees off the floor so they are like a bear on two feet and two hands.

5. Have them complete the following while they have only their two feet and two hands touching the floor:

   Lift one hand off the floor.

   Replace your hand while you move one foot off the floor.

   For older students: replace your foot and slowly move one foot and then one hand off the floor.

6. Starting with two feet and two hands on the floor, have them go through the following motions without stopping:

   Lift your right hand off the floor, then put it down, and quickly move your right foot off the floor, then put it down.

   Then quickly lift your left hand off the floor, then put it down, and quickly move your left foot off the floor, then put it down. (Keep repeating this cycle.)

ACCOMMODATIONS

✔ Observe children's muscular strength and endurance while they carry out the activities to ensure the appropriateness of the activity.

EXTENSIONS

✔ For children who are capable, a leader could ask them to hold each position for a certain amount of time.

✔ Other types of animals could be used as a motivational character for the activity.

PHYSICAL ACTIVITY

Rowboat Warm-up

Rowboat Warm-up can be used as a good agility activity before children play running games or become involved in other locomotor activities.

LEARNING

❋ Cooperation

❋ Warm-up preparation activity

MATERIALS

❋ Floor space

STEPS

1. Have children sit down in pairs so they are facing each other.

2. Tell the children that their legs should be touching the floor and extended so their feet are in contact with their partner's feet.

3. Have children stretch out their arms in front of them and hold the hands of their partner.

4. Once children are set, tell them that they are to move forward and backward holding hands like they are rowing a boat. They should keep their backs straight.

5. As they move back and forth you can ask them to move slow, faster, slower, etc.

6. Children could also try doing the activity while holding only one hand.

 **ACCOMMODATIONS**

✔ The warm-up time can be varied.

 EXTENSIONS

✔ Children could hold onto a bar as they move back and forth.

✔ Pairs of children could be lined up so there is a series of children connected in a synchronized movement.

PHYSICAL ACTIVITY

Balancing Board

Balancing Board is a good activity for children to work on balance. The board takes up little space and offers a variety of extension activities.

LEARNING

✳ Developing a sense of balance

MATERIALS

✳ A 12-by-12-inch piece of board with a small piece of wood nailed to the bottom, which is 2-by-2 inches and 4 inches high

STEPS

1. Provide a child with the balance board.

2. Children first place one foot on one side of the board and then try to stand with both feet on the board.

3. Once children can balance the board with two feet, they can try some other moves:

   Slowly take one foot off and try to balance on one foot.

   From the standing position try to slowly bend down at the knees.

   Try to catch a ball tossed to them and stay balanced.

   Try to rock the board forward and back without having any side touch the floor.

   Try to rock the board side to side.

   Put some weight in one hand and see if you can keep your balance.

4. Children can also invent other activities to do and challenge other children to complete their invented tasks.

ACCOMMODATIONS

✔ When children are new to the activity, assist them in getting on the board the first few times and then have them try to maintain their balance.

✔ If children struggle you may want to use a 2-by-2-by-2-inch base so the board is not elevated as high.

EXTENSIONS

✔ Children can try other movement activities with the board. They can play catch with a partner on a second balance board.

✔ To make the balance board more difficult you can reduce the size of the block underneath the 12-by-12-inch board. It could be 1½-by-1½-by-5 inches at the base.

✔ Have children slowly move both feet around the board while standing on the board.

Balancing Obstacle Course

Balancing Obstacle Course is a good activity to use after you have been working on a variety of balancing tasks for a while. The obstacle course can include a variety of activities used in teaching balance.

LEARNING

* Practicing a variety of balance activities in sequence

MATERIALS

* Balance beam
* Balance board
* Rope
* Stopwatch (optional)

STEPS

1. Set up an obstacle course with balancing activities for children. One possible course could consist of:

   Walking a balance beam in a particular way

   Standing on a balance board for a specific amount of time

   Running on a long rope for a particular distance

   Balancing with specific body parts (one hand, one elbow, and one knee only)

2. Children could be teamed up with a partner or with several other children. Children could be timed or it could be set up like a relay so that when one team member finishes another one starts.

3. The event could also be like a gymnastic event in which all children would first go to the balance beam, then move to the balance board area, and so on.

ACCOMMODATIONS

✔ The events to be set up for the balance obstacle course should challenge children but not be beyond their capability.

EXTENSIONS

✔ The obstacle course could be set up for a extended time period. Children could try to improve their performance over time.

Tube Ball

Tube Ball helps children develop an underhand rolling motion and eye–hand coordination.

MATERIALS

❋ Gym mat or 3-by-6-foot piece of plywood

❋ Plastic tube about 5 inches in diameter (an empty juice or coffee can could also be used)

❋ Tape

❋ Tennis ball

STEPS

1. Set up the gym mat or a piece of plywood on top of a table.

2. Raise one end so it is 6 to 8 inches higher than the other end. Place books or other materials under the end to keep it elevated.

3. Tape a plastic tube about 5 or 6 inches wide to the top of the mat. It should face down the slope.

4. Provide children with a tennis ball. Tell them they are to roll the ball up the mat and into the plastic tube.

5. Give each child five tries.

6. Children earn one point for hitting the tube and three points for getting the ball into the tube.

7. Children can form teams or do the activity individually.

ACCOMMODATIONS

✓ The diameter of the tube or length of the mat can be adjusted up or down to challenge children more.

✓ The mat could be lowered to the floor if the table is too high for some children.

EXTENSIONS

✓ Several different-size tubes could be taped to the elevated end at one time. Points could be given based on the diameter of the tube. The smaller the diameter, the more the points.

✓ The tube could be placed on the bottom end, and children could roll the ball down into the tube.

✓ Rather than tape the tube to the mat, another child could hold the tube and try to move it to where the first child rolled the ball. If the ball hits the tube one point could be awarded, and if the ball goes into the tube three points could be awarded to their team.

PHYSICAL ACTIVITY

Toss into the Tire

Toss into the Tire is a good activity to help younger children toss a ball to a location. It helps develop tossing skills along with eye–hand coordination.

LEARNING

❋ How to toss a ball

❋ Eye-hand coordination

MATERIALS

❋ A used car tire

❋ One or more tennis balls

❋ A grassy surface

STEPS

1. Lay a tire flat on a grassy outdoor surface. Set up tossing lines 4, 6, 8, 10, and 12 feet out from the tire.

2. Give children a tennis ball and instruct them to toss the ball into the tire. Points may be awarded if they hit the tire and if they get the ball into the tire. Some pointers to give children are

   Keep your eye on the tire when tossing the ball.

   Have your fingers pointing to the tire as you toss the ball.

   Take a step forward as you toss the ball.

3. Give children three trials. If the children are successful getting the ball into the tire from the 4-foot line they can move back.

4. Children can keep their own records to see how many times they hit the tire or get the ball into the tire.

ACCOMMODATIONS

✔ Younger children may be given more tosses so they have the opportunity to practice the tossing motion.

✔ The tossing line could be set up further back for older children.

EXTENSIONS

✔ Children could be given a number of different types of balls to toss into the tire. Golf balls, soccer balls, basketballs, or bean bags can be tried. Some balls might be lighter or heavier, as well.

✔ The tire could be set up at different angles to make the target more or less visible.

PHYSICAL ACTIVITY

Catch

Catch is a traditional game that helps reinforce throwing and catching skills. The activity also is helpful in developing eye–hand coordination.

MATERIALS

❋ A ball for each set of partners (tennis ball or rubber ball)

❋ Open area

STEPS

1. Assign children partners and have them stand 6 to 25 inches apart depending on their level of development.

2. Have one child throw the ball using the following techniques:

Place the opposite foot forward as the ball is being thrown.

Keep an eye on the target while throwing the ball.

Have your fingers point towards the target.

Shift your body weight from your back foot to your front foot as you throw.

3. Have the second child catch the ball using the following techniques:

Watch the ball all the way.

Keep your thumbs together if catching above the waist and your pinkies together if catching the ball below the waist.

Relax your hands upon impact of the ball.

4. Have children play catch at close distances until they are successful before moving to greater distances.

ACCOMMODATIONS

✔ Larger plastic balls could be used with younger children.

✔ The distance between partners can be adjusted for the children's ability level.

✔ Children who have more advanced throwing skills could be paired up with children who are still in the beginning stages of throwing development.

EXTENSIONS

✔ Different-size balls could be used. Children could use large balls for practice catching balls with two hands, small balls for practice catching with one hand.

✔ As children develop they could use two balls at one time.

✔ Balls with different textures and weights could also be tried: tennis, Nerf, beanbags, etc.

✔ For extra fun, water balloons could be used.

PHYSICAL ACTIVITY

Balloon Tapping

Balloon Tapping is an good eye-hand coordination activity for children. The activity helps children prepare for a number of games with balls.

LEARNING

✳ Improved eye-hand coordination
✳ Developing ball-controlling skills

MATERIALS

✳ Balloons (about 8 inches in diameter)
✳ An open area

STEPS

1. Provide each child with a round balloon.

2. Tell the children they are to toss the balloon up into the air about 4 feet above their heads and try to tap the balloon as many times as they can without the balloon touching the ground.

3. Techniques to suggest to the children include:

   Keep your thumbs together with your fingers spread far apart.

   Hit the balloon softly with your fingertips.

   Keep your eye on the balloon.

4. At times have the children try to tap the balloon higher or lower into the air.

 ACCOMMODATIONS

✔ You can adjust the size of the balloons to the children's level of development. Younger children should use larger balloons.

 EXTENSIONS

✔ Children could be required to stay within a certain area while tapping the balloons.

✔ Children could try tapping or hitting the balloons with a racket or stick.

✔ Children could partner up and try to keep the balloon in the air by alternating who taps it.

✔ Various types of balls could be used.

PHYSICAL ACTIVITY

Kick to the Stick

Kick to the Stick *can be used to help children developing kicking skills. The activity also helps children develop eye-foot coordination, kicking control, and accuracy.*

LEARNING

* Kicking with control
* Kicking with accuracy
* Eye-foot coordination

MATERIALS

* A 3-foot stake
* A soccer ball (note several kicking areas could be set up with one stake and one ball each)

STEPS

1. Place a stake in the ground so about 2½ feet of the stake is above ground. About 4 feet from the stake set up a kicking line where a soccer ball will be placed.

2. Tell the children they are to stand behind the soccer ball and use a foot to try to kick the ball so it hits the stake.

3. Make the following suggestions to the children:

   Try to hit the ball with the inside of your foot.

   Try to make an imaginary line between the ball and stake.

   Keep your eye on the ball when kicking.

   Try to have your foot kick straight at the stake.

4. At first have the children stand still when they are trying to kick the ball.

5. After they are successful kicking the ball with their preferred, or dominant, foot have them try to kick with their other foot.

6. As children become successful in kicking the ball to the stake, have them try to step up to the soccer ball and kick it in one motion.

7. Have children start two steps behind the ball. They should move the foot they are going to kick the ball with first, then move the opposite foot, and then kick the ball with the foot they used for their first step: step with right foot, step with left foot, step and kick with right foot.

8. The soccer ball can be moved further away from the stake as children become more accurate with their kicks.

(continued)

PHYSICAL ACTIVITY

Kick to the Stick *(continued)*

ACCOMMODATIONS

✔ The distances to kick the ball can be adjusted.

✔ For younger children boards could be set up about 3 feet apart to serve as borders between the kicking area and the stakes so the ball can be contained in a particular area.

EXTENSIONS

✔ Two stakes could be set up, and children could be asked to kick the ball between the stakes.

✔ The distance between the stakes could be adjusted to make the kicking task more challenging.

✔ Children could try to kick a slow moving ball. The child would stand in one spot and another child or the teacher would slowly roll the ball in a path in front of the child. The objective still would be to hit a stake or drive the ball between two stakes.

✔ Children could be paired up and asked to kick the ball straight to the partner across from them.

PHYSICAL ACTIVITY

Dribble the Ball

Dribble the Ball is a good activity to use in teaching children to control a ball by dribbling it. The activity is useful in developing eye–hand coordination and to prepare them for games and sports.

LEARNING

* The skill of dribbling
* Improved eye-hand coordination

MATERIALS

* Basketballs or other balls for dribbling
* An open area

STEPS

1. Provide children with a basketball. Alternatively, a smaller ball could be used.

2. Explain that they are going to learn how to dribble a ball.

3. When dribbling a ball they will need to practice the following techniques:

Keep their eye on the ball to start with.

Spread their fingers far apart so they cover more of the ball.

Practice a pushing-down motion rather than a slapping motion.

Try to dribble the ball to the same height each time.

Keep the ball close to your body but away from your feet.

4. As children begin to dribble the ball with some success the following may be emphasized:

Dribble the ball while looking to the right or left of the ball.

Dribble the ball to different heights.

Dribble the ball while taking one step.

CRITICAL THINKING CHALLENGE

Additional dribbling drills could be set up for children who are more advanced in their dribbling:
1. Dribble while moving forward, backward, or side to side.
2. Dribble while moving around or between objects.
3. Dribble two balls at one time.
4. Dribble a ball that has more or less bounce to it.
5. Dribble with alternating hands.

ACCOMMODATIONS

✔ The size of the balls can be changed to meet the developmental needs of children. Lighter and smaller balls could be used by younger children.

PHYSICAL ACTIVITY

Chapter 13

Fitness

Activities developed for this chapter fit the areas of flexibility, exercise, and muscular development. Activities involving flexibility help children to practice stretching activities and have children develop a wide range of movements for their body parts. Flexibility activities can serve as good warm-up activities for sports and physical games. Activities in the category of exercise are helpful for stretching and for developing endurance. They also provide children with a good set of healthy cardiovascular activities to use to become physically fit. Muscular development activities help children develop muscular strength and endurance.

Toe Touching

Toe Touching is a good activity to use as a warm-up to games, sports, or other exercise activities. It is also a good flexibility activity for working on body movements.

MATERIALS

✳ An open play space
✳ Gym or floor mats (optional)

STEPS

1. Have the children spread out in an open indoor or outdoor area. Start by having them stand up straight and try to touch their toes, bending at the waist. Use gym mats or floor mats if they are available.

2. Have children try to touch their right toe with both hands, then their left toe with both hands. Children can also try to touch their left toe with their right hand, a crossing over movement.

3. While children are touching their toes, count to 5 or 10 before they stop.

4. Have children sit straight up on the floor with their legs extended. Have them slowly bend forward and try to touch their toes with their hands. They can also try to touch their right toe with their left hand, their left toe with their right hand, and so on.

CRITICAL THINKING CHALLENGE

Have children come up with other types of stretching activities involving their toes, elbows, or knees. For example, how many different body parts can you use to touch your knees?

ACCOMMODATIONS

✔ If children are not flexible enough to touch their toes, they could instead touch their ankles or knees.

✔ Children could also be given short sticks to assist them in touching their toes.

EXTENSIONS

✔ Have children keep track of their flexibility movements.

PHYSICAL ACTIVITY

Touch the Sky

Touch the Sky can be used to develop flexibility in the movements of children. It can also be used as a warm-up activity before participating in active games and sports.

LEARNING

✳ Developing flexible body movement
✳ Practicing a warm-up activity
✳ Developing a sense of balance

MATERIALS

✳ A space for children to lift their arms without touching other children

STEPS

1. Have the children stand so they are not touching one another. They could be in a gym, behind their chair in the classroom, or in another appropriate location.

2. First have children stand flat-footed and tell them to slowly move their arms from their sides over their heads. They should reach as high to the sky as they can with their feet flat on the ground. Tell them to hold the position for 5 to 10 seconds.

3. Have them slowly lower their arms back down to their sides.

4. Repeat the activity.

5. Instruct children to slowly raise their arms over their heads to the sky again, but this time they should stand on their tiptoes.

6. Count to 5 or 10 again.

7. Have them slowly lower their arms to their sides.

8. Have children raise only their right arm (their left arm should stay at their side) above their heads to the sky with their feet flat on the ground. Count to 5 or 10 and then have them slowly lower their arms.

9. Have the children repeat the activity using their left arm.

10. Have the children go through the same activities trying to stand on only one leg.

ACCOMMODATIONS

✔ The teacher should attempt only those activities for which children can maintain a certain degree of balance.

✔ The length of time to hold one's position can increase or decrease depending on the continued performances of the children.

EXTENSIONS

✔ Children can also be asked to stretch their arms out as far as they can to their right or left sides while keeping their feet flat on the ground.

✔ Children could repeat many of the same movements with their arms while in a sitting or kneeling position.

PHYSICAL ACTIVITY

Shadow Images

Shadow Images is a fun activity that allows children to develop flexibility in their movements.

LEARNING

* Developing flexibility in movements
* Developing creative ways to demonstrate flexibility

MATERIALS

* Large white bed sheet
* Bright lamp or other lighting source

STEPS

1. In a darkened room hang a large white bed sheet to be used as a screen.

2. Set up a lamp or other lighting source 5 feet behind the screen so the light shines through the sheet.

3. Have two children at a time go through a set of flexibility movements standing behind the sheet with the light behind them. The other children can observe their movements from in front of the sheet.

4. Inform the children that one part of their body must be stationary for each flexibility movement they do. They can stand on one foot while they slowly bend or move their arms. They could keep two hands on the floor along with one foot while the other foot moves about.

5. Each set of children should take a turn.

ACCOMMODATIONS

✓ Children could also move outside and use the sun to create shadow movements.

EXTENSIONS

✓ Children could act out simple events using flexible movements. For example, they could demonstrate the life cycle of a human: baby, child, adult, older adult.

✓ An option would be to have children draw a card with a flexibility challenge such as one elbow, one hand, and one foot must be touching the ground.

PHYSICAL ACTIVITY

Move to the Music

Move to the Music is a fun activity for all children. The activity allows for children to develop their imagination as they do flexible movements to music.

LEARNING

✳ Developing creative body movements

✳ Developing flexibility and balance

MATERIALS

✳ Several types of music to move to (could be loud, fast, etc.)

✳ Open space

✳ Radio or CD player

STEPS

1. Have children spread out in an open indoor or outdoor area. They could be asked to stand on a square piece of carpeting or stand within a hoop.

2. Tell children that you are going to play some music for them. When they hear the music they are to create some flexible movements and move with the music.

3. Remind children that while they are doing their movements at least one body part must be stationary and touching the ground.

4. Use several types of music for children to move to.

ACCOMMODATIONS

✔ To create interest, appropriate music that children are familiar with (popular music) could be mixed in with less-familiar music.

EXTENSIONS

✔ Children could be asked to create movements with partners or groups of three or four.

✔ Children could practice doing synchronized movements to music. Each group of children could come up with its own set of movements.

Rope Movements

Rope Movements *is a great activity to use with children to encourage invented flexible movements.*

LEARNING

* Inventing flexible movements
* Developing flexibility in body movements

MATERIALS

* Open space
* 2-to 3-foot rope for each child

STEPS

1. Give each child a piece or rope about 2 to 3 feet long.

2. Tell the children they are to hold onto the end of the ropes with their hands.

3. Once children are ready, tell them they are going to try to move the rope around their body in different ways.

4. As a warm-up activity have each child take his or her rope (being held by both hands) and to try to lift his or her leg and slide the rope over his or her foot so it is on the inseam side of the leg. (Tell children that jumping rope is not a movement to include at this time.)

5. Tell the children that they can stand, sit, kneel, or lie on the floor while they move the rope around their different body parts. For example, while they are on the floor they could try to slide the rope under their legs and all the way up past their back and over their head.

6. After children have a chance to invent their own movements with the rope, they can volunteer to share their favorite movement. The other children could be asked to reproduce the movement.

CRITICAL THINKING CHALLENGE

Children can work together and see if they can move one or both ropes under, over, or around each other or both of them at the same time.

ACCOMMODATIONS

✓ The length of the rope can be changed to make the activity more or less challenging.

✓ Children might be given more examples to begin with to gain a better understanding of what is expected of them.

EXTENSIONS

✓ Elastic material could be used.

PHYSICAL ACTIVITY

Self-Paced Race

Self–Paced Race is an activity that helps children utilize a variety of locomotor movements as part of an exercise program. The activity allows children to practice running, skipping, and hopping over a predetermined distance.

LEARNING

* ❋ Demonstrating the ability to run, skip, and hop
* ❋ One way to exercise

MATERIALS

* ❋ A space to run some distance
* ❋ Whistle

STEPS

1. Have the children line up in one corner of the gym or playground area.

2. Tell them that they are going to participate in a distance movement activity in which they will run, skip, and hop.

3. Tell children that some of them may complete more laps, which is OK. Each child should try to get as far as he or she can.

4. The first time the activity is used, you might want to observe when fatigue sets in for children and end the activity. As children become less fatigued the time can be extended.

5. The number of laps to be completed can be determined by the area available. In a small gym you might have children do more laps.

6. Tell children that they will start the self-paced race running. When they hear the whistle blow they will be told to start skipping and so on.

7. Adjust the distances for each of the movements. Children could be asked to run a lap, skip only one side of the gym, etc.

8. At times they can be asked to do some of the movements backward.

9. The activity can take place over time, allowing children time to improve their personal best distance.

 ACCOMMODATIONS

✔ The types of movements you include and how far children are to perform each can vary depending on the developmental abilities of children.

✔ A specific amount of time to cover the distance can also be varied depending on the age levels of the children.

 EXTENSIONS

✔ With older children you could try to measure and record their pulse rates before and after the race.

✔ Additional movements such as galloping, walking, and leaping could be added.

✔ As you identify the distances that individuals cover you could pair up children who complete the same distances. The pairs could work together to set new goals for themselves.

PHYSICAL ACTIVITY

Step Up and Down

Step Up and Down *helps children develop leg strength and endurance.*

MATERIALS

✳ Curb or some other object to step onto and off

STEPS

1. Use a curb around the school grounds. If a curb is not available, railroad ties or a 4-by-6-inch piece of wood could be used.

2. Tell the children they are going to practice stepping up and down on the curb to learn another way to exercise.

3. Announce the time in 30-second intervals after they start. Each child should try to go as long as he or she can.

4. The technique to use is

   Step up onto the curb with one foot.

   Bring the second foot onto the top of the curb.

   Bring one foot down off the curb.

   Bring the second foot down off the curb.

   Continue to repeat the same pattern.

5. When starting the activity you might want to pace the children by saying, "on the curb, off the curb" at a particular speed.

6. To vary the activity, you can increase or slow down the tempo.

ACCOMMODATIONS

✔ The tempo for stepping on and off the curb along with the total amount of time for the activity can be adjusted to the individual needs of children.

EXTENSIONS

✔ Higher or lower objects might be tried, or children may start on the curb.

PHYSICAL ACTIVITY

Move to the Music

Move to the Music is a good exercise activity for children. Children can be in constant motion while following the tempo of the music.

LEARNING

❋ Creative way to exercise
❋ Developing endurance through movement

MATERIALS

❋ Radio or CD player
❋ Large open space
❋ Music (some that has an upbeat tempo and some with a slow tempo)

STEPS

1. Have the children spread out in an open play area. Inform them that they are going to exercise by moving to music.

2. Tell the children they can do any movements they want. This is not a dance activity.

3. In performing their movements they should try not to touch or bump into other children.

4. Start with the music that has a slow tempo, and then play the music that has an upbeat tempo. Finish the movement activity with some slow-down music.

5. The first time you do the activity you may want to observe when fatigue sets in. This will help you determine the appropriate time length for the activity. As time goes on, the time period can be extended.

6. For younger children you may want to model some movements to get them started.

 ACCOMMODATIONS

✔ To motivate children you may want to select some music that children are familiar with.

✔ The length of time for the music to play can be adjusted depending on the developmental level of the children.

 EXTENSIONS

✔ You can have children pair up and have them try to make some movements in unison.

✔ Children could be asked to make movements like a butterfly, a tree being blown by the wind, a monkey, etc.

Ribbon Motion

Ribbon Motion *can be a fun activity for young children to use as part of an exercise program. The activity also helps children to become more agile.*

LEARNING

* Developing agility
* Developing endurance
* Knowledge of a way to exercise

MATERIALS

* Music (radio or CD player)
* Open space for movement
* Two ribbons per child about 4 feet long (all one color or a variety of colors)

STEPS

1. Have children space themselves some distance from one another in an open area.

2. Pass out a ribbon to each child.

3. Tell them that they are to make movements using the ribbons as they listen to some music.

4. Play a short segment of a song, and model the ribbon movement activity.

5. Start the music and allow children to create their own movements.

6. Pass out a second ribbon to each child, and repeat the activity.

7. Observe children to see when they start to get fatigued.

 ACCOMMODATIONS

✔ Shorter ribbons could be given to younger children.

✔ The length of time children are to move with their ribbons to the music can be adjusted depending on the age of the children.

 EXTENSIONS

✔ Children could take turns showing a ribbon movement and having other children try to reproduce the movement. Movements in unison could also be tried between two children.

Children's Walk-a-thon

Children's Walk-a-thon is a fun way of having children exercise using a variety of movements. Children's balance is also reinforced through the activity.

LEARNING

❋ How to exercise with walking
❋ Developing balance

MATERIALS

❋ An open area or trail

STEPS

1. Find a trail for children to walk on. An open area in a gym or on a playground could also be used.

2. Tell the children they are going to go on a walk. While on the walk they will be asked to walk in some unusual ways. Start by having children walk like they normally do.

3. After the walk has started, suggest different ways children are to walk. Some possible different ways to walk would be

sideways	with toes pointing out
on toes only	with toes pointing in
on heels only	backward
with arms at one's side	with arms over one's head
taking short steps	taking long steps
slowly	faster
with high steps	with low steps

4. Determine the length or amount of time for the walk based on the energy level of the children. The length of time or distance can be extended as the activity is repeated.

ACCOMMODATIONS

✔ The distance and amount of time assigned to the different walking styles may be adjusted depending on the abilities of the children. For example, younger children may walk on their toes for a very short time.

EXTENSIONS

✔ The walking activities can be mixed with running or other locomotor movements.

✔ Children could practice walking in unison at different speeds, two abreast or four abreast.

✔ Young children could reinforce the concept of left and right by calling out "right, left" as they walk.

Curl It Up

Curl It Up is a traditional form of exercise. It can develop endurance as well as muscular strength.

LEARNING

❋ Using curl ups as a form of exercise
❋ Building endurance
❋ Building muscular strength

MATERIALS

❋ Gym or another open area
❋ Gym mats or rugs (optional)

STEPS

1. Have the children lie down on the floor. Providing gym pads or rugs for the children would be helpful.

2. Have them clasp their hands behind their necks.

3. Have them bend their knees so they are several inches off the ground.

4. Tell the children they are to use their arms to lift their head up several inches off the ground.

5. Tell children to take their time and try several curls.

6. Observe to ensure children are doing curls correctly.

7. After a few trials, have children start their curls together and have them hold their heads up off the floor while you count to 10. Then they are to let their heads down slowly. If they get tired they can slowly let their heads down before 10.

ACCOMMODATIONS

✔ Allow children to move their head as far as they are able to and hold their head off the ground until they need to let their head back down.

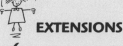

EXTENSIONS

✔ As children become familiar with the activity you can have them try different movements with their arms as they lift their head off the ground. For example, once their head is lifted off the ground, children could try to move their arms and head from left to right.

✔ A variation could be tried in which children move their arms from behind their head to their chest area.

PHYSICAL ACTIVITY

Elastic Tug-of-war

Elastic Tug-of-war is a good activity to work on body strength as well as balance and agility.

LEARNING

✳ Developing body strength

✳ Developing control of one's body

MATERIALS

✳ 12-foot elastic rope

✳ Ribbon

✳ Winning place marker

✳ Grassy or sandy area

STEPS

1. Put together an elastic rope about 10 to 12 feet long with a ribbon tied to the middle of the rope. Have two or three children form a team and stand at each end of the rope.

2. Set the rope up in the grassy or sandy area.

3. Start by having each team get positioned on their side of the rope, holding the rope with both hands. Make sure the ribbon is in the middle between the two teams.

4. Draw a line or set a narrow board underneath the ribbon to mark the winning line.

5. The object is to pull all three opposing team members across the line.

ACCOMMODATIONS

✔ If a 12-foot elastic rope is not available a regular rope can be used, or two shorter pieces of rope could be tied to a shorter elastic piece that would be set in the middle.

EXTENSIONS

✔ Smaller or larger teams can be formed.

✔ One end of the rope could be tied to a wagon (not held by a second team) with rocks added to it, and each team could try to pull the wagon across the winning line.

✔ The rope could be tied to a set of car tires, and each team would be challenged to pull as many tires as possible past the winning line.

PHYSICAL ACTIVITY

Leg Push

Leg Push helps children develop leg strength.

2. Tell them that when they are told to they should push as hard as they can against the wall for 10 seconds.

3. When the 10 seconds are up, they should relax until they are told to repeat the pushing.

4. Have children complete the activity about five times to start with. The number of trials can be increased each day as children continue to do the exercise.

ACCOMMODATIONS

✔ Younger children can be asked to push as hard as they can for shorter amounts of time or be assigned to do fewer repetitions at the start.

EXTENSIONS

✔ Children could be paired up across from each other and be asked to push their feet against each other.

✔ To work with different amounts of force, children could be asked to start each pushing movement with light pressure, then increase the pressure, hold the increased pressure, and finally lighten up the pressure.

PHYSICAL ACTIVITY

Hang Time

Hang Time is a muscular development activity that helps children develop their shoulder strength.

MATERIALS

❋ A chin-up bar or another secured type of hanging pole

❋ Step stool

STEPS

1. Have the children line up in front of a chin-up bar. Tell them that each child will have an opportunity to participate.

2. The bar should be at a height such that children's feet will not touch the ground if their chin is above the pole.

3. Tell the children that the object of the muscle development activity is to see how long they can hang from the bar using their hands to hold them up with their chin remaining above the bar.

4. Tell children that you will help lift them so their chin is above the bar, *or* they can use a small step stool to step up.

5. When a child is ready tell him or her you will let go or move the step stool. You can help children down or replace the step stool when they need to end.

6. Tell children they should try not to swing or move while hanging on the bar.

ACCOMMODATIONS

✔ A mat can be placed below the pole so children can drop down safely.

EXTENSIONS

✔ Two children could hold a pole or stick with their arms out straight and pull as hard as they can without moving the other child.

PHYSICAL ACTIVITY

Bridge Making

Bridge Making is an excellent activity to use to help children develop endurance using their leg, arm, and shoulder muscles.

LEARNING

❋ Developing muscular endurance

❋ Developing balance

MATERIALS

❋ Open grassy area (other surfaces could be used)

STEPS

1. Have them spread themselves out on a grassy surface.

2. Tell them they are going to make bridges with their bodies. Ask them if they have gone over bridges. What did they notice about the bridges?

3. Have the children start out by positioning themselves so their hands and feet are the only body parts touching the ground. They should be facing the ground with their hands and feet about as far apart as their shoulders.

4. After children demonstrate their bridges, have them rest by placing their knees on the ground.

5. Tell the children they are going to make a series of different types of bridges. They should hold the bridge position until they are told to go back to the rest position or until they can no longer hold it.

6. Have children rebuild their bridge with two hands and feet touching the ground.

7. Ask them to build a tall bridge: move their feet closer to their hands so their backside moves up high into the air.

8. Other bridge positions children can try are

   Make a low bridge.

   Make a narrow bridge with your hands and feet positioned next to each other.

   Make a wide bridge with your hands and feet positioned far out to your sides.

   Make a bridge with two hands and one foot touching the ground.

   Make a swaying bridge (move back and forth).

9. A reminder: after children make each of the different bridges they should be allowed to go back to their rest position with their knees touching the ground.

(continued)

PHYSICAL ACTIVITY

Bridge Making *(continued)*

ACCOMMODATIONS	**EXTENSIONS**
✔ The type of bridges to be made might vary depending on the strength children have.	✔ Children could be paired up to try to find creative ways of making longer bridges by using two people.
✔ If needed, children could have a cushion or other object placed under their midsection to give them support as they move their feet or hands further apart.	✔ Children could use the same techniques to try to build hills. For example, they could be asked to make a high, steep hill.
	✔ Children could use a chair to make bridges. They could place their feet or hands on top of a chair and move their hands or feet closer to or further from the chair.

Games

Chapter 14

This chapter on games provides teachers with a series of activities to use in developing physical as well as social skills. The games listed are designed to have children participate together or individually. Many games foster collaboration or goal setting with self-improvement options for children. The games also allow for the development of physical skills such as locomotor movement, balance, agility, muscular strength, or creative movements.

Kick Golf

Kick Golf is a fun game that reinforces kicking accuracy in children.

LEARNING

❋ Developing kicking accuracy

❋ Reinforcing addition skills

MATERIALS

❋ Five or six flags, cups, or tincans filled with heavy material for holes

❋ Kick ball

❋ Scorecards and pencils

❋ Open area

STEPS

1. In an open grassy area set up five or six golf holes. Flags can be stuck into the ground, or tin cans filled with heavy material can be set out to serve as the golf holes. Set up a tee area (starting point) for each hole.

2. Tell children that the objective is to try to hit the flag or cup with as few kicks as possible.

3. Each time a child kicks the ball he or she has to wait for the ball to stop before kicking it again. The child continues to kick the ball until the ball hits the flag or can for the hole.

4. Children can be given a simple scorecard to keep track of their scores. After they finish the last hole they can add up their scores. The computation can be checked and scores recorded on individual charts.

Kick Golf Scorecard						
Name	Hole 1 Score	Hole 2 Score	Hole 3 Score	Hole 4 Score	Hole 5 Score	Score Total

ACCOMMODATIONS

✓ The length of the course can be adjusted to the abilities of the children.

✓ The layout of the course can be made easier (all flat) for beginners.

EXTENSIONS

✓ Adjustments could be made in the course to have children practice making short or long kicks. For example, the course may provide for a shortcut to practice controlling the distances they kick the ball.

✓ Cardboard boxes and other materials could be set up on the holes to have children kick the ball in different directions with control.

✓ Children could go around the course using their dominant foot or less dominant foot.

✓ Children could play in teams, with each child on the team taking a turn kicking the ball.

Balloon Volleyball

Balloon Volleyball is a fun game for children to participate in. The game reinforces tapping skills along with eye-hand coordination. Any number of children can play.

LEARNING

* Following rules
* Developing tapping skills
* Developing eye-hand coordination

MATERIALS

* Balloon 8 inches or more in diameter
* Ropes or board for the centerline marker and boundaries of the court

STEPS

1. Form two teams with an equal number of players. Teams will be on opposite sides of the court, which is marked off by a rope on the ground.

2. Boundaries can be set up by marking each side and the back of the court.

3. Start by having a child on one team tap the balloon (serve) across the centerline.

4. Each team must have at least three different players tap the balloon on their side before it can be tapped back across the rope to the other team. No player can tap the balloon twice in a row.

5. Children should rotate positions on the courts each time a point is scored.

6. If the balloon touches the ground while a team is hitting it on their side of the net the other team gets one point. Likewise, if the team hits the balloon across the net outside the boundaries, the other team gets one point.

7. The first team to get 15 points wins the match.

PHYSICAL ACTIVITY

ACCOMMODATIONS

✔ The size of the court can be made larger for older children.

✔ Smaller teams of three or four can be used so children get more chances to tap the balloon.

EXTENSIONS

✔ Two or more balloons could be put into play at one time if a larger group of children was playing.

Sticker Hop-Tag

Sticker Hop-Tag is a fun game that helps children develop balance, hopping skills, and muscular endurance.

LEARNING

* Developing balance
* Developing the skill of hopping
* Developing muscular endurance

MATERIALS

* An enclosed play area
* Stickers

STEPS

1. Set up a game space large enough for your children to move around somewhat freely. An area of 20-by-20 feet is appropriate for 20 children.

2. Form two teams with an equal number of children on each team.

3. Tell the children that the only way to move around in the game is by hopping on one foot.

4. Each game will have two sets. In the first set each member of Team A will be given a sticker. The objective is for each member of Team A to slap (lightly) a sticker on a member of Team B. Only one sticker can be placed on a person.

5. Once a member of Team B is slapped with a sticker he or she has to freeze and hold one arm in the air to let players know he or she has been stuck.

6. Team A will have 15 seconds to try to slap a sticker on each member of Team B.

7. One point will be awarded for each member of Team B who is slapped with a sticker.

8. In the second set, Team B will be given the stickers and try to stick each member of Team A. The same procedures will be followed.

9. Depending upon the amount of time available, a number of games can be played.

ACCOMMODATIONS

✔ The play area can be made larger for older children who can hop faster and further.

✔ If not all children can hop well on one foot, children could be required to jump with two feet.

✔ The amount of time for each set could be extended.

EXTENSIONS

✔ Children could use different locomotor movements as they play the game. For example, in the first round they could be required to hop on one foot and in the second round they could be asked to skip.

PHYSICAL ACTIVITY

Rope Race

Rope Race is a fun game that allows children to practice the locomotor movements of running and skipping. The activity also requires children to make accommodations for the movement of others.

LEARNING

❋ Developing running and skipping skills

❋ Accommodating for the movement and speed of others

MATERIALS

❋ Racing area or track

❋ One rope about 6 feet long for each team

❋ Paper to record results

STEPS

1. Set up an area or track for team racing. Assign children to teams so each team has three or four members.

2. Give each team a rope about 6 feet long.

3. Tell children that all teams will race from the starting line to the finish line. As they run the race all team members have to have at least one hand on the rope.

4. Run a practice race. After the practice race give children some time to talk about how they can better coordinate their team running.

5. Have children run the first race. How children finish can be recorded. A team is finished when all members cross the finish line.

6. Next tell children that in the second race children will have to run backward holding onto the rope.

7. Let children practice for a while.

8. Run the second race. Results can be recorded.

9. For the third and last race, tell children that teams have to skip holding the rope.

10. Run the race. Results can be recorded

ACCOMMODATIONS

✔ The length of the race can be adjusted to meet the endurance levels of different children.

✔ If some younger children cannot skip, skipping can be eliminated from the race.

✔ Team members could be mixed up after each type of race so that more children have a chance of finishing in the top positions.

EXTENSIONS

✔ Teams could race one at a time and be timed with a stopwatch. Each team could run two races to see if they can better their time.

✔ Team members can be required to hold hands rather than use the rope to help develop more shoulder and arm strength.

Waist Pull

Waist Pull is a fun game for children that helps develop muscular strength and endurance.

LEARNING

* Developing muscular strength and endurance
* Peer coordination

MATERIALS

* Tape

STEPS

1. Assign two children to a team.
2. Tell the children that they will participate in a waist pulling game.
3. One member of each team will stand in front with his or her arms extended and hold both hands of a member of the second team. The second member of each team will stand behind his or her teammate and wrap his or her arms around the teammate's waist.
4. Use tape to make a line on the ground an equal distance between the two teams.
5. When told to start, each team must try to pull both the members of the other team over the line. The team that pulls the other team across the line is awarded the win.
6. If a player's hands pull away from a teammate's waist, the game is over and the other team is awarded a win.

 ACCOMMODATIONS

✔ Efforts should be made to have the team members average out in terms of height and muscular strength.

✔ Rather than holding hands, the teams could hold onto a short rope.

 EXTENSIONS

✔ For older children, teams can be made with more than two members.

Beanbag Horseshoes

Beanbag Horseshoes is a good game to help children work on eye-hand coordination and the skill of tossing.

LEARNING

* Improved eye-hand coordination
* Developing the skill of tossing
* Skip counting (add) by 3s

MATERIALS

- Three beanbags
- Two hoops (hoops could be formed by forming a rope into the shape of a circle or square)

STEPS

1. Set up two hoops in a line about 10 feet from each other.
2. Give the first child three beanbags.
3. Tell the child the object of the game is to get the beanbags to fall inside the hoop.
4. The child should stand alongside one hoop and toss a beanbag underhand to the hoop on the other side.
5. The child gets three points for each beanbag that lands on or in the hoop.
6. When the child is finished tossing the three beanbags, he or she should walk down to the hoop and add the points up.
7. The child will then toss the three beanbags back to the other hoop following the same procedures.
8. The goal is to try to earn 21 points.
9. Children can be paired up or teams can be formed.

ACCOMMODATIONS

✔ The distance between the two hoops can be adjusted depending on the success level of the children. If the beanbags consistently fall short of the hoop, move the hoop closer.

✔ The size and weight of the beanbags can be modified.

EXTENSIONS

✔ Several different-size hoops could be placed on the ground at each end. More points could be assigned when the beanbag lands in a smaller hoop.

PHYSICAL ACTIVITY

Lawn Curling

Lawn Curling a great game to use to help children develop muscular control.

LEARNING

✳ Muscular control

MATERIALS

✳ Paint or chalk
✳ Grassy surface
✳ Three softballs or other balls 4 to 6 inches in diameter

STEPS

1. Set up a curling field on a grassy surface.

2. On one end of the curling alley set a foul line, a line that children have to stay behind when rolling their ball.

CRITICAL THINKING CHALLENGE

Different-size balls or balls with different weights can be tried to vary the amount and type of muscular control to develop.

3. About 10 feet from the foul line down the grass alley, paint or use chalk to create an outer circle 4 feet in diameter and an inner circle 2 feet in diameter.

4. Tell the children that the object of the game is to roll a ball from behind the foul line down the grass alley and have it land within one of the circles.

5. Children will be given three balls to toss for each turn.

6. Five points can be awarded if the ball stops in the smaller circle and three points can be awarded if the ball lands in the larger circle.

7. The object is to get 18 or more points.

8. The game can be played by an individual, pairs, or larger teams.

ACCOMMODATIONS

✔ The size of the circles can be modified depending on the success of the children.

✔ The distance between the foul line and the circles can also be adjusted.

Hit the Shape

Hit the Shape is a good game to use to help children increase their ability to toss or throw an object to a target. The game can also increase children's understanding of shapes.

LEARNING

* Developing tossing and throwing skills
* Knowledge of shapes

MATERIALS

* Glue
* One 4-by-4-foot piece of plywood (thick cardboard could also be used)
* Different-size laminated shapes
* Four beanbags

STEPS

1. Glue a set of different-size laminated shapes to a 4-by-4-foot piece of plywood.
2. Give children the four beanbags to throw or toss.
3. Make a foul line (line not to be crossed by children when tossing or throwing the ball) about 10 feet from the plywood.
4. Children are to toss or throw the beanbags at the piece of plywood from behind the line so that they land on the different shapes.
5. Shapes can have different point values. The smaller the shape, the larger the point value.
6. Children can play against one another, or teams can be formed.
7. The child or team to earn a certain number of points first is identified as the winner.

CRITICAL THINKING CHALLENGE

Spelling words, vocabulary words, or other content to be learned could be placed on the shapes to add to the experience.

PHYSICAL ACTIVITY

ACCOMMODATIONS

✔ The distance the beanbags are to be tossed can be modified based on the tossing or throwing ability of the children.

✔ The size of the shapes used can also be modified.

✔ Young children can use easy shapes (square, oval, etc.), and older children can use harder shapes (octagon, trapezoid, etc.).

EXTENSIONS

✔ Children could be asked to toss the ball with their nondominant hand.

✔ Velcro objects could be tossed on an upright target.

Three Ball Soccer

Three Ball Soccer is a game that helps children to develop eye–foot coordination and to learn about angles.

LEARNING

* Developing eye-foot coordination
* Beginning understanding of angles

MATERIALS

* Four soccer balls
* Four soccer nets (large cardboard boxes could be substituted)
* Playing field about 20-by-20 feet

STEPS

1. Establish a playing field on grass about 20 feet wide and 20 feet long. Place a soccer net or large cardboard box in each corner of the playing area, similar to how bases are arranged on a baseball field.

2. In the middle of the field, set three soccer balls of different colors (or marked differently) next to each other in the form of a triangle.

3. Set a fourth, white soccer ball 5 feet from first three soccer balls. This will serve as the cue ball to start the game.

4. The object of the game is to have each of the participating children take turns kicking the cue ball into one of the other colored soccer balls in order to drive the ball into one of the four nets.

5. Points can be awarded to each child who kicks a soccer ball into a net (optional).

ACCOMMODATIONS

✔ The playing space can be enlarged to make the game more challenging.

✔ More nets could be added to provide more targets to kick the soccer balls into.

✔ The size of the nets could be changed to make the game easier or harder.

EXTENSIONS

✔ Children could use a plastic bat to try to hit the balls rather than kick them as they play the game.

PHYSICAL ACTIVITY

Wall Ball

Wall Ball is a game for older children in which they develop eye–hand coordination with a moving object.

LEARNING

❋ Improved eye-hand coordination

❋ Hitting moving objects

MATERIALS

❋ Wall or surface to hit tennis balls off

❋ Tennis balls

❋ Tape

❋ Different images for targets

STEPS

1. Use tape to make a rectangular border on the gym wall about 6 feet high and 8 feet wide.

2. Tape five or six 1-by-1-foot images inside the rectangle.

3. Tape a line on the floor about 6 feet from the wall.

4. Tell children the object of the game is to hit a tennis ball at the wall and try to hit an image on the wall. Three children could be lined up at each wall area.

5. Children should stand behind the line, drop the tennis ball, and hit it as it bounces up off the floor with their hand toward one of the images on the wall.

6. Point values can be assigned to the images (optional).

ACCOMMODATIONS

✔ The line can be moved closer to or farther from the wall to accommodate the abilities of the children.

✔ Young children could be asked to simply toss the ball at the larger images.

✔ Images used could reflect different classroom concepts, types of foods, etc.

EXTENSIONS

✔ Children could try to keep the ball moving by hitting it back to the wall each time without catching it and bouncing it off the floor.

✔ Children could use tennis rackets or other types of rackets.

PHYSICAL ACTIVITY

Tile Jump

Tile Jump is a fun strategy game for children to engage in.

LEARNING

* ❋ Reinforcing jumping skills
* ❋ Strategy making with movement

MATERIALS

* ❋ Tiles or square pieces of carpet (1-by-1-foot cardboard squares could be taped to the floor if tiles are not available)
* ❋ A number of 3-by-5-inch cards
* ❋ Music and radio or CD player

STEPS

1. Set out a number of tiles or square pieces of carpet on a playing surface. Have three fewer tiles than the number of children.

2. Explain to the children that they are to start jumping from one location to another (not on the tiles) when they hear the music playing. They cannot jump up and down in the same location near a tile.

3. When the music stops they are to jump onto one of the tiles on the floor.

4. Two children cannot jump onto the same tile.

5. Give a card to the three children who do not have a tile to jump onto. Children will also get a card if they do not jump to different locations while the music is being played.

6. The goal of the game to avoid getting any cards.

7. Once the cards are passed out, all children will get set for the next round.

8. The teacher can determine the number of times the music will play.

ACCOMMODATIONS

✓ The length of time the music plays should be aligned with the endurance levels of the children.

EXTENSIONS

✓ Other locomotor movements could be used, such as skipping and walking.

Falling Styrofoam™

Falling Styrofoam™ is a noncompetitive game that helps children develop their eye-hand coordination.

LEARNING

❋ Developing eye-hand coordination

MATERIALS

❋ Hats or caps (children are to bring them from home)

❋ Styrofoam™ packing peanuts (pieces of paper cut into 1-inch squares or other soft material could be substituted)

❋ Small boxes

❋ Large sheet for floor to help with cleaning up (optional)

STEPS

1. Have children bring hats or caps from home for this game.

2. Six children can play the game at one time.

3. Fill several small boxes full of Styrofoam™ packing peanuts.

4. Tell children you are going to throw Styrofoam™ packing peanuts into the air one box at a time.

5. With their hats turned upside down, the children are to catch as many of the falling Styrofoam™ packing peanuts as possible. The teacher may wish to place a large sheet on the floor ahead of time to help with cleaning up.

6. Children should be instructed to hold their caps slightly above their heads so they can keep their eyes on the Styrofoam™ peanuts as the peanuts are falling.

ACCOMMODATIONS

✔ For younger children more Styrofoam™ pieces should be used to help children have more success catching.

EXTENSIONS

✔ Older children could try to catch the pieces with their hands.

✔ Children could be paired up and given small plastic grocery bags to try to catch the Styrofoam™ pieces.

✔ If safety glasses are available, Ping-Pong balls and other slightly harder objects could be used with older children.

PHYSICAL ACTIVITY

Milk Jug Catch

Milk Jug Catch is a fun activity to use in helping children improve their throwing and catching skills.

LEARNING

❋ Developing throwing and catching skills
❋ Improving eye-hand coordination

MATERIALS

❋ 1-gallon plastic milk jugs with the bottom cut out (baseball caps could be substituted)
❋ Tennis balls
❋ Open play area
❋ Whistle

STEPS

1. Have children form teams with five or six children on a team.

2. Have two teams line up about 10 feet apart. The children on each team should stand in a row about 10 to 12 feet apart from one another.

3. Each player should have a 1-gallon plastic milk jug with the bottom cut out so the handle and narrow top end (turned up side down) can be used as a glove.

4. When the whistle blows, the first child on each team is to throw a tennis ball to the second child on his or her team, who is to catch the ball using the milk jug.

5. If the child does not catch the ball, the ball needs to be thrown back to the first team member, who is to throw it again. Later, if the third child does not catch the ball from the second team member, the ball goes back to the second player to be thrown again.

6. The team whose last team member catches the ball first is considered to be the winning team.

ACCOMMODATIONS

✔ Older children could use smaller containers for catching the ball.

✔ The distance between the team member throwing the ball and the team member catching the ball can be shortened depending on the children's throwing skill level.

EXTENSIONS

✔ Children could be asked to throw the ball backward over their heads to the team members.

✔ On hot days the plastic milk jugs could be set aside and water balloons might be used.

✔ Children could be required to throw two separate tennis balls, with each team member being required to catch two in a row.

PHYSICAL ACTIVITY

Get Me if You Can

Get Me if You Can is a fun game for children to play while they are working on ball-kicking skills. The game also helps children to improve their perception of moving objects.

LEARNING

✳ Developing kicking skills

✳ Improving perception of moving objects

MATERIALS

✳ Open play area

✳ Three utility balls about 1 foot in diameter

STEPS

1. Have a group of children form a circle about 20 feet in diameter. (The diameter may vary depending on how many children are participating in the game.)

2. Assign three or four children to move into the middle of the circle.

3. Pass out three utility balls about 1 foot in diameter to three children forming the circle.

4. Inform the children forming the circle that they are to try to hit the children in the middle of the circle by kicking the ball. Be sure to tell the children to kick the ball gently.

5. Inform the children in the middle of the circle that they are to try to avoid being hit by the kicked balls.

6. The game ends when there is only one child left in the middle of the circle.

TEACHER NOTE

Caution should be taken to ensure that children are not kicking the ball too hard or too high.

 ## ACCOMMODATIONS

✔ The size of the circle may vary depending on the kicking strength of the children participating in the game.

✔ More or fewer balls could be added to slow down or speed up the game.

 ## EXTENSIONS

✔ The game could be played by having children roll or throw the balls.

✔ Two teams could be formed. Each team would take turns being the kickers. The winning team could be determined by the number of players left in the circle after a specific time limit.

PHYSICAL ACTIVITY

The Seven-Event Challenge

The Seven-Event Challenge is a great event for children to participate in.
A variety of physical activities can be built into the event.

LEARNING

❋ Reinforcing physical development

MATERIALS

❋ Parent volunteers
❋ Golf ball
❋ Basket
❋ Soccer ball
❋ Two cans
❋ Five hoops (or five pieces of rope to form the hoops)
❋ Small beach ball
❋ Eight folding chairs

STEPS

1. Set up the following seven-event physical obstacle course for children to participate in:

Event 1   *Skip* 10 yards.

Event 2   *Throw* a golf ball into a basket 6 feet away.

Event 3   *Kick* the soccer ball through two cans 8 feet away.

Event 4   *Jump* from hoop to hoop (five consecutive hoops placed 2 feet apart).

Event 5   *Balance* on one foot for 10 seconds.

Event 6   *Catch* a small beach ball from a person 8 feet away.

Event 7   *Run* through a row of 8 chairs (3 feet apart), then hop to the end line.

2. The course can be set up in a large circle on a playground or in a gym. One parent volunteer could be stationed at each event to assist children.

3. Each child's time can be recorded (optional).

ACCOMMODATIONS

✔ The events can be adjusted to meet the physical levels of children.

✔ The number of events can be modified.

EXTENSIONS

✔ Teams could be formed and the times of all team members added up.

✔ The obstacle course could be set up as a series of individual events to form a kind of physical development track meet for teams.

✔ Creative movement events can also be added, along with judges.

PHYSICAL ACTIVITY

Line Tag

Line Tag is an excellent game to use to develop balance, movement, and choice making in children.

LEARNING

* Developing body balance
* Choice making during movements

MATERIALS

* Large hard surface
* Tape

STEPS

1. Set up a series of interconnecting straight and curved lines on a gym floor or hard outdoor surface. The area should be large enough to accommodate your class.

2. Inform children that five of them will play *Line Tag* at one time.

3. The rules are as follows:

   * One child will be identified at the start as the tagger.
   * The tagger is to try to touch another child, who then will be the tagger.
   * Children must try to avoid the tagger.
   * All children must walk or run on the lines. If they step off a line to avoid a tag, they will become the tagger.
   * The game will last for 1 minute. At the end of the game whoever is the tagger will remain the tagger.

4. The tagger stays in the next game and starts as the tagger. A child cannot be a tagger for more than two games.

ACCOMMODATIONS

✓ Teachers should try to emphasize the movements of the children rather than focus comments on who is the tagger after each game.

✓ More children could be added to the game if there is enough space for children to move around in.

EXTENSIONS

✓ Children can use other movements such as walking backward and hopping on the line.

✓ More than one person could be the tagger when playing the game.

✓ If snow is available, pathways could be made in the snow to serve as the lines.

PHYSICAL ACTIVITY

Body Parts Memory Game

Body Parts Memory Game is a fun game for children to play. It helps reinforce knowledge of body parts and develops short-term memory.

LEARNING

* ❋ Knowledge of body parts
* ❋ Short-term memory development
* ❋ Following directions

MATERIALS

* ❋ Open area for movement

STEPS

1. Tell the children they are going to play a memory game. They will be told to touch different body parts in a particular sequence.

2. Start the game with a warm-up sequence: touch your right eye with your right hand and then touch your right ear with your left hand.

3. Once the sequence is given the teacher will say, "Start now."

4. After the children perform the sequence, model the sequence to reinforce the initial request.

5. All children can start on a line and if they get the sequence correct they can take one step forward (optional).

6. The following sequences could also be used:

   Touch your right knee with your left hand, then touch your right thumb to your nose.

   Shake your left foot, then bend your right arm at the wrist.

   Stand on your right foot, lift your left arm into the air, then touch your belly with the pinkle finger on your left hand.

   Jump in the air twice, scratch your left cheek with your left hand, then yawn once.

   Take one step back with your right foot, bend and touch your right foot with your left hand, then smile.

CRITICAL THINKING CHALLENGE

Students could be asked to create their own set of directions for other students within certain limits. For example, give other children a three-sequence memory task.

ACCOMMODATIONS

✔ Younger children may be given fewer directions to follow. For example, bend forward and touch your right hand with your nose.

✔ Older students could be given more detailed directions and more difficult body parts to identify. For example, touch the location of your right kidney with two fingers from your left hand.

EXTENSIONS

✔ Objects could be added to the memory game. Twirl the scarf with your right hand over your head, then drag the scarf with your left hand over your head starting at the back of your head and moving the scarf to the front of your head.

PHYSICAL ACTIVITY

Pass the Ball

Pass the Ball *is a game that develops flexibility in the movements of children.*

LEARNING

✳ Developing flexibility of movement

MATERIALS

✳ Utility ball or beach ball about 15 inches in diameter

✳ Open space

STEPS

1. Have children form two or more lines with at least five children in each line.

2. Tell the children that they are going to play a game called *Pass the Ball*. Inform the children that they will be passing the ball to the individual behind them. All teams are to stop once the pass has been passed back to all the players on their team.

3. Tell children there is a challenge to the game. They will not be using their hands to pass the ball.

4. Children will pass the ball back the first time by holding the ball with their elbows. Demonstrate to children how the ball can be held with the elbows. The player passing the ball should hold it with his or her elbows while the player getting the ball grabs it with his or her elbows.

5. If the ball is dropped it goes back to the player passing it to try again.

6. Emphasis should be on passing the ball without dropping it. Winners need not be identified.

7. Subsequent rounds could have the children pass the ball by

    using the back of their hands

    using their wrists

    using one wrist and one foot

    using two fingers from each hand

ACCOMMODATIONS

✔ Younger children may do some of the activities using one of their hands.

✔ The size of the ball can be adjusted.

✔ More or fewer children could be assigned to the groups, depending on how much time it takes to complete each task.

EXTENSIONS

✔ Other materials could be used, such as a stick, a basket, or a large piece of foam.

✔ Children can also be asked to pass a ball using their hands under their legs, over their heads, or around one side of their body.

✔ Children could be asked to pass the ball using their hands while blindfolded.

PHYSICAL ACTIVITY

Hoops and Rulers

Hoops and Rulers has a long history in various forms. The game helps children develop flexibility in their movements.

LEARNING

✳ Developing flexibility of movement

MATERIALS

✳ Hoops
✳ 12-inch rulers
✳ Open area

STEPS

1. Provide each team of four children with a hoop and a ruler.

2. Tell children the object of the game is to stand the hoop upright and move it across the floor by slapping the ruler over the top of the hoop in a forward motion.

3. Each team member should move the hoop 10 feet to a turn-around line and back to the starting point. Each team member will take a turn.

4. If the hoop falls to the ground, the player should pick it up and continue on.

ACCOMMODATIONS

✓ The distance to be traveled can be shortened for some children.

✓ Small bike tires could be used to gain better control.

EXTENSIONS

✓ Smaller objects could be tried. For example, a pencil and tin can could be tried on a minipath across a tabletop.

✓ Thread spools and toothpicks could also be tried to work with small motor flexibility.

✓ Obstacles could also be set up on a trail so children would have to move the hoop around objects.

Wand Balancing

Wand Balancing *can be used to help children improve their ability to balance objects.*

LEARNING

✳ Developing balance with objects

MATERIALS

✳ A wand for each child (An unsharpened pencil can be substituted.)

✳ Open space

STEPS

1. Pass out a wand or similar object to each child. Inform the children that they are going to use the wand to practice balancing techniques.

2. Have children go through the following balancing tasks:

   Balance the wand:

on one finger	on your knee
on your nose	on your chin
on your wrist	on your foot
on your head	on your shoulder

3. Children could try other body parts.

4. Inform the children they should count ("one thousand one, one thousand two," etc.) to see how long they can balance the wand.

ACCOMMODATIONS

✔ The length, diameter, and weight of the wand can vary. Older children may be asked to balance wands of greater length, etc.

EXTENSIONS

✔ Children could be asked to balance two wands at the same time.

✔ Children could also be asked to stand on one foot while balancing the wand on various body parts.

✔ Other objects such as small books, balls, rulers, pencils, and pipes can be tried.

PHYSICAL ACTIVITY

PHYSICAL ACTIVITY RESOURCES

Belka, D. (1994). *Teaching children games: Becoming a master teacher*. Champaign, IL: Human Kinetics.

Brehm, Madeleine, & Tindell, Nancy T. (1983). *Movement with a purpose: Perceptual motor-lesson plans for young children*. West Nyack, NY: Parker Publishing Company, Inc.

Buschner, Craig A. (1994). *Teaching children movement concepts and skills: Becoming a master teacher*. Champaign, IL: Human Kinetics.

Curtis, Sandra R. (1982). *The joy of movement in early childhood*. New York: Teachers College Press.

Flinchum, Betty M. (1975). *Motor development in early childhood: A guide for movement education with ages 2 to 6*. Saint Louis, MO: C.V. Mosby Company.

Hammett, Carol T. (1992). *Movement activities for early childhood*. Champaign, IL: Human Kinetics.

Hinson, C. (1995). *Fitness for children*. Champaign, IL: Human Kinetics.

Metteer, Richard. (n.d.). *Project success for the SLD child: Motor perception*. Wayne, NE: Wayne-Carroll School District.

Payne, G., & Isaacs, L. (1991). *Human motor development: A lifespan approach* (2nd ed.). Mountain View, CA: Mayfield.

Pettifor, Bonnie, (1999). *Physical education methods for classroom teachers*. Champaign, IL: Human Kinetics.

Pica, R. (1990). *Early elementary children moving and learning*. Champaign, IL: Human Kinetics.

Ridenour, M. (Ed.). (1978). *Motor development: Issues and applications*. Princeton, NJ: Princeton Book Co.

Unit 5

Science

The National Science Education Standards were published in 1996. The standards set out to provide schools with an outline of what children at different levels should know and be able to do to be scientifically literate. The elementary science curriculum for schools includes an understanding and knowledge of the following contents.

❋ **Physical Sciences:** Activities included for the physical sciences include investigations with properties and change, electricity, simple machines, magnets, and light and sound. From the activities children can develop an understanding of objects and materials, position and motion of objects, and forms of electricity and magnetism.

❋ **Life Sciences:** Activities included for the life sciences include the study of animals, plants, and humans. Children should develop an understanding of the characteristics of organisms, the life cycles of organisms, and how organisms interact with the environment.

❋ **Earth Sciences:** Activities included for the earth sciences are based on the topics of temperature, rocks and soils, environment, and space. As a result of the investigations and activities children should begin to understand properties and functions of the earth and space.

In addition to the major contents of the life, physical, and earth sciences the activities selected in this unit provide children with the opportunity to work with a number of process skills. Children will be involved in observing, classifying, hypothesizing, controlling variables, generalizing, and recording and reporting findings. In a number of activities students will experience phenomena and become involved in problem-solving situations. Children will participate in a number of investigations that engage them in experiences scientists go through as they discover new knowledge about our world.

Chapter 15

Physical Science

Activities developed for the physical sciences are centered around
the contents of properties and change, electricity, simple machines,
magnets, and light and sound. Children are involved in learning about
the properties of objects and about materials, about position and
motion of objects, and about the different uses and functions of
electricity and magnets. Through investigations they also have the
opportunity to develop their abilities to observe, classify,
hypothesize, control variables, and make generalizations based
on data.

307

See How It Changes

See How It Changes is an activity to be used with children to develop the concept of properties in change. It is a good activity to use to form the process skills of describing, observing, and hypothesizing.

LEARNING

* Changes in properties
* Process skills of describing, observing, and hypothesizing
* Reasoning with changes in properties

MATERIALS

* Three clear 6-to-8-ounce plastic cups per group
* Different substances (about a tablespoon of each) in small containers or packages: meat tenderizer, oregano, cornstarch
* Lab recording sheets for each group

STEPS

1. Tell children that they are going to study changes in properties through a discovery activity.

2. Give each group three cups of water in clear plastic containers. (Children could fill their own cups to a marked level.)

3. Pass out three mystery substances in small containers marked A, B, and C, as well as a lab recording sheet.

4. Instruct children to look at one substance at a time and describe the substance using different senses (yellow-green, soft, sandy, etc.).

5. As each group agrees upon their descriptions they should record their descriptions in column 1.

6. After the descriptions are recorded, children are to hypothesize what they think will happen to each substance after it is placed into the cup of water for 3 minutes. Their hypothesis should be placed in column 2.

7. Each substance should be placed into the cup of water once the hypotheses are made, and children are to observe the immediate changes. After 3 minutes children should describe and record what happened to the substance in column 3.

8. After the discovery activity is completed by each group, the class as a whole can compare their descriptions in column 1, their hypotheses in column 2, and the recorded results in column 3.

CRITICAL THINKING CHALLENGE

A second discovery activity could follow the first using new mystery substances, some of which would have properties similar to the original set of substances, to see if groups' hypotheses are based on information learned from the first discovery activity. For example, if they found out that cornstarch had a specific reaction when placed in water, might they predict a substance like flour would have the same reaction?

(continued)

See How It Changes (continued)

Sample Lab Sheet		
Description of Substance Column 1	Hypothesis Column 2	What Happened Column 3
Substance A (meat tenderizer)		
Substance B (oregano)		
Substance C (cornstarch)		

ACCOMMODATIONS

✔ When working with younger children, the teacher could have the class discuss the descriptions as a large group and record the descriptions on a board. Hypotheses and results could also be shared as a class. However, children can be placed in groups for the pouring of substances into the water and the observing of the changes in substances.

EXTENSIONS

✔ After groups compare their descriptions of the substances the teacher could ask the class if they can come to an agreement on how the substances should be described.

SCIENCE

Which Object Is It?

Which Object Is It? can be used to help children learn to reason when given information about objects based on their properties.

LEARNING

* Reasoning about properties
* Identifying objects based on properties described

MATERIALS

* A variety of objects with different properties/attributes (hard/soft, green/yellow, cylinder/cone, rough/smooth, etc.) (For example, a white fork, a white tennis ball, a yellow pencil, a silver paper clip, a green eraser, etc.)

STEPS

1. Set up in front of the children a series of objects six to eight that contain some similar and different properties.

2. Inform the children that they are to determine which object the teacher is thinking of.

3. Tell them they will be given clues one at a time. When they have all the clues they need they are to state which object you were thinking of.

4. The challenge for children is to make sure their answers are based on the clues given.

5. After you give each clue, ask the children if they now know which object is the one you are thinking of. For example, you may start with the clue, "The object I am thinking about is hard. Does anyone know which object I am thinking about?"

6. Once the appropriate object is identified the children can share why certain objects may not have been the correct one based on the property clues given.

 ACCOMMODATIONS

✔ The properties of objects selected could be considered when working with younger or older children.

✔ The number of objects can vary.

✔ Pictures of objects could be substituted for real objects.

 EXTENSIONS

✔ This activity could be applied to a number of different areas of science. If children are learning about the characteristics or classification of plants or animals, a number of picture cards could be presented and the children could be given one clue at a time to determine which plant or animal the teacher is thinking about.

✔ Older children could lead the activity by identifying an object they are thinking about.

SCIENCE

Solid or Liquid

Solid or Liquid is a fun activity for younger children to introduce them to the solid and liquid states of matter. Children learn that some solids can become liquids and some liquids can become solid.

LEARNING

* Identifying solids and liquids
* Classifying solids and liquids
* Understanding that some solids and liquids can change their property

MATERIALS

* Table
* Set of objects classified as liquid (water, soda pop, corn oil, etc.)
* Set of objects classified as solid (rock, hard candy, piece of wood)
* An ice cube in a cup

STEPS

1. On a table in front of children set items that are solid and items that are liquid.

2. Inform the children that they will learn about objects that are classified as solids and objects that are classified as liquids.

3. Have the children look at the table. Show them several objects that are classified as liquid. Ask what they notice about these items. Record their observations on the board and discuss them.

4. Show the children several objects that are solid. Again ask them what they observe about the objects, and record their responses.

5. After the observations have been recorded ask children to tell what the differences between liquids and solids are.

6. Have children list other objects they can think of that are a solid or liquid.

7. Next ask children if they can think of any objects that could be a solid sometimes and a liquid at other times.

8. Bring out an ice cube and ask children if the ice is a solid or liquid. Ask children what might happen to the ice cube if it is left in the room for one hour. Tell children this would be an example of a solid becoming a liquid. Have them identify other solid objects that could become liquid or liquid objects that can become solid.

(continued)

SCIENCE

Solid or Liquid *(continued)*

ACCOMMODATIONS

✓ Younger children can be shown very recognizable objects that are clearly defined as liquid and solid.

EXTENSIONS

✓ The matter of gas could be added by adding a setup for steam.

✓ Children could make up a list of items at school or at home that are classified as solid or liquid.

✓ Children could make up a list of items that change from solid to liquid or liquid to solid.

SCIENCE

When Will It Boil?

When Will It Boil? is a change of matter activity that helps children look at differences between changing properties.

LEARNING

✳ Observation of different rates of change for properties

✳ Understanding different chemical properties of solids

✳ Hypothesis making

✳ Concept of boiling

MATERIALS

✳ A cup each of water, soda, rubbing alcohol

✳ Electric burner

✳ Small boiling pot

✳ Cooking or submersible thermometer

✳ Gloves or other heat protection device

STEPS

1. Place an electric burner or other heating source on a table a safe distance from the children. Near the heating source place three containers containing a cup each of different liquids: water, soda, and rubbing alcohol.

2. Ask children if they think all three liquids will begin to boil at the same temperature. If not, which do they think will boil at higher or lower temperatures? You may want to review the standard boiling temperature of 212 degrees Fahrenheit.

3. After children's hypotheses are noted and recorded, place the cup of water into a pot with a cooking thermometer, and turn on the burner. Once the water begins to boil remove the thermometer from the pot using gloves or other another heat protection device, and record the temperature.

4. Complete the same steps for the soda and rubbing alcohol.

5. After the temperatures have been recorded for all three, have children discuss and compare the results.

ACCOMMODATIONS

✔ Older children may become more involved in the investigation by removing the thermometers, etc.

✔ More familiar liquids can be used with younger children, while older students could use other liquids with different chemical properties they may be learning about.

EXTENSIONS

✔ Children could be asked to hypothesize how long it might take 2 cups of water, soda, or rubbing alcohol to boil and compare the results with 1 cup of each.

✔ The activity could be adjusted to find out the melting points of solid objects by submitting each of them to heat and recording the temperature at which the object melts. For example, a tablespoon of butter, finger gelatin, or chocolate bar could be used.

SCIENCE

Mystery Bag

Mystery Bag is an excellent activity for children of a variety of ages to learn how to describe objects through the sense of touch.

LEARNING

❋ Describing objects by touch
❋ Discriminating between different properties of objects

MATERIALS

❋ A bag
❋ Objects to be placed in the bag along with identical objects to be set out (objects that reinforce properties being covered in the curriculum)

STEPS

1. Place into a bag an object that has a number of different properties that can be described by children. The objects selected can include properties to be learned as part of their science curriculum. For example, a wood block could be placed into the bag with different types of materials glued on each side (sandpaper, cotton, Velcro, etc.). Some of the material could be put on more than one side.

2. Place an identical set of objects outside of the bag.

3. Have children take turns placing their hand into the bag and describing the object inside. One description should be given at a time so the other children can listen to the description and compare it with the set of objects presented. To involve more children, one child could give one description, a second child could give the second description, and so on.

CRITICAL THINKING CHALLENGE

Children could be asked to feel and identify the object (e.g., spoon) in the bag and then have children guess the object based on its function or where it might be found. For example, the object in the bag feels like something you might find on a table when eating.

ACCOMMODATIONS

✔ Teachers could construct objects that might better relate to the properties of the curriculum they are using.

✔ Larger objects and bags might be appropriate for younger children.

✔ Older children may not need to have a set of objects placed in front of them to consider.

EXTENSIONS

✔ Two objects can be placed into the bag and children could be asked to describe how they are the same or different.

SCIENCE

Light the Bulb

Light the Bulb is a discovery activity that asks children to get a lightbulb lit using several materials. Children need to problem solve using electricity and need to use illustrations to represent their solutions.

LEARNING

❋ Problem solving with electricity

❋ Using illustrations to present solutions

❋ Experiencing a simple electric circuit

MATERIALS

❋ D battery (one for each team)

❋ Two pieces of wire for each team (coated wire with the ends stripped bare would be best)

❋ Flashlight lightbulb for each team

❋ Paper and pencils for illustrations

STEPS

1. Tell the children they are going to have to solve a problem. The situation is that they have a piece of wire, a lightbulb from a flashlight, and a large battery. Their challenge is to get the lightbulb to light.

To light the bulb using one wire:

❋ Set the bulb on the knob at the top of the battery (+).

❋ Press one end of the wire to the bottom (−) middle of the battery, and position the other end of the wire so that it is touching the metal on the bottom side of the lightbulb on top (+) of the battery.

2. Pass out a set of materials to each team (one wire, one battery, and one lightbulb). Tell children that for the next 5 minutes they are to try using the three materials to get the lightbulb lit.

3. If they get the lightbulb lit they are to illustrate on a sheet of paper how the materials were placed.

4. Once they finish they can help other teams.

5. After 5 minutes are up, ask children to share how they got the lightbulb lit.

6. For their next challenge pass out a second piece of wire. Ask children how they might now get the lightbulb lit. Give them another set amount of time to see if they can light the bulb using two wires, a bulb, and a battery.

CRITICAL THINKING CHALLENGE

Children who are successful with getting one lightbulb lit then could try to get two lightbulbs lit given a third wire.

To light the bulb using two wires:

❋ Have one wire touch the knob at the top of the battery (+) and one wire touch the middle of the bottom (−) of the battery.

❋ Place the two other ends of the wires so they are touching the metal part of the lightbulb. (Make sure the wires do not touch each other.)

(continued)

SCIENCE

Light the Bulb *(continued)*

ACCOMMODATIONS

✔ Teachers may want to have an illustration available for children if they become frustrated in trying to solve the problem on their own.

✔ Simple information about circuits or makeup of batteries could be shared before the discovery activity.

EXTENSIONS

✔ Children could try to use other materials rather than wire (aluminum foil) to see if the lightbulbs will light.

SCIENCE

Does Cotton Conduct It?

Does Cotton Conduct It? *is an activity to use to help children understand what conduction is and which types of materials serve as conductors.*

MATERIALS

✳ An instrument to test for conduction (see directions below)

✳ Objects made of different materials (cotton, wood, metal, rubber, cloth, etc.)

✳ Two containers: one marked *Conducts* and one marked *Does Not Conduct*

STEPS

1. Tell the children they are going to investigate what materials are conductors of electricity. Conductors of electricity allow the current to flow.

2. Place in front of the children an electrical system setup for testing whether materials are conductors of electricity.

3. Show the children that the lightbulb goes on when the two open wires touch and that the lightbulb stays off when the wires do not touch.

4. Take a nail and have the two wires touch the nail at different ends. Ask the children what happened. Since the lightbulb went on we can say this nail is a conductor of electricity.

An electrical system setup to test for conduction can be made as follows:

✳ Have two wires clipped to and extending from the opposite ends of a battery holder.

✳ One wire from the holder should be curved and clipped to a lightbulb holder (holding a bulb), opposite from the battery holder. The second wire from the battery holder should extend from the other end of the battery holder toward the lightbulb so it is *not* near or touching the lightbulb holder.

✳ A second wire from the lightbulb holder should extend back to the unattached wire of the battery holder to form a circuit.

✳ If the open wires from the battery and lightbulb holders touch the lightbulb it will go on.

✳ To use the electrical system for conduction you touch the material with the two open-ended wires. If the lightbulb goes on it means the material is a conductor of electricity. If the lightbulb stays off the material is not a conductor of electricity.

5. Touch a piece of cotton with the two wires. Ask what happened. Since the lightbulb did not go on we can say that this piece of cotton does not conduct electricity.

6. Tell children that they will be shown a set of materials and be asked if they think each material is a conductor or nonconductor of electricity.

(continued)

SCIENCE

Does Cotton Conduct It? *(continued)*

7. As each material is tested place it into a container marked *Conducts* or *Does Not Conduct*. After all materials are tested, review the contents of both containers to determine whether children can make generalizations about materials that conduct or do not conduct.

ACCOMMODATIONS

✔ For older students objects may be selected that make children think again about what things conduct and what things do not conduct. For example, do all types of nails conduct?

✔ Older children could be asked to first set up their own instrument to test for conduction.

EXTENSIONS

✔ As mentioned under the "Accommodations" section, rather than checking whether different types of materials conduct, children could check to see if all of the same type of material conducts (nails, cups, wire, etc.).

✔ Children might go on a scavenger hunt to find materials that serve as conductors.

✔ Children might try to find objects for which part of the object serves as a conductor while another part of the same object may not, for example, a wooden pencil that has a metal band and an eraser. What part of the pencil is a conductor of electricity?

SCIENCE

Make a Switch

Make a Switch can be an extension to the activity Does Cotton Conduct It? *for older children. In this activity children are asked to make a simple switch that will turn a lightbulb on or off.*

LEARNING

✳ Problem solving

✳ Concept behind a simple switch

MATERIALS

✳ An instrument to test for conduction (as explained in the *Does Cotton Conduct It?* activity)

✳ One 3-by-5-inch card per group

✳ Two brass fasteners per group

✳ One large paper clip per group

STEPS

1. Show the children the system that was set up to test materials for conduction (explained in the preceding activity, Does Cotton Conduct It?).

2. Tell them that they are to try to make a simple switch that will allow the lightbulb to be turned on or off.

3. Pass out the following materials to each group of children: a 3-by-5-inch card, two brass fasteners, and a large paper clip. Tell children they are to try to make a switch with the materials. They should also be told the switch needs to be fastened to the wires of the light system setup for testing of conduction.

4. Set a certain amount of time for the children to work on the challenge.

5. As groups come up with a solution have them attach the two wires from the tester to see if the lightbulb turns on and off.

(continued)

SCIENCE

Make a Switch *(continued)*

One possible way to make the switch:

✳ Place the two brass fasteners into the 3-by-5-inch card so they are a distance apart equal to the length of the paper clip.

✳ Pull one of the fasteners out from the card, attach the paper clip to it, and reinsert the fastener into the card with the paper clip attached between the card and fastener.

✳ On the back of the card where the ends of the fasteners come through, split and push the prongs apart so they are touching the card.

✳ Attach the two wires from the tester so one wire is around each of the fasteners.

✳ Turn the card over.

✳ Rotate the paper clip so it touches the second brass fastener. When it does the light should come on. By touching or not touching the paper clip to the second fastener the light will come on or go off, creating a switch.

One solution for a switch:

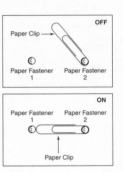

CRITICAL THINKING CHALLENGE

Children could be given a variety of materials and be asked to make a switch.

ACCOMMODATIONS

✔ To make the task easier for younger children the teacher can pass out a sheet showing how part of the switch might look.

Pick Up Slips

Pick Up Slips is an activity that helps children understand the concept of static electricity. The activity can also be used to have children use past data to make hypotheses.

LEARNING

✳ Concept of static electricity
✳ Using data to form hypotheses

MATERIALS

✳ Two medium balloons for each team
✳ A number of 1-inch pieces of paper for each team
✳ One paper plate for each team
✳ One Recording Chart for each team

STEPS

1. Explain to the children that they are going to pick up slips of paper by producing static electricity. They are to produce static electricity by rubbing a balloon on their hair.

2. Have them make hypotheses about the number of pieces of paper that might be picked up.

3. Pass out two balloons, a plate, and a number of 1-inch paper squares per team of children. The balloons may be blown up or could be blown up by the children. Also pass out a record keeping chart for the students.

4. Tell the children that they are going to complete two trials for the activity. In trial 1 they are to rub a balloon on their hair (one child's head per team) for 10 seconds, then place it on the plate with the pieces of paper for about 1 second. They will then pick the balloon up off the plate and count the number of pieces of paper attached to the balloon. Before they start trial 1 they are to guess how many pieces of paper might be picked up. Their guess and actual answers will be recorded on their chart. Once the data has been recorded, children will discuss their guesses and the different results.

5. In trial 2 children should be told they are to rub the balloon on a child's head for 20 seconds. Before they rub the balloon for 20 seconds they are to make a guess as to how many pieces of paper it will pick up this time based on what they learned from trial 1. Their guesses should be recorded on their charts. After guesses are made, the same child in each group will rub the second balloon on his or her head for 20 seconds. Children will record answers on their charts.

6. After trial 2 is completed children will compare their hypotheses and results.

(continued)

SCIENCE

Pick Up Slips *(continued)*

Recording Chart			
Trial	Time Rubbed Hair	Guess (Paper Pieces Picked Up)	Actual Number of Paper Pieces Picked Up
1	10 seconds		
2	20 seconds		

ACCOMMODATIONS

✓ Balloons could be blown up for children.

✓ Larger or smaller balloons and pieces of paper could be used.

✓ The teacher could time the balloon rubbings and indicate when the balloons should be removed from the plates.

EXTENSIONS

✓ Other materials could be used to produce static electricity. Hair combs or brushes could be used, or students could rub their feet on carpets.

✓ Materials other than paper might be used to see if more of one material might be picked up.

✓ Children could compare long versus short hair to see which might pick up more or less paper.

Electromagnetic Nails

Electromagnetic Nails is an activity that shows children how electricity can be used to magnetize a nail. Through problem solving, children will also learn how to make the nail more magnetically strong.

LEARNING

✳ Electric current can be used to create a magnet (magnetic field)

✳ Problem solving to strengthen the magnet

MATERIALS

✳ 6-volt battery

✳ Long nail

✳ 2-to-3-foot piece of insulated wire (about 18 gauge) with the ends stripped about 1½ inches

✳ Box of paper clips

STEPS

1. Set in front of the children a 6-volt battery, a piece of wire about 2 to 3 feet long, and a large iron nail.

2. Tie or clamp one stripped end of the wire to one battery post. Wrap the middle part of the wire around the large nail about five times, leaving some wire to be attached to the other post of the battery.

3. Place a set of paper clips or other metal objects (tacks) below the nail, with the pointed end of the nail facing down toward the objects.

4. Tell the children that you are going to place the other end of the wire on the other battery post and they are to watch what happens to the paper clips right below the nail.

5. Children will discover that a number of paper clips will attach themselves to the nail.

6. Have children count the number of paper clips that are attached.

7. Ask children how they think they could use the same battery, wire, and nail to pick up more paper clips. Try out each suggested method.

8. If none of their methods work, indicate that you will wrap the wire around the nail four or five more times. You could also suggest that the wire be wrapped more closely together to see if more paper clips can be picked up.

9. When you have finished with the trials, ask children to share what they know about making an electromagnet and what they may have learned about making an electromagnet (the nail) stronger.

TEACHER NOTE

Making an electromagnet can cause the nail to get hot. Make sure you disconnect the wire end that you are holding after each trial or if the nail is getting too warm.

(continued)

SCIENCE

Electromagnetic Nails (continued)

ACCOMMODATIONS

✓ Adult supervision is needed if you permit children to wrap the nail, connect one end of the wire to the battery, etc.

EXTENSIONS

✓ Children could try smaller batteries (size D, C) using the same setup to see if they can make an electromagnet nail.

✓ Different sizes of nails could be used to see which picks up the most paper clips.

✓ Different-size paper clips could be used to have older children work with proportions or ratios.

SCIENCE

Rock Lifting

Rock Lifting reinforces the workings of the lever as a simple machine. Children have the opportunity to problem solve with the lever as they attempt to lift small rocks.

LEARNING

❋ Understanding how the lever helps lift or raise objects up

❋ Problem solving with moving the position of the fulcrum

Lever

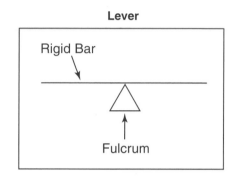

MATERIALS

❋ Rocks of different weights

❋ Rigid bar (a piece of wood 1 inch thick, 4 to 6 inches wide, and about 4 feet long) Note: you may want to nail a small piece of wood (2-by-2 inches) 6 to 8 inches from the ends of the bar so the rock and books do not slide

❋ A fulcrum (a triangular piece of wood with a flat rather than pointed top or a small round pole about 3 inches in diameter)

❋ A set of textbooks of the same size

STEPS

1. Have students gather in a circle somewhere in a play area outside. Tell children they will attempt to lift some rocks of different sizes using a lever, one of several simple machines people can use to do work.

2. Review with children that a **lever** is a simple machine that has a rigid bar and a balancing piece called a fulcrum normally placed underneath the bar.

3. Tell them that by moving the fulcrum to the right or left under the bar may make it harder or easier to lift the rocks.

4. Set the lever up so that the fulcrum is underneath the middle of the bar. Place a rock on one end of the lever. Tell children they are going to use books as weight at the other end of the fulcrum to try to lift the rock off the ground.

5. Set the lever up and put a rock (about 6 inches in diameter) at one end of the bar. Have one child place one book at the other end and continue to add books until the rock is lifted.

6. Record the number of books it took when the fulcrum was in the middle of the board. Remove the books.

7. Place the fulcrum about 6 inches closer to the rock. Have children guess how many more or how many fewer books it will take to lift the rock. After guesses are made have another child start stacking the books until the rock is lifted.

(continued)

SCIENCE

Rock Lifting *(continued)*

8. Compare the results of this second trial with the first. Check to see whether children identify the concept that the closer to the fulcrum the object is, the less weight (work) is needed to lift it.

9. Continue the activity by having students move the rock closer to or further away from the fulcrum to determine how many books it will take.

CRITICAL THINKING CHALLENGE

Explore other concepts, such as if you double the weight of the object to be lifted, will you need to double the amount of weight to lift the object?

ACCOMMODATIONS

✔ The size of rocks and lever to be used can be adjusted to the age level of the children.

✔ If sufficient levers are available children could work in teams and record the different results.

EXTENSIONS

✔ Rulers, a pencil, and pennies could also be used in the classroom to teach the same concept.

✔ Older students working with proportions could record the different amounts needed to lift objects based on moving the fulcrum 2 inches closer or further away from the rock.

SCIENCE

Pull Up the Bucket

Pull Up the Bucket can be used to help children explore how pulleys work. The activity allows children to see how using a different size pulley can make a task easier or harder.

LEARNING

* How pulleys are used
* How the size of a pulley makes work easier or harder
* Reasoning about pulley size

MATERIALS

* Small bucket with rope or sturdy string attached to the handle
* 2 cups of beans
* A 4-foot pole (about 1 inch in diameter)
* Several simple pulleys of different sizes
* Rope
* Wire to attach pulleys to the pole
* Two chairs (other setups could be used to attach the pulleys to)
* Tape

STEPS

1. Set in front of children the several pulleys of different sizes and a small bucket with some beans inside and a rope or sturdy string attached to the handle.

2. Tell them that they are going to try to lift the bucket about a foot off the floor using the different pulleys.

3. Place two chairs from the classroom about 2 feet apart, and place a pole across the top of the chairs. Tape the pole to each chair so it does not move (or have two children hold the bar, one for each chair). The pulleys can be wired to the pole.

4. Put the rope from the bucket around the smallest pulley, and ask a child to pull the other end of the rope until the bucket is about 1 foot off the ground. (A marker could be used to identify 1 foot in height.)

5. Then remove the bucket rope and put it around a larger pulley. Ask the child to again lift the bucket about 1 foot off the ground. Ask the child to tell if it was easier or harder to lift.

6. Continue with other size pulleys and involve other children.

CRITICAL THINKING CHALLENGE

Children could be given two pulleys and asked to arrange them in different patterns to see if one pattern makes it easier to lift objects than another pattern.

(continued)

SCIENCE

Pull Up the Bucket (continued)

ACCOMMODATIONS

✔ The weight of the bucket can be adjusted to the lifting ability of the children. More beans could be added for older children.

EXTENSIONS

✔ A second bucket could be attached to the other end of the rope and objects of the same weight could be added (e.g., golf balls). Kids could estimate how many more or fewer objects it might take to lift the bucket 1 foot.

✔ A second pulley or double pulley could be introduced and used to determine whether two pulleys make the task easier.

Sock Pull

Sock Pull is a good activity to use with younger children to help them understand how an inclined plane can be used to move objects more easily.

LEARNING

✳ How inclined planes work
✳ How to make an inclined plane

MATERIALS

✳ A sock or socks filled with sand and tied with a loop at the end
✳ A board or boards (6 inches wide, 1 inch thick, 2 feet long)
✳ Three books

STEPS

1. Show the children a sock filled with sand and tied at the top end with a loop hanging out. Attach a sturdy piece of string to the loop from the sock.

2. Set the sock on a table next to three books stacked one on top of the other. (If available, you could have several sets of socks and boards set up to involve more children.)

3. Have a child come up and lift the sock up off the table and place it on top of the set of books. Ask the child how hard it was to lift the sock up.

4. Place a board with one end overlapping the top of the books by about an inch and the other end on the table. Place the sock at the bottom of the board.

5. Tell the child to pull the sock up the board until it is sitting on top of the stack of books.

6. Ask the child if it was easier to get the sock on top of the books by lifting it up or by pulling it up on the board.

7. Allow other children to try the same activity.

8. Ask children if they can think of times when it might be helpful to use an inclined plane.

 ACCOMMODATIONS

✔ The sock could be filled half full and children could try lifting it with one or two fingers.

✔ Other material could be put into the sock to make it easier or more difficult to lift.

 EXTENSIONS

✔ The board could be elevated higher or lower, and children could be asked to identify whether the angle of an inclined plane makes it easier or harder to use.

✔ The concept of friction could also be explored using inclined planes of different materials or different surfaces. For example, compare an untreated board and a board that has been polished.

SCIENCE

The Box Splitter

The Box Splitter is an excellent activity to use to teach children about a simple machine, the wedge. Children learn how a wedge can be used to penetrate or split apart objects.

LEARNING

❋ How a wedge works
❋ Using a wedge to penetrate an object

MATERIALS

❋ Two pieces of Styrofoam™ about 4 inches thick and 6 inches wide (other sizes may be tried)
❋ Pole (12 inches long and 1 inch in diameter)
❋ Screwdriver (about ¼ or ½ inch wide at the end)

STEPS

1. Set on a table the two pieces of Styrofoam™, the small pole, and the screwdriver.

2. Tell children that they are going to put holes in the Styrofoam™. Give the small pole to a child and ask the child to push down on the pole to try to make a hole in the middle of one of the Styrofoam™ pieces.

3. After the child's attempt, check to see if a hole has been made. If a hole was made, ask how hard it was to make the hole.

4. Next give the child a screwdriver and ask the child to make a hole with it in the second Styrofoam™ piece. Then observe whether a hole was made and ask how hard it was to make the hole.

5. Have different children take turns trying to make a hole in each piece of Styrofoam™ using the pole and the wedge.

6. When finished, discuss with children the benefit of using a wedge to make holes or split things apart.

 ACCOMMODATIONS

✔ Adjustments can be made to the size of the pole.

✔ For younger children you can use screwdrivers with points that are not as sharp.

 EXTENSIONS

✔ Older children could be asked to use real wedges with a hammer to try to split a small log.

✔ Wedges of different weights could be used to determine whether weight is a factor when using the simple machine.

✔ Wider or narrower wedges could be tried to see which might be easier to use or take less time to complete a given task.

SCIENCE

Up, Up, and Over the Chair

Up, Up, and Over the Chair is a problem-solving activity for older children using different simple machines. Children are asked to identify how they could use a set of different simple machines to lift an object over a structure.

LEARNING

❋ Problem solving with simple machines

❋ Demonstrating how to use simple machines

MATERIALS

❋ Chair for each group

❋ Block (about 4 inches wide, 4 inches high, and 6 inches long) (one 4-by-4-inch piece of wood could be cut into 6-inch lengths)

❋ Pulley for each group

❋ Wedge for each group

❋ Inclined plane for each group

❋ Lever with fulcrum for each group

STEPS

1. Set a student's chair before the children. Tell the children their group is to use a variety of simple machines to move a block of wood up onto the seat of the chair (stage 1), then over the back of the chair (stage 2), and finally from the back of the chair back to the ground (stage 3).

2. Tell them there are three rules they need to follow in moving through the three stages to get the block back to the ground on the other side of the chair.

   ❋ They can only use their hands to tie or secure the wood block to a simple machine. They cannot move the block up or across the chair with their hands.

   ❋ They must use at least two different type of machines to complete the task.

   ❋ They can use any simple machine more than once.

3. Tell children that the goal is to use a set of simple machines that will allow them to complete the task with the least amount of work.

4. Provide each group with a chair and a set of simple machines. (one pulley, one inclined plane, one wedge, one lever with fulcrum)

5. Tell the children that they should work on one stage at a time.

6. Move from group to group and provide ideas only if groups are getting frustrated.

(continued)

SCIENCE

Up, Up, and Over the Chair *(continued)*

ACCOMMODATIONS

✔ The type of simple machines selected could be modified depending on availability and the types being introduced to the children.

✔ The size of structure and object could be adjusted to fit on a desktop or perhaps a playground area.

EXTENSIONS

✔ Teachers could suggest moving objects across waterways like rivers to present different circumstances in which children could use simple machines.

✔ Children could identify different situations for which simple machines could be used and, if appropriate (safe), enact the situations and use the simple machines.

SCIENCE

My Soap-Powered Boat

My Soap-Powered Boat is a fun activity to be used with younger children to help them begin to experience the concept of magnetic pull.

LEARNING

* Concept of magnetic pull
* Making simple guesses
* Compare the effects of different substances in investigations

MATERIALS

* Piece of aluminum foil
* Small piece of soap (1 inch wide and long enough to have about ½ to 1 inch below the water level of the boat
* Two tubs of water, one warm and one cold

STEPS

1. Set out two tubs containing water, one tub with cold water and one tub with warm water.

2. Fold a piece of aluminum foil into the shape of a boat. Set the boat into the warm water at one end of the tub and ask children to observe what happens (does not sink, etc.).

3. Take the boat back out of the water and tape a narrow piece of soap to the back of the boat so that part of the soap is submerged in the water.

4. Place the boat with soap back into the warm tub at one end. Have children observe what happens now. (The boat should begin to move around slowly.)

5. Explain to children that the boat moves from the soapy water to the clear water because the clear water has a stronger pull.

6. Next place the boat with the soap into the tub of cold water. Ask children to observe if the boat is moving faster or more slowly than it did when it was in the warm water.

7. Compare and discuss the results.

ACCOMMODATIONS

✔ The boats could be put into larger plastic swimming pools so they would have more room to move about.

EXTENSIONS

✔ Children could make their own boats and try them out in the water.

✔ Children could compare different brands of soap so see if some cause the boats to move faster or more slowly.

✔ Other liquids could be substituted for water to see if there is more or less movement.

✔ Hard and soft water could be compared.

✔ Other materials such as sugar candies could be attached to the boat to see if they make the boat move.

SCIENCE

Make a Magnet

Make a Magnet is an activity in which children make their own magnet. The activity can also be used to help children explore how they might be able to make their magnet stronger.

LEARNING

✳ How to make a magnet
✳ Ways to make a magnet stronger

MATERIALS

✳ Large bar magnet for each child or group
✳ Large paper clip for each child or group (straight nails could be substituted)
✳ Pieces of steel wool for each child or group (small metal objects could be substituted, such as small, lightweight washers)

STEPS

1. Have each child take a large paper clip that is spread out to form a straight line.

2. Have the children take the straightened paper clip and set it on top of small pieces of steel wool. Ask children if the paper clip attracts and picks up any of the pieces of steel wool.

3. Give the children a bar magnet and tell them they are to rub the wire with one end of the magnet. They should rub the magnet only down the magnet, in one direction *not down and back.*

4. Children should rub the magnet down the paper clip about 25 times.

5. Next children should again take the paper clip and place it on the steel wool pieces, then pick it up to see if pieces of steel wool are attached.

6. The steel wool should be removed.

7. Ask children how they think they might make the magnet even stronger. Suggest that perhaps they could rub the magnet against the paper clip 50 times.

8. Have children rub the magnet against the paper clip 50 times, again using a down-only motion.

9. Have children compare their results. Did rubbing the magnet against the paper clip twice as many times allow the paper clip to pick up more steel wool?

 ACCOMMODATIONS

✔ The teacher could go through the activity as a demonstration if not enough magnets are available.

 EXTENSIONS

✔ Children could rub magnets against other metal materials or nonmetal materials to classify materials that can or cannot be magnetized.

✔ A variety of sizes and types of magnets could be tried to compare differences in the strength of magnetic pull on objects.

Magnet Power

Magnet Power is an activity children can use to see if the magnetic field passes through different kinds of materials.

LEARNING

❋ What materials a magnetic field can pass through

❋ Generalizations about magnetic fields

MATERIALS

❋ A bar magnet

❋ Different pieces of materials about 1 foot by 1 foot (a piece of glass, a plastic cutting board, a place mat, a narrow piece of plywood, a piece of Styrofoam™, a piece of carpet, etc.)

❋ Thumbtack or other iron material

❋ Cardboard

STEPS

1. Show the children a bar magnet and ask them if they think that a magnet will be able to move an object if a piece of cardboard is placed between the bar magnet and the object.

2. Place a metal thumbtack on top of the cardboard and place the bar magnet underneath the piece of cardboard, aligned with the thumbtack. Move the magnet underneath the cardboard and see if the thumbtack moves along with the magnet.

3. Bring out the different materials and have children follow the same steps. Try to make sure all the materials are about the same thickness.

4. Children can set up a chart identifying those materials that do or do not allow the magnetic field to pass through.

 ACCOMMODATIONS

✔ Teachers may want to set up a platform for children to place the materials on.

 EXTENSIONS

✔ The teacher may provide children with materials that are of different thicknesses to determine the thickness at which the magnetic field may no longer pass through.

SCIENCE

Waste Hike with a Magnet Stick

Waste Hike with a Magnet Stick is a fun outdoor activity that allows children to discover what kinds of objects can be picked up by magnets. Children are also able to identify materials that are not attracted by magnets.

LEARNING

* Observing objects that are attracted to a magnet stick
* Using a magnet to collect waste

MATERIALS

* Outdoor area
* Sticks (3 to 4 feet long) for each team
* A magnet for each team
* 2 white garbage bags for each team
* 1 black marker for each team
* Tape

STEPS

1. Give each team of children two white garbage bags, a stick, and a magnet. Tell them that they are going on a hike to clean up the environment.

2. To prepare for the hike, ask teams to tape the magnet to the end of the stick. Also ask them to write with a black marker *magnet pickup* on one garbage bag and *non-magnet pickup* on the other.

3. Before the teams leave tell them to pick up each piece of waste they find with the stick. If the waste material does not attach itself to the stick with the magnet it should be placed in the *non-magnet pickup* bag. If the waste material is picked up by the magnet stick it should be placed in the bag marked *magnet pickup.*

4. After teams return from the hike they will sort out the waste that was picked up with the magnet stick and those waste materials that were not.

5. Students will make generalizations as to what type of trash could be picked up with a magnet stick.

CRITICAL THINKING CHALLENGE

Children could be asked to think of ways they could use magnet sticks to help people, work situations, or the environment.

ACCOMMODATIONS

✓ Children should be encouraged to pick up only small objects.

✓ If needed the teacher could set out some metal objects to ensure that some materials can be picked up by the magnet stick.

SCIENCE

Seeing through It

Seeing through It *helps children discover which materials allow light to pass through them.*

LEARNING

* Discovering materials that allow some light to pass through them
* Concept of translucent

MATERIALS

* Flashlights
* White mailing envelope
* Several coins
* Book
* Square piece of aluminum foil
* Box of translucent and nontranslucent materials (white sheet of paper, piece of thick cardboard, black piece of plastic, white piece of plastic, piece of wood, pieces of cloth, piece of metal, piece of wax paper, leaf, egg, etc.)

STEPS

1. Tell the children they are going to find out what materials are **translucent**. Explain to them that translucent materials allow some light to pass through them.

2. Hold up a white mailing envelope with several coins sealed inside it.

3. Press a flashlight tight against the envelope, with the flashlight turned off.

4. Tell children that there is an object inside the envelope. Have them guess what it might be.

5. Turn the classroom lights off and turn the flashlight on. Hold the envelope so that it is facing the children. Now ask children what they see. Again ask them what they think is in the envelope.

6. Turn the classroom lights back on and review with children what they could see when the flashlight was turned off and what they could see when the flashlight was turned on. Remind them that since they could see images from the light the envelope is a translucent material.

7. Next, with the flashlight turned off, place a book in front of the children with a square piece of aluminum foil inside it. Ask children what might be inside the book.

8. Turn the classroom lights off and turn on the flashlight. Children will observe no difference. They will not be able to see the square piece of aluminum foil.

9. Turn the classroom lights back on and review with children that the book is not a translucent material.

10. Have children get into groups, and pass out a flashlight and a box of materials to each group. Tell the children they are to investigate which of the materials are translucent and which are not translucent.

11. After all groups complete their investigations, review the concept of translucent and have children share materials that are or are not translucent.

12. Children can also look around the room and identify materials that they think might be translucent based on their earlier findings.

(continued)

Copyright © 2005, Thomson Delmar Learning

Physical Science • **337**

Seeing through It *(continued)*

ACCOMMODATIONS

✓ Flashlights that give off a brighter light should be used if the children are in a large classroom.

✓ Some windows could be covered to give a better impression of materials that are translucent.

EXTENSIONS

✓ Children could try to classify translucent materials based on *how* translucent they are, letting through more or less light.

✓ Children could pick up different leaves and classify them by how translucent they are.

✓ Children could make up a translucent puppet show by using a sheet of white paper taped to the front of a shoebox, with lights coming from behind the paper and the characters and objects in between.

SCIENCE

Sun Pictures

Sun Pictures is a fun project that helps children see the effects of the sun's infrared rays on materials.

MATERIALS

* White sheets of paper (8½-by-11 inches)
* Colored construction paper
* Scissors
* Tape
* Source of bright sunlight (hot lights or heat lamps may work)

STEPS

1. Show children a piece of white paper. Then fold the paper in half and then in half again.

2. Use scissors to cut out pieces of the paper along the folded sides to make symmetrical patterns.

3. Unfold the paper and show children the different shapes.

4. Pass out a sheet of paper to each child. Have them fold the paper as you did and cut out their own symmetrical patterns.

5. When children are finished they can share their symmetrical patterns.

6. Next tell children that they are going to place a colored piece of construction paper behind the white paper with the symmetrical patterns cut out.

7. Tape the sides so the white paper is in front and the colored construction paper is in back.

8. Tell the children they are going to place the pictures in the sunlight for two days.

9. After two days have passed, have children cut the tape and pull the colored sheet of construction paper away.

10. The colored sheet of construction paper should have faded, leaving the symmetrical imprints on it.

11. Discuss with the children that the imprints were made by the sun's infrared rays.

(continued)

SCIENCE

Sun Pictures *(continued)*

ACCOMMODATIONS

✔ The paper could be folded just once if young children struggle with trying to cut through the paper when it is folded twice.

✔ Some children may need assistance with folding the paper.

EXTENSIONS

✔ Hole punches and other materials could be used to make the patterns on the white sheet of paper.

✔ Other materials such as wax paper could be tried instead of the standard white sheet of paper.

✔ Some pictures could be placed in sunlight and others under lamps to see the different effects on the colored construction paper. Did they fade equally? Did one source of light have less of an effect on the paper?

✔ Different colors (black, tan, green, yellow, blue) could be tried to see if some colors are more affected by the light.

SCIENCE

Shrinking Shadows

Shrinking Shadows is an activity that allows children to see how shadows change based on light rays and distance.

LEARNING

* How light creates shadows
* How the distance from a light source affects shadows

MATERIALS

* Filmstrip projector or equivalent light source
* Filmstrip projector screen (white sheets or a white wall could be used)
* Cardboard image of a bird about 1 foot long and 6 inches high
* Small stand for the bird image
* Darkened room

STEPS

1. Place a filmstrip projector on a table so it is at the same level as a white screen set up about 6 feet away (or so its light fills the whole screen). A white wall or white bed sheet could be used if a projection screen is not available.

2. Turn on the filmstrip projector light, and turn off the classroom lights.

3. Stand before the film projector light and show children a cardboard cutout of a bird set in a small stand about 1 inch high. Tell the children to look at the screen. No image will appear.

4. Place the bird 6 inches in front of the projector so the bird is between the light and the screen. Ask children to discuss what they see when the bird image is placed 6 inches from the light source.

5. Tell children you are now going to move the bird image about 2 feet from the light source. What do they think will happen to the image?

6. Move the bird image 2 feet away and let children react to what they notice.

7. Ask children, based on what they have seen, what they think will happen if the bird image is placed 3 feet from the light source.

8. Move the bird image 3 feet from the light source and have children make their observations.

9. From the investigation you can ask children to explain what they have learned about the effect of distance on light and shadows.

CRITICAL THINKING CHALLENGE

Children could observe changes in shadows based on the direction from which the light source hits an object. Does the shadow change if the light source hits an image straight on or from the side?

(continued)

SCIENCE

Shrinking Shadows *(continued)*

 ACCOMMODATIONS

✓ Larger images could be used with younger children.

✓ Children could explore with flashlights in a darkened room before the activity.

✓ The shadow images could be traced on sheets of paper placed over the screen to permit children to recall the differences between the sizes of the shadows at the different distances.

 EXTENSIONS

✓ Transparent colored sheets of paper could be placed over the projector light to observe how the shadows appear with different colors.

✓ Two light sources could be used at the same time coming from different locations.

SCIENCE

Making Phones

Making Phones *is an activity that helps children to explore how sound carries. Children investigate which types of materials help to carry sound.*

MATERIALS

* String, wire, yarn, ropes, plastic tubing, etc. to serve as telephone wire
* Two large boxes
* Cans of different materials/sizes, different shapes/sizes of plastic bottles, etc.

STEPS

1. Have two children come up to the front of the classroom. Give each child a tin can with a string acting as a phone line between the two cans. Have one child step outside the classroom and close the door most of the way leaving room so the string is not pinched. The string must be pulled tight.

2. Have one child say something while the other child listens to hear what is being said. Note: you should experiment ahead of time to ensure some sound can be heard.

3. Tell children they are to investigate whether or not other materials in combination will carry sound. Have children form investigation teams.

4. Set out two large boxes in front of the children.

   In box 1 have pairs of different hearing devices: cans of different sizes and metals, plastic bottles, foam can holders, etc.

   In box 2 have different types of materials to use as wire: string of different sizes, different strips of wire, yarn, etc.

5. Tell the children that they are to pick out one set of hearing devices and one type of wire at a time. Using tape they are to make their phones and test them out to see how well they can hear.

6. Children should record the different combinations of materials tried and note whether the sound *did not come through*, *came through but was somewhat hard to hear*, or *came through clearly*.

7. The activity can be ongoing with children bringing in other types of materials to try out.

8. When children have completed their investigations they can discuss which types of materials produced the best sound.

(continued)

SCIENCE

Making Phones (continued)

ACCOMMODATIONS

✓ If not enough materials are available you could assign each team to try out one combination and share the results.

✓ With younger children, the teacher can make the different phones beforehand and have children try them out and vote on which one carries the sound the best, and which the least well.

EXTENSIONS

✓ Children could make the same type of phone but vary the length of the phone wire to determine the minimal or maximum distances sound might travel.

Comb Instruments

Comb Instruments is an activity to be used to help children learn how vibrations produce sound.

LEARNING

* Concept that vibrations produce sounds
* Controlling variables

MATERIALS

* Combs
* Tissue paper
* Different pieces of material: aluminum foil, wax paper, writing paper, construction paper, cloth of different types, thin cardboard

STEPS

1. Show children a small comb covered with a piece of tissue paper.

2. Have one child come up and hold the comb to their lips and hum. Have the child stop humming after 10 seconds. Have children explain what they heard.

3. Tell the children that the humming produced vibrations, which created the sound.

4. Bring out several additional (sanitary) combs and pass them out to small teams of children. Also set out a number of different types of materials.

5. Tell children they are to place the different materials over the combs to see if no sound is produced or if different sounds are produced.

6. Tell children they need to use the same type of humming voice and sequence.

7. Have children demonstrate the different types of sounds that were produced by their humming instruments.

ACCOMMODATIONS

✔ The teacher could have one child demonstrate the different sounds if there are not enough combs to go around.

✔ Children should be reminded that only one child should blow on each different material so they do not pass germs.

EXTENSIONS

✔ Children could form a band by each humming the same tune with different materials attached to their combs.

✔ Children could explore whether the sound changes if you use big combs or small combs.

SCIENCE

Sounding Boards

Sounding Boards is a simple yet excellent activity to use to help children discover how different sounds can be produced by different vibrations.

MATERIALS

❋ Two wooden boards about 15 inches long, 12 inches wide, and 1 inch thick
❋ 16 wood nails 2 inches long
❋ Four wires the same length but different thicknesses (mil)
❋ Four wires the same thickness but different lengths
❋ Hammer

STEPS

1. Start by using two wooden boards. On board 1 pound eight nails so there are four columns of two nails about 8 inches apart.

2. Set up board 2 so there are four columns but each column has the nails spaced different distances apart (column 1: 2 inches apart, column 2: 4 inches apart, column 3: 6 inches apart, column 4: 8 inches apart)

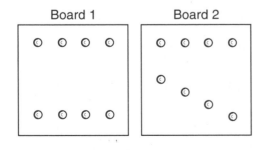

3. Set up board 1 by wrapping different-size (mil) wire around each of the four sets of nails, with the first wire being thinnest and the last wire being thickest.

4. Set up board 2 so that the same size (mil) of wire is used for all four sets of nails.

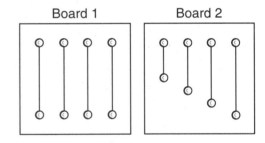

5. Start with board 1. Strike the first wire and have the children listen to the sound. Strike the second wire and have children make comparisons between the two.

6. Based on what the difference was between the first two, have children share what they think the third wire will sound like, then what the fourth wire will sound like.

7. Strike the third and fourth wires and have the children listen to the sounds and comment on the accuracy of their predictions.

8. Set board 1 aside and show the children board 2. Ask them what difference they see between the two boards. You may tell them that all the wires are the same thickness on board 2.

9. Strike the first wire and have children listen to the sound. Strike the second wire and have children compare the two sounds.

(continued)

10. Based on what the difference between the two sounds, have children predict how the third wire might sound when it is struck.

11. Strike the third wire and have children identify whether their predictions were accurate. Repeat the same sequence for the fourth wire.

12. When finished, have children review the differences between the sounds from board 1 and board 2. What are the effects on sound when wires of different sizes or lengths are struck?

 ACCOMMODATIONS

✓ Children could take turns striking the wires.

✓ The wires could be struck several times to ensure that the sounds are heard clearly.

✓ Try to ensure that the children are sitting close enough to hear the sounds.

 EXTENSIONS

✓ A third board could be set up with a number of different types of wires (copper, steel, etc.) to see if different types of wire produce different sounds.

✓ Elastic materials such as rubber bands of different sizes and thicknesses could be substituted for wire.

✓ Children could use a variety of the board types to make instruments for a band.

SCIENCE

Chapter 16

Life Science

Activities developed for the life sciences are centered on the areas of animals, plants, and humans. Children are involved in learning about the characteristics of different organisms and how organisms relate to their environments. Through investigations they will also have the opportunity to develop their abilities to observe, classify, hypothesize, control variables, and make generalizations based on data.

Neighborhood Animals

Neighborhood Animals *is an activity to be used to help children become familiar with animals in their neighborhoods.*

LEARNING

* Learning about animals that are in children's neighborhoods
* Observing differences in animals

MATERIALS

* Camera (or one camera per group of children)
* Film

STEPS

1. Inform the children they are going to walk around their neighborhood taking pictures of animals. (Digital cameras would work well.)

2. Ask children to pick out animals to be caught on camera. Remind them to observe not only bigger animals but smaller animals as well.

3. Children will go on the neighborhood walk pointing out pictures to take. If necessary, each child could be allowed to identify two animals to be photographed.

4. After the neighborhood walk is completed and once the photos of animals are available, have children review the pictures. Emphasis could be placed on those animals that children are least familiar with.

ACCOMMODATIONS

✓ The type of animals to be photographed could be limited if there are too many animals to be photographed in an area.

✓ The teacher could have children take the pictures during the neighborhood walk.

EXTENSIONS

✓ If children are studying a certain classification of animals, the photos to be taken could be limited to a particular classification, such as mammals, for example.

✓ Children could make animal storybooks after the photos have been discussed.

SCIENCE

Animal Classification Children's Style

Animal Classification Children's Style *is a good activity to use in introducing animal classification systems to children.*

LEARNING

❋ Observing different characteristics of animals

❋ Grouping animals by specific characteristics

MATERIALS

❋ Sets of 10 animal pictures for each group of children

STEPS

1. Pass out a set of 10 animal pictures to each group of children. Tell the children they are to create a way of grouping the animals so that each group has at least two common characteristics.

2. Tell the children they are to put the 10 animals into no more than four major groups.

3. After children classify the 10 animal pictures into four categories, they are to give each category a name.

4. After each team has developed their classification system, they can share the system with the class.

CRITICAL THINKING CHALLENGE

Children could add new categories as they look for other animal pictures.

 ACCOMMODATIONS

✔ When working with younger children it might be helpful to work with toy animals.

 EXTENSIONS

✔ Children could be asked to continue to look for pictures during the week, cut them out, and add them to the classification categories they devised.

SCIENCE

Neighborhood Habitats

*Neighborhood Habitats is a similar activity to Neighborhood Animals.
In Neighborhood Habitats children learn about where
animals in their neighborhood live.*

LEARNING

❋ Observing where animals live

❋ Matching animals with their habitats

MATERIALS

❋ Camera

❋ Film

STEPS

1. Tell the children they are going to take photographs of the habitats of animals found in their neighborhood. (If you have already completed the activity *Neighborhood Animals* you can tell the children that you are going to take pictures of the homes of animals you already photographed.)

2. Have the children talk about different types of habitats they know about.

3. Lead the children on a walk of the neighborhood telling them they each can find one habitat to photograph.

4. After the neighborhood walk, once the pictures are available, ask children to match pictures of habitats with the corresponding animals.

ACCOMMODATIONS

✓ Teachers may permit children to take the pictures.

✓ Teachers should remind children that they should not disturb or touch the different habitats they are to photograph.

EXTENSIONS

✓ As indicated above, if pictures were previously taken of animals in the neighborhood, children could be asked to match the animal pictures with the habitat pictures.

✓ Children could classify animals by their habitats.

SCIENCE

Community Zoo Model

Community Zoo Model is an excellent activity that allows children to create a model of a zoo that includes different classes of animals from their community area.

LEARNING

* ❋ Developing a representational model of neighborhood animals
* ❋ Reinforcing understanding of animal classes

MATERIALS

* ❋ Clay to construct animals
* ❋ One or more large flat cardboard boxes for the zoo grounds
* ❋ Clay, twigs, sand, and other materials for building living spaces for the zoo animals
* ❋ Toothpicks for animal identification signs
* ❋ Small pieces of construction paper for animal identification signs

STEPS

1. Have the children make a list of different classes of animals they have found in their community. (Children could use the information from the *Neighborhood Animals* activity in this section of the book.)

2. Once they identify different mammals, birds, insects, fish, etc., have some children begin to build clay models of several animals, about 2 inches in size, for each class of animal that is most common to the community.

3. While the animals are being constructed several other children can make little identification signs for the animals using toothpicks and small pieces of construction paper. The signs could be color coded to represent the different classes of animals.

4. Another group of children can make the zoo using a large flat cardboard box. Sand, small twigs, clay, and other materials can be used to form living spaces for the animals.

5. Children can set the model up as a display area for others to study.

 ACCOMMODATIONS

✔ It may be easier for younger children to cut out pictures of animals and glue or tape them to sticks instead of building clay animals.

✔ Small boxes could be used for the animal living spaces in the zoo.

 EXTENSIONS

✔ If children are studying a particular class of animals, an aquarium or other living environment can be used in place of the zoo.

✔ Children could build the zoo on a cart and take it from room to room to explain the classes of animals in the zoo that reflect those found in their neighborhood.

Hunting Animal Parts

Hunting Animal Parts *is an activity in which children match different body parts of animals. Through this activity children gain experience in identifying animal classifications based on animal body parts.*

MATERIALS

✳ Pencils
✳ Zoologist's Animal Parts Guide Sheets
✳ Nature walk area

STEPS

1. Pass out the Zoologist's Animal Parts Guide Sheet that follows. Tell the children that on the sheet in the left-hand column there is a list of body parts that they are to find while on a nature walk. In the right-hand column there is space for them to write down the types of animals that have those body parts.

2. Tell the children they can work with a partner to identify as many animals as they can find that have the same body parts. Remind them to keep a watch for very small animals as well as those that are bigger and easier to see.

3. Set a time limit for the nature walk.

4. Once children return from the nature walk, they can share the types of animals they found for each body part.

Zoologist's Animal Parts Guide Sheet	
Animal Body Parts to Find	Animals That Have the Body Part
Wings	
Claws	
Fins	
More Than Two Legs	
Fur Covering	
No Arms or Legs	
Tails	
Antlers or Antennae	
Ears	

(continued)

Hunting Animal Parts (continued)

ACCOMMODATIONS

✔ If a nature walking area is not available, children could look through a set of pictures or use magazines to identify animals with the body parts listed.

EXTENSIONS

✔ Children could be asked to identify other characteristics of animals such as making different sounds, moving in specific ways, or eating different types of food.

Ants on the Move

Ants on the Move is an activity that allows children to see how ants live and move about. As part of the activity children can be involved with caring for ants.

LEARNING

❋ Practice observing
❋ Recording data
❋ Caring for animals

MATERIALS

❋ Large jar
❋ Soil
❋ 10 to 15 ants
❋ Black strip of construction paper
❋ Rubber bands
❋ Fine wire netting
❋ Water
❋ Small wet sponge
❋ Sugar, honey, and bread crumbs

STEPS

1. Present children with a large jar filled with lightly dampened soil. Place a small wet sponge on top of the soil.

2. Put 10 to 15 ants in the jar along with a small amount of sugar.

3. Cover the top of the jar with a fine wire screen to keep the ants in the jar and to allow air in.

4. Wrap a black piece of construction paper around the jar so it covers the sides of the jar to about one inch from the top or at least an inch past the top of the soil line. Place a rubber band around the black paper to hold it onto the jar. The black paper is used to keep the ant habitat dark.

5. Once the ant habitat has been set up tell children that they will need to water the ant home daily with a small amount of water. They can also dampen the small sponge.

6. Children can also feed the ants with a small amount of sugar, bread crumbs, or honey.

7. A watering and feeding chart can be made up, and different children can be assigned to carry out these tasks each day.

8. Once the habitat is set up, tell the children that each day the black paper will be removed for a short time period and they will be asked to illustrate what they see. They can record the different tunnels they see in the jar over time.

ACCOMMODATIONS

✔ Children can be given magnifying glasses so they can observe more detail in the ants and tunnels.

✔ The daily drawings of tunnels can be put into a journal to show different tunnel paths over time.

EXTENSIONS

✔ Children can observe the ants and try to draw their different body parts.

✔ Children can record how many ants they see each day when the black paper is removed for a short time period.

SCIENCE

Bird Watch

Bird Watch *is a good activity for children to participate in as they work on developing a deeper understanding of how to classify animals.*

LEARNING

❋ Observing small details in animals
❋ Different characteristics of one class of animals

MATERIALS

❋ Pencils
❋ Binoculars (optional)
❋ Copy of the Bird Watchers Log Sheet for each child

STEPS

1. Inform the children that they are going to learn how to be bird watchers. One of the important things bird watchers must learn is how to identify differences in birds by looking at their characteristics.

2. Have children make a list of birds that they commonly see in their community.

3. If necessary, children could go on a bird watching walk and the children and teacher could point out different birds they know.

4. Pass out the Bird Watchers Log Sheet to the children. Tell them that they are to identify the specific characteristics of each of the birds they see.

5. Children can go on bird watching walks for several days if necessary to complete the task. Children could use binoculars if they are available.

6. When the task is completed, children can compare results and display their Bird Watchers Log Sheets can be displayed.

Bird Watcher Log Sheet					
Type of Bird	Beak Color	Wing Color(s)	Breast Color	Eye Color	Length of Bird

(continued)

SCIENCE

ACCOMMODATIONS

✓ The type of birds selected could appear to be more closely alike for older children.

✓ The characteristics of birds to be observed can be modified: color underneath the wings, type of feet (how many toes), etc.

✓ Pictures of birds could be used if ample birds are not available for bird walks.

EXTENSIONS

✓ Children can observe the different characteristics of males and females of the same bird type.

✓ Observations can be made of birds' movements. Which birds fly and stay in trees, which birds hop on the ground, which birds move upside down on trees, etc.?

SCIENCE

Moving Goldfish

Moving Goldfish is a fun activity that can be used to help children learn about controlling variables. The activity also helps children to learn to work with data.

LEARNING

❋ How variables can be controlled or changed

❋ Observing changes

MATERIALS

❋ Two goldfish bowls the same size

❋ Two goldfish (similar looking)

❋ Stones (equal number to be placed in the bottom of each bowl)

❋ Optional: other objects to be placed in the goldfish bowls (model trees, etc.)

❋ CD player with music

STEPS

1. Place two goldfish bowls in front of the children. Each bowl should have one goldfish in it. The two goldfish should look similar.

2. Ask children to observe the bowls and identify all the things that are the same between the two goldfish bowls. Make a list: same size bowl, both have stones in the bottom, both have the same kind of goldfish, etc.

3. Explain to children that these are all things that are the same and are being controlled for in an investigation they are going to do with the goldfish.

4. Tell them they are going to find out if playing soft music next to the goldfish bowl makes a goldfish swim around the bowl more. The music will be the thing that is different, the variable that is changed in their investigation.

5. Have children share what they think about music's ability to make goldfish swim more in the bowl.

6. Set the two goldfish bowls about 15 feet from each other. Children should be able to see both bowls.

7. Place a CD player next to the one bowl with the volume set low. You can select the type of music you want to play. Turn the speakers toward the one bowl so the music faces away from the other goldfish bowl.

8. Tell the children they're to observe both bowls while you turn on the music for 1 minute. Children are to see if the goldfish in the bowl next to the music moves more than the other goldfish.

9. Play the music for 1 minute then turn off the music for two minutes before turning the music back on for another minute.

10. Have children share their observations.

11. The teacher could raise the issue of whether or not there would be any change in movement if the music were played for longer amounts of time, for instance, 10 minutes.

CRITICAL THINKING CHALLENGE

Different types of music could be tried to see if there are any movement changes between the two goldfish.

(continued)

SCIENCE

Moving Goldfish *(continued)*

ACCOMMODATIONS

✔ The volume could be adjusted depending on how close or far away the bowls are. Some sound, though not as noticeable, will most likely carry to the second bowl.

EXTENSIONS

✔ Rather then music, other types of noises could be tried such as a light tapping next to the bowl.

✔ Older students could systematically record movement by marking tallies at 15- or 30-second intervals. A tally would be recorded for each fish if it were moving at each 15-second mark.

SCIENCE

Caterpillar to Butterfly

Caterpillar to Butterfly can be used to teach children about the life cycle of animals. The activity can also be used to help children make predictions about events.

LEARNING

* ✻ The life cycle of an animal
* ✻ Making predictions

MATERIALS

* ✻ A large jar with holes punched in the lid
* ✻ Twigs and leaves
* ✻ Caterpillar
* ✻ Line drawing of a butterfly
* ✻ Markers, crayons, or colored pencils

STEPS

1. Bring a jar to class that contains a caterpillar. The jar should have holes in the lid and be filled with twigs and several moist leaves.

2. Ask the children if they know what might happen to the caterpillar in the environment.

3. As children share or discover that the caterpillar will form a chrysalis, have children discuss how long they think it will take the caterpillar to form the chrysalis. Record the children's predictions.

4. Observe the caterpillar each day until the caterpillar forms the chrysalis.

5. Once the chrysalis is formed ask children what will happen to the chrysalis. When they determine a butterfly will form, ask how long they think it will take for the butterfly to form.

6. Pass out a small line drawing of a butterfly and ask the children to color the butterfly the color it will be when it comes out of the chrysalis.

7. Once the butterfly hatches, have children review their predictions about the length of time it would take for the butterfly to hatch and the color(s) the butterfly would be.

 ACCOMMODATIONS

✔ Children may be given the opportunity to change their predictions if it appears that none of the predictions is close.

✔ The teacher may want to post pictures of the life cycle of the butterfly.

 EXTENSIONS

✔ Children may go on a caterpillar hunt to find their own caterpillars for the activity. Teams could be formed, and each team could scout for one caterpillar.

✔ Children could do research before the event to discover what is the best way to care for the caterpillar.

✔ Children could investigate beforehand what is the best way to have the butterfly return to its natural environment after it has hatched.

SCIENCE

Neighborhood Plants

Neighborhood Plants is a good activity to use to introduce children to the different types of plants that grow where the children live.

LEARNING

* Identifying neighborhood plants
* Observing characteristics of neighborhood plants

MATERIALS

* Camera (digital or Polaroid would be best)
* Film
* 3-by-5-inch cards
* Pencils or markers

STEPS

1. Tell the children they are going on a nature hike to take pictures of different types of plants they have in their neighborhood (trees, bushes, flowers, etc.).

2. While on the nature walk the teacher and children can take pictures of a number of different trees, bushes, and flowers they see.

3. After children return to the classroom they can write the plant names on separate 3-by-5-inch cards.

4. The teacher can set the plant pictures and the set of cards with plant names at a learning station or on an interactive bulletin board for children to match up the pictures and cards.

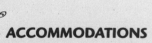

ACCOMMODATIONS

✔ The teacher may want to take the nature walk before the children do to identify the type of plant life available.

✔ Younger children could look at broad categories (bush, tree) on the walk, while older students could look for more specific categories (oak tree, white oak, ponderosa pine, red maple).

EXTENSIONS

✔ If more than one camera is available, children can be broken into groups with each group taking a certain number of pictures with its camera.

✔ Children can focus their picture taking to just trees or flowers.

✔ Children can make a book about plants in their neighborhood. They could glue each plant picture to a page and write the name of the plant underneath it.

SCIENCE

Flower Detectives

Flower Detectives *can be used to help children learn about how to see differences and similarities between flowers.*

LEARNING

❋ Differences between flowers
❋ Recording information

MATERIALS

❋ Five different types of flowers
❋ Name plates for in front of each flower
❋ Vases for each flower (or some other clear container)

STEPS

1. Set up on a table five different types of flowers that can be found in gardens around the neighborhood(s) where the children live.

2. Set up name plates in front of each flower so children can learn and remember what they are called.

3. Have children look at each of the flowers and tell which one(s) they like.

4. Direct children to a chart drawn on the board with the following information on it.

Detective Clues					
What is my name?	How many petals do I have?	How big is my flower?	What color(s) am I?	What do my leaves look like?	How am I different?

ACCOMMODATIONS

✔ Other parts of the flower could be identified for the children to observe in their role as detective.

✔ Pictures of flowers could be used in lieu of real flowers.

EXTENSIONS

✔ After the flowers have been compared and the differences listed, the flowers could be used to identify different flower parts.

✔ Flowers common to different geographical areas that are being studied by children could also be used.

SCIENCE

Leaf Classification

Leaf Classification *is an activity that allows children to develop their own classification system of leaves before they study standard classification. The activity has children use reasoning skills to group leaves based on criteria they identify.*

LEARNING

* Identifying a classification system for leaves
* Reasoning skills

MATERIALS

* An outdoor area that provides for a variety of leaves
* Bags for collecting leaves
* Recording chart for children's invented classification categories

STEPS

1. Have the children take a short walk with the instructions to pick up different kinds of leaves they find on the ground.

2. After children collect the leaves, have them sit down in an appropriate area outdoors (or they can return to the classroom) and have them divide the pile of leaves they collected into groups based on their invented criteria.

3. After children classify their leaves, have them share their systems with the other children.

4. Record their categories for leaf classification on the board.

5. The categories could be saved for later when children study a standard system for leaf classification.

 ACCOMMODATIONS

✔ It may be helpful to younger children if they first share some ideas as to how leaves might be put into groups (color, type of edges, general shapes, etc.).

✔ If a good variety of leaves is not available, the teacher may ask children to bring leaves from home.

 EXTENSIONS

✔ After children have finished classifying the leaves they collected they could gather books from the library to see if they can match each leaf with the name of the tree it fell from.

✔ Children could make their own leaf book in which they explain how leaves differ.

SCIENCE

Parts of a Plant

Parts of a Plant is an activity to be used to help children understand that a plant has different parts. Children can also learn about the function of certain parts of a plant.

LEARNING

* Different parts of a plant
* Functions for some plant parts

MATERIALS

* Potted nonflowered plant
* Potted flowered plant
* Flowered plant for each group (optional)

STEPS

1. Show the children a nonflowered plant and explain that they are going to learn about the different parts of the plant.

2. Remove the plant from the soil and show children the root system. Ask children what they think the root does for the plant. Functions to emphasize are bringing in water and dissolved minerals for the plant and roots helping hold the plant in place.

3. Have children next look at the stem. Ask the children what they think the stem does. Functions of a stem to emphasize are bringing water from the roots to the leaves, bringing dissolved minerals up from the roots to the leaves, conducting food down from the leaves to the roots, and holding many plants erect.

4. Have children look at the leaves. Ask them what they think leaves do for the plant. The main function of the leaf is to make food for the plant. The leaf also helps the plant to digest food and changes the food into energy that the plant needs.

5. After children review the parts and functions of the nonflowered plant, show them a flowered plant. Take the flowered plant out of the soil, and let children observe the parts of the plant they just studied. Then ask the children what they think the function of a flower is. The flower part of the plant is used to produce new plants of the same kind. People also use the flower for decoration because of its beauty.

6. After children have the chance to review the parts of a plant and the functions of the different parts, divide children into small groups and provide each group with a small plant (taken out of soil) to explore. Children could cut apart the different plant parts and place them on a sheet identifying each part.

(continued)

SCIENCE

Parts of a Plant *(continued)*

ACCOMMODATIONS

✔ If sufficient plants are not available for groups a picture of a plant could be presented to children and they could color or cut apart and name the different plant parts.

✔ It might be helpful to have the main functions of the plant prewritten on charts for children to review. The charts can be posted and remain available for children to see for several days.

EXTENSIONS

✔ Children could study the major parts of the flower (sepal, petal, stamen, and pistil).

✔ Children could be shown a variety of plants and then investigate different root systems.

SCIENCE

Classroom Terrarium

Classroom Terrarium is a project children can develop that will provide a model of the living plants that are most frequently found in their neighborhood.

LEARNING

* Developing a indoor environment for neighborhood plants
* Modeling skills

MATERIALS

* Glass container with a lid
* Assortment of small neighborhood plants
* Soil for plants
* Decorative objects (optional)

STEPS

1. Tell the children they will be developing indoor environments called terrariums for plants that are found in their neighborhood to grow.

2. Review with the children the different types of plants that grow in the neighborhood.

3. Show the children a number of small plants they just discussed. Parents or community individuals may be asked to help provide a number of small plants.

4. After the discussion, have children gather in groups and have each group identify three or four different plants they would like to grow in their terrarium.

5. Have each group pick up their plants along with a glass container and lid, some soil, and small rocks or any other decorative materials they might want to add.

6. Have children add about 2 to 3 inches of soil to their container.

7. Demonstrate how to set the plants in the terrarium and add rocks and other decorative objects.

8. Once the plants are planted have each team lightly sprinkle them and slide the lid partway over the glass container.

9. Children can also make a small sign identifying the type of plants contained in the terrarium.

10. Inform children that they will be responsible for maintaining their terrarium.

CRITICAL THINKING CHALLENGE

Modifications could be made to the amount of sun, air, and other variables to see the effects on plants in terrariums.

(continued)

Classroom Terrarium *(continued)*

 ACCOMMODATIONS

✔ If granted permission, children could go to different areas of the neighborhood to gather the small plants.

✔ The class could work as a group to have one larger terrarium instead of the group terrariums.

 EXTENSIONS

✔ Plants could be classified and then placed in like groups in the terrariums.

Mold Garden

Mold Garden is a fun activity for children that helps them to understand how certain conditions such as moist, dark locations affect food.

LEARNING

❋ The effects of moist and dark conditions on food

❋ Observation and recording of changes in food

MATERIALS

❋ Large glass jar with lid

❋ Sand (fill the glass jar about ⅓ full)

❋ Small pieces of food (cheese, bread, orange, and others picked by children)

❋ Recording chart as illustrated

❋ Camera (optional)

STEPS

1. Ask the children if they know what mold is. Can they think of any foods that get moldy? Make a list of the items children suggest.

2. Tell the children they are going to make a mold garden. They are going to observe and record their observations of food becoming moldy.

3. Set out a large glass jar filled about ⅓ full of sand. Pour some water on the sand.

4. Place a piece of an orange, a small piece of bread, and a small piece of cheese inside the jar and screw the lid on tight. Take a picture of the food items (optional).

5. Ask children how long it might take each of the items to begin to form mold. Record predictions on the board.

6. Tell children that tomorrow you will bring in some additional foods that children had mentioned at the start of the lesson.

7. Place the jar in a dark area of the classroom, or cover it with a box.

8. Each day have children observe and record if they see mold on the different food items. When the activity is finished take another picture to show the changes in the food items (optional).

Food	Day 1	Day 2	Day 3	Day 4	Day 5	Day 6	Day 7	Day 8	Day 9	Day 10
Orange										
Bread										
Cheese										
Apple										
Meat										

Put a NO in the box if there is no mold on the food and put the word MOLD in the box if there is mold on the food item.

(continued)

SCIENCE

Mold Garden (continued)

ACCOMMODATIONS

✓ The teacher may show children pictures of mold on food and nonfood items to help reinforce what mold is.

EXTENSIONS

✓ Children may also predict which foods may not form mold over time.

✓ Each individual child may be asked to bring in his or her own jar along with several food items he or she thinks will form mold.

✓ If pictures are taken, children can create a class book reporting how long it took the different types of food to form mold.

SCIENCE

Plants Break Rocks

Plants Break Rocks is a fun activity for children. It helps them see the amazing strength of plants.

LEARNING

✳ The strength of plants

MATERIALS

✳ Prepared plaster mix
✳ Clear plastic cup
✳ Two bean seeds

STEPS

1. Pour plaster mix (mixed but not hardened) into a clear plastic cup.

2. Gently push two bean seeds into the plaster so the beans are just below the surface.

3. Place the cup near the window.

4. Ask children if they think the seeds will grow. If the seeds grow, what do you think the plants will look like?

5. Let the plaster containing the seeds set. Each day have children observe the cup to see if any growth is taking place.

ACCOMMODATIONS

✔ Children could prepare the plaster mix, and each child could plant his or her own bean seeds into a cup.

EXTENSIONS

✔ Children could try to plant different types of seeds.

✔ Children could plant the seeds into other moistened materials such as clay, rocks, and flour and observe the results.

SCIENCE

Using Our Senses

Using Our Senses is a good activity to use to help children become aware of the senses they use when encountering different objects in their environment.

LEARNING

❋ The senses used by humans
❋ Awareness of the different senses to use when encountering objects

MATERIALS

❋ Chart paper and marker
❋ Objects for identifying senses: orange, whistle, cotton ball, cup of vinegar, flower, cookie, clock (one that ticks)
❋ Basket to hold the objects

STEPS

1. Place the basket of objects in front of the children.

2. Hold up the orange and ask the children which senses they could use to describe the orange:

   Can they taste part of it?

   Can they smell part of it?

   Can they see part of it?

   Can they hear any part of it? Could it make noise?

   Can they feel any part of it?

3. Check off the senses used to identify the orange on a chart as shown on pg 372.

4. After children identify which senses they use to identify the orange, have children go through each of the objects.

5. Have children add up the number of check marks for each column and ask them: Which senses were used the most? Which were used the least? You could also ask which sense children think they use the most each day.

CRITICAL THINKING CHALLENGE

Children could problem solve to determine how a different sense might be used to identify an object. Is there a way an orange can make a sound?

(continued)

SCIENCE

Using Our Senses *(continued)*

Senses					
Object	See	Hear	Touch	Smell	Taste
Orange	/		/	/	/
Whistle					
Cotton Ball					
Vinegar					
Flower					
Cookie					
Clock					

ACCOMMODATIONS

✔ A variety of other objects could be used. The objects selected may allow for more than one sense to be used to describe a single object.

EXTENSIONS

✔ Children could be asked to identify a number of other objects over the course of a week and identify which senses might be used to describe them. At the end of the week totals for each sense could be identified, and children could be asked to make a generalization about which senses we use most frequently.

✔ Children could discuss which senses might be most important for different types of jobs, such as baker, detective, painter, etc.

SCIENCE

Post It on My Body Part

Post It on My Body Part can be used to help children learn the location and function of different parts of their bodies. Both external and internal body parts can be used.

MATERIALS

❋ Small stickers

STEPS

1. Have the children stand in a circle. Tell them they are going to take turns asking children to locate different body parts. When a child identifies a body part children will place a sticker on their body where the part is located.

2. Provide children a list of body parts to choose from. After the body parts are located children can be asked to tell what the function of the body part is.

3. Children will take turns asking for, locating, and explaining the function of the different body parts. If the children disagree about the location or function they are to check with the teacher for clarification.

4. Listed below are some possible body parts for children to consider.

eyes	shoulder	heart	lung area
nose	wrist	artery	trachea
ears	knee	place to	molar
chin	elbow	feel a pulse	stomach
		air passage	

TEACHER NOTE

The teacher may want to observe children closely if partners are used to ensure that children place stickers on "appropriate" body parts only.

(continued)

Post It on My Body Part *(continued)*

ACCOMMODATIONS

✔ Stickers could be placed on life-size drawings of the children in lieu of on each child.

✔ The teacher could stand in the middle of the circle while the children are being asked to locate body parts to see if children are identifying the correct location.

EXTENSIONS

✔ If different body parts were being reviewed the stickers could be color coded to reflect the circulatory system, respiratory system, etc.

✔ Children could use life-size body drawings to place illustrated pieces of internal body parts (liver, small intestine, etc.)

✔ Partners could work together with guidance from the teacher.

The Animal Most Like Me

The Animal Most Like Me *is a fun exercise that can be used to help children reinforce their understanding of body components.*

LEARNING

＊ Body components

＊ Comparing body components between a person and animal

MATERIALS

＊ Models of different types of animals (bird, horse, fish, rabbit, monkey)

STEPS

1. Set up several different animal models for the children to look at.

2. Tell the children they are going to try to determine which of the animals has the most external body parts in common with humans. For each animal they are to list the body parts that are similar to humans'.

3. When children are finished they are to share each of their lists and identify which animal they think has the most body parts similar to a human being.

ACCOMMODATIONS

✔ The teacher could review human body parts.

✔ The teacher may wish to identify the names of the different body parts of animals with younger children.

EXTENSIONS

✔ Children could use the library, the Internet, or other resources to identify the internal body parts of the animals and make comparisons of internal body parts.

✔ Specific body parts such as teeth, skin, toes, etc. could also be compared separately.

SCIENCE

Fingerprint Me

Fingerprint Me is a good activity to use with children to identify what fingerprints look like and what they are used for.

LEARNING

❋ What a fingerprint is

❋ Comparing fingerprints

❋ What fingerprints are used for

MATERIALS

❋ Transparency pieces cut into 2-inch squares

❋ Washable ink pads

❋ Wet wipes or water, soap, and paper towels

❋ Overhead projector

STEPS

1. Find out from the children what they know about fingerprints. After the discussion tell them each of their fingerprints is unique and that fingerprints can be used to identify people.

2. Have children come up one at a time and have them press the thumb of their left hand onto an ink pad. The teacher should help make the thumbprint impression.

3. Have each child remove his or her thumb from the ink pad and with the help of the teacher press it onto a 2-by-2-inch piece of transparency.

4. Have the children clean their thumbs with wet wipes or soap and water.

5. After children make their thumbprints, place four of the transparency pieces on an overhead projector and have the children compare the fingerprints. Repeat this until all children's fingerprints have been shown.

6. Have children discuss other reasons they might use fingerprints.

ACCOMMODATIONS

✔ Younger children may need more assistance from their teacher with making their fingerprints.

EXTENSIONS

✔ Children could make fingerprints of both their thumbs and compare them.

✔ Two sets of fingerprints could be made for each child. One set of their fingerprints could be mixed up with others, and children could see if they could find their own fingerprints.

SCIENCE

Hair

Hair is a classification activity that allows children to observe differences in hair. The classification experience provides children with the opportunity to invent a classification system based on criteria they observe.

LEARNING

* ✳ Inventing a classification system
* ✳ Observing similarities and differences
* ✳ Making generalizations

MATERIALS

* ✳ A variety of hair samples for each child or small group of children (Human and/or animal hair could be used.)
* ✳ Magnifying glasses for each child or group (optional)

STEPS

1. Provide each child or small group of children with eight to 10 pieces of hair of different appearance, texture, and color. (Sanitary conditions should be monitored when using hair)

2. Tell the children they should take some time to observe the hair.

3. Provide each child or group with a magnifying glass so they can make finer observations of the pieces of hair (optional).

4. After the children have had time to observe the hair, ask each child or group to put the hair into different piles so that each pile of hair is the same somehow.

5. Have children come up with a name for each pile of hair.

6. All children or groups can share their invented classification systems for hair.

7. Once all classification systems have been shared, ask children if there are any generalizations they might make about different types of hair.

ACCOMMODATIONS

✔ Younger children could complete the activity as one large group. Several pieces of hair could be passed out at once for children to make observations about.

EXTENSIONS

✔ Children could make comparisons between human and animal hair.

✔ The hair could be observed under a microscope to make closer observations regarding the different hair samples.

SCIENCE

Charting the Foods We Eat

Charting the Foods We Eat is a good activity to help children become aware of their good and poor eating habits.

LEARNING

❋ Monitoring the good and bad foods one eats

❋ Understanding of the food pyramid concept

MATERIALS

❋ Blank Food Pyramid Sheet for each child

❋ Copy of food pyramid to display

STEPS

1. Review with the children the food pyramid. (If children have not been introduced to the food pyramid, you should provide several lessons on the pyramid before completing this activity.)

2. Tell the children that understanding the food pyramid is good for healthy living. More important, however, they need to be aware of how well they apply the food pyramid to their daily living.

3. Provide each child with a handout containing a blank pyramid. Tell children they are to write down on the pyramid the foods they eat each night for one week. At the end of the week they will discuss how healthy their diet has been.

CRITICAL THINKING CHALLENGE

Children could prepare menus at school for snacks that reflect good eating habits.

Food Guide Pyramid
A Guide to Daily Food Choices

Fats, Oils, & Sweets
USE SPARINGLY

KEY
☐ Fat (naturally occurring and added) ☐ Sugars (added)
These symbols show fat and added sugars in foods.

Milk, Yogurt, & Cheese Group
2-3 SERVINGS

Meat, Poultry, Fish, Dry Beans, Eggs, & Nuts Group
2-3 SERVINGS

Vegetable Group
3-5 SERVINGS

Fruit Group
2-4 SERVINGS

Bread, Cereal, Rice, & Pasta Group
6-11 SERVINGS

Source: U.S. Department of Agriculture/U.S. Department of Health and Human Services

(continued)

SCIENCE

Charting the Foods We Eat *(continued)*

✔ ACCOMMODATIONS

✔ Teachers could have children draw or glue pictures of the different food groups they have at each evening meal at home.

✔ Children can do the activity in a large group by having them review the food items that were on the school lunch menu each day.

EXTENSIONS

✔ Older students could also investigate the number of calories in certain foods they eat.

✔ Children could examine menus for restaurants and select a well-balanced meal.

SCIENCE

Chapter 17

Earth Science

Activities developed for the earth sciences are centered around the topics of temperature, rocks and soils, environment, and space. Children are involved in learning about the properties of earth and space. Through investigations they also have the opportunity to develop their abilities to observe, classify, hypothesize, control variables, and make generalizations based on data.

Daily Temperature Readings

Daily Temperature Readings *is a good activity to use to determine children's ability to read and compare outdoor temperatures.*

❋ Reading and recording outdoor temperatures

❋ Comparing daily range of temperatures

MATERIALS

❋ Outdoor thermometer

❋ Daily recording sheet for three separate temperature readings

STEPS

. Stick an outdoor thermometer to a window in your classroom so it does not receive direct sunlight.

. Have the children review how a thermometer is read in Fahrenheit.

. Tell children that for the next two weeks (or another time period) children in pairs will read and record the temperature three times each day: when they come into the classroom in the morning, before lunchtime, and before they leave school.

4. At the end of each day the three temperature readings can be reviewed, and children can note the change in temperature throughout the school day.

5. At the end of the two-week time period children will review the temperatures and compare the daily changes. The following questions could be raised:

Which day had the highest temperature reading?

Which day had the highest *average* temperature reading?

Which day had the lowest temperature reading?

Which day had the lowest *average* temperature reading?

Which day had the biggest change in temperature readings?

Which day had the smallest change in temperature readings?

Were the changes in temperature between morning and noon normally bigger or smaller than the changes between noon and afternoon?

(continued)

SCIENCE

Daily Temperature Readings *(continued)*

 ACCOMMODATIONS

✓ If the activity is used while children are learning how to read temperatures, a larger thermometer might be used so all children can read the temperature together.

✓ If the outdoor thermometer cannot be attached to a window or be placed out of direct sunlight, another outdoor location could be used.

 EXTENSIONS

✓ Children could go online and compare the temperature reading at their school with the temperature reading for their community, state, etc.

✓ Children could color on thermometer templates the daily temperature readings to create a visual representation of the changes.

SCIENCE

Keeping Hot Chocolate Warm

Keeping Hot Chocolate Warm *is a fun activity for helping children practice reading thermometers. The activity also provides children with the opportunities to work with the process skill control of variables.*

LEARNING

* Reading thermometers
* Controlling variables
* Carrying out an investigation
* Hypothesis making

MATERIALS

* Plastic cup
* Styrofoam cup
* Coffee mug (ceramic)
* Four submersible thermometers
* Container of hot chocolate

STEPS

1. Place three cups in front of the children: one plastic, one Styrofoam, and one ceramic coffee mug. Ask children which cup they think would keep hot chocolate the warmest and why they think so.

2. Have children make an initial guess and provide an explanation.

3. After some guesses and reasons are shared, take a vote of the class to see which type of cup is thought to be most likely to keep the hot chocolate the warmest.

4. Bring out a container of hot chocolate. Place a submersible thermometer into the container for several minutes. Read and record the temperature.

5. Place an equal amount of hot chocolate (about 6 ounces) into each of the three cups along with a submersible thermometer in each. Wait 5 minutes and then read and record the temperature on each thermometer.

6. Have children analyze the results. Did their choice of cup (plastic, Styrofoam, ceramic) keep the hot chocolate the warmest?

(continued)

SCIENCE

Keeping Hot Chocolate Warm *(continued)*

ACCOMMODATIONS

✔ The initial temperature of the chocolate may vary depending upon whether the teacher or the children are going to do the pouring and reading.

✔ For children who have not yet learned how to read thermometers, the teacher could start with *warm* hot chocolate and have children compare which cup keeps the hot chocolate the warmest by tasting it.

EXTENSIONS

✔ Additional containers could be tried, such as cups made of tin or glass.

✔ After the results have been obtained, children may be asked if they think the same cup that kept the hot chocolate the warmest might also keep a glass of cold water the coldest.

✔ Children could use only one type of container and measure to see if different substances that start off at the same temperature are kept equally warm over a particular amount of time. For example, does a plastic cup keep hot water, hot chocolate, and hot tea at the same temperature over 5 minutes?

SCIENCE

Effects of Two Ice Cubes

Effects of Two Ice Cubes can be used to have children reason about temperature changes when variables change. This activity provides children with the opportunity to make a hypothesis using known data.

LEARNING

❋ Changes in temperature

❋ Effects of changes in variables

❋ Hypothesis making using known data

❋ Reasoning skills with temperature changes

MATERIALS

❋ Two cups of water of equal amounts set out at room temperature

❋ Two submersible thermometers

❋ Three ice cubes

STEPS

1. Ask the children what they think will happen when one ice cube is placed into a cup of water that is at room temperature.

2. Tell children that they are going to measure the temperature of two cups, one marked A and the other marked B, both containing water at room temperature.

3. Place submersible thermometers into the cups, wait 2–3 minutes and then remove them. Measure and record the readings for cup A and cup B.

4. Next tell children that they are going to put an ice cube into cup A and let it stand for 5 minutes.

5. Place the ice cube and submersible thermometer into cup A. While children are waiting the 5 minutes to read the new temperature, have them make guesses as to how much colder they think the water will be after the ice cube has been in the cup for 5 minutes. Guesses can be recorded on the board.

6. After 5 minutes read and record the temperature. Compare the results with the initial guesses.

7. Place cup A off to the side and show the children cup B. Review the temperature that was recorded for cup B.

8. Have children review how much cooler cup A was after one ice cube was placed in it for 5 minutes.

9. Tell children that two ice cubes will be placed into cup B. Based on what they learned about cup A, how much cooler do they think cup B will get if two ice cubes are put into it for 5 minutes?

10. Have children make their guesses and provide rationales for their thinking.

11. Place two ice cubes into cup B along with the submersible thermometer, and wait 5 minutes. Read and record the new temperature.

(continued)

SCIENCE

Effects of Two Ice Cubes (continued)

12. Compare the results with their guesses, and then observe the different results between cup A and cup B. Since two ice cubes were put into B, did it cool off twice as much over the 5 minute period?

 ACCOMMODATIONS

✓ The teacher could read the thermometers if the children are unable to.

✓ Children would not need to make a guess about the temperature change for cup A.

 EXTENSIONS

✓ Children could be asked to guess how long it might take the ice cube to melt in cup A and in cup B.

✓ Older children could record the results from cup A and cup B and then, based on the percent of change, make an estimate for the change if a third cup was added and three ice cubes were placed into it.

Temperature Chase

Temperature Chase is a good activity to use with children who have some experience with reading thermometers. The activity provides children with a deeper understanding of how temperatures can vary from one location to another.

LEARNING

✳ How temperatures can differ

✳ Making predictions regarding temperature based on location of the thermometer

MATERIALS

✳ Thermometers for each group of children

STEPS

1. Set out two thermometers in the classroom and read their temperatures. After you share the readings of the two thermometers (they should be similar), place one in an area away from an external wall and place the second one inside the classroom so it is up against an external wall that is exposed to the sun. Wait several minutes. Read both thermometers. Discuss the readings.

2. Tell children that sometimes temperatures in a single room may be different depending on a number of factors.

3. Divide children up into small groups. Inform them each group will be given a thermometer to measure the temperature outside.

4. They are to place the thermometers in different locations around the school building for several minutes and read the temperatures. They should record the temperatures and locations on a sheet of paper. They could be placed on the ground, in shaded areas, near wooded objects, on cement, near dark areas, etc.

5. After children return to the classroom, ask them to share their findings.

6. Older children may be asked if they see any patterns to temperature readings and locations.

ACCOMMODATIONS

✔ The teacher could double-check the children's thermometer readings before they are recorded if children are still learning how to read thermometers.

✔ The teacher could read the thermometers and have children identify the locations.

EXTENSIONS

✔ Children could measure temperatures of different locations in the classroom.

✔ Children could read thermometers that have been placed under different colored sheets of paper that have been placed in direct sunlight.

SCIENCE

Warm Up to My Lightbulb

Warm Up to My Lightbulb can be used to have children compare lightbulbs and the heat they generate. Students can discover how much heat is generated by lightbulbs of different wattages.

LEARNING

* Making comparisons
* Hypothesizing based on known data

MATERIALS

* Four lamps
* Four lightbulbs: one with a 40-watt bulb, one with a 60-watt bulb, one with a 75-watt bulb, and one with a 100-watt bulb
* Four thermometers

STEPS

1. Set up four lamps without lamp shades. Use a 40-watt lightbulb in lamp A, a 60-watt lightbulb in lamp B, a 75-watt lightbulb in lamp C, and a 100-watt lightbulb in lamp D.

2. Place a thermometer about 6 inches from each lightbulb. Check to make sure all thermometers have the same temperature reading before you start. Record the temperature of each thermometer on a small card in front of the lamp for children to see.

3. Tell the children they are going to discover how much heat lightbulbs generate.

4. Turn on lamps A and B for 5 minutes. Then read the thermometers and record the temperatures on the cards for lamps A and B next to the starting temperatures.

5. Before turning on lamp C, have children discuss the differences in wattage and temperatures for lamps A (40 watts) and B (60 watts). Based on their findings, have children make a prediction as to what the temperature might be for lamp C, which contains the 75-watt bulb.

6. After the predictions have been made, turn on lamp C for 5 minutes and then record the temperature. Compare the temperature readings with the children's predictions.

7. Go through the same procedure for lamp D. Have children make a prediction based on the temperatures for lamps A, B, and C. Turn on lamp D for 5 minutes and record the temperature.

8. Have the children review the results.

CRITICAL THINKING CHALLENGE

Different types of bulbs with the same wattage could be used. Does a clear bulb with 40 watts put out more or less heat than a white, frosted bulb? Does a yellow (bug) lightbulb put out as much heat as a regular white frosted bulb?

(continued)

SCIENCE

Warm Up to My Lightbulb *(continued)*

ACCOMMODATIONS

✔ One lamp could be used, with the light-bulbs being replaced after each temperature reading.

✔ Children can take turns reading the thermometers.

✔ The temperature readings could be recorded on a chart so children could read the different temperature increases for the different bulbs.

EXTENSIONS

✔ Temperatures could be recorded with a single lightbulb over longer time periods to observe patterns. What is the temperature of the lamp with the 40-watt bulb after 5 minutes? After 10 minutes?

Fahrenheit to Celsius

Fahrenheit to Celsius is an activity to be used to teach older children how to convert temperature readings from Fahrenheit to Celsius. The activity can also be used to practice reading temperatures in Fahrenheit and Celsius.

LEARNING

❋ Converting temperature readings from Fahrenheit to Celsius

❋ Reading temperatures in Fahrenheit and Celsius

STEPS

1. On the board write down the freezing (32) and boiling (212) points for Fahrenheit in one column and the freezing (0) and boiling (100) points for Celsius in another column.

2. Have children determine the range between freezing and boiling points for each (Fahrenheit, 180, and Celsius, 100). One degree Fahrenheit is equal to about 5/9 of a degree Celsius. Knowing this, ask children how many degrees Celsius is equivalent to a change of 10 degrees Fahrenheit (18).

3. Ask the children what the degree difference is between the freezing points of Fahrenheit and Celsius (32).

4. Knowing the above information, tell children that the way to convert Fahrenheit to Celsius is to:

   Subtract 32 degrees from Fahrenheit so both start at the same base.

   Then multiply Fahrenheit by 5/9 to account for the difference in range of degrees (Fahrenheit, 180, versus Celsius, 100).

   So, Celsius is equal to Fahrenheit minus 32 degrees times ⁵⁄₉.

   $$C = (F - 32) \times ⁵⁄₉$$

   So, if Fahrenheit is 80 degrees, Celsius would be 26.6 degrees: 80 degrees Fahrenheit minus 32 degrees equals 48 degrees; 48 degrees times ⁵⁄₉ equals 26.6 degrees Celsius.

5. Have children practice making several Fahrenheit-to-Celsius conversions.

Fahrenheit to Celsius	
Fahrenheit Temperature	**Celsius Temperature**
90 degrees	
120 degrees	
40 degrees	
72 degrees	

(continued)

SCIENCE

Fahrenheit to Celsius *(continued)*

ACCOMMODATIONS

✔ Younger students who do not have a computational understanding of how to multiply fractions could make estimates of Fahrenheit to Celsius conversions.

✔ Children could make the Fahrenheit-to-Celsius conversions by reading a thermometer that records both Fahrenheit and Celsius.

EXTENSIONS

✔ Children could learn how to do reverse conversions, converting Celsius to Fahrenheit using the formula:

Fahrenheit = ⅘ of Celsius + 32 degrees.

✔ Children could take daily temperatures in Fahrenheit and convert and report the temperatures in both Fahrenheit and Celsius.

SCIENCE

Food Temperatures

Food Temperatures can be used reinforce children's ability to read thermometers and to make estimates about the temperature of objects.

LEARNING

✳ Reading standard and food thermometers
✳ Estimating temperatures of foods we eat

MATERIALS

✳ A variety of foods at various temperatures (hot dog, cooked rice, gelatin, scrambled eggs, pickle, french fries, ice cream, and others)
✳ Food thermometer (regular thermometer may work)
✳ Plates for the food
✳ Oven, toaster oven, microwave oven, or heating lamp (to keep foods at serving temperatures)
✳ Cooler (to keep foods at serving temperatures)

STEPS

1. Ask the children what they think are the temperatures of different foods we eat.

2. Ask them what they think are the temperatures of the following foods when they are put on their plates: hot dog, cooked rice, gelatin, scrambled eggs, pickle, french fries, and ice cream. (The teacher may choose to make substitutions.)

3. Record some responses on a chart.

4. Show children a thermometer used in cooking. Tell them they will be taking the temperature of the foods they just discussed.

5. Bring out one food at a time and have children measure the temperature of the food.

6. Record on the chart the temperature of each food after the thermometer has been in the food for about 4 minutes.

7. After children have a chance to observe and discuss the recorded temperature of each food, bring out several new food items that might normally be the same temperatures as those foods that were already recorded.

8. Ask children to estimate how hot these foods might be based on what they discovered about the temperatures of the other foods. Record their guesses on a new chart.

9. After the estimates are made, measure the temperature of each of the foods and compare the children's guesses with the actual temperature results.

10. Have children look at how close their guesses were to the actual food temperatures of the first group, and then compare the guesses and actual temperatures for the second set of food. Is the children's second set of guesses more accurate than the first set of guesses?

(continued)

Food Temperatures (continued)

Food Temperatures		
Food	Temperature Guess	Actual Temperature
Hot Dog		
Cooked Rice		
Gelatin		
Scrambled Eggs		
Pickle		
French Fries		
Ice Cream		

ACCOMMODATIONS

✔ Other foods may be used.

✔ To maintain the serving temperature of foods the activity could be done in a kitchen.

EXTENSIONS

✔ Thermometers could be kept in the food to determine how long it takes food to cool off.

✔ Different types of serving plates could be used to see if french fries, for example, stay warm longer on one type of plate (Styrofoam™) than another (paper).

✔ The temperatures of liquids could also be investigated. What are the temperatures of such liquids as hot water, hot chocolate, chilled lemonade, and chilled milk?

SCIENCE

Stone Sorting

Stone Sorting is a good activity to use while children are working on classification and sorting skills in science. Children can invent stone groupings before they are introduced to more formal rock classifications.

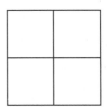

LEARNING

❊ Inventing a classification system for stones

❊ Observing similarities and differences among stones

MATERIALS

❊ Bags with a different assortment of stones for each group

❊ 8½-by-11-inch of paper for each group

STEPS

1. Provide each small group of children with a bag of stones

2. Have children observe the similarities and differences among the stones found in their bag.

3. Provide each small group with an 8½-by-11-inch piece of paper with lines drawn on it to make four rectangles.

4. Tell the children they are to put rocks into groups in the rectangles so that the rocks in each rectangle are the same somehow. They do not have to use all four rectangles. If they can find a way to group the stones in more than four ways, they can get another sheet of paper.

5. Once children have finished with the task, bring the small groups together and have them share their grouping criteria. The criteria can be recorded on a board or chart.

6. After all groups have shared their grouping criteria, have them review kinds of things that can be looked at when studying stones and review the different ways in which stones were grouped.

ACCOMMODATIONS

✔ For younger children the teacher may try to select some stones that are visually very different to make the groupings of stones an easier task.

✔ Different-size stones may be used to provide a category for size.

EXTENSIONS

✔ Before the stone sorting activity takes place, children could go on a stone collecting hike to pick up and identify stones common to their area.

✔ Children could be provided picks in order to group stones by how they are affected by being picked at.

Water and Soil

Water and Soil can be used to introduce children to different types of soils and how they react differently to water.

LEARNING

✳ Different types of soils

✳ How soils react to water

MATERIALS

✳ Water

✳ Three small clear plastic cups

✳ Three different types of soil (sand, garden soil, potting soil, or other soil)

✳ Lab sheets

STEPS

1. Set up three small clear plastic cups filled with different types of soils to within 1½ inches of the top of the cup.

2. Place ⅓ cup of water into each of the cups at the same time. Have children observe each cup over time, and have them notice what happens to the water in each cup.

3. After several minutes have children look at the bottom of the cup to observe how much water has settled down at the bottom.

4. Have children discuss what they have seen.

5. Pass out a lab sheet with three cups illustrated in the middle of the paper. Tell children they should illustrate what happened to the water in each of the cups. Children are also to label each cup with the type of soil that was in it.

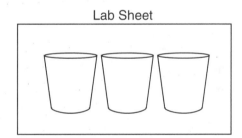

Lab Sheet

ACCOMMODATIONS

✔ If children are unable to illustrate the contents of the cup the teacher could take pictures of each cup with a tag identifying the type of soil contained in it.

EXTENSIONS

✔ Children could observe the top part of each soil and record how long it takes to dry.

✔ Different types of liquids could be put into the cups to observe the differences. For example, milk, water dyed red, or orange juice might be used in lieu of water.

✔ The effects of hot versus cold water could be studied with the same soils.

SCIENCE

Soil Samples

Soil Samples is a good activity to introduce children to the study of soils, minerals, and rocks. Children learn to observe what is found in different soils.

LEARNING

❋ Properties that make up different soils
❋ Differences in soils

MATERIALS

❋ Bags of soil collected from different locations (paper or reclosable plastic bags)
❋ Magnifying glasses for each group
❋ Piece of newspaper for each group
❋ Blank sheet of paper for recording observations
❋ Clear plastic cup for each group

STEPS

1. Take the children on a nature walk to collect soils from different locations.

2. Have them bring along paper or reclosable plastic bags to place the soil samples in.

3. Children should record where they pick up the soil sample from: by the river, by the palm tree, in Paul's garden, and so on.

4. When children return to the classroom, have them form small groups. Each group should be given a magnifying glass, a piece of newspaper, a clear plastic cup, and a blank sheet of paper.

5. Give each group a bag of soil from the field trip, and tell the children to dump the soil onto the newspaper. They are to spread the soil out and identify and record on the blank sheet of paper what they find: dirt, small pebbles, roots, dark-colored dirt, etc.

6. When children finish with their observations and recordings, have them put the soil into the plastic cup. Have the children bring the plastic cups along with their observation recording sheets to an area set up for display.

7. Instruct children that as they have time over the next several days they can examine the different cups and they can add other observations to the sheets.

ACCOMMODATIONS

✔ Teachers can have children in a large group observe and discuss the things they see in each of the soil bags if children are just beginning to work on the process skill of observing.

✔ Teachers could collect soil types ahead of time to ensure that there is a variety of things to see in the soils selected.

EXTENSIONS

✔ Children could review all the properties from the soils to see if some properties are more common than others. For example, is there a strong possibility that small pebbles will be found in soil?

Edible Soil

Edible Soil is a fun activity that has children work on the process skill of model building in science. Through the activity children also have the opportunity to add depth to their understanding of soils.

LEARNING

* Building models
* Using observation to create different soil types

MATERIALS

* A bag of potting soil for each table
* A variety of food materials to make the model soil (chocolate cake, brown sugar, sugar cubes, chili powder, and other seasonings)
* Forks for mixing or chopping
* Bags for the edible soil models

STEPS

1. Provide children with a small bag or container of potting soil.

2. Tell children that they are going to try to make up a second bag of foodstuff so that it looks the same as the bag with the potting soil.

3. Place children in small groups around tables. Each child can work separately or with a partner.

4. On each table there should be a bag or two of the soil to be imitated.

5. Also on each table there should be the collection of edible foods that can be used to develop a model of the potting soil. The food materials selected should have properties similar to those found in the potting soil used. Forks or other objects for breaking down the sugar cubes or mixing the food materials should also be provided.

6. After children create their model of the soil they are to place the contents in another bag. The bags with the edible soil might be coded differently from the bags containing the real soil.

7. When all children are finished, the bags containing the real soil and the bags containing the edible model soil should be placed alongside each other. Children can discuss which of the bags with the made-up soil appear to be most like the bags with the real soil.

CRITICAL THINKING CHALLENGE

Children could also be given the challenge not only to create a model soil that looks like the real soil but also to create a good-tasting mock soil.

ACCOMMODATIONS

✔ Potting soils with few different elements might be selected for younger children.

EXTENSIONS

✔ Children could be asked to make up recipe cards for their model soil explaining what ingredients were used.

SCIENCE

Rock Shower

Rock Shower is an exciting activity for children to observe. It provides children with the opportunity to see the effects of temperature changes on solids.

LEARNING

✳ The effects of temperature change on rocks

MATERIALS

✳ A large clear plastic container with a cover (with a 2-inch hole in the cover)
✳ Small pot of boiling water
✳ Safety glasses
✳ Frozen rock (several different rocks may be tried)

STEPS

1. Place a very cold flint or rock into a large clear plastic container. Depending upon the climate one lives in, a rock from outdoors may be used, or you may place a rock in a freezer until it reaches the temperature in the freezer.

2. Place the container some distance from the children. The teacher should put on a pair of safety glasses.

3. Cover the container with a lid with a small opening, about 2 inches in diameter.

4. Tell the children you are going to pour some boiling water over the rock. Ask them what they think might happen when the boiling water is poured over the rock.

5. Slowly pour the boiling water over the rock and observe the rock. The rock should begin to explode as the outer layers begin to heat and expand faster than the layers in the center of the rock.

 ACCOMMODATIONS

✔ Several children at a time wearing safety glasses could stand closer to the container to better see the reaction.

 EXTENSIONS

✔ A variety of frozen rock types could be tried. Give children the responsibility of identifying different effects the boiling water has on each of them.

✔ Metals, glass, and other solids could also be used in the investigation.

SCIENCE

Mineral Jar

Mineral Jar helps children experience how layers of the earth are formed.

LEARNING

* How layers of the earth are formed

MATERIALS

* Medium glass jar
* Small pebbles
* Soil
* Sand
* Water
* Lab sheet with an empty jar drawn on it for each child

STEPS

1. Tell the children that they are going to perform an activity to demonstrate how different layers of the earth are formed.

2. Show them a medium-size jar. Ask different children to come up to add different types of earth materials to the jar. Some earth materials to use are small pebbles, sand, and soil from a garden. More materials could be added.

3. Once each child carefully dumps the earth material into the jar, add some water.

4. Have several children take turns slowly shaking the jar so all the earth materials are well mixed.

5. Tell children they are going to let the jar sit until tomorrow.

6. Pass out a sheet of paper with a picture of an empty jar on it. Ask children to draw a picture of how they think the jar will look in one day.

7. The next day have children check the jar and compare what they see with the pictures they drew.

8. Hold a discussion regarding the different layers of earth materials they see.

ACCOMMODATIONS

✔ Rather than draw pictures the children could take a vote as to which earth material they think will be at the bottom, in the middle, and on the top. The different earth materials could be poured into the jar in the order voted on for a more realistic comparison with what happens in the jar under investigation.

EXTENSIONS

✔ A collection of man-made materials could be used in the jar: wood chips, potting soil, etc.

✔ Dye could be added to the water and the investigation could also be used as an art project when the earth study investigation is completed.

SCIENCE

Waste Collectors

Waste Collectors is a good environmental activity for children to participate in. It helps children gain a real sense of what types of waste materials are present in our communities.

LEARNING

* Types of waste materials found in communities
* What can be done to limit waste materials
* A sense of caring about our environment

MATERIALS

* Garbage bags for collecting waste materials
* Large plastic or canvas sheet to place waste materials on
* Latex or other gloves to be used by children when picking up and sorting waste materials
* Appropriate containers to dispose of waste materials (for plastic, paper, aluminum, and other)

STEPS

1. Provide each child or group of children with a plastic garbage bag.

2. Explain to the children that they are going on a walk in the neighborhood around their school. You may want to identify a walking route before the activity to ensure there are waste materials to be found.

3. When they go on the walk children are to pick up waste materials that have been left by people on the ground, in bushes, and in other places.

4. Have a discussion with the children about what kind of things might be considered waste materials of people: soda cans, candy wrappers, cigarette butts, parts of old newspapers, etc.

5. Before children go on the walk you may want them to put on latex or another type of gloves as a precaution.

6. Have the children go on the walk picking up waste materials along the way and putting them in their plastic bag.

7. When children return they can take all the waste materials out of their bag. The waste materials can be placed on a large plastic or canvas sheet in the middle of the room or on the playground.

8. Ask children to observe the different types of waste materials they found. When finished, provide children with the appropriate containers to place the waste materials in so that they are disposed of properly.

(continued)

SCIENCE

Waste Collectors *(continued)*

ACCOMMODATIONS

✓ If latex gloves are not available, the teacher and other adults should wear gloves to pick up materials identified by the children.

✓ Older students could use bigger garbage bags, go on longer walks, and collect more waste materials.

EXTENSIONS

✓ A follow-up activity to the initial walk could be to go on a second walk and have each group of children pick up a specific type of waste material. For example, two groups may be responsible for picking up plastic items only.

✓ The classroom could adopt a route along which they would periodically go out and pick up waste materials.

✓ If recycling centers are nearby, children could take their collected waste to the centers.

✓ A display board could be made of waste materials commonly found in the community.

SCIENCE

School Beautification Day

School Beautification Day could be adopted as an annual project by a classroom or school. The project, which may take several weeks or months to complete, helps older children to understand what types of plants and trees are native to the area.

LEARNING

* Experience beautifying an outdoor space
* Identifying plants and trees native to an area
* Experiencing the organization of an environmental project

MATERIALS

* Plants and trees to be planted on School Beautification Day.

STEPS

1. Show the children pictures of plants and trees that are common to the area around their school.

2. Explain to them that they are going to prepare for an event called School Beautification Day, which will take place several weeks (or months) from today.

3. In preparing for School Beautification Day, they will need learn about and do several things.

   know what types of trees and plants would grow around their school

   identify a fund raising project to earn money to buy plants and trees

   learn where they might possibly plant their items around the school

   get permission from the school board to plant their items

4. Divide the children into teams, and give each team one of the above responsibilities. Provide a time each week for the teams to meet and work on their part of the project.

5. Time should be provided once a week for all teams to share. Children will find out the importance of knowing what each team is doing. For example, the team that is preparing to take its project to the school board may need to know what types of plants and trees are being considered. The team may also need to know where around school another team is planning on planting the items.

6. Depending on the progress of the teams and the best time of the year for planting, set the date for the School Beautification Day.

7. Children will all participate in the School Beautification Day planting event.

CRITICAL THINKING CHALLENGE

Children could create a model for the School Beautification Day project. The model could be shown to the school board.

(continued)

SCIENCE

Copyright © 2005, Thomson Delmar Learning

School Beautification Day (continued)

ACCOMMODATIONS

✓ Children could make plans for a Classroom Beautification Day if the option of planting items around the school grounds is impractical or impossible. Children can discuss plants for the classroom and perhaps request permission from the principal.

EXTENSIONS

✓ Children could complete the project in the community. Permission could be obtained to plant different items in different locations.

SCIENCE

Acid Rain Destruction

Acid Rain Destruction is an excellent activity that allows children to observe the effects of acid rain on plant life.

LEARNING

❋ Harmful effects of acid rain on plant life

❋ Observation and measuring changes in plant life

❋ The controlling of variables in an investigation

MATERIALS

❋ Two identical plants of about the same height in the same type of pots

❋ Two containers to hold water and vinegar

❋ Water

❋ Vinegar

❋ Chart to record growth

STEPS

1. Present two like plants to children. Tell them that they are going to do an investigation with the two plants.

2. Set out two containers. Fill one container about half full with tap water. Fill the second container ¼ full with water and ¼ full with vinegar. Tell children that the second container is like **acid rain**.

3. Tell the children that over the next several weeks the two plants will receive the exact same treatment including the same amount of moisture, except one will receive water and the second will receive the acid rain.

4. Each morning have children observe the two plants. Have them also measure and record the growth of each plant on a line graph.

5. At the end of each week have children review the differences between the two plants.

 ACCOMMODATIONS

✔ Small, inexpensive plants can be used for the investigation.

✔ Pictures of the plants could be taken each day to compare results.

 EXTENSIONS

✔ Children could add other solutions to the water to see if the results are the same as the acid rain solution used in the investigation. For example, liquid soap could be added to the water.

✔ Rather then making acid rain by mixing vinegar with water, other materials might be added to the soil (oil) to determine other harmful effects on plants.

SCIENCE

Would You Breathe That Air?

Would You Breathe That Air? is an activity that helps children visually see the effects of polluted air.

LEARNING

❋ What polluted air looks like up close

❋ How air becomes polluted

MATERIALS

❋ Two mediumsize jars with lids (the size of a medium peanut butter jar)

❋ Three small wooden matches

❋ Pictures of air pollution, industrial smoke, etc.

STEPS

1. Set up the two medium-size jars for children to view.

2. Close the lid of one jar . Ask children what they see. Share with children that the jar contains clean air.

3. Turn the second jar upside down and light three small wooden matches next to it. Blow the matches out and put the jar over the burnt matches so that the smoke rises into the jar. Quickly put the lid on the jar so it retains the smoke.

4. Pass the two jars around to children, and ask them which one they think is healthier to breathe.

5. Ask the children how they think pollution gets into our air. References can be made to smokestacks on factories, as well as smoke coming from vehicles, wood burning stoves, and other sources.

6. Pictures of polluted air may be shown.

7. Ask children what they might do to reduce the amount of polluted air in their neighborhood.

ACCOMMODATIONS

✔ Pictures could be gathered from the neighborhood to bring about a more realistic understanding of how pollution gets into the air.

EXTENSIONS

✔ Discussions could take place regarding the effects of polluted air on people.

✔ An investigation could take place with plants. Place one plant into a clean air environment, and put one in an environment that receives a dosage of smoke frequently.

SCIENCE

Rocket Blastoff

Rocket Blastoff is a good activity to introduce children to rockets and space science. The activity gives children a basic understanding of how rockets lift off into space.

LEARNING

✳ How a rocket blasts off

MATERIALS

✳ Paper towel tube for each rocket
✳ Sheet of construction paper (for cone and wings) for each rocket
✳ 35mm film canister with lid for each rocket (clear plastic canisters work best)
✳ Teaspoon of water for each rocket
✳ Seltzer tablet for each rocket
✳ Tape

STEPS

1. Pass out an empty paper towel tube, some paper, a 35mm film canister, some water, and a seltzer tablet.

2. Have the children make a 1½-inch cone from construction paper and tape it to the top of the paper towel tube. Then have them make three wings (fins) from construction paper and tape them to the bottom part of the rocket.

3. Place the film canister upside down into the paper towel tube.

Sample

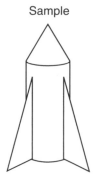

4. Turn the paper rocket upside down, and place the seltzer tablet into the film canister.

5. Add a teaspoon of water to the canister, quickly put the film lid on tightly and set the rocket right side up. The rocket should blast off in about 10 seconds.

6. Ask the children why they think the water added to the seltzer made the rocket shoot up.

CRITICAL THINKING CHALLENGE

Children could make adjustments to the type of cone or wings that are used.

(continued)

SCIENCE

Rocket Blastoff *(continued)*

ACCOMMODATIONS

✓ Teachers may prebuild the rockets for younger children or prepare the cone and wings for children to tape on.

✓ With younger children the teacher may want to add the water to the seltzer and place the lid on the rocket before turning it right side up.

✓ If paper towel tubes are not available, a tube could be made by rolling up an 8½-by-11-inch piece of paper.

EXTENSIONS

✓ Children could explore what effect the length of a rocket has on the distance it travels.

SCIENCE

Planets in Inches

Planets in Inches is a useful activity for older children to gain some idea of the order, size, and distances of planets in relation to the sun.

LEARNING

* Order of the planets
* Relative size of the planets
* Relative distance of the planets
* Determining ratios for distances

MATERIALS

* Paper to cut out planets
* Tape

STEPS

1. Display a chart showing the order of the planets from the sun:

   Sun – Mercury – Venus – Earth – Mars – Jupiter – Saturn – Uranus – Neptune – Pluto

2. Pass out an information sheet on the size of each planet and the distance of each planet from the sun.

3. The sun's diameter would be 62½ inches using the scale of 1 inch per 16,000 miles.

4. Have children fill in column C to identify the number of inches in diameter each planet would be if the planets were scaled down so that 1 inch equals 16,000 miles. For example, Mercury has a diameter of 3000 miles. If Mercury were scaled down to inches using this scale, Mercury would be about .18 inches, or about ²⁄₁₀ of an inch. (3000 divided by 16,000)

5. Have children fill in column E to represent each planet's distance from the sun using the scale of 1 inch equaling 36,000 million miles.

6. After columns C and E have been filled in, have children take paper and build the sun and planets to scale using the diameters determined in column C.

7. Have children place the planets in the appropriate order and distances from the sun using the scaled measures listed in column E.

8. Have children observe the size and distances from across the room.

(continued)

Planets in Inches *(continued)*

Column A	Column B	Column C	Column D	Column E
Planets: Sizes and Distances from the Sun (Also Scaled to Inches for Diameter and Distances)				
Planet	Diameter in miles	Planet's diameter scaled: 1" equals 16,000 miles	Distance from Sun in miles	Distances scaled: 1" equals 36 million miles
Mercury	3000	.18 inch	36 million	1 inch
Venus	7550		69 million	
Earth	7926		93 million	
Mars	4200		142 million	
Jupiter	88,700		484 million	
Saturn	74,000		891 million	
Uranus	29,000		1.8 billion	
Neptune	28,000		2.8 billion	
Pluto	1500		3.7 billion	
Sun	865,400			

ACCOMMODATIONS

✓ Younger children may have the diameters and distances in inches predetermined for them. They would have the responsibility of making the planets and spacing them out using the distances assigned.

EXTENSIONS

✓ Children could also determine the amount of time it takes each planet to revolve around the sun. The earth, for example, takes 365¼ days to revolve once around the sun.

SCIENCE

Moon Calendar

Moon Calendar is an activity that helps children to see how the appearance of the moon changes. After the activity children are prepared to discuss and demonstrate why the moon changes.

LEARNING

❋ Observing the phases of the moon

❋ Recording the phases of the moon

MATERIALS

❋ Blank calendar for the month to fill in moon phase pieces

❋ Moon phase pieces (two pieces of each moon phase)

❋ Glue

❋ Scissors

STEPS

1. Before the start of a new moon for a month, pass out a blank calendar to children. Tell children that they are to observe the moon at home every third night.

2. Pass out a sheet with the different phases of the moon to be cut out. Tell children that after they look at the moon each night they should cut out and glue the picture of the moon that looks most like the real moon for the day.

October

S	M	T	W	T	F	S
1	2	3	4	5	6	7
8	9	10	11	12	13	14
15	16	17	18	19	20	21
22	23	24	25	26	27	28
29	30	31				

Moon Phase Pieces

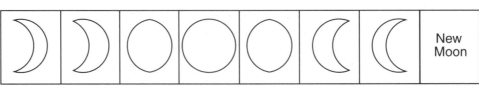

(continued)

SCIENCE

Moon Calendar *(continued)*

3. Remind children that if no moon appears it is a new moon.

4. Have children bring their calendars to school each week to compare the recorded moon phase.

ACCOMMODATIONS

✔ Children could draw in the phases of the moon rather then glue on the moon pieces.

✔ Different time periods for recording the phases of the moon could be recorded.

✔ You may want to start the activity on the first day of the month rather than when a new moon is going to appear.

EXTENSIONS

✔ As each part of the moon appears the teacher could demonstrate with a flashlight (sun), globe (earth), and ball (moon) how that phase of the moon is made.

✔ After the activity is completed for one full cycle of the moon, a new calendar could be passed out and children could predict when the different phases of the moon will appear based on the calendar they filled out for the last moon cycle.

SCIENCE

Telling Time by the Sun

Telling time by the Sun helps children understand the movement of the sun throughout the day. Children can also learn about the time of day based on their shadows.

LEARNING

❋ Telling time by the sun

❋ Observing the movement of the sun throughout the day

MATERIALS

❋ Large round piece of cardboard or white tagboard

❋ Dowel or pole

❋ Four cards with one of the following written on each: north, south, east, west

❋ Compass

STEPS

1. Tell the children they are going to learn to tell time with the help of the sun. They will use an instrument called a **sundial**.

2. Have children stand in a large circle on the playground on a sunny day.

3. Place a large circular piece of cardboard or white tagboard in the middle of the circle.

4. Stick a large dowel in the middle of the cardboard.

5. On the edge of the cardboard, place small cards with the ordinal directions listed on them: north, south, east, and west. You can use a compass if you are not sure which direction north is on the playground. Make sure that 12 o'clock is lined up with north.

6. Once the sundial is set up, tell children they are going inside and will come back out at, for example, 10:00 o'clock, noon, and 2:00 o'clock. They will then mark the current time on the cardboard where the dowel's shadow is. On a subsequent day, students could look at where the dowel's shadow falls in relation to the marks they have made in order to determine what time it is.

 ACCOMMODATIONS

✔ Each child could make his or her own sundial using a small board about 1 foot across.

 EXTENSIONS

✔ Children could record the length of the dowel's shadow during one season of the year and then observe the length of the shadow at another time of the year to see if the shadow gets longer at certain times during the year.

✔ Children could be asked to report the time in hours as a supplemental activity to learning how to tell time.

SCIENCE

Rotate or Revolve

Rotate or Revolve is an activity that helps children to understand that the earth rotates counterclockwise on its axis while it revolves around the sun.

LEARNING

❋ The concept of earth's rotation

❋ The concept of the earth revolving around the sun

MATERIALS

❋ Large orange ball (a string could be taped to it to hang from the ceiling)

❋ Small Styrofoam™ ball with a stick placed through it

STEPS

1. Set a large orange ball in the middle of the room or hang it from the ceiling. In your hand, hold a smaller Styrofoam™ ball with a stick placed through it.

2. Explain to children that the earth **rotates** on its axis in a counterclockwise direction at a slight angle (about 23½ degrees).

3. Demonstrate to the children how the earth rotates at its axis, on an angle and in a counterclockwise direction.

4. Pass the Styrofoam™ ball around for different children to practice rotating the earth on its axis.

5. Set the Styrofoam™ ball several feet from the large orange ball. Explain to the children that while the sun rotates on its axis in a counterclockwise motion it also **revolves** around the sun in a counterclockwise direction.

6. Demonstrate to the children how the earth rotates on its axis moving counterclockwise while it revolves around the sun in a counterclockwise motion.

7. Have children practice the movement.

 ACCOMMODATIONS

✔ Younger children may practice revolving the earth around the sun first before they are asked to have the earth rotate on its axis while revolving around the sun.

✔ Younger children may need to practice what a counterclockwise movement is.

 EXTENSIONS

✔ Children could use themselves to demonstrate the concepts of rotating and revolving. One partner could play the role of the sun and stay stationary. The other child could turn around in a counterclockwise motion and then slowly move around the sun (partner) in a counterclockwise direction. Children can reverse roles.

SCIENCE

SCIENCE RESOURCES

Branley, F. (1996). *What makes a magnet?* New York: Harper-Collins.

Charlesworth, Rosalind, Lind, Karen K., & Fleege, Pam. (2003). *Math and science for young children* (4th ed.). Clifton Park, NY: Thomson Delmar Learning.

Cobb, Vicki. (1972). *Science experiments you can eat.* New York: Scholastic, Inc.

Diehl, J., & Plumb, D. (2000). *What's the difference?: 10 animal look-alikes.* New York: Kingfisher.

Fiarotta, Phyllis, & Fiarotta, Noel. (1999). *Great experiments with light.* New York: Scholastic, Inc.

Herbert, Don. (1980). *Mr. Wizard's supermarket science.* New York: Random House.

Langley, A. (2001). *The Oxford first book of space.* New York: Oxford University Press.

Levine, S., & Crafton, A. (1992). *Projects for a healthy planet.* New York: Wiley.

Lind, Karen K. (1991). *Exploring science in early childhood: A developmental approach.* Clifton Park, NY: Thomson Delmar Learning.

Lorbeer, George C. & Nelson, Leslie W. (1992). *Science activities for children* (9th ed.). Dubuque, IA: Wm. C. Brown Publishers.

Markle, Sandra. (1980). *Primary science sampler.* Santa Barbara, CA: The Learning Works.

National Science Resources Center. (1991). *Electric circuits: student activity handbook.* Burlington, NC: Carolina Biological Supply Company.

Press, Hans J. (1967). *Simple science experiments.* West Germany: Otto Maier Verlag Ravensburg.

Project Learning Tree. (2001). *Environmental education activity guide pre k-8* (8th ed.). Washington, DC: American Forest Foundation.

VanCleave, Janice P. (1991). *Earth science for every child: 101 easy experiments that really work.* New York: John Wiley & Sons, Inc.

VanCleave, Janice P. (1991). *Physics for every child: 101 easy experiments in motion, heat, light, machines, and sound.* New York: John Wiley & Sons, Inc.

VanCleave, Janice P. (1995). *The human body for every child: Easy activities that make learning science fun.* New York: John Wiley & Sons, Inc.

Wyler, Rose, & Ames, Gerald. (1963). *Prove it!.* New York: Scholastic Book Services.

SCIENCE

Unit 6

Social Studies

The activities in this unit incorporate important aspects of the ten themes for social studies that the National Council for Social Studies organizes its curriculum standards upon. These themes are:

❋ Culture

❋ Time, Continuity, and Change

❋ People, Places, and Environment

❋ Individual Development and Identity

❋ Individuals, Groups, and Institutions

❋ Power, Authority, and Governance

❋ Production, Distribution, and Consumption

❋ Science, Technology, and Society

❋ Global Connections

❋ Civic Ideals and Practices

With these themes firmly in mind, we have divided our social studies unit into these five chapters:

* **Geography:** The activities in this chapter are meant to promote mapping skills and to help children become more familiar with the various landforms and countries that make up our world.

* **History:** This chapter emphasizes learning about the past—what has changed and what remains the same—and how we remember and record the past through written histories, museums exhibits, photographs, artifacts, etc.

* **Economics and Careers:** These activities introduce the children to our working world and the people and products that are an intricate part of it.

* **Civics:** This chapter has to do with our government, promoting pride in our country, and our responsibilities toward our country and others in our democratic society.

* **Multiculturalism:** The activities in the multiculturalism chapter are intended to open the children's eyes to the wonders of the our big world beyond their backyards and allow them to see the interconnectedness of all people.

The hands-on activities in these five chapters are meant to be relevant to the children's lives and to teach them valuable social studies concepts through doing, creating, discussing, and problem solving. The goal is for our world in all its great variety to be presented as an exciting and dynamic place to learn about.

Chapter 18

Geography

Activities in this chapter provide several varied experiences with map making and map reading as well as activities intended to improve the children's understanding of landforms and countries and where they are on our earth.

Environment Dioramas

In Environment Dioramas children choose an environment (desert, rainforest, tundra, etc.) to represent in the form of a diorama using natural materials, as well as other realistic-looking materials.

LEARNING

❋ There are several different types of environments found in our world.

❋ Models or dioramas present a visual 3-D method to show an understanding of these.

MATERIALS

❋ Pictures, videos, and books on various landscapes or environments

❋ One shoebox for each landscape

❋ A variety of materials to work with, such as rocks, sticks, cardboard, Styrofoam, clay, etc. (Children can also search the great outdoors around their school or home for materials.)

❋ A bottle of glue for each group or individual child

STEPS

1. Discuss the various landscapes or environments of the world with the children using pictures and videos to enhance your discussion and increase understanding.

2. Have individuals or groups of children choose a landscape to portray. Provide books to add to their ideas and understanding of what the landscape they choose actually looks like.

3. Have each group brainstorm materials they wish to use to create the diorama of that landscape. Children can then ask at home to see if they can locate some of these materials.

A supply of a variety of materials, such as Styrofoam, cardboard, etc., you have collected, as well, will aid in their collection of materials they wish to use.

4. Each group will also need a shoebox. A note sent home prior to this project requesting these should bring in an adequate supply.

5. Once they have the necessary supplies, allow the children to construct their landscapes.

6. Display the finished and labeled landscapes on an eye-level shelf or a table.

CRITICAL THINKING CHALLENGE

Locate each type of landscape on a map of the world and discuss what it might be like to live in each environment represented, or discuss the animals that live there. (Plastic figures of animals and/or people could also be added to the dioramas.)

ACCOMMODATIONS

✔ This project can be adjusted to suit a variety of age groups and ability levels by increasing or decreasing the number and types of landscapes discussed.

✔ Another idea would be to pair a younger child with an older child for this project.

SOCIAL SCIENCE

My Garden Map

In My Garden Map, using seed catalogues to find pictures of garden plants, the children create a garden map on paper laid out according to a plan.

LEARNING

❋ Gardeners plan out their gardens in a certain way.

❋ A map can be made of the finished garden.

MATERIALS

❋ Several seed catalogues or other catalogues with pictures of plants

❋ Brown paper

❋ Scissors

❋ Glue

STEPS

1. Have the children cut out several pictures of garden plants they wish to "plant" in their gardens. They need several pictures of each plant.

2. On brown paper, have them arrange their plants as you might see in an actual garden and then glue them on once they are satisfied with their plan.

3. Next have them explain how to get from one type of plant to another without stepping on any plants (by following the rows) using such phrases as, "First walk up the third row, turn toward the pumpkins, go by the carrots, then walk down the row between the carrots and the corn, and the beans will be halfway down that row."

CRITICAL THINKING CHALLENGE

Discuss why gardeners plant certain plants where they do, such as, because they take up a lot of space or because they discourage animals from coming into the garden and thus are planted on the borders.

ACCOMMODATIONS

✔ By adjusting the size of the garden (brown paper) and number and variety of plants within the garden, this activity can serve many levels of learners.

SOCIAL SCIENCE

Follow the Clues

In Follow the Clues *children will use their map–reading abilities to solve a problem.*

LEARNING

✳ It is important to follow map directions carefully in order to end up where you wish to be!

MATERIALS

✳ Sandwich-size plastic reclosable lunch bags

✳ Small treats such as individually wrapped crackers, miniature candy bars, etc. divided into enough bags to match your number of groups

✳ 3-by-5-inch note cards for writing your directions

STEPS

1. Before the children arrive, hide bags of treats around the classroom or playground. You will need the same number of bags of treats as groups you will divide the children into. Groups should be no larger than three or four children.

2. Next write down simple directions to locate each bag, such as, 1. Go out the front door of our building. 2. Follow the sidewalk to the grass by the bench. 3. Find a bush next to the bench. 4. Look under it to find your surprise! You need as many sets of different directions as there are bags.

3. Divide your children up into small groups and give each group a set of directions. Allow the children to follow the directions to their treats!

ACCOMMODATIONS

✔ By grouping children by ages you can give more complicated directions to older children and simpler directions to younger children.

✔ Use multi-age groupings of children so that older children can help younger children in the same group.

EXTENSIONS

✔ Allow the children to write their own directions to find hidden objects.

✔ At Easter, plastic eggs with candy inside might be hidden.

SOCIAL SCIENCE

Find the Words–Solve the Mystery

Find the Words–Solve the Mystery *is a variation of* Follow the Clues. *This time the children use a map to find hidden word cards that spell out a sentence when they are all located.*

LEARNING

❋ A map can be read to direct us to specific locations.

MATERIALS

❋ Something to hide

❋ Note cards and markers

❋ A large class map that uses symbols and a key to identify objects in the room

STEPS

1. Before the children arrive, select something to hide and write a sentence telling where it is, such as, "The ball is in the closet," placing one word on each note card. Number the cards in order.

2. Now place the note cards in different spots around the room.

3. Write the number of each card on a classroom map to indicate where it can be found in the room.

4. When the children arrive, tell them you've hidden the ball but by reading the map carefully and collecting the word cards they will be able to solve this problem and find the ball.

5. Show them how to use the map as you work together to locate the cards in numerical order. Lay these cards on the table with the numbered sides facing up as they are each located using the map.

6. Now have children turn the cards over to reveal the sentence they make and discover the location of the ball.

 ACCOMMODATIONS

✔ The number of cards and vocabulary level of the words written on the cards can be adjusted to your group's needs.

 EXTENSIONS

✔ You could divide children into groups and give each group a smaller map with a different mystery to solve in this manner.

✔ Children could make up their own mysteries to solve. Maps could be laminated as could blank cards for them to write on to make this an activity that is easy to use over and over again!

SOCIAL SCIENCE

All Around Our Town

In All Around Our Town, the children will figure out where one of their classmates is going each day by the address given and place his or her picture card on a large map of the city at the correct location.

LEARNING

✳ Addresses help us locate places on a map.

MATERIALS

✳ Places and addresses in the community in a hat

✳ A large city map or a map of the area near your site

✳ A small picture of each child

✳ A method for attaching pictures to the map

STEPS

1. Each day have a designated child pull the name of a place and its address in the community out of a hat.

2. Have the group help him or her find that location on the map.

3. Then have the child attach the picture of himself/herself to the map at that address.

ACCOMMODATIONS

✔ The area you are working with and the names and types of locations could be adjusted to suit the abilities of the group.

EXTENSIONS

✔ Children could write down addresses for others to locate on the map or name places for others to find using an address.

✔ They could also direct a child from one spot to another on the map.

SOCIAL SCIENCE

Find the Landmark

Find the Landmark *is an activity in which children use coordinates to locate landmarks on a grid.*

LEARNING

✳ Coordinates help us to locate information on a grid.

MATERIALS

✳ Chalkboard and chalk or cardboard strips and a bulletin board
✳ Pictures of landmarks cut from magazines
✳ A method to attach the pictures to the grid

STEPS

1. Using several long strips of cardboard and a blank wall or a chalkboard, form a grid pattern of 25 squares.

2. Label each column across the top with a letter of the alphabet (A to E).

3. Now label the rows on the right edge with the numbers 1 through 5 going upward, one number next to each box.

4. Place pictures of landmarks in several of the boxes.

5. Have the children name the coordinates that tell where the landmarks are located, for example, B3. If your chalkboard is magnetic, you may want to attach a piece of magnetic tape to the back of each landmark picture so that the landmarks can easily be switched around.

ACCOMMODATIONS

✔ The size of your grid and number of landmarks can be adjusted up or down to suit the group.

EXTENSIONS

✔ Allow the children to rearrange the pictures in the grid and to add their own pictures or use pictures of the children themselves!

✔ A large grid could be drawn on the blacktop with sidewalk chalk and the children could find their spots on the grid using coordinates.

State in a Bag

In State in a Bag, through the use of visual props, each child will tell about a state he or she has visited or is interested in.

LEARNING

✳ Each state has its own special features that make it unique.

MATERIALS

✳ Paper lunch bags
✳ A map of the United States
✳ A United States puzzle

STEPS

1. Ask each child to discuss with his or her parents the states he or she has visited or knows some facts about.

2. Give each child a paper lunch bag and have him or her draw the shape of the state he or she chooses on the bag and label it with the name of that state.

3. Have the child take the bag home and place items in it that symbolize that state. For example, a bag about Iowa might include a can of corn, a plastic hog figure, something from the Hawkeyes football team, and a postcard of the Amana Colonies.

4. As the bags are returned, allow each child to show what he or she brought to symbolize his or her state.

5. As each state is talked about, the corresponding puzzle piece could be added to a puzzle of the United States.

6. After the children have all presented their chosen states, you could discuss the states that are left and things that represent those states. Making books about the states available throughout this activity would be very helpful for ideas.

 ACCOMMODATIONS

✔ The number of objects a child is expected to bring in and your expectations in presenting this information should be adjusted to the ages and ability levels in your group.

 EXTENSIONS

✔ Children could create a brochure or poster about their state or write to the state government for more information.

✔ Videos about various states might also be viewed.

✔ A graph of which states the children have been to and how many children have been to each could be created.

SOCIAL SCIENCE

A Snowy/Sandy Adventure

A fun activity on a snowy winter day is to make a footprint map in the snow for the activity A Snowy/Sandy Adventure! *If snow is not available, a sandy area is a great alternative.*

LEARNING

✳ Routes can be mapped out and followed.

MATERIALS

✳ Sticks and cardboard to make the trail name markers

STEPS

1. You will need to wait for a snowy day in the north or look for a sandy place if snow is not common in your area.

2. Next plan out the routes you wish to create on a piece of paper.

3. Help the children to walk out these routes so their footprints make trails.

4. Have them show you which trail leads to the swings, flagpole, etc.

5. Make signs on sticks to name the trails.

6. Have the children give each other directions to follow using the trail names and other landmarks to watch for.

7. Have the children describe and show each other the shortest routes to various spots on the trails and alternative routes they could use to get to the same places.

ACCOMMODATIONS

✓ Adjust the length and number of trails for your age group.

✓ Allow older children to work with younger children

EXTENSIONS

✓ For a fun game at recess, these trails can be used for a game of tag in which children cannot go off the trails.

✓ Provide maps for the children to study that have routes marked out on them, such as maps of buildings or maps to get from one person's house to another that are drawn with a line leading from one place to another.

So Much Earth to See

In So Much Earth to See the children create an earth-shaped collage of pictures of landforms from around the world such as mountains, mesas, cliffs, etc.

LEARNING

✳ Our world is made up of many and varied landforms.

MATERIALS

✳ Magazines featuring natural sights such as *National Geographic, Arizona Highways*, etc. (Travel brochures may also work.)

✳ One large sheet of sturdy paper for each child or one very large sheet of paper for the entire class to use together

✳ Scissors

✳ Glue

STEPS

1. Take out the magazines or travel brochures featuring natural sights.

2. Have each child draw a large circle on a heavy sheet of paper and cut it out. An alternative would be to make one huge circle for the entire group's use.

3. Next have the children cut out pictures from the magazines depicting various landforms.

4. These can then be glued to the "earth paper" in collage fashion.

ACCOMMODATIONS

✔ For children who have difficulty cutting, tearing pictures out of the magazines might work just as well and give the collage a rugged effect.

✔ Another idea would be to have children divided into picture finder, picture cutter, and picture gluer groups, each taking on just one part of the task. This would work for making the entire class collage or with three people making one collage.

EXTENSIONS

✔ Children could create landforms out of clay or make a relief map.

SOCIAL SCIENCE

426 · Geography

Box City

In Box City, using a variety of cardboard boxes of many shapes and sizes, children create a model of their community or town.

LEARNING

✳ Our town is made up of many different buildings that serve different purposes.

MATERIALS

✳ Boxes of several different shapes and sizes (Call on parents and businesses to contribute boxes.)

✳ A variety of papers, including construction paper and contact paper

✳ Several colors of tempera paint, paintbrushes, and paint smocks

✳ Black tagboard strips for roads

✳ As your town develops, you may need other readily available materials that can be donated. Encourage the children to be creative with the resources and materials available.

✳ Camera and film

STEPS

1. Initially you will need to call on parents and businesses to contribute boxes of many different shapes and sizes.

2. While you are doing this, you will want to take several pictures of buildings in the area. You might also go on walks around the neighborhood with the children pointing out the various buildings they see and their characteristics.

3. Once you have several boxes, you are ready to begin this project.

4. The children should select buildings in the town that they'd like to make.

5. Using the pictures you took, their memories, and paper and paint, allow them to create their buildings.

6. When these are finished you can move on to making streets out of black tagboard, street signs, bridges, playgrounds, etc., all related to their community. Adding toy cars and trucks will enhance your town.

7. If space is an issue, use small boxes that can be stored in a tub when not in use.

ACCOMMODATIONS

✔ By adjusting the size of the project, you will adjust the level of ability it requires. It doesn't really matter if one building is more accurately done than another. The concept that a town has many different types of buildings will still be emphasized.

EXTENSIONS

✔ Have a city planner come to visit to talk about why things are where they are in a town—that a town has a plan to its layout.

✔ You could also help the children create a map of the town they created.

SOCIAL SCIENCE

Country Corner

Country Corner is appropriate in a room where it can stay set up for a period of time. A corner of the room is set up to depict a country you wish to feature.

LEARNING

✳ There are many countries in our world, each with different characteristics it is known for.

MATERIALS

✳ VCR
✳ Videos about the country featured
✳ Props that represent characteristics of the country. Be creative and include the children in deciding what is needed and locating it.
✳ A map of the world or globe
✳ Books about the country featured
✳ Simple passports made for each child

STEPS

1. Decorate a corner of the room to represent a country. For example, for Switzerland you could cover large boxes with white sheets to represent snow-covered mountains, stand a pair of skis in the corner, and provide warm scarves, mittens, etc. If there's room on the wall, you could add a mountain scene with a chalet drawn on paper. Children could also watch a video about the country.

2. Next add a map or globe for locating the country featured.

3. Books of varying degrees of reading difficulty and with good pictures depicting the country should also be a part of this area.

4. Stamp each child's passport when he or she visits the country during free time. With a different country featured each month, the children will have the opportunity to "travel" to many countries.

 ACCOMMODATIONS

✔ Consider countries children may be more familiar with.

✔ Have a variety of reading levels covered within your book assortment.

 EXTENSIONS

✔ Children could "send" postcards they've made to their friends when they visit the "country corner."

✔ This activity could also be done featuring the United States.

SOCIAL SCIENCE

Do You Know Your Landforms?

Do You Know Your Landforms? challenges the children with a game in which all the questions have to do with landforms. The description of this game is long but, once you've read through it, you will see clearly how the game works.

LEARNING

* There are many landforms on our earth that we can identify.

MATERIALS

* A large piece of light-colored laminated tagboard cut into several rectangles
* Question cards and a dry erase marker of a dark color that will show up on the cards
* A book depicting many landforms to get your definitions from (You must be accurate!)
* A pocket chart (or a chalkboard you can tape things to)
* Placement ribbons for winners (optional)

STEPS

1. Laminate a large sheet of light-colored tagboard and cut it into several equal-sized rectangles. You will need two rectangles for each question.

2. Write a question about a landform on a card and the answer on the back with an erasable marker. (For example, Question: What is a piece of land called that is totally surrounded by water? Answer: An island)

3. On another card write a number of points on one side and leave the other side blank.

4. Make your questions progressively more difficult as you increase the point value.

5. Set up the game board (pocket chart) with the question cards facing you, and then cover each one with a point card that is visible.

6. Arrange the board so that the difficulty of questions and point values increases as you go down the board.

7. Divide the group into equal-size teams. If you have extra children, they can participate as scorekeepers or card removers.

8. Now you are ready to play the game with each team selecting a point value and answering the question under that value to earn those points. If one team doesn't know an answer, let the next team try to give it and earn the points.

9. Total up the points at the end of the game and praise everyone for their knowledge and good sportsmanship. A round of applause for the winning team is appropriate and yet not too hard on those who didn't win. Or you could have placement ribbons for each group.

(continued)

SOCIAL SCIENCE

Do You Know Your Landforms? *(continued)*

ACCOMMODATIONS

✓ You can make the questions as easy or as difficult as your group can handle.

✓ Your point values can also be set up to require addition at the level the children can handle. They can help you add up the totals to practice their addition skills!

✓ You could have questions for older children to choose from and others for younger children to choose from (for example, the top two rows for younger children and the bottom two rows for older children).

✓ One way to reduce the anxiety of not having any points yet is to start out with each team having a small amount of points already!

EXTENSIONS

✓ This game format and the materials allow it to be used over and over again with other topics or subjects.

✓ You could set up a tournament format playing the game once a week for several weeks.

SOCIAL SCIENCE

All Dressed Up!

The activity All Dressed Up! integrates history and geography. Children research the traditional costumes of different countries and then "dress" outlines of their bodies in them and match them to the countries they represent.

LEARNING

※ There are traditional costumes that are associated with various countries.

MATERIALS

※ Resource materials—books, pictures, videos, etc.—that depict traditional costumes of several countries

※ Large sheets of butcher paper—the length of each child

※ Pencils to trace with

※ Scissors to cut out body forms

※ Materials to decorate body forms with—paint, markers, construction paper, etc.

※ Sticky tack for hanging forms on the walls

STEPS

1. Supply the children with the resource materials that depict the traditional costumes of several countries.

2. Have each child choose which costume he or she would like to "try on."

3. Next have the children take turns lying on sheets of paper as long as they are tall. One child can trace around another child's body, and then they can switch tasks. Both will need to cut out their individual body forms.

4. Using paint, crayons, markers, or construction paper, have each child "dress" his or her body to represent the country of his or her choice.

5. As these are completed, tape them up on the walls with the country names, shapes, and flags above the corresponding costumed figures.

ACCOMMODATIONS

✔ Older children may help younger children with tracing and cutting.

✔ You could lessen the scope of this activity by supplying each child with a smaller generic body form to "dress."

✔ If you attach a craft stick to the back of each the above completed figure, they could be stuck into slits in a cardboard box in order to stand next to each other.

✔ Each figure could hold in its hand a flag of the country it represents.

EXTENSIONS

✔ It would be a good idea to discuss how children from each country usually dress. These traditional costumes are not their everyday wear.

✔ You could point out certain features of the costumes that may have special meaning.

SOCIAL SCIENCE

Find My Egg

In Find My Egg each child hides a plastic Easter egg with his or her name on a slip inside it. He or she identifies on a map where the egg is hidden, and another child uses the map to locate the egg.

LEARNING

❋ Maps are used to locate things.

MATERIALS

❋ Plastic Easter egg for each child
❋ Small slips of paper to write names on
❋ A map of a specific area for each child

STEPS

1. Draw a map of an area that is familiar and accessible to the children.

2. Make copies of this map so that each child can have one.

3. Give each child a plastic Easter egg.

4. Have each child write his or her name on a slip of paper and place it inside the egg.

5. Allow each child to look at the map and decide where to hide the egg.

6. One at a time, with an adult assistant, have each child hide the egg with his or her name in it and identify the spot on his or her map.

7. When all the eggs have been hidden, have the children exchange their maps. (Be sure each child has put his or her name on the map to indicate where he or she has hidden an egg.)

8. Now allow the children to use the maps to find the eggs. They will be able to match the name on the map and the egg to see if they found the correct egg.

 ACCOMMODATIONS

✔ Maps can be made as detailed as is appropriate for your age group.

✔ For multi-age groups you could pair a younger child with an older one for this activity or make one less-detailed and one more-detailed map and divide the children by age.

✔ Another idea would be to use a smaller area for younger children and a larger one for older children.

 EXTENSIONS

✔ Hopefully, this activity will stimulate lots of map making from your children as they hide things for others to find.

✔ Another idea would be to do a traditional Easter egg hunt having the children use maps to find the eggs.

SOCIAL SCIENCE

Chapter 19

History

Activities in this chapter are intended to add to the children's understanding and appreciation of the past and to give them an understanding of the various ways in which the past is recorded.

History Comes Alive!

History Comes Alive! gives the children an opportunity to "meet" important people who shaped history.

LEARNING

❋ People from the past have influenced our world in many ways that we can learn about.

MATERIALS

❋ Children's books depicting facts about the lives of famous people in history

❋ Simple props that would be appropriate for the character you are presenting (For example, for Betsy Ross you could wear a long dress and carry a flag. Ben Franklin might have a kite.)

STEPS

1. Find a children's true story about an important person who influenced our world.

2. Select the details about this person's life that you wish to share with the children.

3. Select some simple props that will add to your presentation.

4. Then take on the role of that person and tell the children about yourself.

5. Allow the children to ask you questions and answer as if you are that person. Stay in character!

CRITICAL THINKING CHALLENGE

Have the children come up with props to represent famous people they can then tell about.

ACCOMMODATIONS

✔ Keep your vocabulary and information at your group's level.

EXTENSIONS

✔ Encourage the children to read the true stories of famous people to share with the group.

✔ Help them choose facts to share and allow them to write them down to read to the group.

✔ Visit a historical site where the guides stay in character.

My History

My History affords the children the opportunity to record the important events in their lives on personal timelines.

LEARNING

✳ A timeline is used to record events in chronological order.

MATERIALS

✳ 3-by-5-inch note cards for each child (The amount depends on the age and ability levels of the children.)

✳ Photos of memorable events

✳ A paper strip for each child wide enough and long enough to accommodate the number of note cards provided the child

✳ Glue or sticky tack to attach the cards to the paper strips

STEPS

1. Write down ten important happenings in your life on 3-by-5-inch note cards. (A picture to accompany each one would definitely add to your information—it could be a snapshot or something you've drawn.)

2. As you discuss each event, place the card in chronological order on a timeline drawn on the chalkboard—use the chalk tray or tape to do this.

3. Give each child a manageable number of 3-by-5-inch cards to take home and fill out with memorable events from his or her life with the help of an adult. Encourage the children to bring photos to go with the events or to hand draw them. Allow a reasonable amount of time for this assignment.

4. When all the children have returned the cards, give each child a strip of paper long enough to hold all his or her cards in a row.

5. Have the children line the event cards up on the strip of paper in the order they occurred. Do not worry about exact dates—just that the cards are in chronological order.

6. The cards can then be attached to the paper strip in a manner appropriate for the materials provided. Be sure to treat actual snapshots with special care so as not to damage them.

7. Have the children pair up to share their personal timelines before you display them.

ACCOMMODATIONS

✔ For children who do not write yet or have difficulty with writing, allow an adult to fill out the cards.

✔ Vary the number of cards with the ages and abilities of the children.

EXTENSIONS

✔ Locate timelines in books to show the children how they help organize events chronologically.

✔ Begin a class timeline to fill out as memorable events happen in the classroom or community. One child could draw a picture of each event as it occurs or a photo could be taken.

SOCIAL SCIENCE

Where Have I Been? What Have I Seen?

Where Have I Been? What Have I Seen? calls for the children to create their own postcards of historic places they might visit.

LEARNING

✳ Postcards can supply us with information about historic places.

MATERIALS

✳ Sample postcards of historic sites or historic places in your community or nearby

✳ Tagboard cut to the same size as a postcard and with a line drawn down the middle of one side to separate the message area from the address area (one for each child)

✳ Colorful markers or crayons for drawing the postcard pictures. Actual pictures could be copied from the Internet, as well, and cropped to postcard size to glue to the tagboard.

✳ Resource books or Internet access to research the historic sites chosen

✳ All the students' names written on slips of paper and placed in a container to be drawn from

✳ Chalkboard space to write the school address for children to copy onto the postcards

STEPS

1. Gather together the postcards and allow the children to look at them. Show them where information about the historic site pictured is featured on the postcard. Also point out where the person sending the postcard can write down more information he or she gathered while visiting the site.

2. Have each child show the postcard you gave him or her and tell what he or she learned by reading the postcard.

3. Now tell the children to pretend that they have just won a vacation to go visit the historic site of their choice. Give examples, such as the Statue of Liberty, Mount Rushmore, the White House, Gettysburg, etc. Tell them that this vacation is not to an amusement park or entertainment area but to a place that is important in the history of our country.

4. Once they have chosen where they will go, they will need to do some research using books you've provided or the Internet to find out some interesting or important facts about the place they chose to visit.

5. Now give each child a piece of tagboard cut to the size of a postcard.

6. On one side they are to draw a colorful picture of what they saw.

7. On the other side they are to add the information found. A brief sentence or two should go up in the left-hand corner with a personal message below which will contain more information about the historic site and will start with "Hi" and end with the writer's name.

(continued)

Where Have I Been? What Have I Seen? (continued)

8. This postcard will be delivered to a class-mate whose name will be drawn out of a hat. The postcard will be addressed to the child with his or her name and the school address (which should be written on the board after you discuss this part of the activity.) Have the children keep the name of the person they drew a secret.

9. Each child should add a picture of a stamp drawn in the right-hand corner with the correct postage written on it.

10. Collect the postcards and tell the children they will be delivered to the correct people tomorrow.

11. Deliver the postcards to the children's desks or cubbies before the children arrive at school the next day.

12. Allow each child to share the postcard he or she received with the class—both the picture and the information on it.

ACCOMMODATIONS

✓ Help the children choose sites that they will be able to find information about that they will understand. For example, Gettysburg is better for an older child, whereas the Statue of Liberty would be more appropriate for a younger child.

✓ Children can write information and a number of sentences to suit their abilities.

EXTENSIONS

✓ Encourage children to bring in postcards they receive to share with the class.

✓ You could use a map to tie these places to where they are actually located by placing the postcards on the edges of a bulletin board with a map of the United States in the middle and connecting string from the postcards to the locations of the sites on the map.

SOCIAL SCIENCE

When Did That Happen?

When Did That Happen? *incorporates historic events with calendar activities.*

LEARNING

✳ Important events in history happened on many different dates.

MATERIALS

✳ A calendar with large squares to add information

✳ Information on important events in history and when they occurred

STEPS

1. Select important historical events you wish to teach the children about.

2. Add these to a large calendar on the dates they occurred with a brief notation or a small picture.

3. Then when that date occurs, be prepared to share information about that event with the children. This will take a little research on your part, but it will be well worth it.

4. Discuss the fact that some events were so important that we do special things to commemorate them on specific dates—such as Memorial Day and the Fourth of July.

 ACCOMMODATIONS

✔ Choose historical events that the children will grasp and that influence them and their lives in some way.

 EXTENSIONS

✔ Allow the children to suggest the addition of other historical dates as they learn about them through other means such as another class or a television program, etc. Let the child who suggests the date describe its significance.

✔ Give each child a small calendar of his or her own to fill out as you do the larger one.

Famous People in Our City's History

Every city has a person or people who were important in its early years and, through the activity Famous People in Our City's History, *the children will have the opportunity to learn about this part of their city's history.*

LEARNING

❉ It took people to establish cities and get them growing.

MATERIALS

❉ Information on the people who were instrumental in starting the city where your school is located

❉ Pictures of the founders of the city

❉ Note cards

STEPS

1. Do some research to find out a little about how the city where your school is located got started. You are sure to discover a name or two of someone who is remembered because he or she had an important roll in this. If you have a local historian, talk to him or her or, better yet, invite him or her to your classroom. Your local historical society can also be a great resource for this type of information, as well as museums in the area and a Website your city may sponsor.

2. Present this information to the children or help them locate it themselves.

3. Now have them compile a list of all the streets, buildings, parks, etc. that commemorate these famous people of the city's past.

4. If you can find pictures of these people, the children can write down facts about them on note cards to display with the pictures. "The Famous Founders of (city's name)" might be a good title for this display.

 ACCOMMODATIONS

✔ Keep the information presented and the materials used to locate it appropriate to your group's abilities.

 EXTENSIONS

✔ Add information about the city's history whenever you find it.

✔ Invite in an older person who has lived his or her whole life in the city to tell the children how it has changed over the years.

SOCIAL SCIENCE

Who Is on My Money?

In the activity Who Is on My Money? *the children do a little research to find out whose pictures grace their money and why.*

LEARNING

❋ The people whose pictures appear on our coins and paper money were important to our history in some way.

MATERIALS

❋ Real pieces of money, both paper and coins, or realistic replicas or pictures of the money

❋ Green, gray, and brown construction paper

❋ Resources for the children to use to do their research

STEPS

1. Bring in several different pieces of real money, including coins and bills or realistic replicas of the money. Show the children each piece of money and ask them who is on that piece.

2. Once you have a list of the people on the money, let the children form small research groups that each find out more about the person on one piece of money, such as a dime, fifty-cent piece, or dollar bill. Make sure each piece of money represented will have a group of children to research the person on it.

3. Provide children researching people on bills with large bill replicas made out of green construction paper with the amount written in the corners. For those researching the people on the coins, provide construction paper cut into circles proportionate in size to the real coins. Use gray paper for all the coins except the penny, which needs to be brown. These children will write the facts they find about their people on the bill or coin replicas.

4. Provide resources for the children to use for their research. Be sure these are written at their level. Each child in the group could be responsible for writing two facts that the group has found working together.

5. Once this is done, have the members of each group share what they found out about the person they researched. The person who wrote each fact should tell or read it. After the facts are given about the person researched, speculate why he was given the honor of appearing on the coin or bill.

ACCOMMODATIONS

✔ If your group is multi-aged, try to pair an older child or two with younger ones to help carry out the research.

EXTENSIONS

✔ Discuss the fact that some coins and bills are less common such as the two dollar bill, and Sacagawea coin, and that we didn't always have money in these forms.

What's in My Wagon?

What's in My Wagon? deals with the decisions the pioneers had to make when they loaded their wagons for the long, hard trip west. The children fill their construction paper wagons with the supplies they need.

LEARNING

❋ The pioneers had to make tough decisions when deciding what to take west as their space was very limited.

MATERIALS

❋ Information about the pioneers and their journey west

❋ A sheet of paper with an outline of a covered wagon on it and a pencil for each child

❋ A large sheet of paper with a large outline of a covered wagon on it and a marker to use to write on it

STEPS

1. Discuss the forms of transportation the pioneers used to go west. Families usually rode in a covered wagon, which had to hold them and everything they needed for the trip and immediately when they got to their destination. Discuss the length of the journey—several months—and the fact that the weather would change in that amount of time, as would the conditions of the trails.

2. Discuss what kinds of things the pioneers might need to take, and list as many as the children can think of on the board. This should be a fairly long list. Talk about how important these decisions were for the pioneers.

3. Now tell the children that they can only take a portion of the things on the list. This amount will depend on the length of the list you made.

4. Hand out a covered wagon outline copied onto paper for each child. Tell the children that they are to write the things they think they most need to take on their journey inside the covered wagon outline. Tell them to think carefully about their choices.

5. When the children have all filled their wagons, have them share their choices and why they made them with the others. Keep a list of the choices most often named, and write them on a larger outline of the wagon drawn on a larger sheet of paper. Discuss how many of the children felt these were the most important things to take, and explain that is how you decided which items to put in your wagon: you used their

(continued)

What's in My Wagon? *(continued)*

good advice. Discuss how the wagon masters and other pioneers who had already made the trip probably gave this sort of advice to new travelers to help them make the best decisions, too.

6. Ask the children whether they would have liked to make the journey the pioneers did and why they feel as they do.

ACCOMMODATIONS

✔ A list of possible things to take can be written on the board. The children should then be able to copy off their choices with some help provided in reading the items off the board or they can dictate to someone what these choices are and have that person record them on the child's wagon.

EXTENSIONS

✔ If you have access to a computer, the program "The Oregon Trail" deals with the issue of the pioneers' needs, as well, and is appropriate for children in third grade and above.

Chapter 20

Economics and Careers

Activities in this chapter are meant to introduce the children to the world of work and the many people and businesses involved in the intricacies of keeping our world functioning well economically.

443

Everybody Gets a Job!

Through Everybody Gets a Job the children produce greeting cards assembly–line fashion.

LEARNING

✳ When things are produced on an assembly line, each person is responsible for one part of the whole.

MATERIALS

✳ Box of greeting cards with a simple design on front

✳ Four seasonal shapes—one for each season—cut out of paper (as many of each shape as there are children in the class, plus extras)

✳ Four colors of light-colored construction paper cut to the size (5-by-8 inches) to be folded for the greeting cards (as many of each color as there are children in the class, plus extras)

✳ Four markers or crayons

✳ Four glue sticks

✳ Four boxes for the finished cards—one for each season, labeled with that season's name

STEPS

1. Prepare a simple shape cut from construction paper that can serve as design for the front of a card—a sun for a summer card, an orange leaf for a fall card, a snowflake shape for a winter card, and a simple flower shape for a spring card. If you have access to a die-cutting machine, it will be very easy to cut out many shapes that are all the same. You can also buy packages of shapes that are the same at school-supplies stores. Otherwise, you will need to spend some time cutting out enough shapes so that each child has one of each, plus extras.

Several sheets of paper can be cut through at once with good scissors and maybe a parent or two would be willing to do this for you with some advance notice, if you provide the patterns and paper.

2. Tell the children that when we make a one-of-a-kind greeting card by hand we are using the process of unit production.

3. Now show the children the box of greeting cards you purchased.

4. Explain that we can make our own greeting cards that all look the same, if we agree on what they should look like. Tell the children that the class will be working together to make greeting cards for each season of the year so that each classmate will have one card for each season that is the same as everyone else's.

5. Write the word "Happy" and then the name of each season on the board.

6. Have the children sit at four tables—four children to a table. Each group will make cards for one season.

7. Now give one child in each group the paper to use to create the cards—use a different color for each season's cards. He or she will need at least as many precut sheets of paper as there are children in the class.

8. The child seated to this child's right needs the seasonal shapes for his or her table's season and a glue stick.

9. The next child needs a marker or crayon to write the message ("Happy Spring," etc.) in the cards. Have him or her choose one color of marker or crayon that will show up well on the card's background color. *(continued)*

Everybody Gets a Job? *(continued)*

10. The last child in the group is the quality inspector.

11. Tell each child that he or she will do the same job as many times as it takes to make a card for each child in the class.

12. The first child in each group should carefully fold the paper for the card in half. The second child in the group should glue the seasonal shape on the front of the card. The third child should neatly write the message inside the card. The fourth child should check to see that the card is of good quality—that it is folded correctly, that the seasonal shape is on securely, and that the message is neat and with correct spelling. If the card passes inspection, then the inspector should place it in a box on a separate table marked with the appropriate season. If the card isn't correct, the inspector should place it in a separate pile at the table where his or her group is working to be discarded and replaced with a new card later.

13. Remind the children that this is not a race but that the idea is to work as fast as you can at your job and still do it correctly.

14. Once all the cards have been made and the discarded cards have been replaced with new ones (provide a small amount of extra materials for this), the assembly line process is complete.

15. Discuss when and why businesses use assembly-line production (when the finished products will all look the same; to speed up production, so each person can specialize in just one phase of the construction, etc.). Compare assembly-line production with unit production, in which one person does all the jobs necessary to make the finished product.

16. Remind the children that on the first day of each season, they will have a card to give or send to someone. If you start this project before fall officially begins, you will be able to remind the children when to send each card as its season comes up. This is a way to announce the start of each season to the children. Keep the cards in the boxes labeled with each season. Then on the day that season begins, pass out the cards so that each child has a card to give or send to someone special.

ACCOMMODATIONS

✔ Divide the jobs to suit the abilities of the individual children in each group.

✔ If you think one particular job will take longer than the others, you could assign two children to that job, if there are enough children in the class.

✔ The number of steps to make each card can also be adjusted to suit the number of children in the entire group.

✔ Consider adding or adjusting tasks to accommodate more children. For example, one or more children could select a seasonal card from each box and group these together in a plastic sandwich bag for each child in the class to have.

EXTENSIONS

✔ Observing an assembly line at work at a real business would be a great experience for the children.

✔ Use assembly-line production at some other appropriate time, such as to make a snack item.

SOCIAL SCIENCE

Walk Around the Block Game

The Walk Around the Block Game uses the sidewalk of a city block as a giant board game. The children answer questions in teams and one person from each team serves as the team's game piece.

LEARNING

✳ We can review many facts we've learned through playing board games.

MATERIALS

✳ Questions prepared by the teacher ahead of time that have to do with information about businesses the children know about in the city. There should be enough questions to keep the children going all the way around the block on the sidewalk squares. Questions should be written on cards with the answers on the backs and be accompanied by point values. If you have fewer questions, use larger point values and, if you have more questions, use smaller point values. You may want to walk around the block before you write down the questions and count how many sidewalk squares there are.

✳ A city block with sidewalk sections in squares all the way around

STEPS

1. After learning about some of your city's important businesses, create several cards with questions about them on one side and the correct answers and point values that depend on the difficulty of the questions, on the other side.

2. Divide the children into equal teams of five or fewer members each. Write down a number between one and 20 on a piece of paper for each group. Then have the children guess the number you wrote down for their group. The child in the group who guesses closest to the number you wrote down will be that team's playing piece.

3. Have all the "playing pieces" line up on the sidewalk at the place you choose to start the game. Name each team by the name of its playing piece, such as Jack's team, Tammy's team, etc.

4. Ask the first team a question that you wrote on a card, such as, "How many grocery stores does our city have?" or "What product is made at the Smith Company?" Allow the team members to try to come up with the correct answer. If they do, their playing piece gets to move the same number of sidewalk squares as the point value on that card. If they don't get the answer right, another team can answer and steal their move. This should keep all the children listening to the questions and keep them involved in the game. Continue, in like manner, for each team. Then ask the first team another question. The team members will follow their playing piece around the block until the playing piece reaches the starting line once more. Keep the questions easy enough for the children to generally have success at the game and the point values close enough so that the playing pieces stay relatively close together to keep the game manageable.

(continued)

SOCIAL SCIENCE

Walk Around the Block Game? *(continued)*

5. The first playing piece and team to circle the block are declared the winner of the game and get a round of applause. See if one of the businesses will donate a prize for each child in the class for being such good gamers! For instance, an ice cream company might donate an ice cream treat.

CRITICAL THINKING CHALLENGE

Have the children write their own questions about things they have learned, along with the answers and point values, for the game.

ACCOMMODATIONS

✔ Divide the children into groups with a range of ability levels so that there is help for the children who may not know many answers.

✔ You could also draw a large game board with sidewalk chalk on the blacktop playground surface.

EXTENSIONS

✔ Use this game format to practice solving math story problems. The number of squares to move could be determined by the answer to the story problem.

SOCIAL SCIENCE

Just Gotta Have It!

Just Gotta Have It! encourages the children to think about new products
that children would like and how to get people to buy the products.

MATERIALS

* Video clip of television commercials geared toward children, such as those for toys, clothes, and snack foods. By videotaping the commercials you can erase some if necessary to make sure that all the commercials presented are appropriate for your age group and advertise products they would want.
* VCR
* Large sheet of drawing paper for each group

STEPS

1. Videotape some television commercials geared toward advertising children's products.

2. As you show these to the children, discuss how the advertisers try to get the children "hooked" on the products. Some ways are: by making it sound like everybody really needs this product, by making it seem like the people who have this product are popular, by making it appear that this product does fantastic things, by offering gimmicks such as a prize in the package, by claiming this product is better than a competitor's similar product, etc.

3. Brainstorm ideas for new products that the children would like to see on the market to get their creativity going.

4. Then divide the children into small groups of three to four. Have them decide on a new product they want to sell to the other children. They may either draw their product on a large sheet of paper or use a prop as the product.

5. Have them create a commercial to advertise their product to the class.

6. Share the commercials with the entire group and discuss what method or methods the advertisers used to get you to buy their products.

CRITICAL THINKING CHALLENGE

You could have each group try to sell the same product and discuss which group made the children want to buy that product the most and why.

(continued)

Just Gotta Have It? *(continued)*

ACCOMMODATIONS

✓ Pair up children who you feel will work well together and encourage the sharing of ideas and responsibilities within the commercial. You may have to help the children negotiate with each other in making their commercials.

EXTENSIONS

✓ You could videotape the commercials, if you have the equipment available to do so, and the children could watch each group's commercial.

SOCIAL SCIENCE

I Can't Have Everything I Want

Through the activity I Can't Have Everything I Want *children learn about the decisions we must make when spending our money.*

MATERIALS

✳ Pictures of items that children might like to purchase and a price on a price tag attached to each

✳ A place to display the pictures and prices

✳ A copy of the form provided and scratch paper for each child

✳ Pretend money to spend—the same amount for each child

STEPS

1. Cut out large catalogue pictures of things that children might wish to have.

2. Assign a price, actual or imaginary, that each item will cost and write the price on a large price tag to attach to each item. Display the items along the chalkboard tray or on a bulletin board where they can easily be seen by the children.

3. Give each child an amount of pretend money to spend that is insufficient to buy all the items.

4. Provide each child with a copy of the form below to record his or her purchases from the items displayed and figure out how much of his or her money was spent. Any child who is over the amount of money given to spend must subtract an item and see if now he or she is at or under the amount of money given. If not, another item must be subtracted until the amount spent is at or below the amount of money given to spend. Give each child a piece of scratch paper to do his or her figuring on.

Item Purchased	Money Spent
Total Spent:	

5. Once the children are all within their budgets, discuss how they made decisions on what to buy and what not to buy. Also, if they were over the amount they had to spend, how did they decide what to give up?

6. Ask if these decisions were hard to make and why they had to be made.

(continued)

SOCIAL SCIENCE

I Can't Have Everything I Want *(continued)*

7. Tell them that many people have this dilemma—unlimited wants but limited resources. It is important to make good decisions so that money isn't wasted on things we won't use or can do without and so that we will have money to buy those things we can't do without like food and shelter.

ACCOMMODATIONS

✔ Limit the prices to amounts of money the children can handle adding and subtracting.

EXTENSIONS

✔ You can include new items for the children to buy that they cut out of catalogues and assign prices to.

✔ You can vary the amount of money each child is given to illustrate that sometimes our financial situations limit the choices available to us.

What's Sold Here?

In the activity What's Sold Here? *the children create signs for local businesses that indicate by their shapes what is sold.*

LEARNING

✳ We can combine pictures with words to make business signs that clearly tell viewers what the businesses sell. Signs such as these draw customers to a business even if they are unfamiliar with the specific business but know the product they want.

MATERIALS

✳ Pictures of businesses in the community whose signs show what the businesses sell. If there are no signs of this sort in your community, try to find some in books, nearby communities, etc. as these pictures will help the children understand how to do the activity.

✳ Construction paper and markers or crayons

✳ A chalkboard or chart paper to write on

✳ Business directory (optional)

STEPS

1. If there are businesses in your area with signs that by their shape tell what the businesses sell, bring in pictures of these to show the children. There may be an ice cream store with a sign in the shape of an ice cream cone or a car dealership with a car-shaped sign. Discuss how such signs immediately let us know what is sold at a business even if we are unfamiliar with the business by name and that long ago many people could not read and these types of signs helped them get to the right businesses for their needs.

2. Have the children name several of the businesses they are familiar with in your community. Discuss what each business sells. If no one knows, help the children find out using a business directory or a company Web site. Remind the children that some companies, such as libraries and hospitals, provide a service even if they do not sell a product.

3. After you have a list of businesses and their products, have the children each choose a business to make a sign for. Provide construction paper for this purpose. Remind them to include the name of the business on the sign as companies want us to associate their specific businesses with the signs. When the signs are finished, encourage each child to share his or her sign with the entire group. The signs could then be displayed along with the words "Businesses in Our Community."

(continued)

What's Sold Here? *(continued)*

ACCOMMODATIONS

✓ Try to include businesses for which the shape the sign could be is fairly obvious. A department store is harder to create a sign for than a flower shop.

EXTENSIONS

✓ You may be able to arrange to send the signs the children make to the businesses for them to display. Many businesses are very willing to do this. Children could address large envelopes for this purpose.

✓ When a new business comes to town, have a volunteer make a sign for that business to add to the class display. Some research may need to be done to find out what the company sells.

SOCIAL SCIENCE

Here's to You, Whatever You Do!

Here's to You, Whatever You Do! *develops children's appreciation for the people who do the jobs we need done. This is a good activity to do in conjunction with Labor Day in September.*

LEARNING

❋ All jobs are important and the people who do them should be appreciated.

MATERIALS

❋ Construction paper
❋ Writing and drawing tools
❋ Envelopes (optional)

STEPS

1. Have each child name a job he or she can think of that someone does. Write all these jobs on the chalkboard and comment on how many different jobs there are that need someone to do them. Aren't we glad we have people who do these jobs?

2. Tell the children that one way to show our appreciation for the people who do the jobs we need done is to write them thank you notes. Have the children think of someone they know who does his or her job well and should be thanked for that.

3. Give each child a piece of construction paper to fold in half to make a card. On the front of the card the child should write "Thank you" and draw a picture of the person doing his or her job. On the inside of the card the child should write a brief message thanking that person for the job he or she does.

4. The children can either deliver their thank you cards in person, if practical, or the cards can be mailed to the recipients. If you limit your recipients to school personnel, or parents or guardians, the cards can very easily be hand delivered.

 ACCOMMODATIONS

✔ For children with limited writing abilities, the message to be put in the card could be dictated to an adult who could write the message down.

 EXTENSIONS

✔ As the teacher, you could write the children thank you notes for the good job they do of going to school and trying their hardest.

SOCIAL SCIENCE

What Do I Do?

What Do I Do? calls for the children to match job titles with the description of the jobs.

LEARNING

✳ Different people do different things in their jobs.

MATERIALS

✳ Pictures of persons with different job titles

✳ Job title sheets and job description sheets in equal amounts so that each child can have one or the other

✳ Glue

✳ Two sheets of construction paper for each job. All sheets need to be of the same color.

STEPS

1. This is a matching game. Glue a picture of a person, such as a nurse, businessperson, farmer, etc., on a sheet of construction paper with a job title written under the picture.

2. Now, for every job title, write a job description on another sheet of paper.

3. Pass these all out randomly among the children. Each child's job will be to find the person who has the job title and picture or the job description that goes with his or her info on the sheet of paper.

4. Once all the partners have been found, have one child in each pair share the picture and job title and the other partner read the job description while the rest of the class listens to see if the match is correct.

5. The children might wish to tell you which job of those used in this activity they might like to do someday and why they chose that job.

ACCOMMODATIONS

✔ Keep the job titles and descriptions at the children's level of understanding and reading ability.

✔ If you have an uneven number of children, allow one child to hand out the cards for you.

EXTENSIONS

✔ Allow the children to pair up to prepare more matches. Each pair should create a job title sheet and a matching job description sheet. Then use these sheets to play the same type of matching game. The children may need help writing the job descriptions, as many children know the title for a job but have no idea what a person with that job title does.

SOCIAL SCIENCE

Chapter 21

Civics

Activities in this chapter involve learning about our democratic society and how it functions. We all have rights and responsibilities as citizens of this great land we are privileged to live in.

It's Great to Be a Citizen

Through It's Great to be a Citizen *the children learn what it means to be a citizen and that people born in the United States can automatically become citizens of our country as well as those born to at least one U.S. citizen anywhere in the world. Others must go through a process to receive citizenship.*

LEARNING

❋ Citizens are people who are entitled to all the civil rights a country offers.

❋ We can become U.S. citizens through birth in our country or by going through a process called naturalization in the United States.

MATERIALS

❋ Information on rights of citizens in the United States. Read the Bill of Rights and discuss it in language the children can understand

❋ A speaker who has become a citizen of the United States through naturalization

❋ Drawing paper

❋ Writing utensils

STEPS

1. Begin with a class discussion about what it means to be a citizen of a country. Tell the children that in the United States there is a document called the Bill of Rights that tells what our rights are as citizens of the United States. Go over these rights. Discuss that not all countries grant their citizens the same rights.

2. Ask the children how they became citizens of the United States or another country.

3. Discuss how a person who is not born in a country may have to go through a process to become a citizen.

4. Bring in a speaker who has become a citizen of the United States through naturalization. Have the speaker discuss this process and why he or she wanted to be a citizen of our country. Also have the speaker discuss what rights he or she has gained now.

5. Have each child draw a picture entitled "It's Great to Be a Citizen" depicting something he or she has the right do or will have the right to do as an adult if he or she is a citizen of the United States, such as vote, run for office, worship where he or she chooses, etc. If a child is not a citizen of the United States, do some research to find out about the rights he or she has or will have as an adult in his or her homeland. Discussing this with the child's parents will be very helpful and will be a great source of information.

6. Have each child add sentences to his or her picture telling about the right depicted in the picture.

CRITICAL THINKING CHALLENGE

Have the children consider why we have or do not have certain rights. Do we have the right to take other's property? Why not?

(continued)

It's Great to Be a Citizen *(continued)*

ACCOMMODATIONS

✓ Consider the amount and complexity of the information you want to cover for the abilities of the group members.

✓ Be sensitive to children who are not U.S. citizens and respectful of the countries they are citizens of and the rights given by those countries.

EXTENSIONS

✓ Tie the rights of citizens of a country to the rights of citizens of the classroom. Create a classroom "bill of rights". Such statements as "We have the right to our opinions." or "We have the right to feel safe in our classroom." can be a part of the classroom "bill of rights."

SOCIAL SCIENCE

Special Days, Weeks, and Months

Special Days, Weeks, and Months encourages children to do activities that commemorate special themes that have been designated for specific days, weeks, or months.

LEARNING

❋ Many days, weeks, and months through the year are set aside to emphasize specific themes. Special activities and events occur during these times.

MATERIALS

❋ A book or calendar that specifies days, weeks, or months that have special designations, such as "Fire Prevention Week" (in October) and "Black Poetry Day" (October 17). There are many of these readily available. (See resources section.)

❋ Materials you need to do the activities you choose to go with the special days, weeks, or months

STEPS

1. Become aware of days, weeks, and months that are designated with specific themes.

2. Sometime during that day, week, or month, do an activity in honor of that time period. Some examples are: For Veterans Day (November 11) the children could make cards to thank former soldiers for helping keep our country free and delivering them to the local VFW hall. On National Magic Day (October 31) you could teach everyone a magic trick. There are designated days, weeks, and months for a huge variety of things such as United Nations Day (October 24), National Clown Week (first week in August), and National Courtesy Month (September). Your activities can be as broad or as narrow in scope as you choose and you don't have to do every day, week, or month—just a few now and then that catch your fancy!

3. Tell the children that many of these special times were designated through official proclamations by Congress, the President, governors, or mayors.

CRITICAL THINKING CHALLENGE

Give days, weeks, and months designations the class chooses, such as Hat Day, Silly Poems Week, or Appreciate the Cooks month and let the children come up with ideas to honor these times.

ACCOMMODATIONS

✔ Choose special times and activities that are appropriate for your group of children.

EXTENSIONS

✔ Ask the principal to make an official proclamation over the speaker system, or make one yourself as the teacher.

✔ See if you can get the whole school involved in promoting worthy themes.

SOCIAL SCIENCE

Patriotic Days

There are several Patriotic Days *during the year and special, meaningful ways for children to celebrate them.*

LEARNING

✷ We can show our patriotism in special ways on specific days honoring our country and its military heroes.

MATERIALS

✷ A small American flag for each child (These can be purchased fairly cheaply or you may be able to get them donated by a civic organization.)

✷ Patriotic marching band music

STEPS

1. Flag Day (June 14), Veterans' Day (November 11), Independence Day (July 4), and Memorial Day (May 31) are days that give us a great opportunity to show our patriotism or pride in our country. Use these days to discuss what it means to be patriotic.

2. Placing small American flags on the graves of soldiers at a local cemetery for Memorial Day will emphasize to the children that many people fought for our country and worked to keep it free. Encourage the children and their parents to attend the ceremonies often held on Memorial Day at cemeteries.

3. On Flag Day you could have a parade with the children waving flags as they march to military marching tunes. Discuss what our flag symbolizes to us.

4. Veterans Day is a great time to discuss, first of all, that a veteran is someone who was in the military (army, navy, etc.). He or she may be living or dead. A thank you note written by each child and given to the local VFW hall to distribute to veterans in the area would be appreciated by the veterans and would help the children realize how important our soldiers are to our country. This is also a great time to emphasize that women as well as men serve in the armed forces. If a child has a parent or relative who is a veteran, invite that person to speak to your group about what he or she did in the armed forces.

ACCOMMODATIONS

✔ Gear what you tell about these days to your group's level of understanding.

EXTENSIONS

✔ Older children might be willing to do some research about these special days to share with younger children, such as when the days were first officially recognized and what events led up to them being officially added to the calendar.

✔ If you have children from countries other than the United States, see if you can find out what patriotic days are celebrated in those countries and compare the celebrations with those here.

SOCIAL SCIENCE

Who Says So?

Through the activity Who Says So? the children realize that there are many people who have the right to make rules we must follow.

LEARNING

✳ We all must follow rules that others have the right to make.

MATERIALS

✳ A chart to record the rules that the children decide on for their classroom

STEPS

1. This is a good activity to do the first day or week of school.

2. Hold a discussion about rules. What are some rules we must obey? Who makes them? Discuss such rules as "20 mph in a school zone," "You must be in bed by eight," and "You must write your name on your paper," as well as who gets to make these rules.

3. Ask why we have rules and speculate about what would happen if we didn't have any rules.

4. Ask the children if they have ever had the opportunity to make rules. Tell them that today they will get to make some rules for their classroom. Help the children to decide on two to five rules that they feel are important in order for the classroom to run smoothly and to be a safe and secure place for everyone in it. Having a say in the rules that need to be followed helps the children learn to take responsibility for their actions and gives them a sense of control over their environment.

CRITICAL THINKING CHALLENGES

1. Discuss the rules that various groups of people, such as drivers, homeowners, citizens, athletes, etc., must follow and why.

2. Discuss what happens when rules aren't followed.

ACCOMMODATIONS

☑ The younger the children, the fewer the rules. Help the children to come up with practical and appropriate rules that are manageable for the group.

SOCIAL SCIENCE

Let's Vote On It

In Let's Vote On It *the children have the opportunity to decide specific issues that affect them through voting.*

LEARNING

✳ In a democratic society, the voting process lets us have a say on the issues that affect us.

MATERIALS

✳ A ballot box with a cover that can be removed to take out the ballots

✳ Red, white, and blue paper

✳ Ballots made up for the issue being decided

STEPS

1. Cover the box and its lid with red, white, or blue paper. Then decorate it patriotically with red, white, and blue paper, as well. You may want to include stars and red, white, and blue stripes. Make a slit in the top of the box cover for the ballots to slide through.

2. Now when an important classroom decision needs to be made, you or a child can prepare a ballot for the children to use to vote on the matter.

3. Explain that the class will agree on the choice with the most votes. This is called majority rule. It is not what everyone wants but what most of the people want. This is the way it works when adults vote, as well. Then have the children use the ballots to mark their choices and place these in the ballot box you made. Remind the children that their votes are secret and they don't have to share their choices with anyone else. Count the ballots and tally the votes for the children to see which choice has the most votes and thus, will be carried out.

 ACCOMMODATIONS

✔ Limit the different choices to an amount appropriate for your group.

✔ Be sure the choices are appropriate and realistic.

 EXTENSIONS

✔ Encourage the children to accompany their parents or guardians when they go to the polls to vote to see how this is officially done.

✔ Hold your own mock election for President of the United States when that election comes up.

Surveys, Anyone?

Surveys, Anyone? familiarizes the children with surveys and allows them to administer their own surveys.

LEARNING

✳ Surveys are a method used to gather and record information people share.

MATERIALS

✳ Paper for recording the responses from the surveys

STEPS

1. Conduct a simple survey with the children, such as to find out their favorite flavors of ice cream or their favorite television shows.

2. Show them a method to chart their results, such as a bar graph, tallies, etc.

3. Discuss how to compare the responses recorded. Emphasize that we are not looking for a winner and that it is fine to be the only person with a particular preference.

4. Discuss why we do surveys.

5. Allow the children to conduct their own surveys and to arrange their data in a way that shows the responses they got.

CRITICAL THINKING CHALLENGE

Discuss how the responses to a survey might help the company or organization doing the survey.

ACCOMMODATIONS

✔ Gear the survey you conduct to the interests and knowledge level of your group.

✔ Allow children to work together to plan and carry out a survey.

EXTENSIONS

✔ Bring in surveys you find to show the children how they are laid out and completed.

SOCIAL SCIENCE

Chapter 22

Multiculturalism

Activities in this chapter are intended to give children a broader view of our world and the many different people who inhabit it. The interconnectedness of our world is emphasized. We need each other, enjoy each other, and depend on each other.

Eating Around the World

Eating Around the World helps the children appreciate where the foods they eat come from and to locate those places on a world map.

LEARNING

✳ We are dependent upon many different countries for the foods we eat.

MATERIALS

✳ Snack foods the children generally eat (Pictures of food can also work.)

✳ A map of the world attached to a wall or bulletin board

✳ Yarn

✳ Tape or tacks

✳ Books that describe the food products produced in different countries of the world or a computer with Internet access

STEPS

1. Help the children identify where the foods served for snacks come from. (Check the labels on packaged foods or help the children do some research on the foods served to discover where they come from.)

2. Tape the package itself or a picture of the food near a large map of the world attached to the wall and extend a piece of yarn from the package to the country where that food comes from.

3. Emphasize our dependence on others for many of the foods we eat.

ACCOMMODATIONS

✔ None are necessary.

EXTENSIONS

✔ Use this activity as a springboard to encourage children to try foods they are unfamiliar with that come from foreign countries.

✔ Try to find foods from countries not yet represented on the map.

✔ A field trip to a grocery store to hunt for foods from around the world or to listen to a food buyer describe where some of the foods come from would be appropriate.

✔ Read labels and packaging to find products other than foods that come from foreign countries.

SOCIAL SCIENCE

Class Pen Pals

Having Class Pen Pals from another country is a great and authentic means of learning about another country through the eyes of children.

LEARNING

* People live all over the world and yet there are many similarities among us as well as differences.

MATERIALS

* A method of connecting with children of the same ages as your group in another country
* Letter writing materials

STEPS

1. A personal way to plan for having class pen pals is if you have a connection to another country via friends there or if you know a foreign exchange student who could connect you to an elementary school in the area he or she is from. There are also methods set up on the Internet that you might wish to investigate. Try to find a classroom of children the same ages of your group so that they will have lots in common. Be sure you are corresponding with a classroom in which the children speak English or you are fluent in the language they speak. Alternatively, the classroom teacher may also be able to translate your letters into their native language and their letters into English. So, you see, some preliminary research must be done before you begin this project with children!

2. When you are ready to include the children, begin by exchanging a class letter that provides general information about the class, a picture with the students identified on it, and a map of where your school is located within the United States.

3. Use a map to show your students where this information will be sent.

4. As the year progresses you can discuss the things going on in the classroom. Be sure the children give you input into the letters' contents. Include pictures drawn by students, cards, holiday gifts, etc. Remind the children to ask questions of their pen pals and ask about their school activities, as well. This will make the learning more meaningful and at the interest level of the students. By making this a class project, rather than having individual pen pals, you will assure that the letter writing is kept up regularly and that the content of the letters is appropriate and will add to your children's understanding of the children and their country.

(continued)

SOCIAL SCIENCE

Class Pen Pals *(continued)*

ACCOMMODATIONS

✔ Consider the ages of the children when deciding what topics to cover in your letters. Letting the children dictate what they wish to include will give you a good idea of what interests them.

✔ Bring in books about the country where the foreign school is located to add to the children's understanding of the country.

EXTENSIONS

✔ A video of your children speaking to their pen pals would be a great thing to send, but check on the equipment the foreign school has available and if it is compatible with yours.

✔ E-mailing is another way to correspond. Again, check on the availability of e-mail at the school you are corresponding with.

SOCIAL SCIENCE

Celebrations Around the World

In Celebrations Around the World the children learn about many ways that people celebrate the important events in their lives.

MATERIALS

✳ Resources with information about the celebrations of different countries, including such things as stories, crafts, foods, and music associated with the celebrations

STEPS

1. Decide on which countries you wish to explore—too many different countries and traditions may confuse the children and lead to misunderstandings about who does what and why. Also stick to celebrations that the children can relate to—birthdays, holidays, etc.

2. Be sure the children understand why the activities are done and the meaning behind what is celebrated.

3. Some of the children's parents may be more than willing to help with the celebrations and may have valuable background information and ideas to share about countries they are from or are very familiar with. This first-hand information is invaluable to making your celebrations authentic.

4. Choose countries from different continents to get a good variety of types of celebrations and also choose celebrations from different times during the year.

5. Since you will want to do some solid research for each celebration, try to do no more than one per month or maybe even per season. Doing one celebration well is far better than briefly touching on many. The children will still get the idea that we all celebrate but in many different and unique ways!

ACCOMMODATIONS

✔ Include activities from the celebrations that all the children in your group can participate in.

✔ Choose celebrations that your children can understand.

EXTENSIONS

✔ You may wish to expand your study of a specific country far beyond the celebrations, if time allows you to do so. Studying another country in depth is a valuable and interesting experience for children and can be adjusted to fit the group's abilities.

SOCIAL SCIENCE

The Same Yet Different

Many of our favorite fairy tales and folktales have versions told in several other cultures or countries. In The Same Yet Different the children compare a fairy tale or folktale from our culture with that tale as it is told in another culture or country using a Venn diagram and discuss reasons for any differences.

LEARNING

✳ Some traditional stories (fairy tales and folktales) are told in many cultures with some variations but with the basic story intact.

MATERIALS

✳ Two versions of a fairy tale or folktale as told in two different countries or cultures

✳ Chalkboard and chalk

STEPS

1. Locate a well-known fairy tale or folktale written in two different versions from two different countries or cultures. There are many of these.

2. Read one version of the story one day and the other the next.

3. Now draw a large Venn diagram on the chalkboard with the title of the story from one country or culture over one circle and the title of the other story over the other circle but not where the circles intersect.

4. Explain that the details about the stories that are the same will be written in the section where the two circles intersect. The details about the stories that are different will be written in the circle parts that don't intersect under each story title.

5. Discuss why these differences might occur and that some things are the same in other countries or cultures and some things are different. One story is not better than the other—It is just different. And isn't it interesting that both countries or cultures have such similar stories?

ACCOMMODATIONS

✔ Select a fairy tale or folktale that is the appropriate length and subject for your group and is one that they are familiar with.

EXTENSIONS

✔ The children could write and perform plays for the two fairy tales or folktales.

✔ There may also be books and videos of fairy tales and folktales in which some of the details we are familiar with have been changed. Some compilers of these tales delete or change actions and words that may seem violent by today's standards.

Day of Swings

In Day of Swings the children celebrate this June holiday of Korea.

LEARNING

✳ Different holidays are celebrated in different cultures around the world.

MATERIALS

✳ A swing set
✳ A bell
✳ Crepe paper streamers of red and white to decorate the swings with. The streamers can be wound in and out of the chains with longer lengths hanging down, or they can be tied to swings' covered chains so that they fly out behind the swings as they go back and forth.

STEPS

1. Tell the children about the Korean holiday called "Day of Swings," which generally falls during June. Briefly, it is celebrated by decorating swings on which the children swing high in an effort to be the first to ring a bell strung high in front of the swing. The first one in the group to ring the bell wins.

2. Go out to the playground and decorate the swings with streamers of red and white crepe paper, the same colors that are used to decorate the swings in Korea.

3. Then have the children take turns swinging high until you ring a bell. Then it's the next group's turn to swing high. If there is a way to string bells for the children to ring with their feet, then you can play the game exactly as it's done in Korea. That will depend on the location of your swing set and the objects nearby. Be sure the bells are large and each hangs by a separate string down from the main string they are strung on so there is no way that the children's feet could become entangled in the main string. As soon as a bell is rung by a child's feet, all the children must slow down and stop trying to swing higher.

ACCOMMODATIONS

✔ Gear how high you wish the children to swing by their ages and abilities.

✔ Children could also be pushed on the swings if they are unable to make them go on their own. Older children could push younger children if they are able to do it safely.

EXTENSIONS

✔ Explore other holidays celebrated around the world with fun activities that are a part of the celebrations.

SOCIAL SCIENCE

We All Play Games

In We All Play Games *the children play games from around the world that are similar to the games we play here.*

LEARNING

* There are many similarities in people all around the world and in the things they do.
* We are more alike than different.

MATERIALS

* The book *Children's Traditional Games: Games from 137 Countries and Cultures* by Judy Sierra and Robert Kaminski
* Items that are needed to play the games you select

STEPS

1. Use the book *Children's Traditional Games: Games from 137 Countries and Cultures* or another book similar to it that features games from around the world. (See Social Studies Resources.) Many of these games have striking similarities even though they were developed in different places by different people. They are all arranged by their similarities to other games, so it is easy to find two games that will be easy to compare.

2. Play the games that are similar as they are generally played in this country and as they are played in another part of the world. Point out the country the game is from on a world map.

3. Discuss the similarities and differences between the games and what things might be responsible for the differences.

CRITICAL THINKING CHALLENGE

Have the children come up with ways the games resemble other games the children are familiar with.

ACCOMMODATIONS

✓ Keep the games at the skill level appropriate for your group.

EXTENSIONS

✓ If the children are able, allow them to pick out the games and teach them to the rest of the class as well as point out the countries where the games are played on the world map.

SOCIAL SCIENCE

The Japanese Haiku

In this activity, The Japanese Haiku, *the children are introduced to a form of poetry from Japan and experiment with writing their own haikus.*

LEARNING

❋ Different forms of poetry are developed in different parts of the world.

❋ In Japan one traditional form of poetry is the haiku.

MATERIALS

❋ The book, *Hands Around the World: 365 Creative Ways to Build Cultural Awareness and Global Respect* by Susan Milford

❋ A haiku you have written yourself or picked from a book copied onto chart paper with a picture you've drawn to accompany it (optional)

❋ A haiku poem form (see Steps below) for each child to write his or her poem on

❋ Drawing paper and markers or crayons

❋ Glue

STEPS

1. Using the book *Hands Around the World* (See Social Studies Resources.) or another good source, read the information given about the form of poetry called haiku to share with the children. Share some haikus Japanese poets have written as well as where Japan is on the world map compared to where the children live. The haiku is a poem about nature that follows a specific pattern of syllables. Here is an example:

Spring

The snow has melted.

The bright sun warms the brown earth.

Life begins anew.

The pattern is three lines with five syllables in the first line, seven syllables in the second line, and five syllables in the third line. Obviously, for this activity the children will need to have a working understanding of what syllables are.

2. Write your sample haiku on chart paper, and help the children see how the poem was written as far as topic (nature) and syllables. Then give the children the opportunity to write their own haikus. Brainstorm ideas for the poems that have to do with nature. A poem form with a line drawn for each syllable will aid in the children's writing of haikus. It would look like this:

_____ (title)

__ __ __ __ __ (5 syllables)

__ __ __ __ __ __ __ (7 syllables)

__ __ __ __ __ (5 syllables)

The children need to understand that each blank is for a syllable and not necessarily a word, unless it is a one-syllable word.

3. When the children have their poems written, they can each draw a picture to illustrate their poems and glue the poem sheets on the drawing paper next to the pictures. These could then be displayed or bound together as a book.

(continued)

The Japanese Haiku *(continued)*

✔ ACCOMMODATIONS

Writing a poem together might work well for this activity if the children will have a difficult time dealing with the syllable requirements. Copies could be made of the class poem for each child to illustrate in his or her own way.

EXTENSIONS

✔ You could try a poem format from a different country, such as a limerick from Ireland, and follow the procedure above. *Hands Around the World* has information about limericks, as well.

We Depend On Each Other

Through the activity We Depend On Each Other *children come to realize that we depend on many other countries for many of the products we use every day.*

LEARNING

✲ Countries around the world are interdependent.

MATERIALS

✲ A variety of items produced in countries other than the one the children live in, such as pieces of clothing, toys, canned or boxed foods, electronics, etc.

✲ A world map

✲ A chalkboard

STEPS

1. Gather up items that are produced in countries other than your own.

2. Give each child an item to examine to see if he or she can find out where it was produced. Write each country where a product was produced on the chalkboard and show where that country is located on a map of the world. Emphasize that we use these products from other countries every day. Ask if the children think other countries use products from their country. Do a little research to find out where some products from their country go and share this information with the children. Emphasize the fact that countries are interdependent—that they depend on each other.

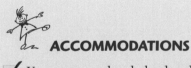

ACCOMMODATIONS

✓ You may need to help the children find the name of the country where a product was produced on its tag or label.

EXTENSIONS

✓ Ask the children to locate two products at their houses that come from two different countries than their own. Have them write down each product and where it came from to share with the class. Locate these countries on the map, as well.

SOCIAL SCIENCE

How Do You Say It?

In the activity How Do You Say It? *the children are encouraged to try out languages other than their own.*

LEARNING

✳ We don't all speak the same language, but we say many of the same things.

MATERIALS

✳ Specific words from other languages that have direct counterparts in English

✳ A chalkboard to write the words on

STEPS

1. Locate and learn to say some specific words in several different languages, such as "Hello," "Yes," "No," and "Thank you." Be sure you are pronouncing the words correctly.

2. Then once a week have a day on which you introduce these words in one language. Write them on the board next to their English counterparts. Do be aware that not all words can be directly translated from one language to the next, however. Avoid these for this particular activity.

3. Now have the children use these foreign words all day long whenever they wish or need to say, "Hello," "Yes," "No," or "Thank you."

4. Discuss how we all communicate with words but that those words don't all sound the same.

CRITICAL THINKING CHALLENGE

Older children could write sentences or make captions for cartoons using words from the language they are learning.

ACCOMMODATIONS

✔ If you have children who speak other languages, start with words from these languages. Ask them to share their languages with the other children.

✔ Invite a bilingual adult to teach the children some words from his or her native language and maybe a song or poem.

SOCIAL SCIENCE

SOCIAL STUDIES RESOURCES

Allocca, Donna Marsh. (1997). *Create a community*. Torrance, CA: Fearon Teacher Aids, A Division of Frank Schaffer Publications, Inc.

Brown, Jeff. (1992). *Flat Stanley*. New York: HarperCollins Publishers.

Flowers, Barbara, Meszaros, Bonnie, & Suiter, Mary C. (1993). *Economics and children's literature*. St. Louis, MO: SPEC Publishers, Inc.

Gibbons, Gail. (1996). *Deserts*. New York: Holiday House.

Jenkins, Steve. (1998). *Hottest, coldest, highest, deepest*. Boston: Houghton Mifflin.

Knowlton, Jack. (1998). *Geography from a to z*. New York: Crowell.

Kourilsky, Marilyn. (1992). *KinderEconomy +*. New York: Joint Council on Economic Education.

McKinnon, Elizabeth. (1989). *Special day celebrations*. Everett, WA: Warren Publishing House, Inc.

Milford, Susan. (1992). *Hands around the world: 365 creative ways to build cultural awareness and global respect*. Charlotte, VT: Williamson Publishers.

Milford, Susan. (1996). *Tales of the shimmering sky: Ten global folktales with activities*. Charlotte, VT: Williamson Pub.

Phipps, Barbara J. (1995). *Teaching strategies K-2*. New York: National Council on Economic Education.

Reinke, Diane Wilcox, McGuire, Margit, & Reinke, Robert W. (1989). *Exploring the community market place*. New York: The Community Publishing Company.

Sierra, Judy. (1996). *Multicultural folktales for the feltboard and readers' theater*. Phoenix, AZ: Oryx Press.

Sierra, Judy, and Kaminski, Robert. (1995). *Children's traditional games: Games from 137 countries and cultures*. Phoenix, AZ: Oryx Press.

Sweeny, Joan. (1996). *Me on the map*. New York: Crown.

Van Cleave, Janice. (1993). *Geography for every kid*. New York: Wiley.

Resources

Introduction:

Bandura, A. (2001). Social cognitive theory: An agentic perspective. *Annual Review of Psychology*, 52, 1–26.

Berk, L. E. (2005). *Infants, children, and adolescents.* 5th ed. Boston: Allyn and Bacon.

Bredekamp, S. (1987). *Developmentally appropriate practice in early childhood programs serving children from birth through age 8.* Exp.ed. Washington, D.C.: NAEYC.

Gardner, H. (1983). *Frames of mind: The theory of multiple intelligences.* New York: Basic Books.

Gardner, H. (1993). *Multiple intelligences: The theory in practice.* New York: Basic Books.

Lubeck, S. (1996). Deconstructing child development knowledge and teacher preparation. *Early Childhood Research Quarterly.* 11(2), 147–167.

McCarthy, B. (1980). *The 4MAT system: Teaching to learning styles with right/left mode techniques.* Oak Brook, Illinois: Excel, Inc.

New, R. (1994). Culture, child development and developmentally appropriate practices: teachers as collaborative researchers. In B. Mallory & R. New (Eds.), *Diversity and developmentally appropriate practices: challenges for early childhood education* (137–154). New York: Teachers College Press.

Palincsar, A. S. (1998). Social constructivist perspectives on teaching and learning. *Annual Review of Psychology*, 49, 345–375.

Pressman, H., and Deblin, P. (1995). *Accommodating learning differences in elementary Classrooms.* New York: Harcourt Brace.

Walberg, H. J. (1986). Synthesis of research on teaching. In M.C. Wittrock (ed.), *Handbook of research on teaching.* 3rd ed., 214–229. New York: Macmillan.

Unit 1: Fine Arts Resources

Ashliman, D. L. (2004). *Folk and fairy tales:A handbook.* Pittsburg, PA: Greenwood Press.

Bahti, Mark, and Baatsoslanii, Joe. (2000). *A guide to Navajo sandpaintings.* Tucson, AZ: Rio Nuevo Publishers.

Bisson, Lynn. (1989). *3–D art projects that teach.* Nashville, TN: Incentive Publications, Inc.

Boiko, Claire. (1997). *Children's plays for creative actors.* Plays, Inc.

Carle, Eric. (1966). *The grouchy ladybug.* New York: Harper Trophy.

Cole, Joanna. (1989). *Anna banana: 101 jump rope rhymes.* New York: Beech Tree Books.

Consortium of National Arts Education Associations. (1994). *National Standards for arts education: What every young american should know and be able to do in the arts.*Washington, D.C.:

Douglas, Kathy. (2001). *Open-ended art.* Torrance, CA: Totline Publications.

Hart, Avery, and Mantell, Paul. (1993). *Kids make music*. Charlotte, VT: Williamson Pub. Co.

Koehler-Pentacoff, Elizabeth. (1989). *Curtain call*. Nashville, TN: Incentive Publications, Inc.

Marx, Pamela. (1997). *Take a quick bow: 26 plays for the classroom*. Glenview, IL: Good Year Books.

Mecca, Judy Truesdell. (1992). *Plays that teach: Plays, activities and songs with a message*. Nashville, TN: Incentive Publications.

Meish, Goldish. (2001). *50 learning songs sung to your favorite tunes*. New York: Scholastic Professional Books.

Sanders, Sandra. (1970). *Creating plays with children*. New York: Citation Press.

Smolinski, Jill. (1998). *50 nifty super animal origami crafts*. Chicago: Contemporary Books.

Storm, Jerry. (1995). *101 music games for children*. Alemeda, CA: Hunter House.

Unit 2: Language Arts Resources

Brenner, R. (1997). *Valentine treasury: A century of valentine cards*. NJ: Judith Yankeilun Lind, Roseland Free P. L. (Reed Business Information, Inc.).

Love, Marla. (1977). *20 reading comprehension games*. Belmont, CA: Fearon.

Moore, Joe, Moore, Jo E., Tryon, Leslie, and Franco, Betsy. (1994). *How to do plays with children*. Monterey, CA: Evan-Moor, Corp.

Novelli, Joan. (2002). *40 sensational sight word games*. New York: Scholastic Professional Books.

Potts, Cheryl. (1999). *Poetry play any day with Jane Yolen*. Fort Atkinson, WI: Alleyside Press.

Prelutsky, Jack (selected by). (1993). *A. nonny mouse writes again: Poems*. New York: Knopf: Distributed by Random House.

Roeber, Jane A. (1990–1999). *1990 through 1999 summer library program manuals (each based on a different theme)*. Madison, WI: Wisconsin Department of Public Instruction.

Silverstein, Shel. (1974).*Where the sidewalk ends*. New York: Harper Collins Publishers.

Unit 3: Mathematics Resources

Bacarella, Dawn H. (1997). *1–100 Activity book: Activities and worksheets for the hundred board*. Vernon Hills, IL: Learning Resources, Inc.

Bresser, Rusty, & Holtsman, C. (1999). *Developing number sense grades 3–6*. Sausalito, CA: Math Solutions Publications.

Carter, Rik. (1996). *Exploring measurement grades 5–6: Length, area, volume, mass, time*. Rowley, MA: Didax Educational Resources, Inc.

Charlesworth, R. (2000). *Experiences in math for young children* (4th ed.) Clifton Park, NY: Thomson Delmar Learning.

Copley, Juanita V. (2000). *The young child and mathematics*. Washington, DC: National Association for the Education of Young Children.

May, Lola J. & Frye, Shirley M. (1995). *Down to earth mathematics: Activities for building strong math foundations*. Rowley, MA: Didax Educational Resources, Inc.

Overholt, James L., White-Holtz, Jackie, & Dickson, Sydney. (1999). *Big math activities for young children*. Clifton Park, NY: Thomson Delmar Learning.

National Council of Teachers of Mathematics. (1999). *Mathematics for young children*. Reston, VA: Author.

National Council of Teachers of Mathematics. (2000). *Principles and standards for school mathematics*. Reston, VA: author.

Reys, Robert E., Suydam, Marilyn N., & Lindquist, Mary M. (1995). *Helping children learn mathematics*. (4th ed.). Needham Heights, MA: Allyn and Bacon.

Richardson, K. (1999). *Developing number concepts, Book 1: Counting, Comparing, and pattern.* Parsippany, NJ: Dale Seymour Publications.

Richardson, K. (1999). *Developing number concepts, Book 2: Addition and subtraction.* Parsippany, NJ: Dale Seymour Publications.

Richardson, K. (1999). *Developing number concepts, Book 3: Place value, multiplication, and division.* Parsippany, NJ: Dale Seymour Publications.

Richardson, K. (1999). *Understanding geometry.* Bellingham, WA: Lummi Bay Publishing.

Silverman, Helene, & Oringel, Sandy. (2001). *Math activities with dominoes: Grades K–3.* Vernon Hills, IL: Learning Resources, Inc.

Smith, Nancy l., Lambdin, Diane V., Linquist, Mary M., & Reys, Robert E. (2001). *Teaching elementary mathematics: A resource for field experiences.* New York: John Wiley and Sons.

Smith, Susan S. (1997). *Early childhood mathematics.* Needham Heights, MA: Allyn and Bacon.

Wakefield, Alice P. (1997). *Early childhood number games: Teachers reinvent math instruction.* Needham Heights, MA: Allyn and Bacon.

Unit 4: Physical Activity Resources

Belka, D. (1994). *Teaching children games: Becoming a master teacher.* Champaign, IL: Human Kinetics.

Brehm, Madeleine, & Tindell, Nancy T. (1983). *Movement with a purpose: Perceptual motor-lesson plans for young children.* West Nyack, NY: Parker Publishing Company, Inc.

Buschner, Craig A. (1994). *Teaching children movement concepts and skills: Becoming a master teacher.* Champaign, IL: Human Kinetics.

Curtis, Sandra R. (1982). *The joy of movement in early childhood.* New York: Teachers College Press.

Flinchum, Betty M. (1975). *Motor development in early childhood: A guide for movement education with ages 2 to 6.* Saint Louis, MO: C.V. Mosby Company.

Hammett, Carol T. (1992). *Movement activities for early childhood.* Champaign, IL: Human Kinetics.

Hinson, C. (1995). *Fitness for children.* Champaign, IL: Human Kinetics.

Metteer, Richard. (n. d.). *Project success for the SLD child: Motor perception.* Wayne, NE: Wayne-Carroll School District.

Payne, G., & Isaacs, L. (1991). *Human motor development: A lifespan approach* (2nd ed.). Mountain View, CA: Mayfield.

Pettifor, Bonnie, (1999). *Physical education methods for classroom teachers.* Champaign, IL: Human Kinetics.

Pica, R. (1990). *Early elementary children moving and learning.* Champaign, IL: Human Kinetics.

Ridenour, M. (Ed.). (1978). *Motor development: Issues and applications* (ed.). Princeton, NJ: Princeton Book Co.

Unit 5: Science Resources

Branley, F. (1996). *What makes a magnet?* New York: Harper-Collins.

Charlesworth, Rosalind, Lind, Karen K., & Fleege, Pam. (2003). *Math and science for young children.* (4th ed.). Clifton Park, NY: Thomson Delmar Learning.

Cobb, Vicki. (1972). *Science experiments you can eat.* New York: Scholastic, Inc.

Diehl, J., & Plumb, D. (2000). *What's the difference?: 10 animal look-alikes.* New York: Kingfisher.

Fiarotta, Phyllis, & Fiarotta, Noel. (1999). *Great experiements with light.* New York: Scholastic, Inc.

Herbert, Don. (1980). *Mr. Wizard's supermarket science.* New York: Random House.

Langley, A. (2001). *The Oxford first book of space.* New York: Oxford University Press.

Levine, S., & Crafton, A. (1992). *Projects for a healthy planet.* New York: Wiley.

Lind, Karen K. (1991). *Exploring science in early childhood: A developmental approach.* Clifton Park, NY: Thomson Delmar Learning.

Lorbeer, George C. & Nelson, Leslie W. (1992). *Science activities for children* (9th ed.). Dubuque, IA: Wm. C. Brown Publishers.

Markle, Sandra. (1980). *Primary science sampler.* Santa Barbara, CA: The Learning Works.

National Science Resources Center, (1991). *Electric circuits: student activity handbook.* Burlington, NC: Carolina Biological Supply Company.

Press, Hans J. (1967). *Simple science experiments.* West Germany: Otto Maier Verlag Ravensburg.

Project Learning Tree. (2001). *Environmental education activity guide pre k–8* (8th ed.). Washington, DC: American Forest Foundation.

VanCleave, Janice P. (1991). *Earth science for every child: 101 easy experiments that really work.* New York: John Wiley & Sons, Inc.

VanCleave, Janice P. (1991). *Physics for every child: 101 easy experiments in motion, heat, light, machines, and sound.* New York: John Wiley & Sons, Inc.

VanCleave, Janice P. (1995). *The human body for every child: Easy activities that make learning science fun.* New York: John Wiley & Sons, Inc.

Wyler, Rose & Ames, Gerald. (1963). *Prove it!* New York: Scholastic Book Services.

Unit 6: Social Studies Resources

Allocca, Donna Marsh. (1997). *Create a community.* Torrance, CA: Fearon Teacher Aids, A Division of Frank Schaffer Publications, Inc.

Brown, Jeff. (1992). *Flat Stanley.* New York: Harper-Collins Publishers.

Flowers, Barbara, Meszaros, Bonnie & Suiter, Mary C. (1993). *Economics and children's literature.* St. Louis, MO: SPEC Publishers, Inc.

Gibbons, Gail. (1996). *Deserts.* New York: Holiday House.

Jenkins, Steve. (1998). *Hottest, coldest, highest, deepest.* Boston: Houghton Mifflin.

Knowlton, Jack. (1998). *Geography from a to z.* New York: Crowell.

Kourilsky, Marilyn. (1992). *KinderEconomy +.* New York: Joint Council on Economic Education.

McKinnon, Elizabeth. (1989). *Special day celebrations.* Everett, WA: Warren Publishing House, Inc.

Milford, Susan. (1992). *Hands around the world: 365 creative ways to build cultural awareness and global respect.* Charlotte, VT: Williamson Pub.

Milford, Susan. (1996). *Tales of the shimmering sky: Ten global folktales with activities.* Charlotte, VT: Williamson Pub.

Phipps, Barbara J. (1995). *Teaching strategies K–2.* New York: National Council on Economic Education.

Reinke, Diane Wilcox, McGuire, Margit, & Reinke, Robert W. (1989). *Exploring the community market place.* New York: The Community Publishing Company.

Sierra, Judy, (1996). *Multicultural folktales for the feltboard and readers' theater.* Phoenix: Oryx Press.

Sierra, Judy and Kaminski, Robert. (1995). *Children's traditional games: Games from 137 countries and cultures.* Phoenix: Oryx Press.

Sweeny, Joan. (1996). *Me on the map.* New York: Crown.

Van Cleave, Janice. (1993). *Geography for every kid.* New York: Wiley.

Developmental Milestones

Language Arts
Primary Grades (K–3)

Learns to express self through written format

Experiments with different forms of writing: stories, poetry, letters

Shares written work with others

Speaks in front of groups for short time periods

Volunteers ideas and opinions when communicating with others

Enjoys being read to and learning to read silently

Comprehends age-appropriate stories, poems

Listens to short poems and stories

Makes predictions about what will happen next

Changes language to suit audiences, purpose, or situation

Selects age-appropriate books to read or be read to

Begins to use writing to communicate in a variety of situations

Expands speaking and listening vocabulary

Uses invented spelling

Writes but may lack standard conventions

Benefits from guided reading

Intermediate Grades (4–6)

Expresses self more clearly through writing

Writes increasingly complex stories, poems, letters

Evaluates written work of others

Speaks more comfortably and competently in front of groups

Explains and defends ideas and opinions

Reads silently for increasing periods of time

Comprehends increasingly complex material

Listens for sustained periods of time to readings

Makes accurate predictions based on information presented

Changes language effectively to suit audience, purpose, or situation

Develops favorite genres of literature

Increasingly uses written language to communicate

Amount and complexity of written and spoken language increases

Uses many standard writing conventions

Becomes more accurate in spelling

Selects age-appropriate materials independently

Fine Arts

Primary Grades (K–3)

Experiments with a variety of tools and media such as pencils, brushes, scissors, etc.

Experiments with creative art techniques: drawing, painting, collages, weaving, etc.

Uses drawings to reproduce impressions of people, events, and objects

Recognizes the basic colors and begins to mix colors to create new colors

Notices differences in artistic creations

Recognizes and uses basic shapes, lines, textures, forms and color in artwork

Recognizes and experiments with two- and three-dimensional art forms

Plays with classroom instruments

Sings variety of age-appropriate songs, demonstrating some rhythm, pitch, phrasing, tempo, and volume

Moves in response to sounds, beat, and rhythms

Recognizes simple melodies, tempos, and rhythms within musical pieces

Begins to recognize a variety of styles of music

Creates simple music with vocal, environmental, and instrumental sounds

Participates in age-appropriate performances

Expresses personal feelings about musical pieces

Enjoys pretending in play and has great imagination

Gains confidence in performing in front of others

Makes and manipulates simple puppets

Intermediate (4–6)

Uses an expanding variety of tools and media including adhesives, drawing utensils, fiber

Produces individual works of art through drawing, painting, sculpting, printing, illustrations, and weaving

Draws more detailed and intricate pictures

Effectively mixes colors to create an array of new colors for specific purposes

Shows individuality in artwork

Produces light and dark qualities of colors

Describes in detail art objects and materials after observation using appropriate senses

Recognizes and uses increasingly complex shapes, lines, textures, forms, and color in artwork

Creates two- and three-dimensional artworks

Maintains interest and focus for longer periods of time

Uses a wide variety of classroom instruments to make music

Singing demonstrates increasingly complex rhythms, phrasing, and tempos

Movements to musical sounds, beats, and rhythms become more complex

Recognizes increasingly complex or subtle melodies, tempos, rhythms within music scores

More self-conscious and needs encouragement by teacher

Plans and directs own creative performances

Moves in more intricate ways

Creates detailed puppets and puppet theaters

Begins to write own puppet plays

Math

Primary (K–3)

Sorts, classifies, and orders objects by different properties: size, number, shapes

Moves from using concrete objects to symbols to demonstrate computations of addition, subtraction, multiplication, division

Uses objects, illustrations, and later symbols to solve different type of story problems

Understands concept of fractions to one-tenth

Skip counts by twos, fives, tens to three- or four-digit numbers

Reads, writes, and orders numbers to four-digits

Rounds numbers to the nearest ten and hundred

Begins to sense the magnitude of hundreds and one thousand

Recognizes, compares, and begins to build two- and three-dimensional shapes

Begins to describe attributes of two- and three-dimensional shapes

Forms one shape from other shapes

Recognizes and constructs symmetrical images

Relates ideas of shape to number and measurement

Recognizes concepts of length, volume, weight, area, and time

Measures using nonstandard, standard, and metric units

Selects appropriate tools for measurement

Makes estimates of units in terms of length, weight, time

Represents data using objects, pictures, and simple graphs and charts

Identifies probability of events happening as likely or unlikely

Intermediate (4–6)

Understands base-ten number system beyond one thousand

Understands fractions and decimals beyond tenths

Understands equivalent forms of normally used fractions

Explores numbers less than zero

Works with higher levels of division and multiplication

Uses calculators, estimation, and mental computation when computing whole numbers

Identifies commutative, associative, and distributive properties of whole numbers

Expresses mathematical relationships using equations

Analyzes patterns and functions using words, tables, graphs

Classifies two- and three-dimensional objects based on properties

Explores congruence and similarity of geometric shapes

Investigates subdividing, combining, and transforming shapes at higher levels

Understands attributes of length, weight, volume, and size of angles

Measures with standard and metric units and makes simple conversations

Explores relationship between area and perimeter

Collects data using observations, surveys, and experiments

Represents data using tables, graphs, line plots, bar graphs, and line graphs

Physical Activity
Primary (K–3)

Uses fork effectively

Cuts with scissors following lines

Copies and later draws shapes

Uses knife to cut food

Ties shoes

Draws person with five to six parts

Draws two-dimensional objects and some evidence of three-dimensional objects takes place in the form of shapes, etc.

Copies and later writes numbers

Walks with alternating feet

Runs smoothly

Gallops and skips on one foot

Throws and catches balls with smooth motions

Rides a bicycle with training wheels then without

Intermediate (4–6)

Improves writing ability in cursive writing

Drawing of geometric shapes makes substantial gains with three-dimensional objects

Running speed increases substantially

Skipping movements and side-stepping movements improve

Vertical jumping improves from around 4 inches to 12 inches by age 12

Throwing, catching, and kicking improve

Batting and dribbling improve

Balancing and agility skills improve with more rapid and accurate movements in games

Force also improves from the primary years, throwing the ball farther etc.

Science

Primary (K–3)

Begins to understand that objects are made up of different properties

Groups and classifies objects and substances

Observes changes in temperature, speed, direction, and other physical properties

Understands states of matter

Begins to construct simple models

Observes objects at rest and in motion

Begins to understand energy and its different forms

Begins to understand basic concepts of light, electricity, sound, and magnetism

Identifies simple machines and how they are used

Investigates how magnets work on materials

Understands vocabulary for rocks, minerals, and soils

Begins to identify land and water masses

Identifies stars, sun, moon, and planets, and notes changes in movement patterns

Understands terms relating to clouds, temperature, changes of seasons, and forms of precipitation

Differentiates between living and nonliving things

Investigates plants, animals, and humans with regard to food, habitats, life cycles

Intermediate (4–6)

Increases understanding of properties and substances

Understands how simple electrical currents work to form light, sound, heat

Identifies materials that transmit, reflect, or absorb light and sound

Examines how forces act on structures

Investigates how pulleys and gears work

Observes and investigates pull of magnets

Works with electromagnets

Understands the different human organs and major bodily systems

Demonstrates phases of the moon

Increases understanding of habitats and comunities

Explores diversity of living things

Understands how plants are classified and major concepts such as photosynthesis

Social Science

Primary (K–3)

Develops time concepts of past, present, and future

Sees differences in cultures as frightening or strange

Needs concrete experiences that allow for hands-on learning

Learns through repetition

Eager to make sense of immediate environment (home, community, school)

Develops sense of direction through physical movement (up, down, left, right)

Aware of changes physically experienced

Shows interest in maps and their usage

Understanding of spatial concepts improves to allow child to draw simple maps

Aware of rules but sees them as unchangeable

Sees ones view as the right view that everyone has

Develops simple economic concepts such as earning money for work, need for money, etc.

Intermediate (4–6)

Develops more accurate sense of time

Identifies and accepts similarities and differences in cultures

Develops appreciation for others' points of view

Begins to think more abstractly and understands map symbols, directions

Relates new concepts to past learning

Understands right, left directions

States how environmental changes affect humans

Realizes need for maps and can complete more detailed maps

Improved understanding of spatial concepts leads to more accurate mapping abilities

Sees need for others in our world and the need for interdependence

Sees value of rules and understands they can change

Makes economic decisions, what to buy, how much to spend, etc.

Materials List

Appendix **C**

Unit One
Chapter 1

Make Your Own Music

✴ Various recyclable items and odds and ends (*see step # 1* on page 4)

✴ Tools and materials to produce the instruments

Musical Characters

✴ Rhythm instruments—either traditional or created—enough for each child to have one to represent a character. More than one child may have the same instrument.

I'm in a Mood!

✴ A rhythm instrument for each child in the group.

Instrument Pantomime

✴ Video featuring band and/or orchestra instruments and television with VCR

✴ Large pictures of the instruments with the names of the instruments on them

✴ Small cards with pictures of the instruments and their names

✴ A small container

✴ Work well in multi-age groups

What Do You Hear Now?

✴ Rhythm instruments—either commercial or handmade

Musical Patterns

✴ One rhythm instrument for each child (*see* page 9, *for examples*)

Musical Animal

✴ A variety of rhythm instruments

✴ A box or screen to hide the instruments behind

Musical Bingo (Mingo)

✴ 1 × 1 inch square pictures of 25 marching band instruments on a 5 × 5 inch square sheet of paper, copied—one sheet for each child plus one extra sheet for the teacher

✴ 5 × 5 inch square sheets of paper with blank 1 × 1 inch squares on them—5 per row and five rows—one for each child

✴ 25 (1 × 1 inch square) pieces of cardboard for the teacher to mount one set of pictures on to make the calling pieces

✴ Scissors and glue for the children to use to prepare the game cards

✴ A container for the calling pieces

You're the Conductor

* A variety of rhythm instruments—for this activity it is fine if several are the same kind of instrument
* A baton for the conductor

New Year's Parade

* Noisemakers and hats from New Year's Eve celebrations

Jump Rope Jingles

* Jump rope jingles
* Large sheets of chart paper and a dark, thick marker
* Jump ropes (optional)

Music on the Move

* A xylophone or another instrument on which to play musical scales
* Music that contains fairly substantial changes in pitch throughout the piece

Music That Makes Us Move

* A piece of classical music that incorporates a variety of different rhythms
* Device to play the music—CD player, tape recorder, etc.—depending on the format the music is recorded on
* Scarves or streamers

Musical Messages

* A familiar tune
* A message that you wish to send written out to fit the tune

It's All Music

* Music characteristic of the culture you are emphasizing

Let's Have a Parade

* Marching music
* Rhythm instruments to play or flags to wave

Classical Cartoons

* Video recorded children's cartoons that incorporate classical music scores in their sound tracks
* A variety of classical music pieces that have different tempos and rhythms

The Music of the Week

* Music of several different types—Libraries often carry a nice variety of selections of good quality musical pieces you could borrow
* A good system

Let's Dance

* Music for the dance songs
* A large open space for dancing

So Many Songs to Sing

* Selections of songs from many different categories
* Props to go with the categories

Chapter 2

Styrofoam Snowflakes

* Waxed paper sheets cut into circles and styrofoam
* A piece of cardboard for each child cut a bit bigger than the circles
* Glue in squirt bottles—enough for each child to have one
* Fishing line for hanging

Colors of My Rainbow

* Red, yellow, and blue liquid tempera paint
* Styrofoam plates to use as paint pallets (one for each child)
* A paintbrush for each child
* Styrofoam cups to hold water for washing paintbrushes out after creating each new color and painting each stripe

* White and blue construction paper
* Scissors
* Glue

Nature Prints

* A variety of natural objects such as rocks, leaves, shells, feathers, etc.
* Tempera paint of various colors
* Paint brushes and aluminum pie tins
* Construction paper

Leaf Roll

* A variety of fresh leaves—they need to be flat or should be flattened under heavy books before being used for this activity
* Tempera paint
* Blank newsprint paper
* Rolling pins or cylindrical blocks of rolling pin length

Window Art

* Clear contact paper—enough for each child to have two identical pieces
* Construction paper to cut shapes out of or flat materials like leaves or confetti which will stick to contact paper. Construction paper is also needed for borders.
* A hole punch and yarn or string for hanging

Seeds Say It All

* A variety of seed packets—Families of the children may have some to donate. Gardeners often have unused seed packets that contain seeds too old for planting but perfect for this project! Garden shops and other stores that sell seeds may be willing to donate seed packets left over after planting season, as well.
* Sturdy paper or cardboard
* White glue in bottles
* Crayons

Two Halves Make a Whole

* Colorful pictures of interest to children, cut from magazines
* Sheets of white paper large enough to allow for the entire picture
* Scissors and glue
* Markers or crayons

Real Cool Trees

* One three to five foot tree branch with smaller branches attached
* Wallpaper sample books (These can usually be obtained free from wall decorating stores once the styles in the books are out of print or date.)
* Brown yarn, scissors for children, and a hole punch
* A piece of earth tone clay suitable for your branch size and a piece of cardboard to place it on

Ribbons and Color

* Two same size and shape sheets of construction paper for each child
* Tempera paint in squirt bottles.
* Lengths of yarn or ribbon (any width will work) a few inches longer than the paper length

Wall Art Bulletin Board Backgrounds

* Various painting supplies such as rollers, painting sponges, plastic wrap and feather dusters
* Tempera or latex paint
* A large bulletin board covered with a sheet of heavy paper

Sand Paintings

* Authentic sand paintings or pictures of these
* Information to share about sand painting
* Containers with tight fitting lids
* Dry sand

* Several colors of liquid tempera paint
* A corrugated cardboard square for each child
* White glue in small squeeze bottles
* A tub for left over sand
* A pencil for each child
* A self-adhesive label for each child

Decorative Garden Rocks

* A rock for each child that is six inches to a foot in diameter and has a broad flat surface
* Tempera paint and brushes and/or permanent markers
* White glue and water

Welcome Flags

* Enough light colored fabric for each child to have a 7 × 10 inch piece
* One clear plastic sheet protector for looseleaf paper sheets for each child
* Fabric paints or fabric markers of a variety of colors
* Enough sturdy wire for each child to have a five foot length
* A piece of corrugated cardboard a bit larger than the fabric piece for each child
* Four stick pins for each child

Plastic Bird Feeder

* An 8 oz. or smaller plain plastic tub for each child. Parents could be asked to supply a tub for their child.
* Enough string or fishing line for each child's feeder to have three equal length pieces
* A hole puncher and permanent markers
* Some sort of hook for each feeder that will allow for hanging the feeder
* Bird seed
* A guidebook for bird watchers. These can be purchased at bookstores.

I'm Puzzled

* Tag board cut into the size of puzzles you wish to have the children make
* Markers
* Sealant (*see* page 43 *for details*)
* Heavy books
* Paper cutter
* Clear plastic self-sealing food bags
* Camera
* Clear tape

Build Me a SandCastle/Snow Sculpture

* Snow or sand of the consistency to hold together when molded
* Plastic containers of various sizes and shapes
* Spray bottles filled with water dyed with food coloring (snow sculptures only)

Cupcake Liner Flowers

* Multicolored cupcake pan liners—two sizes—enough for each child in the group to have 1 of each size for the number of flowers the child wants to make plus the larger size green liners to cut into leaf shapes. One green liner should be enough to make 4–5 leaf shapes.
* One green pipe cleaner for every flower that will be made. The slightly larger and thicker pipe cleaners will work well for these flowers
* A short length of yarn for each bouquet made

Picture This!

* A variety of large garden seeds—about a cup per child depending on the size of the seeds
* Clear plastic lids such as those from coffee cans—one per child
* White glue
* Water

* A container to mix the glue and water in and a spoon for mixing
* A cup with a pouring spout
* Pop top lids—one for each child
* Permanent markers

Paint Mystery

* Liquid tempera paint
* A variety of items to paint with
* Sheets of paper to paint on

Edible Art

* Large white marshmallows—3 per child
* Cookies frosted with white icing to use as a "snowy" base—one per child
* Corn syrup
* Aluminum foil
* Small white paper plates—one per child
* One black and one orange container of paste food coloring available at cake decorating supply stores
* Two toothpicks for each child
* One large gumdrop candy for each child

Let's Create Scarecrows!

* An old long sleeved shirt and a pair of pants of compatible size for each scarecrow to be made
* A roll of somewhat heavy string cut into workable lengths of string (*see* page 53 for directions)—six pieces per scarecrow
* Two short pieces of wire (six inches each should do) for each scarecrow
* A sturdy stick an inch or two in diameter and as long as the length of the scarecrow from the pant seat bottom to a half foot above the shirt neck
* A plastic jack-o-lantern head like that used to gather Halloween candy for each scarecrow with a hole the width of the stick cut into the

middle of the bottom and the handle removed

* An old hat of some type for each scarecrow
* A strong piece of string to secure the scarecrow to a tree or a cross type stand for the scarecrow of a "T" shaped design and string to secure the scarecrow to that

Animal Stamp

* Several colors of liquid tempera paint
* Pie tins to hold the paint
* Fake fur, leather, feathers, etc. cut into small pieces to use for stamping
* Sturdy paper of several colors
* Drawing utensils
* Scissors

Chalk Mural

* Enough sidewalk chalk of several colors for the group to share
* Real or pictured murals to observe

Famous Artist Gallery

* Prints of masterpiece works of art—these may be found over the internet or in books and copied onto heavy paper to display on a bulletin board that can be used for this purpose throughout the year along with paper or cardboard frames
* The art mediums and other supplies for the child to create their own masterpieces in the styles of the famous artists
* Art smocks and an easel or table to work on

Chapter 3

Here We Are at the Amusement Park

* None Needed

Give Me the Microphone

* Music to sing along to
* Samples of singers from good children's musicals to use with a T.V. and VCR

* A toilet paper roll and half Styrofoam ball to fit over one end, glue, black tempera paint, paintbrush, and a three foot long piece of heavy black yarn per child
* Or a hair clip that opens at one end only, a small black Styrofoam ball painted black, and glue for each child

Are You a Copy Cat?

* A large open floor space

I'm Walking on Clouds

* A large space for movement

I Felt So Bad I Could Have Cried

* A story to tell that includes many different emotions
* A paper plate for each child and drawing utensils
* A bulletin board for displaying the faces

I'm Changing

* Space to move

Now I'm a Statue, Now I'm Not

* Music that will encourage movement
* A tape recorder or CD player to play the music on

Let's Picnic

* A large green blanket
* A picnic basket

Paper Plate Masks

* Paper plates
* Materials to decorate the masks—paper, cardboard, markers, glue, yarn
* Elastic and a stapler to make the masks wearable
* Play scripts
* Props (optional)

Stories with Props

* A familiar story
* Simple props to go with the story when its acted out

Shadow Shows

* A white bed sheet and a method to hang it above a table
* A light source such as a floor lamp with the lamp shade removed of the height to shine on the sheet
* A table with the front below the top covered so that one cannot see under the table
* An idea for a puppet show
* Puppets for the show cut as silhouettes from cardboard and mounted on tongue depressors

Magnetic Puppet Theatre

* A shoebox with a curtain (optional) attached
* Puppet figures made from light weight cardboard that can stand up. A paper clip needs to be attached with clear tape to the bottom of each
* A magnet strong enough to move the figures through the box bottom
* A puppet play to perform

Overhead Puppet Shows

* Overhead projector
* At least two sheets of overhead film per puppet show—more if you want to use more than one background or several puppets
* Permanent as well as dry erase markers in a variety of colors

Sock It to Me Puppet Show

* One tube type sock per child
* Materials to create the puppets—see above
* Craft glue and scissors

* Paper for drawing the puppet designs on and writing out the puppet show plays
* A table and a large sheet of roll paper or tablecloth to cover below the table so one can't see under it

Unit Two
Chapter 4
Alphabet People

* One foot by one foot pieces of white cardboard with the capital letters of the alphabet on one side and the corresponding small letters on the other
* A hole punch and string to make the letter cards so they can be worn around the neck.

Alphabet Snake

* The letter cards made for the "Alphabet People" activity.

Alphabet Dominoes

* Alphabet domino cards (see steps for directions to make these)
* A large, flat playing surface.

Fishing for Letter Sounds

* A set of Fishing For Sounds cards as described above

Letter Match Game

* A bulletin board covered with paper you can write on
* A dark marker for writing on the bulletin board
* A tack for each letter included
* Different colored yarn strings that reach from each letter on one side of the board to each letter on the other side of the board
* shapes and their names.

Rhyming Word Ball Toss

* A ball to toss
* A word that can be rhymed with many other words

Categories Race

* A category that has many words that fit it

Categories

* Items that can be categorized—enough for each child to have an item (*see steps* on page 91)
* A box large enough to hold all the items you have for that category
* A method to label the boxes—if you tape a piece of clear plastic to each box leaving an opening at the top, the category can be written on a card and placed in the plastic pocket. Then the categories can be easily changed and the boxes used over and over again for different categories.

Words of the Season

* Long sheet of light colored paper
* Dark thick marker for recording words. Attach it by a long string to the wall by the chart so you can easily add words as they come up.

Go Together Race

* Heavy sheets of words that can be combined to make compound words cut into separate word pieces and placed into plastic sandwich bags with zipper-type closures—one bag for each child.
* A minute timer

Personal Word Finds

* Grid paper with large enough squares for children to write a letter in each square

Describing Words

* A large old fashioned schoolhouse shape cut out of red paper

* A dark marker to write with
* Paper of several different colors for the children to make their shapes on
* A vacant space to display the children's work

I Am So Lucky

* Ideas for categories that will work for this activity.
* Your imagination!

Sentence Challenge

* Word cards depicting all parts of speech and capable of forming sentences.
* Erasable cards would work great for this so that the "game" can be played over and over again.

Silly Sound Sentences

* Letter cards
* Writing utensils
* Scratch paper for each child
* Drawing paper for each child

Answer in a Sentence

* A question to ask each child

Listen to Me Read

* A tape recorder
* A blank cassette tape for each child
* A private place to read orally

What's Your Favorite Book?

* A favorite children's book of the teacher to share with the group
* Favorite books for the children to share
* Space for the children to spread out and read

Two Very Different Mice

* A copy of the story "Country Mouse/City Mouse"
* A chalkboard to write on

Chapter 5

What a Picture! What a story!

* Colorful and interesting pictures cut from magazines that show action
* Writing paper suitable for the age and ability of the writers

How Many? Who? How?

* The story, "The Three Billy Goats Gruff"
* Writing paper
* Cardboard to make the book covers and a method to attach them together with the pages in between

ABC Story

* A long sheet of chart paper or a flip chart with several pages with the letters of the alphabet written one below the other all the way from A to Z and with room after each letter to write a sentence
* A dark marker to write with

My Me Book

* Paper, cardboard, yarn, a hole puncher, and contact paper to make books
* A camera and film for picture taking
* White glue or glue sticks
* Writing utensils—markers or dark crayons would work well for this project
* Catalogs and magazines

Sound Rebus Story

* A children's story involving a variety of animals in a format so that the children can visually follow along as the teacher reads it

Resolutions

* Official looking documents copied onto sturdy paper with the wording as stated in the steps above. One for each child and yourself!

* Construction paper to make a folder the document can be stapled to so that it is covered up but can be peeked at

My Favorite Treat Recipe

* Notes written out to explain the project to the children's families—one for each child

* Recipe type cards made up that are large enough for your children to write clearly on. Send an extra with each child as well in case the information won't fit on the front of just one card. Remind the child to only write on one side of the card.

* Materials to compile the recipes in a book

Picture This!

* A rebus story written on large chart paper

* A copy of a story which has many words that could be replaced with pictures and space between the lines of words for the children to draw pictures where appropriate for each child

* A copy of a rebus story that has spaces in the places where pictures can go instead of words for each child

* Writing paper that has space between the lines so that there is room to draw in pictures to replace words for each child

Let's Be "Reason-a-Full"

* An issue that the children are interested in and might have definite opinions about to discuss as a group

* Another issue that fits the above description written on the board for the children to copy on writing paper

Letters to the Stars

* Chart paper containing the format for writing a friendly letter and addressing the envelope

* Addresses of famous people the children might be interested in writing to

* Letter writing paper and envelopes

* A stamp for each child's envelope

* A loose leaf binder with enough clear loose leaf sleeves for each letter and picture to go in. Each sleeve will hold one letter and one picture.

Be My Valentine!

* A variety of valentines that incorporate the clever use of words to make their point

* Materials for making the valentines such as red, pink, and white paper, markers, glue sticks, doilies, ribbon, etc.

Chapter 6

What's the News? What's the Weather?

* One large appliance box (Stores that sell such appliances are often willing to donate one to a good cause.)

* A cutting utensil that will cut through the cardboard

* Brass fasteners

* News sources such as newspapers, television and radio news programs, etc.

* Optional: a video camera and a television and VCR

* A map to use for reporting the weather

Introductions

* Someone to introduce

Interviews

* A chalkboard and chalk

* Paper to write the children's questions on

* A copy machine

I Hear You Loud and Clear

* A microphone

* Material for each child to read that he/she is very familiar and comfortable with

Say Hello to My Pet

* A stuffed animal for each child
* An answer sheet for each child to fill out
* Questions which call for information on the answer sheets written out on index cards

How Do You Do It?

* Each child will need something to demonstrate and the equipment or materials to do this
* Chart paper—one sheet for each child

Haven't I Said That Before?

* Short plays for the children to perform
* Tape recorders and blank tapes
* Materials to use to make the sound effects

Unit Three

Chapter 7

Sort Our Shoes

* Children's shoes or sandals
* Recording paper and marker

Can the Objects

* 3 or 4 cans of sufficient size to hold objects used for classifying
* Different sets of objects with common attributes for each set
* Paper to record attributes

Which Numbers Belong Together

* Number cards for each child or group of children
* Sheet with Boxes for classifying the numbers

Number Hunt

* Number sheets with numbers listed in categories
* Large recording sheet for numbers collected by all children

* A walking area containing a variety of signs, etc. that include numbers

Group These Fractions

* Sheet containing a number of fractions to be grouped
* Scissors

Animals in a Row

* A number of different types of toy animals of different colors, sizes, etc.

Bolt it Right

* A tub containing bolts, nuts and washers (colored bolts, nuts and washers could also be used to add another attribute)

Number Decoder

* *Secret Code Sheets* for each child or group
* Pencils

100's Board Skip Counting

* 100's counting board for each child
* A set of markers for each child (coins, beans, etc.)

Ordering Shapes Memory Game

* Sets of paper shapes for each child of different color and size
* Paper clips for each child
* A set of shape sequence cards (teacher made)
* Blank strips of paper

It Will Not Work That Way

* Sheets of paper to work out answers

Block Building

* Blocks or 1 inch square pieces of paper

Chapter 8

Mini-muffins are the Best

* Bakery items for the Breakfast Bakery Sale
* Tables and chairs

* Record sheet tally items sold
* Graph or chart paper

Making Bar Graphs
* Different sets of colored objects (buttons, beans, candy, pasta, blocks, etc.)
* Stripes of colored paper matching the colors of the colored objects
* Glue
* White sheets of paper "8½ by 11"

More Zippers or Buttons
* Pictures of zippers and buttons the same size
* Scissors

Analyze This
* Paper for report writing
* Survey forms (see sample)

The Red, White, or Blue Gum Ball
* Gum ball machine (a clear jar with a lid can be substituted—a whole slightly bigger than the size of the gum balls should be made in the lid)
* A number of gum balls perhaps twice the size of the class

Chances are it will be a 1980's
* 2 Rolls of coins (pennies) for each team
* Board and marker to record data

My Forecast
* Weather recording charts
* Thermometer

Drop Those Beans
* Cups
* Sets of 6 beans with two different colored sides (red and white)

Chapter 9

Shape Find
* A set of attribute blocks, geoblocks or paper shapes of different types and sizes

Shape Designers
* Sets of paper shapes

It's My Puzzle
* Sheets of paper 8" by 8" (size can be modified)

Pack It Tight
* Boxes that are the same in size (shoe boxes, envelope boxes, wet-wipe tubs, etc.)
* Sets of objects of different sizes and shapes (geoblocks, lids, marbles, wooden blocks, bottle caps, sugar cubes, etc.)

Rope It Square
* A tied rope for each group of children (yarn or string could also be used)

Square to Triangle
* 8" by 8" sheets of paper (cloth or other material could be tried)
* A display board can be used for displaying various shapes formed by the square.

Arrange Eight
* Provide children with 8 triangles cut from an 8" by 8" piece of paper (Cut the piece of paper in half and then cut each half again to make (4) 4" by 4" sheets.)

Count My Sides and Points
* A collection of three dimensional objects (cubes, cones, prisms, etc.)
* A data collection chart

It Looks Different From Here
* A number of small 1 inch blocks

Drawing Sides

* A number of three dimensional objects: cubes, cylinders, prism, cones, etc.
* Paper and pencils

Chapter 10

Toothpicks Long

* Toothpicks
* String or tape

The Measurement Hunt

* Tape measure 6 feet or longer (if tape measures are not available children could use rulers to measure straight lined objects. Curved objects could be measured by using a string lined up along the objects and then straightening the string out and measuring the string with a ruler)
* *The Measurement Hunt* record sheet
* Pencil

How Many Birds Will It Take

* Pencil and paper

Build the Iguana Cage

* Long sheets of paper (wire would be used if an Iguana were to live in the cage)
* Rulers
* Glue
* Scissors

Which Stuff is Longer

* Ruler or nonstandard measurement tool
* Bag to collect objects in

How Long are My Body Parts

* Standard rulers
* Paper and pencils

Cup to Cup

* 8 clear plastic cups
* A pouring tray

Liquid (water with colored dye or other colored liquid)

* A liquid container with liquid for pouring activities

Fill My Pail

* 3 or 4 different size pails (other containers may be used)
* A number of balls (ping-pong balls, golf balls or tennis balls, etc. could be used)

Super Size Drink

* Construction paper or other sturdy paper
* Tape and rubber bands
* Standard liquid measuring device(s)

Storing My CD's

* Large cardboard boxes to be cut up into strips
* 25 empty CD cases
* Scissors
* Tape

Everything is a Pound

* 1 to 5 small scales
* A pail of sand weighing over 1 pound
* A number of pencils that weigh over 1 pound
* A number of scissors that weigh over 1 pound
* A number of 3" by 5" cards that weigh over 1 pound

Buttered Lite Weights

* 10 to 12 smaller size butter/margarine containers (film canisters can also be used)
* Materials of different weights to be put in the containers

Sort This Junk

* 4 marked tubs or boxes
* A collection of stuff that fit the approximate weight categories being asked for

How Many to Sink Me
* 2 tins made of aluminum foil 3" by 3" with a lip around the tin about ½" high
* Quantities of pennies, nickels, and quarters

My Balancing Act
* 1 balance board 4 inches wide, by 2 feet long by 1 inch thick
* 1 fulcrum board for balancing 4 inches long, by 2 inches wide by 2 inches high
* 1 cup of water
* 1 cup of sand (may have some extra sand available)
* 1 cup of marbles (may have a few extra marbles available)

Squared Up
* 4" by 4" sheets of paper for each child (partners could be used to reduce the number of sheets)
* 3" by 6" sheets of paper for each child
* 25, 1 inch square tiles for each child (set or partners)
* Other sheet with different designs for extra practice

Measure it Around
* 1 foot by 1 foot pieces of cardboard for each child or set of partners
* 1 set of 1 inch strips of paper for each child or set of partners
* 1 large sheet of paper to identify objects and their corresponding perimeters
* 1 marker

Area to Perimeter
* Color pencils or pens for each child
* 8½" by 11" graph paper for each child
* Board to create a chart and record responses

The Wall Mural
* 1 large sheet of paper 8 feet tall and 3 feet wide for each team (long boards can be used to draw the squares on the large sheets—smaller sheets could be used if you adjust the graph squares to ½ feet rather than 1 foot)
* 1 small sheet of graph paper using 1 inch squares
* Drawing pencils
* Tape

My School Day
* A classroom clock (digital, standard, or both)
* Time Sheets for recording time

How Much Time
* Recording sheets for the timed activities and stop watches
* Different materials depending on the timed activities selected

Convert My Time
* Copies of the *Time Conversion Problem Task Sheet*

Time Setting
* 1 standard watch with hour and minute markings
* 1 digital clock
* 1 clock with roman numeral markings
* Other clocks with no minute or hour markings

Chapter 11
Number scrabble
* 3" by 5" index cards (or scraps of paper)
* Pencils for recording
* Grid paper or self-made grid sheets

* 3 dice (spinners with numbers or playing cards could be substituted)

Guess my Number
* Pieces of paper
* Graph paper or self-made grid paper

Move to the Number
* Masking tape
* Teacher made player cards with numbers
* Teacher made player cards with the words, a *lower number* or a *higher number* written on them

Ad Inspector
* Ad sheets from newspapers
* Pencils
* Copies of *Ad Price Sheet*

Number Expansion
* Number Expansion Board
* 49 Teacher made numbered sequenced cards, 1 by 1 inch

Big Strips Little Strips
* Unit strips (9 ones, 9 tens, 9 one hundreds) per individual or team
* *Big Sheets Little Sheets Company Log Sheet*
* Pencils

Fewer Crops This Year
* Pencils
* Copies of *Big J's Farm Report*

Build My Cage
* Cardboard or poster board
* Scissors
* Ruler
* Tape

Snack Bags
* Snack Chart

* Paper
* Pencils

My Stars
* 11½ sheets of paper
* Star stickers or glued on star figures (number depends of level of your children)

Number in the Bundle
* Toothpicks (amount depends on the level of children)
* Rubber bands

Balls in a Jar
* Clear Jar

How Many Now
* Clear bowl or other clear container
* Small cups
* Large bag of colored objects (small colored candies, blocks, marbles, etc.)

Make Me a Guess
* A set of starter numbered cards (numbers at the understanding level of the children)
* A corresponding set of higher numbered cards
* A corresponding set of lower numbered cards

Unit Four
Chapter 12
* Set of hoops of different sizes (rope, taped together, can also be used in lieu of commercial hoops)

Skip on the Trail
* Rope, boards, chalk, or other material to make a trail 20–25 feet long
* Sidewalks could also be used as a skipping area

Animal Walking

* Open play area

Hop the Foot Prints

* Right and Left foot patterns. The foot patterns could be made of paper which is laminated and taped to the flooring. Chalk patterns shaped like feet can also be used.

Leap the Log

* 1 smooth log (start with a log with a diameter of about 3")
* Safety pad
* Starting line marker

Dodge the Balls

* Balls for the children to roll
* Stop watch or watch to time the children (optional)

Broom Handle Race

* Gym or outdoor running space
* 1 broom handle per team (other poles or rope about 5' long could also be used)

Obstacle Course Challenge

* A large outdoor or indoor space
* Small flags to be placed into or on top of the ground
* Bike or car tires for hoping into
* Piece of plywood to skip across
* 2 pieces of rope
* Other appropriate materials for other obstacle course race modifications or additions

Walk the Plank

* A balance beam or elevated boards could be used (sidewalk curbs also could be tried out)

Try One Limb

* Open floor space

The Leaning Body

* Open space area
* Floor mats (optional)

Bear Stand

* Open floor space
* Floor mats optional

Row Boat Warm Up

* Floor space

Balancing Board

* 1 piece of board 12" by 12" with a small piece of wood nailed to the bottom which is 2" by 2" by 4" (high)

Balancing Obstacle Course

* Balance beam
* Balance board
* Rope

Tube Ball

* Gym mat or piece of plywood 3' by 6'
* Plastic tube about 5" in diameter and empty juice or coffee can could also be used
* Tape
* Tennis ball

Toss into the Tire

* 1 used car tire
* 1 or more tennis balls
* 1 grassy surface

Catch

* Ball for each set of partners (tennis ball or rubber ball)
* Open area

Balloon Tapping

* Balloons
* An open space area

Kick to the Stick
* 1 Three foot stake (place about 6" into the ground)
* 1 soccer ball (note several kicking areas could be set up with 1 stake and 1 ball)

Dribble the Ball
* Basketballs or other balls for dribbling
* An open area

Chapter 13
Toe Touching
* An open play space
* Gym or floor mats (optional)

Touch the Sky
* A space for children to lift their arms so they do not touch other children.

Shadow Images
* 1 large white bed sheet
* 1 bright lamp or other lighting source

Move to the Music
* Open space

Rope Movements
* Open space
* 2 to 3 foot rope for each child

Self-Paced Race
* A space to run some distance

Step Up and Down
* Curb or some other object to step onto and off

Move to the Music
* Large open space

Ribbon Motion
* Open space for movement
* 2 ribbons per child about 4' long

Children's Walk-A-Thon
* An open spaced area or trail

Curl It UP
* Gym or another open space area
* Gym mats or rugs (optional)

Elastic Tug of War
* 1 twelve foot elastic rope.
* 1 ribbon
* 1 winning place marker

Leg Push
* Wall (or other locations in which children can push against an object which does not move)

Hang Time
* A chin-up bar or another secured type of hanging pole
* Stepping stool

Bridge Making
* Open space area
* Grassy area (other surfaces could be used)

Chapter 14
Kick Golf
* Flags or cups for holes
* Kick ball
* Score Cards and pencils

Balloon Volleyball
* 1 balloon 8 inches or more in diameter
* Ropes or board for the center line marker and boundaries on the court

Sticker Hop-Tag
* An enclosed play area
* Stickers

Rope Race
* Racing area or track
* 1 Rope about 6 feet long for each team

Waist Pull
* Tape

Bean Bag Horseshoes
* 3 bean bags
* 2 hoops (hoops could be formed by winding a rope into the shape of a circle or square)

Lawn Curling
* Paint or chalk
* Grassy surface
* 3 softballs or other balls 4" to 6" in diameter

Hit the Shape
* One 4' by 4' piece of plywood (thick cardboard could also be used)
* Different sized laminated shapes
* Bean bags

Three Ball Soccer
* 4 Soccer balls
* 4 Soccer nets (large cardboard boxes could be substituted)
* Playing field about 20' by 20'

Wall Ball
* Wall or space to hit tennis balls off
* Tennis balls
* Tape
* Different images for targets

Tile Jump
* Tiles (cardboard squares 1' by 1' could be taped to the floor if tiles are not available)
* A number of 3" by 5" cards

Falling Styrofoam
* Hats (children are to bring them from home)
* Styrofoam package filling (pieces of paper cut into inch squares or other soft material could be substituted)
* Small boxes

Milk Jug Catch
* Two gallon plastic milk jugs with the bottom cut out (caps or other materials could be substituted)
* Tennis balls
* Open play area

Hit Me if You Can
* An open play area.
* 3 utility balls about 1 foot in diameter

The Seven Event Marathon
* Parent Volunteers
* Golf ball
* Soccer Ball
* 2 Cans
* 5 Hoops (or 5 pieces of rope to form the hoops)
* Small Beach ball
* 8 Folding chairs

Line Tag
* Large hard surface
* Tape

Body Parts Memory Game
* Open area for movement

Pass the Ball
* Utility ball or beach ball about 15 inches in diameter.
* Open space

Hoops and Rulers
* Hoops
* 12" Rulers
* Movement area

Wand Balancing
* Wands for each child
* Open space

Unit Five
Chapter 15
See How It Changes
* 3 clear plastic cups per group (6–8 ounce cups)
* Different substances (about a tablespoon of each) in small containers or packages: meat tenderizer, oregano, corn starch
* Lab recording sheets for each group

Which Object Is It
* A variety of objects with different properties/attributes (hard-soft, green-yellow, cylinder-cone, rough-smooth, etc.)

Solid or Liquid
* Set of objects classified as liquid
* Set of objects classified as solid
* An ice cube in a cup

When Will It Boil
* 1 cup each of water, soda, rubbing alcohol
* 1 electric burner
* 1 small boiling pot
* 1 cooking or submersible thermometer

Mystery Bag
* A bag
* Objects to be placed in the bag along with objects to be set out (objects that reinforce properties being covered in the curriculum)

Light the Bulb
* 1 size D battery for each team
* 1 piece of wire (coated wire with the ends stripped bare would be best)
* 1 light bulb for each team (light bulbs from flashlights)
* Paper and pencils for illustrations

Does Cotton Conduct It
* An instrument to test for conduction
* Objects made of different properties/materials (cotton, wood, metal, rubber, cloth, etc.)
* Two containers: 1 marked *Conducts* and 1 marked *Does Not-Conduct*

Make a Switch
* Set up a tester for conduction (as explained in the *Does Cotton Conduct It* activity)
* 3" by 5" cards per group
* 2 paper fasteners per group
* 1 larger paper clip per group

Pick Up Slips
* 2 medium size balloons for each team
* A number of 1 inch pieces of paper for each team
* 1 paper plate for each team
* 1 Recording Chart for each team

Let the Rice Fly
* 1 plastic spoon
* 1 container of rice (puffed)
* 1 piece of woolen cloth

Electromagnetic Nails
* 1 6-volt battery
* 1 long nail
* 1 piece of insulated wire (about 18 gauge) with the ends stripped about 1 and a half inches
* 1 box of paper clips

Rock Lifting

* Rocks of different weight
* Rigid bar (a piece of wood 1" thick, by 4" to 6" wide, and about 4' long) Note: you may want to nail a small piece of wood (2" by 2") 6" to 8" from the ends of the bar so the rock and books do not slide.
* A fulcrum (a triangular piece of wood with the top being flat rather then pointed or a small round pole about 3" in diameter)
* A set of textbooks the same size

Pull Up the Bucket

* 1 small bucket
* 2 cups of beans
* 1 four foot pole (about 1 inch in diameter)
* Several simple pulleys of different sizes and rope
* 2 chairs (other set ups could be used to attach the pulleys to

Sock Pull

* A sock or socks filled with sand and tied with a loop at the end
* A board or boards (6"wide, 1" thick, 2' long)

The Box Splitter

* 2 Pieces of Styrofoam about 4" thick and 6" wide (other sizes may be tried)
* 1 pole (12" long and 1" in diameter)
* 1 screw driver (the end about ¼ or ½ inch wide at the end)

Up, Up and Over the Chair

* Chair for each group
* Block (about 4" wide, 4" high, and 6" long): one 4" by 4" piece of wood could be cut into 6" lengths
* 1 pulley for each group

* 1 wedge for each group
* 1 inclined plane
* 1 lever with fulcrum

My Soap Powered Boat

* 1 Piece of Aluminum foil
* Small piece of soap (1 inch wide and long enough to have about ½ to 1 inch below the water level of the boat
* 2 tubs of water, 1 warm & 1 cold

Make a Magnet

* 1 bigger size magnet for each child or group
* 1 large paper clip for each child or group (straight nails could be substituted)
* Pieces of steel wool for each child or group (small metal objects could be substituted such as small light weight washers)

Magnet Power

* A bar magnet
* Different pieces of materials about 1' by 1'
* Thumbtack or other iron material

Waste Hike with a Magnet Stick

* Sticks (3' to 4' long) for each team
* A magnet for each team
* 2 white bags for each team
* 1 black marker for each team
* Tape

Seeing Through It

* Flashlights
* White mailing envelope
* Box of translucent and non-translucent materials (Examples: white sheet of paper, piece of thick cardboard, black plastic piece, white plastic piece, piece of wood, pieces of cloth, piece of metal, piece of wax paper, leaf, egg, etc.)

Sun Pictures

* White sheet of paper (11½" by 8")
* Colored construction paper
* Scissors
* Tape
* Source of bright sun light (hot lights or heat lamps may work)

Growing Shadows

* Filmstrip projector or equivalent light source
* Filmstrip projector screen (white sheets, or a white wall could be used)
* Bird image about 1" long and 6" high
* Small stand for the bird image
* Darkened room

Making Phones

* String, wire, yarn, ropes, plastic tubing, etc. to serve as telephone wire
* Cans of different materials/sizes, different shapes/sizes of plastic bottles, etc.

Comb Instruments

* Combs
* Different pieces of material: aluminum foil, wax paper, writing paper, construction paper, cloth of different types, thin cardboard

Sounding Boards

* 2 wood boards about 15" long, 12" wide, 1" thick
* 16 wood nails 2" long
* 4 wires the same length but different thickness (mil.)
* 4 wires the same thickness but different lengths
* Hammer

Chapter 16

Neighborhood Animals

* Camera (or one camera per group of children)
* Film

Animal Classification Children's Style

* Sets of 10 animal pictures for each group of children

Neighborhood Habitats

* Camera
* Film

Community Zoo Model

* Clay to construct animals
* One or more large flat cardboard boxes for the zoo grounds
* Clay, twigs, sand and other material for building living spaces for the zoo animals
* Toothpicks for animal identification signs
* Small pieces of construction paper for animal identification signs

Hunting Animal Parts

* Pencils
* *Zoologists Animal Parts* guide sheets
* Nature walk area

Ants on the Move

* Large jar
* 10 to 15 ants
* Black strip of construction paper
* Small wire netting
* Water
* A small wet sponge
* Sugar, honey, and bread crumbs

Bird Watch

* Pencils
* Binoculars (optional)

* Copies of the *Bird Watchers Log Sheet* for each child

Moving Goldfish
* 2 gold fish bowls the same size
* 2 gold fish
* Stones (equal number to be placed in the bottom of both bowls)
* Optional: other objects to be placed in the gold fish bowls (model trees, etc.)
* CD player with music

Caterpillar to Butterfly
* A large jar with holes punched in the lid
* Twigs and leaves
* 1 Caterpillar

Neighborhood Plants
* Camera (digital or Polaroid™ would be better)
* Film
* 3" by 5" cards
* Pencils or markers

Flower Detectives
* 5 different types of flowers
* Vases for each flower (or some other clear container)

Leaf Classification
* An outdoor area that provides for a variety of leaves
* Bags for collecting leaves
* Recording chart for invented classification categories of children

Parts of a plant
* 1 potted non-flowered plant
* 1 potted flowered plant
* 1 flowered plant for each group (optional)

Classroom Terrarium
* Glass container with a lid
* Assortment of small neighborhood plants
* Soil for plants
* Decorative objects (optional)

Mold Garden
* 1 large glass jar with lid
* Sand (fill the glass jar about 1/3 full)
* Small pieces of food (cheese, bread, orange, and others picked by children)
* Recording chart as illustrated

Plants Break Rocks
* Prepared plaster mix
* Clear plastic cup
* Two bean seeds

Using Our Senses
* Chart paper and marker
* Objects for identifying senses: orange, whistle, cotton ball, cup of vinegar, flower, cookie, clock (one that ticks)

Post it on My Body Part
* Small stickers

The Animal Most Like Me
* Models of different types of toy animals

Fingerprint Me
* Transparency pieces cut into 2 inch squares
* Ink pads
* Wet-wipes or water, soap and paper towels

Hair
* A variety of hair samples for each child or small group of children
* Magnifying glasses for each child or group

Charting the Foods We Eat

❋ Blank Food Pyramid Sheet for each child

❋ Copy of food pyramid displayed

Chapter 17

Daily Temperature Readings

❋ An outdoor thermometer

❋ Daily recording sheet for three separate temperature readings

Keeping Hot Chocolate Warm

❋ 1 Plastic cup

❋ 1 Styrofoam cup

❋ 1 Coffee mug (ceramic)

❋ 4 Submersible thermometers

Effects of Two Ice Cubes

❋ 2 Cups of water of equal amounts set out at room temperature

❋ 2 submersible thermometers

❋ 3 ice cubes

Temperature Chase

❋ Thermometers for each group of children

Warm Up to My Light Bulb

❋ 4 Lamps

❋ 4 light bulbs: one with a 40 watt bulb, one with a 60 watt bulb, one with a 75 watt bulb, and one with a 100 watt bulb

❋ 4 thermometers

Food Temperatures

❋ A variety of hotter and cooler foods (Hot Dog, cooked rice, gelatin, scrambled eggs, pickle, French fries, ice cream and others)

❋ Food Thermometer (regular thermometer may work)

❋ Plates for the food

❋ Oven, toaster oven, microwave oven, or heating lamp (to keep foods at serving temperatures)

❋ Cooler (to keep foods at serving temperatures)

Stone Sorting

❋ Bags with a different assortment of stones for each group

Water and Soil

❋ 3 Small clear plastic cups

❋ 3 Different types of soil

❋ Lab sheets

Soil Samples

❋ Collected bags of soil from different locations

❋ Magnifying glasses for each group

❋ Black sheet of paper for recording observations

❋ Clear plastic cup for each group

Edible Soil

❋ Bags of potting soil for each table

❋ A variety of food materials to make the model soil (chocolate cake, brown sugar, sugar cubes, chili powder, and other seasonings)

❋ Forks for mixing or chopping

❋ Bags for the edible soil models

Rock Shower

❋ A large clear plastic container with a cover (about a 2" hole in the cover)

❋ Small pot of boiling water

❋ Safety glasses

❋ Frozen rock (several different rocks may be tried)

Mineral Jar

❋ Medium glass jar

❋ Small pebbles

❋ Soil

❋ Sand

❋ Water

* Lab sheets with an empty jar drawn on it for each child

Waste Collectors

* Garbage bags for collecting waste materials
* Large plastic or canvas sheet to place waste materials on
* Latex or other gloves to be used my children when picking up and sorting waste materials
* Appropriate containers to dispose of waste materials (for plastic, paper, aluminum, and other)

School Beautification Day

* Plants and trees to be planted on *School Beautification Day.*

Acid Rain Destruction

* 2 identical plants in the same type of pots about the same height
* Water
* Vinegar
* Chart to record growth

Would You Breathe that Air

* 2 medium size jars with lids
* 3 small wooden matches
* Pictures of air pollution, industrial smoke, etc.

Rocket Blast Off

* 1 paper towel tube for each rocket
* 1 sheet of construction paper (for cone and wings) for each rocket
* 1 35mm film canister with lid for each rocket (clear plastic canisters work better)
* Teaspoon of water for each rocket
* 1 seltzer tablet for each rocket

Planets in Inches

* Paper to cut out planets
* Tape

Moon Calendar

* A blank calendar for the month to fill in moon phase pieces
* Moon phase pieces (2 pieces of each moon phase should be provided)

Telling Time by the Sun

* Large piece of round cardboard or tagboard
* 1 dowel or pole
* 4 cards with one of the following written on each: north, south, east, and west
* 1 larger orange ball (a string could be taped to it to hang from the ceiling)
* 1 smaller Styrofoam ball with a stick placed through it

Unit Six
Chapter 18
Environment Dioramas

* One shoebox for each landscape
* A variety of materials to work with, such as rocks, sticks, cardboard, styrofoam, clay, etc.
* A bottle of glue for each group or individual child

My Garden Map

* Several seed catalogues or other catalogues with pictures of plants
* Brown paper
* Scissors and glue

Follow the Clues

* Sandwich-size plastic zipper lock lunch bags
* Small treats such as individually wrapped crackers, miniature candy bars, etc. divided into the number of bags to match your number of groups
* 3 × 5 note cards for writing your directions

Find the Words—Solve the Mystery

* Something to hide
* Note cards and markers

✳ A large class map that uses symbols and a key to identify objects in the room

All Around Our Town

✳ A large city map or a map of the area near your site

✳ A small picture of each child

✳ A method for attaching the picture to the map

Find the Landmark

✳ Chalkboard and chalk or cardboard strips and a bulletin board

✳ Pictures of landmarks cut from magazines

✳ A method to attach the pictures to the grid

State in a Bag

✳ Paper lunch bags

✳ A map of the United States

✳ A United States puzzle

A Snowy/Sandy Adventure

✳ Sticks and cardboard to make the trail name markers

So Much Earth to See

✳ One large sheet of sturdy paper for each child or one very large sheet of paper for the entire class to use together

Box City

✳ Boxes of several different shapes and sizes

✳ A variety of papers including construction paper and contact paper

✳ Several colors of tempera paint and paintbrushes and paint smocks

✳ Black tag board strips for roads

✳ As your town develops, you may need other readily available materials that can be

donated. Encourage the children to be creative with their resources and materials available.

Country Corner

✳ Props that represent characteristics of the country featured. Be creative and include the children in deciding what is needed and locating it.

✳ A map of the world or globe

✳ Books about the country featured

Do You Know Your Landforms?

✳ A large piece of light colored laminated tag board cut into several rectangles

✳ A dry erase marker of a dark color so it will show up on the cards

✳ A book depicting many landforms to get your definitions from—you must be accurate!

✳ A pocket chart (a chalkboard you can tape things to will also work)

All Dressed Up!

✳ Large sheets of butcher paper—the length of each child.

✳ Pencils to trace with

✳ Scissors to cut body forms out

✳ Materials to decorate their body forms with—paint, markers, etc.

✳ Sticky tack for hanging forms on the walls

Find My Egg

✳ 1 plastic Easter egg for each child

✳ Small slips of paper to write names on

✳ A map of a specific area

Chapter 19

History Comes Alive!

✳ Children's books depicting the facts about the lives of famous people in history

✳ Simple props that would be appropriate for the character you are presenting

My History

✳ 3x5 note cards for each child. The amount depends on the age and ability levels of the children

✳ A paper strip for each child wide enough and long enough to accommodate the number of note cards provided the child

✳ Glue or sticky tack to attach the cards to the paper strips

Where Have I Been? What Have I Seen?

✳ Sample postcards

✳ Tag board cut to the same size as a postcard and with a line drawn down the middle of one side to separate the message area from the address area for each child

✳ Colorful drawing utensils—markers or crayons—for drawing the postcard pictures. Actual pictures could be copied from the internet as well and cropped to postcard size to glue to the tag board.

✳ Resource books or internet access to research the historic sites chosen

✳ All the students' names written on slips of paper and placed in a container to be drawn from

✳ Chalkboard space to write the school address to be copied by the children onto the postcards

When Did That Happen?

✳ A calendar with large squares to add information

✳ Information on important events in history and when they occurred

Famous People in Our City's History

✳ Information on the people who were instrumental in starting the city where your school is located

✳ Pictures of the founding fathers of the city and note cards

Who is on My Money?

✳ Real pieces of money, both paper and coins or realistic replicas or pictures of the money

✳ Green, gray, and brown construction paper

✳ Resources for the children to use to do their research

What's in My Wagon?

✳ Information about the pioneers and their journey West

✳ A sheet of paper with an outline of a covered wagon on it and a pencil for each child

✳ A large sheet of paper with a large outline of a covered wagon on it and a marker to write on it with

Chapter 20

Everybody Gets a Job!

✳ Four seasonal shapes—one for each season—to correspond with the number of children in the class (see steps above)

✳ Four colors of light colored construction paper cut to the size (5x8 inches) to be folded for the cards to match the number of children in your entire group

✳ A marker or crayon for one child in each small group

✳ Glue for one child in each small group

✳ Four boxes for the finished cards—one for each season labeled with that season's name

Walk Around the Block Game

* Questions prepared by the teacher ahead of time that have to do with information about businesses in the city they know about of an amount to keep them going all the way around the block on the sidewalk squares with the answers on the backs accompanied by point values. If you have less questions, have larger point values and if you have more questions, have smaller point values. You may want to walk around the block before you write down the questions and count how many sidewalk squares there are.

Just Gotta Have It!

* A video clip of television commercials geared toward children. By video taping the commercials you can edit them to make sure that all the commercials are appropriate for your age group and of products they would want.
* A large sheet of drawing paper for each group

I Can't Have Everything I Want

* Pictures of items that children might like to purchase and a price on a price tag attached to each
* A place to display the pictures and prices
* A copy of the form provided and scratch paper for each child
* Pretend money to spend—the same amount for each child

What's Sold Here?

* Pictures of businesses in the community whose signs show what the businesses sell. If there are no signs of this sort in your community, try to still find some in books, nearby communities, etc. as these pictures will help the children understand how to do the activity.
* Construction paper and markers or crayons
* A chalkboard or chart paper to write on

Here's to You, Whatever You Do!

* Construction paper and writing and drawing tools
* Envelopes (optional)

What Do I Do?

* Job title sheets and job description sheets of equal amounts so that each child can have one or the other

Chapter 21

It's Great to be a Citizen

* Information on rights of citizens in the United States—Read the "Bill of Rights" and discuss it in language the children will understand
* A speaker who has become a citizen of the United States through naturalization
* Drawing paper and drawing instruments

Special Days, Weeks, and Months

* A book or calendar that specifies days, weeks or months that have special designations. There are many of these readily available. (See resources section)
* Materials you need to do the activities you choose to go with the special days, weeks, or months

Patriotic Days

* A small flag for each child
* Patriotic marching band music

Who Says So?

* A chart to write the rules on that the children decide on for their classroom

Let's Vote on It

* A ballot box with a cover that can be removed to take out the ballots
* Ballots made up for the issue being dealt with

Surveys Anyone?

* Paper for recording the responses from the surveys

Chapter 22

Eating Around the World!

* Snack foods the children generally eat

* A map of the world attached to a wall or bulletin board

* Yarn and tape or tacks

* Books that describe the food products produced in different countries of the world or a computer with internet access.

Class Penpals

* A method of connecting with a school with children of the ages of your group but in another country

* Letter writing materials

Celebrations Around the World

* Resources with information about the celebrations of different countries

The Same Yet Different

* Two versions of a fairytale or folktale as told in two different countries or cultures

* Chalkboard and chalk

Day of Swings

* A swing set

* A bell

* Crepe paper streamers of red and white to decorate the swings with—the streamers can be wound in and out of the chains with longer lengths hanging down or tied to the ropes or covered chains of those types of swings so that they fly out behind the swings as they go back and forth

We All Play Games

* The book *Children's Traditional Games: From 137 Countries and Cultures*

* Items that are needed to play the games you select

The Japanese Haiku

* A haiku you have written yourself or picked from a book copied onto chart paper with a picture you've drawn to accompany it (optional)

* A haiku poem form (*see* page 472) for each child to write his/her poem on

* Drawing paper and markers or crayons

We Depend on Each Other

* A variety of items produced in other countries than the one the children live in

* A world map

* A chalkboard

How Do You Say It?

* Specific words from other languages that have direct counterparts in English

* A chalkboard to write the words on

Index

developing indoor environment for neighborhood, 366–367

effects of acid rain on, 404

identifying classification system for leaves, 363

making connection between seeds and, 31

making mosaics using seeds, 48–49

native, 402–403

neighborhood, identifying, 361

parts of, and functions of, 364–365

seeing differences and similarities between flowers, 362

strength of, 370

Plays. *See also* Puppet shows

acting out familiar stories as, 69

tape-recording dialogue and sound effects for, 127

Pollution

acid rain, 404

air, 405

Population, understanding of, 155–156

Pose, holding, 67

Positioning

identifying shapes after different, 164–165

problem solving and shape, 169

of shapes, working with, 172

understanding, working with shapes, 167–168

Postcards, of historic places, 436–437

Pounds

and ounces, discriminating between, 195

understanding, 192

Predictions

about events, 360

based on information collected, 346–347

making, based on past trials, 162

regarding temperature, 387

using data to make, 160–161

Pretending

to be on a picnic, 68

to sing (lip-synch) songs, 61

stuffed animals are real pets, 125

to walk on variety of materials, 63

Primary colors, mixing, 27

Print designs, 28

Probability. *See also* Chance

game with beans to experience, 162

gum ball game, to introduce, 157–158

Problem solving, 132, 138–139, 226–227, 230–231, 234, 319–320

with chance, 159

with electricity, 315–316

with measurement, 190–191

with moving position of fulcrum, 325–326

with numbers, 147, 215–216, 217–218

with positioning of shapes, 169

with reasoning, 229

with shapes, 167–168

with simple machines, 331–332

to strengthen magnet, 323–324

with time, 211–212

using chance with, 160–161

using data, 155–156

using, with measurement, 182–183, 184

with volume measures, 192

with weights, 195

Products

dependence on other countries for, 474

thinking about new, 448–449

Properties

changes in, 308–309, 311–312

making up different soils, 396

of objects, discriminating between different, 314

observation of different rates of change for, 313

reasoning about, 310

Props, use of, 70

Public speaking

learning to enjoy, 125

practicing to be comfortable with, 121

Pulleys, 327–328

Puppets

made from overhead projector film, 75

moved by magnets, 73–74

for shadow puppet shows, 71–72

sock, 76

Puppet shows. *See also* Plays

creating shadow, 71–72

overhead, 75

sock puppets for, 76

using magnets, 73–74

Puzzles

creating word find, 95

using drawings to make, 43–44

Q

Quantity, of objects, representing, 154

Questions, using complete sentences to answer, 100

R

Range

identifying, for set of data, 150–151, 155–156

understanding of, 155–156

Ratios, 408–409

Reading, 103

abilities, map-, 420

aloud, evaluating abilities when, 101–102

data from charts, 226–227

food thermometers, 392–393

and recording outdoor temperatures, 381–382